The
Coast Guardsman's
Manual

EIGHTH EDITION

The Coast Guardsman's Manual

Revised by Captain George E. Krietemeyer, USCG (Retired)

with the assistance of
Commander Doug Starr, USCGR (Retired)
and
CWO(MAT) Wayne Truax, USCG

Naval Institute Press
Annapolis, Maryland

© 1991 by the United States Naval Institute
Annapolis, Maryland

First edition published 1952. Eighth edition 1991

Library of Congress Cataloging-in-Publication Data

Krietemeyer, George E.
    The coast guardsman's manual / revised by George E. Krietemeyer,
with the assistance of Doug Starr and Wayne Truax.—8th ed.
        p.   cm.
    Includes index.
    ISBN 1-55750-450-4
        1. United States.   Coast Guard—Seamen's handbooks.   I. Starr,
Doug.   II. Truax, Wayne.   III. Title.
VG53.K75   1991
359.9'7'0473—dc20   91-10944

Printed in the United States of America on acid-free paper ⊗

9   8   7   6   5   4   3   2

The Coast Guard Vision Statement

The United States Coast Guard is committed to continuous improvement of its performance as the world's leading maritime humanitarian and safety organization.

We strive to be the armed force offering the most challenging and rewarding career for the young men and women of our nation while preserving and honoring those customs and traditions that have served the country so well in peace and war.

We are responsive to changing national priorities. We are willing to explore new areas of endeavor and we seek a balance in response to our traditional missions in support of national security, law enforcement, maritime safety and environmental protection.

We are committed to providing for the welfare of our people and their families so that the Coast Guard can stand, always ready, to serve, protect and enhance our nation's maritime interests.

The Coast Guard Work-Life Philosophy

The purpose of the ongoing Work-Life initiative is to strike a reasonable balance between the needs of the Coast Guard and the needs of our members and their dependents. The goal is to create a total quality environment by which the Coast Guard will achieve organizational excellence and continue to provide valued services to our customers.

Work-Life issues are critical to individual and organizational achievement. They will always affect the Coast Guard's mission performance and are certain to impact the future. Work-Life balance enhances diversity, recruitment, retention, and, most important, the job performance of the Coast Guard's work force.

For the Coast Guard to compete effectively as an employer in the twenty-first century, we must build and maintain necessary support systems for our military and civilian members as well as their families.

Contents

THE COMMANDANT OF THE UNITED STATES COAST GUARD
WASHINGTON, D.C. 20593-0001

The United States Coast Guard . . . Our name evokes a range of images in the minds of the American public that is as vast and dynamic as the missions we endeavor to fulfill on a daily basis. For over 200 years, our dedicated men and women have established proud traditions of service to this country in maritime safety, marine environmental protection, maritime law enforcement, and national security. As we pursue each of these missions with equal vigor, we must remember that our greatest strength is in our people . . . the dedicated men and women of the United States Coast Guard. As the present and future leaders of our noble service, you must keep in mind the need to approach all of our operational missions with a sense of balance, for they are all equally important. At the same time we, as an organization, and as leaders, must ensure that our people are provided with the support, tools, and skills to sustain the high level of effectiveness and mission performance that has become our standard.

This manual can be one of your most valuable tools, regardless of your rank, rate or time in service. Its value is attested to by the generations of Coast Guardsmen who have found it to be a ready source of guidance on a broad range of topics. It will serve you well.

Today in the Coast Guard, the future is as bright as it is challenging. We must stand confident in our abilities, yet never lessen our commitment to be truly "Semper Paratus"—Always Ready.

The Master Chief Petty Officer of the Coast Guard

2100 — 2nd Street, S.W.
Washington, D.C. 20593-0001

Today, we look back with pride to a glorious past, a past filled with traditions and honors. The traditions, service, and honors that have served our fellow man, our Coast Guard, and our country will continue to mount as we do our duty. Today we look forward to a bright future, filled with knowledge that we can accomplish anything we put our mind to.

The basic knowledge and skill you are taught in recruit training are reinforced and continue to live on in this book. Remember your time in recruit training with the pride that you accomplished a task that you sought out. Remember the teamwork that you developed with your shipmates. The people you will meet from our Reserve Force, our Auxiliary, and our counterparts in the Department of Defense know your abilities and respect them. You on the other hand must know, respect, and recognize them and their mission.

You have the basics: recruit training and your Coast Guardsman's Manual. Use both wisely as you advance yourself in our Coast Guard.

You are the future of the Coast Guard. Take care of our Coast Guard.

Preface

As we go about our work in the Coast Guard, we often don't realize how much of an impact we have on this country and its people. Because of our "average" day with its average problems and average work, people are saved from the perilous sea, our channels are safely buoyed, ports and vessels are operated safely, the smugglers of death are stopped, incompetent seamen and poor vessels are removed from the sea, and our waterways are cleaner than anytime in recent memory.

A lot of above average Coast Guard people, both military and civilian, make an average day in the Coast Guard something special. Maybe that's the reason our average day isn't so average. Let's take a look at some recent figures.

On an average day, we saved 12 lives. This is only an average but it is certainly a very important one to every person who is alive today because of us. During that same average day we assisted another 315 people and saved $2 million in property. We also serviced 150 aids to navigation.

Coast Guard Marine Safety personnel worked 23 oil or hazardous-chemical spills. They boarded 90 large vessels for port safety checks, inspected 64 commercial vessels, and investigated 17 marine accidents.

Other Coast Guard personnel were involved in seizing 318 pounds of marijuana and 253 pounds of cocaine on our average day. They also interdicted 112 illegal migrants.

You have joined a unique organization dedicated to serving the public in many ways. Welcome to the Coast Guard.

We are grateful to the editors of the seven previous editions of this book: Capt. W. C. Hogan (1952); LCdr. M. M. Dickinson and BMC L. W. Behrens (1954, 1958); Cdr. L. A. White (1964, 1967, 1976); and Capt. R. F. Bennett (1983).

A major revision of a manual of this scope cannot be accomplished by one or two people. You will find throughout your service career that the best way to complete a mission successfully is to put a team of experts together, establish some goals and responsibilities, and then make it happen. That is exactly how this book was put together. The team of experts is listed below—my sincere thanks to each and every one of them.

Editorial and technical review and support: Cdr. D. Starr, CWO (MAT) W. Truax, YNCS V. Patton, and Lt. C. Cashin.

Editing and design: Ms. C. Swartz and Ms. K. White, respectively, of the Naval Institute Press.

Production typing and computer disks: Ms. D. Reid and Ms. M. A. Gehrdes of Techni-Type.

Technical revisions and updating:

USCG Academy: LCdr. J. Miko, QMC W. Webber, Ms. J. Miller, Mr. L. Carpenter.

CG Training Center Cape May: Lt. Seachrist.

CG Institute: Ms. P. Knaup, Ms. M. Sterling.

CG Aviation Technical Training Center: ASM1 G. Waters.

CG Reserve Training Center Yorktown: Lt. B. Smith, BMC F. Good, QMC L. Bailey, CWO D. Hall, Lt. H. Black, DCCM B. Velek, Lt. J. Farthing.

CG Training Center Petaluma: CWO4 S. Milobar, Lt. A. Illobre, YNC T. Brooks, YNC C. Anderson, LCdr. W. Bryant, Cdr. R. Batson, RMC J. Mize, RMCM R. Mercurio, BMCS C. Kennovin, BMCS G. Wilhelm, ETC D. Pier, HSC P. Bold, HSC J. Ramsdell, DCC R. Holzvinger.

CG Headquarters: PA1 C. Kallenbach, Dr. R. Scheina, PACS Pheris, Capt. P. Poerschke, Capt. E. Kiley, PA1 R. Mench, Rear Adm. A. Steinman, YNC Keenan.

CG Information Systems Center: Lt. (j.g.) Douglas.

Retired personnel: CWO4 D. Schmidt, CWO3 P. Grimes.

Special thanks to the staff of the Chief Petty Officers Academy for their in-depth review and constructive criticism.

"SEMPER PARATUS"

From Aztec Shore to Arctic Zone,
 To Europe and Far East,
The Flag is carried by our ships
 In times of war and peace;
And never have we struck it yet,
 In spite of foemen's might,
Who cheered our crews and cheered again
 For showing how to fight.

CHORUS
So here's the Coast Guard marching song,
 We sing on land or sea.
Through surf and storm and howling gale,
 High shall our purpose be,
"Semper Paratus" is our guide,
 Our fame, our glory, too.
To fight to save or fight and die!
 Aye! Coast Guard, we are for you.

"Surveyor" and "Narcissus,"
 The "Eagle" and "Dispatch,"
The "Hudson" and the "Tampa,"
 These names are hard to match;
From Barrow's shores to Paraguay,
 Great Lakes' or Ocean's wave,
The Coast Guard fights through storms and winds
 To punish or to save.

Aye! we've been "Always Ready"
 To do, to fight, or die!
Write glory to the shield we wear
 In letters to the sky.
To sink the foe or save the maimed
 Our mission and our pride.
We'll carry on 'til Kingdom Come
 Ideals for which we've died.

     —Captain F. S. Van Boskerck, USCG

The
Coast Guardsman's
Manual

I.
Welcome Aboard—
Introduction
to the Coast Guard

CHAPTER 1

History and Missions

This chapter describes some of the important events that shaped the United States Coast Guard into the organization it is today, and reviews the primary missions (programs) of the Coast Guard.

By studying the history of our organization you will be able to understand where the organization is going and how you can best fit in. Remember, the operations and missions of today will be the history of tomorrow. You have an important part to play in helping write the history of the Coast Guard.

HISTORY—IN PURSUIT OF NATIONAL PURPOSES

Unlike some federal organizations, the United States Coast Guard did not begin at any one time for any single purpose. Instead, today's Coast Guard is a collection of other federal organizations that no longer exist, most of them long forgotten.

In order to describe the complete organizational evolution of the Coast Guard properly, it would be necessary to begin with the individual histories of each of those old defunct organizations (which are usually referred to as "predecessor agencies"). To write such a history would far exceed the pages available in this manual.

Another way to tell the story is to think of the Coast Guard as being the primary agency involved in the promotion of a whole range

Figure 1-1. Two petty officers from the Revenue Cutter *Rush* during the early 1900s.

of national goals in the maritime arena. That view is less complicated and much more attuned to the actual work the Coast Guard now performs. There are many ways to describe the national objectives that are achieved by the Coast Guard. Sometimes these duties are called missions, sometimes roles, and sometimes programs. In a historical sense, however, we should think of the Coast Guard as carrying out the following traditional primary duties:

promoting safe and efficient maritime transportation;
promoting the collection of national revenues;
promoting measures to enhance national security; and
promoting the preservation of life and property following
    maritime incidents.

You will note that the word "promoting" has been used in describing each of these national purposes. This is fitting for the Coast Guard, because the Latin root word for "promote" means "to move forward." In the Preamble to the Constitution, the authors included the clause "to promote the general welfare." It was this wording that has been used by Congress to justify most of the national purposes assigned to the Coast Guard since 1789. Whereas other federal organizations have been created over the ensuing years to "maintain" various things, Coast Guard predecessors were charged with moving ahead, taking the ball and running with it. Historically, the merging of the predecessor agencies into the Coast Guard took place because, although they were charged with moving forward a national purpose, they took on a "maintain what we have" approach instead.

Coast Guard history can be viewed as a series of important but unrelated events that can be selectively presented because they establish precedents, reinforce traditions, provide a neat comparison with another military organization, or have some special local interest. The Coast Guard is rich in this kind of history, and it encourages pride in our organization. Let's take a look at our history as a reflection of national purpose—highlighted by the important events of the past.

One of the first orders of business our nation's founders had to contend with was maritime trade. In those days almost all trade beyond the borders of the United States was done by ships. Different colonies had taken a number of steps to promote safe and efficient marine transportation, but in their new role as states, it was believed that such promotion ought to be national in purpose and be handled by the federal government—at least insofar as building and maintaining the devices that would assist navigation were concerned. The new states may have been eager to retain control over the pilots who guided vessels into the coastal ports, but the maintenance of expensive structures was something they were happy to pass on to the federal government.

Thus, in 1789 the Coast Guard began the business of maintaining lighthouses. Under the supervision of the Army Corps of Engineers, new lighthouses and beacons were built during the early 1800s with federal funds, and older lighthouses, built by private subscriptions of maritime interests, were taken over by the federal government. The general supervision of this effort to promote safe and efficient marine transportation fell to the secretary of the treasury. For many years, this function was performed by the Fifth Auditor of the Treasury, Samuel Pleasanton. In 1852, a special group within the Treasury Department was formed and called The Lighthouse Board. The board consisted of Army engineers, Navy officers, and civilian scientists.

At about the same time that our new nation realized it had a duty to promote safe and efficient marine transportation, it was faced with a greater, more immediate challenge—collection of revenues. In an atmosphere of almost total disregard by some marine interests for the new customs laws, where smuggling of commodities from foreign countries into the marketplace without paying customs duties was commonplace, this was no small challenge. The collection of revenues arising from customs fees and tariffs was one of the ways the new federal government could raise the money required to run the government; there was no income tax in those days! And there were, indeed, costs involved in running the government, particularly if the government was to "provide for the common defense and promote the general welfare," as stated in the Preamble to the Constitution.

In October 1789, Secretary of the Treasury Alexander Hamilton asked the various collectors of customs about the need for boats to protect and ensure revenue collection. Sharp Delany, the collector at Philadelphia, replied that he was already using a vessel for that purpose and fully endorsed the concept. In April 1790, Hamilton asked Congress to create a Revenue Marine service with a fleet of ten small cutters. As the Continental Navy had been disestablished after the Revolution and would not be reestablished until 1799 no armed federal vessels existed with which a Revenue Marine service could be created.

On 4 August 1790, Congress passed Hamilton's Revenue Cutter

Bill, which provided for construction of the following ten armed cutters:

Scammel	*Active*
Massachusetts	*Virginia*
Argus	*Diligence*
Vigilant	*South Carolina*
General Greene	*Eagle*

Hamilton's first ten armed vessels were not large by modern standards; they ranged in length from 40 to 60 feet. In fact, today we would call them boats, not cutters. Despite their small size and absence of uniformity in design, the law and these vessels established the precedent that all ships of the Coast Guard would forever be called cutters.

The date 4 August 1790 is important to the Coast Guard because it is celebrated as the Coast Guard's birthday. Even though the nation had announced its intention to promote safe and efficient marine transportation a calendar year earlier, our national commitment to construct, maintain, and man a fleet of armed vessels for actual law-enforcement operations is of far greater historical significance. It would not be until 1847 that official consideration would be given toward using federal lighthouse people for other than maintenance and lamplighting. By that time, the role of Hamilton's armed federal vessels had expanded to meet several other national objectives, including the promotion of safe and efficient marine transportation.

Scarcely eight years had elapsed from the time that Hamilton first considered using armed federal vessels to promote revenue collection when a new threat emerged. Foreign armed vessels had begun making unprovoked attacks on our merchant marine. On 1 July 1797, Congress authorized the president to "increase the strength of the several Revenue Cutters . . . to defend the sea coast and to repel any hostility. . . ." Thus, the Coast Guard became "multimission," having the two jobs of providing for the common defense as well as collecting revenues. Over the ensuing decades, other national purposes were served by our revenue cutters—specifically, enhancing the preservation of life by rescuing the shipwrecked, and promoting safe transportation by supporting the lighthouse establishment.

In 1838, Congress responded to a rash of explosions on steamboats. The technology of the steam engine was relatively new, and its application to marine transportation, though economically successful, wasn't always safe when left solely to the steamboat industry. To protect passengers from this risk, Congress enacted a federal steamboat inspection law calling for the enforcement of vessel safety standards. This law and a host of statutes that followed were enforced by federal inspectors whose job was to prevent maritime disasters and the resulting loss of life. Ultimately, they were very successful. Coast Guard inspectors became investigators. The inspector/investigator role expanded to include crew licensing, vessel documentation, protection of ports from dangerous cargoes, the physical security of ports, the safety of waterways, and the preservation of the marine environment. The inspectors, as in the case of other Coast Guardsmen, have become involved in promoting more than one national purpose. In licensing and documentation, they foster safe and efficient marine transportation, and in port safety they advance measures to enhance national security.

As the middle of the nineteenth century approached, our nation's population swelled from shiploads of European immigrants. New York was their destination, and the coastlines of Long Island, New York, and New Jersey became the final resting places for many of the immigrant packet ships that fell victim to winter storms.

Colonial laws also had dealt with the matter of shipwreck as they applied to salvage. Different colonies had different laws, and when the colonies became states, many colonial laws became state laws. Merchants at the principal seaports along our coasts were interested in making sure that the goods carried by ship to and from their ports reached their destinations. Shipowners, on the other hand, did not wish to lose their ships to shipwrecks, and the insurers of those ships had a very great interest in preventing or minimizing the effect of wrecks.

Acting together with the interests of merchants, shipowners, and marine insurers, colonial law combined to create a sort of safety system. Lighthouses were funded and built by local interests. Skilled local navigators, called *pilots*, were required by colonial governments to be employed by masters on board oceangoing vessels transiting the port. Humane societies were founded to care for shipwreck victims, and in some cases, to engage in rescue operations. Colonies, and later states, established government posts, called variously *wreckmasters, commissioners of vendue, vendue masters*, etc., whose job it was to rally local boat crews, row boats out to the wrecks, rescue the people on board, and save the vessel and cargo. Often the laws provided that the boat crew that rescued the people got the salvage job, too. But the safety system was not very well developed, and no lifesaving technology was employed, other than the use of an experienced and skillful boat crew. If boats could not be launched because of sea conditions, there was little that could be done except to care for the shipwrecked victims who were washed ashore and to bury the dead.

On 3 August 1848, a physician from New Jersey named Newell, who was also a member of Congress, introduced an amendment to a lighthouse appropriation bill to provide $10,000 for "surfboats, rockets, and carronades and other apparatus necessary for the better protection of life and property from shipwreck on the coast of New Jersey, between Sandy Hook and Little Egg Inlet." In an impassioned speech calling for this appropriation, Newell dwelt heavily upon the responsibility of the federal government to promote the general welfare—in other words, to promote the preservation of life and property following a maritime incident. The amendment was passed, and the federal government entered into the search-and-rescue business as a specific objective. A chain of coastal rescue stations, manned by paid crew members, was not begun until 1871; nevertheless, Newell's appropriation did provide the immediate basis for a very effective, volunteer, manned rescue system on the coasts of New Jersey and Long Island. In the twenty-two years that the volunteer lifesavers were at work, aided by substantial support from marine insurance interests, 90 percent of all persons on board vessels shipwrecked in their area reached shore safely. In areas not so protected, and during the years before 1848, the existing safety system enabled 50 to 60 percent of those on board wrecks to survive. In the years following the establishment of the full, paid-crew, coastal rescue system, 99 percent of those on board wrecked vessels made it ashore safely. During those later years, the "lifesavers" (as they were called) of the coastal rescue stations were to expand their role beyond that of solely serving to promote the preservation of life and property following a maritime incident.

The lifesavers were of service to Customs, being on the lookout for smuggling; hence, they were involved in collecting national revenues. But perhaps the single most important other service they were involved in was that of national security, when they provided 60 percent of the nation's coastal sentry force during the Spanish-American War.

In discussing the national purposes traditionally assigned to the Coast Guard, law enforcement is not listed, because virtually every-

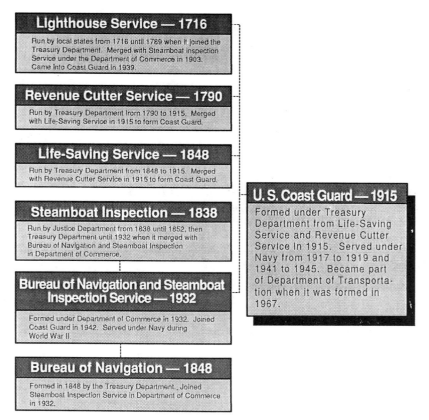

Lighthouse Service — 1716

Run by local states from 1716 until 1789 when it joined the Treasury Department. Merged with Steamboat Inspection Service under the Department of Commerce in 1903. Came into Coast Guard in 1939.

Revenue Cutter Service — 1790

Run by Treasury Department from 1790 to 1915. Merged with Life-Saving Service in 1915 to form Coast Guard.

Life-Saving Service — 1848

Run by Treasury Department from 1848 to 1915. Merged with Revenue Cutter Service in 1915 to form Coast Guard.

U. S. Coast Guard — 1915

Formed under Treasury Department from Life-Saving Service and Revenue Cutter Service in 1915. Served under Navy from 1917 to 1919 and 1941 to 1945. Became part of Department of Transportation when it was formed in 1967.

Steamboat Inspection — 1838

Run by Justice Department from 1838 until 1852, then Treasury Department until 1932 when it merged with Bureau of Navigation and Steamboat Inspection in Department of Commerce.

Bureau of Navigation and Steamboat Inspection Service — 1932

Formed under Department of Commerce in 1932. Joined Coast Guard in 1942. Served under Navy during World War II.

Bureau of Navigation — 1848

Formed in 1848 by the Treasury Department. Joined Steamboat Inspection Service in Department of Commerce in 1932.

Figure 1-2. Organizations merged to form the Coast Guard.

thing the Coast Guard does *is* law enforcement! The concept of our moving forward as an organization means that the Coast Guard has actively promulgated the will of our citizens as expressed through Congress in the passage of legislation that became law. Coast Guard actions have included enforcement operations directed against greedy shipowners whose chief interest was in making money and not in safe and efficient marine transportation; against smugglers who cared little for the national revenue; against saboteurs who would destroy our national security; and against wanton poisoners of our marine environment who would threaten the safety of our lives and property by carelessly or deliberately causing marine pollution incidents. Law enforcement is a way of life for Coast Guard personnel; it is one of the main tools we use in achieving our national objectives. It is a means to an end, but it is not, of itself, an end.

Military Milestones of Coast Guard History

In fulfilling its responsibilities to promote the general welfare, the Coast Guard was charged with many duties that were specifically military in nature. Today, these duties are referred to as military operations; they form a very special portion of Coast Guard history and deserve to be treated separately. The record of our military operations can be traced back to the Quasi-War with France and brought forward to Operation Desert Storm.

Our Coast Guard standard proudly exhibits 31 battle streamers—each one designed to remind us of our heroic predecessors. Many of the men and women who served our country in these campaigns sacrificed their lives for us who now enjoy the freedoms they so jealously guarded. The following paragraphs briefly describe some of these battles, campaigns, and operations.

Quasi-War of 1798-1801

The original ten cutters placed into service in 1791 were soon replaced by larger ones. In 1798, the United States was without a navy, the Continental Navy having been disbanded following the Revolutionary War. Aggressive military and naval activity by France resulted in the seizure of several merchant vessels by armed French vessels on the high seas. The naval response of the United States was to employ the revenue cutters in the defense of our merchant fleet. In these operations, the cutters responded effectively, as they would in future conflicts in support of the nation's naval missions. Especially outstanding were the *Pickering*, Commodore Preble's first command, and the *Eagle*. The *Eagle* fought a memorable engagement with the French privateer *Revenge* in 1799, recapturing the American vessels *Nancy* and *Mehitable*.

War of 1812

From 1801 until the war with England in 1812, the cutters were busy enforcing the Embargo and Non-Intercourse Acts. After the War of 1812 began, the cutter *Jefferson* captured the first enemy prize, in June. The cutter *Vigilant* captured the *Dart*. The most famous action

Figure 1-3. The Revenue Cutter *Vigilant* captures the British privateer *Dart* in a night engagement off Block Island on 4 October 1813.

was fought by the cutter *Eagle*. When she was caught by two British ships, her captain ran the ship ashore on Long Island. The crew dragged guns to a cliff top and beat off the enemy. That night they refloated their ship and headed for New Haven, but she could make little speed and the enemy finally captured her.

The end of the war brought no peace for the cutters. For the next quarter century, they fought pirates, slavers, smugglers, and Indians. The *Alabama* and *Louisiana* broke up the notorious LaFitte gang of pirates in the Gulf of Mexico, and the *Dallas* and *Jackson* fought the Seminole Indians in Florida.

Mexican War

During the war with Mexico (1846–48) cutters performed scout, convoy, towing, and blockade duty, transported troops and supplies, carried mail and dispatches, and put down a mutiny of troops on the *Middlesex*. The cutters *Ewing* and *Legare* delivered rifles to troops before the battles of Monterey and Buena Vista.

Figure 1-4. The revenue cutter *Harriet Lane* forces the merchant steamer *Nashville* to show her colors during the attack on Fort Sumter 13 April 1861.

Civil War

During the Civil War, all the military services were torn by officers who "went South" to fight for their native states. To prevent the cutter *McClelland* from being turned over to the Confederates, Secretary Dix issued a dispatch containing the words that became a rallying cry of the North: ". . . If anyone attempts to haul down the American flag, shoot him on the spot."

In May of 1862, President Lincoln and his staff embarked on the *Miami* and cruised down Chesapeake Bay to Norfolk where the Union transports, loaded with troops, were anchored. Officers claimed that the water was too shoal for a landing, but that night the *Miami* steamed inshore and landed the president on Confederate soil. Safely back aboard the cutter, Lincoln personally ordered the assault for the next day. It was completely successful.

Spanish-American War

Even before the outbreak of war with Spain, a squadron of cutters patrolled the Straits of Florida to prevent violations of American neutrality. Seven vessels were seized, two filibustering expeditions were broken up, and a dozen gun-runners were chased back into American ports. The new *McCulloch*, on a round-the-world shakedown cruise, joined Dewey's squadron at Hong Kong and participated in the defeat of the Spanish fleet at Manila Bay. Meanwhile,

Figure 1-5. The *Hudson* prepares to tow the disabled *Winslow* beyond enemy fire at the battle of Cárdenas, Cuba, 11 May 1898.

the cutters on the East Coast joined naval forces in actions against Spanish forces in Cuba.

World War I

During World War I, 280 lifeboat stations were active, and fifteen cruising cutters patrolled off the coast. Overseas, six cutters patrolled between Gibraltar and England.

Near the end of the war, the *Tampa*, presumably struck by a torpedo, was lost with all hands. During this war the Coast Guard had a higher percentage of personnel killed in action than any other service.

It was in this same period that Coast Guard aviation was born. Lieutenant E. F. Stone, USCG, one of several early Coast Guard flyers, was copilot on the Navy NC-4 flying boat, the first aircraft to cross the Atlantic.

After the war, the job of enforcing the Eighteenth (Prohibition)

Amendment by sea was given to the Coast Guard. This antismuggling duty entailed considerable expansion in both ships and aircraft. Prior to World War I, extensive scouting flights had met with such success that Congress had authorized the establishment of ten Coast Guard air stations. The war stopped the development, but under influence of the Prohibition Amendment, the scouting flights were resumed.

World War II

In September 1941, the cutter *Northland* frustrated a German attempt to set up weather stations in Greenland by capturing the *Buskoe*, the first naval capture in World War II.

Immediately after the Japanese attack on Pearl Harbor on 7 December 1941, cutters were ordered to escort duty. One of the first successful attacks on a German submarine was credited to the 165-

Figure 1-6. The *Taney* fires at Japanese aircraft at Pearl Harbor 7 December 1941.

foot cutter *Icarus*, which forced the submarine to the surface with depth charges and forced her to surrender with a 3-inch "popgun."

Another famous attack was delivered by the *Campbell*. In early 1943 she ran into the center of a wolf pack. One submarine was sunk by ramming after a sharp gun battle. The *Campbell* was badly damaged. The entire crew volunteered to remain aboard, but the captain permitted only a small group to stay. This party kept the ship afloat during a 600-mile tow to port.

Later the same year, the *Spencer* made an attack that involved the difficult feat of tracking a submarine through a convoy. This successful attack was conducted with such skill that the action report became part of the antisubmarine force doctrine.

In World War II, Coast Guardsmen operated escort destroyers, frigates, corvettes, patrol boats, and subchasers, while planes patrolled the coasts and assisted in the war on submarines. Beach patrols and Port Security Units ensured coastal safety.

In the Pacific war, amphibious operations employed thousands of Coast Guardsmen, where their small-boat experience proved invaluable. Over 180,000 Coast Guard men and women served on combat ships and in the support forces, where they manned naval transports, attack transports, supply vessels, and shore units. Douglas Munro, a signalman, was posthumously awarded the only Medal of Honor won by a member of the Coast Guard. He heads a long list of Coast Guard personnel who were cited for courage and skill in action.

As a wartime measure, in 1942 the Bureau of Marine Inspection and Navigation was consolidated with the Coast Guard because of the importance of marine safety laws to the war effort. In 1946 this organizational change was made permanent.

The Korean War

In 1946 a Coast Guard team was sent to Seoul, Korea, to "organize, supervise, and train a Korean Coast Guard." This group became the National Maritime Police. A shipyard was set up, a supply and communications system was arranged, training facilities were established, and nineteen ships were transferred to Korea from the Japanese and American navies.

With the outbreak of hostilities, marked by the invasion by North Korean Communist forces southward across the 38th parallel into the Republic of South Korea in June 1950, the United Nations responded with a "police action," usually called the Korean War. The Coast

Figure 1-7. Signalman 1/c Douglas A. Munro protects withdrawing Marines at Guadalcanal.

Guard manned a number of Navy destroyer escorts, performing a variety of missions in the Western Pacific. A chain of mobile Loran stations was established in the Far East to support the air and sea navigational needs of United Nation forces. One of those Coast Guard stations was situated at Pusan, Korea.

Coast Guard in Vietnam

During the early stages of the Vietnam conflict, the Navy was faced with the problem of preventing the movement of enemy forces and supplies by water, in areas where large combatant naval vessels could not operate. Vietnam's long and irregular coastline and the prevalence of fishermen and coastwise commerce in sampans made it difficult to distinguish friend from foe. The Coast Guard's highly maneuverable craft were ideal for operations there, and in April 1965 it sent seventeen of its 82-footers to Vietnam. The cutters were heavily armed, and their crews received extensive training. Later, nine more cutters joined them.

Coast Guardsmen boarded all suspicious-looking craft, searching for weapons, ammunition, and other contraband. In addition, the cutters took part in hundreds of naval gunfire support missions, assisting ground forces with mortar fire on selected enemy targets.

In 1967 the Coast Guard sent five larger cutters to operate from Subic Bay, Republic of the Philippines, and patrol off Vietnam.

Coast Guard involvement in South Vietnam included an extensive aids-to-navigation operation including port safety teams to supervise off-loading of ammunition from ships, and a merchant marine detail. Loran stations were built in Vietnam and Thailand.

In 1969–79, the Coast Guard turned over to the Republic of Vietnam all of its 82-footers on duty in Vietnam and four 311-foot, high-endurance cutters.

The War on Drugs

For over 200 years, the Coast Guard has been the nation's principal maritime law enforcement agency and is the *only* federal agency with jurisdiction on the high seas, as well as in U.S. territorial waters. An important part of the Coast Guard's enforcement mission is the interdiction of illegal drugs bound for the United States. Coast Guard cutters, boats, planes, and helicopters conduct routine drug patrols and special operations throughout the maritime arena, both over and on waters adjacent to principal source and transit countries and in U.S. coastal waters. The Coast Guard's program emphasis is on interdicting vessels and aircraft smuggling cocaine and marijuana into the U.S., and in tracking, monitoring, and apprehending aircraft suspected of carrying drugs from source and transit countries over the high seas.

Operation Desert Shield/Desert Storm

In August of 1990 the army of Iraq invaded and quickly took control of their neighboring country of Kuwait. A coalition of countries from around the world, led by the United States, quickly responded to the threat to other countries in the area. Coast Guard personnel throughout the world were pressed into service to support the largest buildup of military forces in recent memory.

During Operation Desert Shield the initial Coast Guard efforts included breaking out sixty-eight ships of the Ready Reserve and locating merchant seamen to safely sail the vessels. The loading of hazardous materials and ammunition was supervised in U.S. ports. Three Reserve Port Security Units were deployed to Saudi Arabia to provide waterside security for DOD forces.

The primary objective of Operation Desert Storm was to expel the invading forces from Kuwait and restore the legitimate free government. The swift and decisive victory of the Allied Coalition forces has ushered in a new era and spirit of peaceful international cooperation among the nations of the world.

The Coast Guard's unique operational capabilities and maritime expertise were tapped quickly and often by the Departments of Defense, State, and Transportation and by governments of the Allied Coalition. Law Enforcement Detachments (LEDETS) were dispatched to augment and most often lead the naval boarding teams enforcing the United Nations economic embargo. These teams conducted hundreds of boardings and uncovered tons of illicit cargo. Coast Guard personnel also augmented the staff of the Commander Middle East Forces to coordinate interdiction and SAR efforts of the myriad naval forces deployed in the Persian Gulf and Red Sea. Field units from New York to Guam were engaged in loading explosives, and in port safety and port security operations. Over 800 reservists were on active duty assisting these operations. Three Reserve Port Security Units stood in harms way to assume duties in joint Coast Guard/Navy harbor defense. Coast Guard oil spill experts quickly responded to a request from the Saudi Arabian government to assist them in dealing with the massive oil spill. These experts and Aireye-equipped aircraft provided invaluable technical advice and assistance in combating this act of environmental terrorism. The versatility of our service has never been more impressively displayed.

MISSIONS—WHAT WE DO NOW

It is not possible to separate the history of the Coast Guard from its missions. In order to fulfill the objectives that the citizens have set for us through federal laws, we should understand how and why we got started in the first place. For example, it is important that Coast Guard personnel know that the reason we originally carried out certain safety inspections was to protect ships and their passengers and crew members from ignorant, careless, or greedy shipowners who were not interested in safety. Times change, as do missions, but any Coast Guard person who understands the basic historical reasons for our safety missions should know that the Coast Guard's job is to protect lives and property from maritime accidents and the results thereof. It surely is not to provide a service to the owner of a vessel; the owner has insurance to protect his investment, and the Coast Guard is not in the insurance business. So history is important to know, because it provides us with background and the reasons *why* we do what we do.

Missions, however, are *what* we do; they are the most important and should demand our very best efforts. Coast Guard missions are the specific groups of activities that carry out the national purposes discussed earlier. Sometimes missions are called *programs* or *operating programs.*

One interesting aspect of the Coast Guard is that it is a multimission organization. That means that there are very few operating units that perform only one program or mission. This is unlike most federal civilian agencies. Nearly every Coast Guard operating unit requires the operation of cutters, aircraft, or boats, even if only on occasion, to meet its mission requirements. Some operating units, of course, are cutters; others are the places from which aircraft, boats, and vehicles operate. When Coast Guard personnel are under way, they are multimission because they "carry the flag" with them. The longer Coast Guard personnel remain in the service, the more training and experience they usually have in a variety of Coast Guard missions. It is Coast Guard personnel, and their varied capabilities, that makes us multimission. Multimission saves the taxpayer money. A cutter on law- and treaty-enforcement patrol is also a potential search-and-rescue platform. A harbor patrol boat on a port and environmental safety mission may detect a drug smuggler. All the Coast Guard units at a port will respond during the time of natural or maritime disaster to perform all the missions required, with safety of life as the highest priority. That's multimission!

Programs Briefly Described

A brief description of the major Coast Guard programs/missions follows:

Search and Rescue

Search and rescue is one of the Coast Guard's oldest missions. Rescuing those in peril at sea has priority over all other Coast Guard peacetime missions. The Coast Guard keeps a nationwide system of boats, aircraft, cutters, and rescue coordination centers on 24–hour alert, ready to respond to vessels in distress. The program objective is to minimize loss of life, personal injury and property damage on the high seas and in all United States waters.

Marine Environmental Protection

This program has two major mission areas. Their objectives are:
Marine environmental response. To minimize damage caused by pollutants released in the coastal zone. To overcome or reduce threats to the marine environment posed by potential spills of oil or hazardous substances. To assist in national and international pollution response planning. *Every effort is made to recover costs following a federal response.*

Port safety and security. To safeguard the nation's ports, waterways, waterfront facilities, vessels, personnel, and property from accidental or intentional damage, disruption, destruction or injury. To monitor oil transfer and hazardous cargo operations to prevent spills. To conduct harbor patrols to detect oil or chemical spills, and to enforce pollution regulations.

Enforcement of Laws and Treaties

Enforcement of laws and treaties (ELT) became the first mission of what would evolve into the Coast Guard when in 1790 Alexander Hamilton formed a "fleet of cutters" to suppress smuggling. Today, drug interdiction has made ELT one of the Coast Guard's most visible missions. The program objective's are: to enforce federal law on the high seas and in U.S. waters; to interdict drug smugglers and illegal migrants; to enforce exclusive economic zone laws and regulations up to 200 nautical miles offshore; to inspect domestic and foreign fishing vessels to ensure compliance with U.S. law; and to help other agencies enforce our nation's laws.

Ice Operations

The Coast Guard conducts both *polar ice operations* and *domestic ice operations.* It is the only federal agency that operates icebreakers. Icebreakers provide assistance and oceanographic support to Coast Guard programs—the search and rescue, aids to navigation, and enforcement of laws and treaties programs—and to other governmental and scientific organizations. The program objectives are: to provide icebreaking capability to support our national interest in polar regions; to facilitate U.S. maritime transportation through iceladen domestic waters; and to conduct the International Ice Patrol (initiated in 1912 after the oceanliner *Titanic* struck an iceberg and sank), which observes and charts the positions and movement of icebergs.

Aids to Navigation

The aids-to-navigation program operates long-range electronic *radionavigation aids*—Loran-C and Omega systems—worldwide, as well as domestic radiobeacons. It also maintains *short-range aids to navigation*—lighthouses, fog signals, buoys, daymarkers, and radar beacons—and operates *vessel traffic services*. The program's objectives are: to develop, establish, maintain and operate audible, visible, and radar aids to navigation that help navigators determine their position or safe course and warn of obstructions in or adjacent to navigable waters; to establish, operate, and maintain electronic aids throughout the United States and in other areas of the world in order to provide continuous, accurate, all-weather positioning capability for military and civilian mariners and aviators.

Marine Safety

The Coast Guard's marine safety program consists of two major activities: *commercial vessel safety*, which carries out comprehensive marine inspection and licensing programs; and *recreational boating safety*, which fulfills the legislative mandates of the Federal Boat Safety Act of 1871.

Commercial Vessel Safety. This program's objectives are: to minimize deaths, injuries, property loss, and environmental damage by developing and enforcing federal standards for vessels, offshore facilities, merchant marine personnel, and other facilities engaged in commercial or scientific activity in the marine environment.

Recreational Boating Safety. This program's aim is to reduce the number of deaths, personal injuries, and property damage involving recreational boats; to improve boating safety; and to encourage the development, use, and enjoyment of all U.S. waters.

Defense Readiness

Defense readiness ensures that the Coast Guard can function as an effective armed force. Coast Guard resources are used in both peacetime and wartime. The program's objective is to provide constant Coast Guard military capability and readiness.

CHAPTER 2

Organization

The Coast Guard is a large multimission organization consisting of both full-time active duty military and civilian personnel and part-time reserve and auxiliary personnel. Over 90,000 people are involved in serving their country and fellow men and women as part of this important team. In peacetime the Coast Guard operates under the Department of Transportation, and the commandant receives orders from the secretary of that department. In time of war or when directed by the president, the Coast Guard operates as a service within the Department of the Navy.

ACTIVE-DUTY FORCES—COMMAND STRUCTURE

The Coast Guard organization is structured to accommodate the service's multimission nature and is very complex.

The commandant, a four-star admiral, plans, supervises, and coordinates the overall activities of the Coast Guard. The commandant gives immediate direction to special service units, called headquarters units, which report directly to headquarters even though they are within the geographic limits of districts.

The area commanders, three-star admirals, act for the commandant in coordinating or directing emergency or contingency opera-

Figure 2-1. Coast Guard Raider boats patrolling around the Maritime Prepositioning Ship PFC *Dewayne T. Williams* as it comes into port in the Persian Gulf.

tions within areas where multidistrict coordination is required. The area commanders serve as the intermediate echelon of command between the commandant and intra-area district and maintenance and logistic commanders.

The district commanders, one- and two-star admirals, provide regional direction and coordination for the performance of operational duties by individual field units within the geographic limits of their district.

The maintenance and logistics commanders, one-star admirals, provide maintenance and logistic support to area commanders and district units.

The commanding officers or officers-in-charge are responsible for their particular units and have absolute responsibility for those units unless relieved by competent authority. They may delegate authority to subordinates to carry out details, but this does not relieve them of the responsibility for the safety, efficiency, and well-being of their commands.

Chain of Command

The chain of military command and operational and administrative control ordinarily runs from the commandant to the area commanders, from the area commanders to the district commanders and maintenance and logistics commanders, and from them to commanding officers and officers-in-charge of operational and logistics units. In the case of units reporting directly to headquarters, the chain of command runs directly from the commandant to the commanding officers of those units. Figure 2-2 shows the chain of command.

In very small organizations, managers can normally execute all of their own functions. However, as organizations become larger, managers must delegate part of their functions to subordinates. These subordinates as a group constitute their staffs. The concept of staff is an essential feature of Coast Guard organization.

Staffs assist the commandant, area commanders, district commanders, and maintenance and logistics commanders. Their authority comes from the commandant or their respective commanders. They can take action on a variety of matters; however, they must take action in behalf of, or in the name of, the appropriate staff officer in charge.

In a staff component of an organization, the chain of command runs from the military chief of the component through the military

Figure 2-2. Chain of Command.

assistant chief to subordinates within the component. Where civilians serve as chief or assistant chief of a component, they serve in recognized supervisory roles, but are not in the military chain of command.

Additional command and support levels exist to reduce the wide span of control for district commanders or to handle special geographic areas. Group commanders (within the United States) and sector commanders (outside the United States) provide direction, support, and coordination for assigned units. A special European command—Activities Europe—provides command, support, and coordination for units assigned in that area.

Headquarters Organization

Coast Guard Headquarters is in Washington, D.C. From headquarters, the commandant directs the policy, legislation, and administration of the Coast Guard. He is aided by the vice commandant and assisted by a chief of staff and staff rear admirals heading up the offices shown in figure 2-2.

Each staff office performs specific functions related to a specific area. For example, the Office of Engineering and Development performs functions of an engineering nature, such as the design, construction, repair, maintenance, outfitting, and alteration of vessels, aircraft, aids to navigation machinery, and utilities. The Office of Personnel and Training deals with the procurement, training, assignment, and separation of personnel.

Headquarters Units

Certain Coast Guard units, even though physically within the geographical limits of a district, operate independently of the district commander; they are under the direct control of the commandant. These units, known as headquarters units, were established because they satisfy a total service requirement. For instance, the Research and Development Center at Groton, Connecticut, supports the operational programs of the Coast Guard by conducting research and developing operational techniques, concepts, systems, equipment, and materials. Training centers are classified as headquarters units, since their duty or function is to provide training support to a broad segment of the Coast Guard.

Major headquarters units include the following:

Training Centers (all)	Coast Guard Yard
Aircraft Repair and Supply Center	Coast Guard Academy
Electronics Engineering Center	Marine Safety Center
Intelligence Coordination Center	Pay and Personnel Center

Coast Guard Areas

The ten Coast Guard Districts, and two Maintenance and Logistics Commands, report to two Area Commands—Atlantic and Pacific.

The area commanders are vice admirals who control the operations of designated area units that include major cutters, aircraft, and communication stations. The area commanders, assisted by their staffs, have special responsibilities relating to readiness and mobilization planning, search and rescue and law enforcement operations, and oceanographic and icebreaking functions.

Coast Guard Maintenance and Logistics Commands

MLC Atlantic and MLC Pacific are each under the command of the maintenance and logistics commander, who reports to the respective area commander. The MLCs are tasked with providing internal support to their operational units. The MLC commanders are assisted by their staffs, which are divided into division or staff elements as follows:

Vessel Technical Support	Inspection
Shore Technical Support	Health Services
Finance	Legal
Communication Technical Support	Personnel

Each division provides support or services in its respective logistic area. For example, the Vessel Technical Support Division manages the repair, maintenance, and alteration programs for cutters and standard boats assigned to the area and districts. Likewise, the Health Services Division manages the planning and administration of the health care of eligible beneficiaries.

A variety of units and subunits (subunits are headed by supervisors) exist to provide immediate support services to operating units. The various types of MLC elements include:

Support Centers	Ship Repair Detachments
Facility Design and Construction Centers	Shore Maintenance Detachments
Electronic Maintenance Detachments	Maintenance Assist Teams

The commanding officer or supervisor of an MLC element reports directly to the MLC commander but works directly with the operating units to deliver support services.

Coast Guard Districts

The ten Coast Guard districts are each under the command of a district commander, who is a rear admiral directly representing the area commander in all matters pertaining to the Coast Guard within the district. The district commanders are responsible for the administration of their districts and of the efficient, safe, and economical performance of Coast Guard duties within their districts. The district staff serves as their principal advisors.

The district office divisions include Boating Safety, Operations, Marine Safety, Readiness and Reserve, and Administration. Each division performs functions for specific programs. For example, the Operations Division assures the effective performance of some of the operational programs of the district; maintaining the aids to navigation system also comes under its direction. The Marine Safety Division assures the effective performance of the marine safety and pollution-prevention programs of the district; for example, this division enforces the navigation and vessel inspection laws to prevent accidents to United States merchant ships.

Each district contains many shore units and exercises authority over cutters 180' and smaller. Each unit is headed by a commanding officer or officer-in-charge and is provided with the personnel and material necessary to perform specific operational missions.

District Units

A district unit is under the control of the district commander. In some instances, the district commander may exercise control of a particular unit through a group or section commander. The various types of district shore units include:

Air stations   Group offices
Bases   Marine safety offices
Coast Guard stations

RESERVE FORCES

The Coast Guard Reserve is administered by the chief of the Office of Readiness and Reserve and is organized into 51 groups and 311 units located throughout the United States, Guam, and Puerto Rico.

Figure 2-3. U.S. Coast Guard districts.

Force Structure

Reserve groups are established to assist the district commander, reserve unit commanding officers, and active-service unit commanding officers in identifying, training, and administering members of the Selected Reserve.

Reserve units are shore units whose mission is to maintain a trained reserve to perform the duties of its mobilization assignments while assisting the active service.

Administration of the reserve program is largely decentralized in the district offices around the country. Approximately 19,000 personnel are involved in the various programs.

The Ready Reserve is divided into the Selected Reserve (SelRes) with 12,000 members and the Individual Ready Reserve (IRR) with 6,000 members. Personnel in the SelRes perform inactive-duty training drills and at least 12 days of active-duty training each year. Personnel in the IRR, on the other hand, generally have no contractual obligation to perform either inactive- or active-duty training, but may choose to drill or receive training for retirement points only. There are two flag officers in the Ready Reserve—one for the Atlantic and one for the Pacific.

The Standby Reserve comprises members of the reserve other than the Ready and Retired Reserve who are liable for active duty only in time of war or national emergency as declared by Congress, or when authorized by law.

The Retired Reserve consists of members who have retired for length of service and who may be entitled to retired pay at age 60.

Missions and Mobilization

The primary mission of the Coast Guard Reserve, as with all reserve components, is mobilization readiness.

During a war or national emergency, SelRes training units cease to exist, and the members report to active-duty assignments, generally at active component commands. Recent DoD tasking has resulted in the establishment of three port-security units to train for overseas deployment and three aviation reserve units to support two deployable C-130 squadrons. Many reservists were activated and sent to Saudi Arabia as part of Operation Desert Storm.

Part of the Coast Guard's wartime tasking comes from the continuation of its peacetime statutory missions, such as search and rescue, marine environmental protection, and port security. Some of these

Figure 2-4. A Port Security man 1st class on duty in the Perisan Gulf.

Figure 2-5. Coast Guard reservists respond to aircraft crash in Boston Harbor.

activities, such as port safety, would expand dramatically in wartime since the safety and security of our ports is critical to the flow of military and commercial cargoes.

Coast Guard reservists learn most of their mobilization skills from working alongside their active-duty counterparts performing the peacetime Coast Guard's regulatory and law enforcement duties. In the early 1970s, Congress mandated that the Coast Guard Reserve provide a peacetime return to the taxpayer for the resources spent on mobilization training. This led to the concept of augmentation training, a peacetime mission to support active-duty Coast Guard forces in their day-to-day missions of search and rescue, port safety and security, aids to navigation, and law enforcement. Augmentation accounts for two-thirds of all reserve training and focuses on activities that provide reservists with specific skills needed for their mobilization assignments.

Law Enforcement

Since the Coast Guard Reserve's primary means of training for mobilization is augmentation of the active service, reservists hold a variety of assignments that may involve them in the Coast Guard's drug intervention program. Reservists holding afloat mobilization assignments perform their annual active duty on board medium- and high-endurance cutters engaged in law enforcement patrols. Often they relieve members of the regular crew and, as such, are expected to be qualified in all respects for duties on board these vessels, including being members of boarding teams. Reservists routinely relieve the entire crew of several 82-foot patrol boats and perform law enforcement patrols as well as search and rescue.

In gathering and analyzing intelligence, reservists who are civilian law enforcement officers have proved very useful. Their familiarity with local and state intelligence resources often helps expedite the sharing of information that would otherwise be difficult to obtain.

Reservists have worked with the Air Force and Navy in Southern California and Florida in providing radar watches to support specific Customs Service air interdiction operations. Reserve aviation personnel have been involved in special drug enforcement operation conducted with the Bahamian government.

In addition, at small boat stations, where one will find most Selected Reserve personnel, small boat crews are involved in the boarding of vessels in coastal waters to enforce the law. Port security personnel routinely board merchant vessels, inspect waterfront facilities, and assist Customs in searching containerized cargo ashore.

Emergency Response

As a natural outgrowth of augmentation training, the Coast Guard Reserve is involved in responding to domestic emergencies. The biggest peacetime call-up in the history of the Coast Guard Reserve was in response to the Cuban refugee exodus in 1980. During a five-month period, 1,700 reservists were called upon to augment the active service.

Another example of a domestic emergency for which the Coast Guard Reserve was used is in the clean-up of the *Exxon Valdez* oil spill in 1988.

Readiness

For the Coast Guard to assess its readiness capabilities properly, the readiness plans and the ability of reservists to carry out those plans must be tested periodically. The Coast Guard carries out three types of exercises to do this: command post exercises, field training exercises, and fleet exercises.

Command post exercises test the plans, lines of communication, and staff organization, but do not move resources.

Field training exercises, which are typically joint or interservice exercises with the Navy or another branch of the armed services, test the ability to process reservists for mobilization quickly and efficiently. These exercises test plans and involve resource movement and interservice coordination.

Fleet exercises involve reserve participation in shipboard refresher training or underway NATO fleet exercises. These exercises train reservists who have mobilization billets on cutters and provide a means of assessing a Coast Guard cutter's ability to perform its wartime mission.

AUXILIARY FORCES

The Auxiliary is a nonmilitary organization. It operates a Coast Guard civil function, a role further defined by the commandant, who determines the specific manner in which the Auxiliary may perform civil missions and prescribes the training and qualifications necessary to perform these activities. Auxiliary membership is open

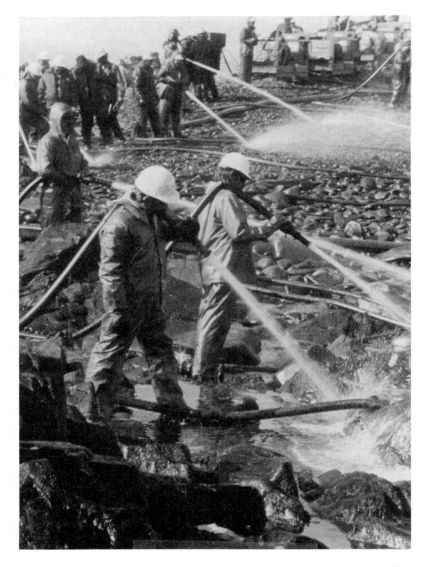

Figure 2-6. Coast Guard reservists assist in cleaning up the Alaskan shoreline after the tanker *Exxon Valdez* ran aground.

to civilian or military men and women, 17 years old or older, who are United States citizens, and who own at least 25 percent interest in a boat, aircraft, or marine radio station. The ownership requirement may be waived if a person has a special talent or skill useful in the boating safety field. The Auxiliary has 40,000 members residing in all 50 states, Puerto Rico, the Virgin Islands, American Samoa, and Guam.

Organization

Although under the authority of the Commandant, the Auxiliary is internally autonomous, operating on four organizational levels: flotilla, division, district, and national.

The chief director, who is a senior Coast Guard officer, is a member of the National Executive Committee and directs the administration of the Auxiliary on policies established by the commandant. The overall supervision of the Coast Guard Auxiliary is under the chief, Office of Navigation Safety and Waterway Services.

Missions

The Auxiliary has four basic missions: vessel examinations, public education, operations, and fellowship. Members may participate in any or all four activities. Auxiliarists must complete correspondence courses and pass examinations, similar to those in the Coast Guard, before participating in the first three activities. The fourth activity is important, as it promotes informal dialogue among members of the entire "Coast Guard family."

Vessel Examinations

The Courtesy Marine Examination (CME) is a free service Auxiliary volunteers provide to pleasure boaters. A CME is a check of the boat's safety-related equipment. Any discrepancies that fail to meet the required standards are not reported to the Coast Guard or any other law enforcement agency. Instead, the Auxiliary examiner points out to the owner the safety equipment lacking and faults needing repair or replacement. If a boat passes the exam, it receives the "Seal of Safety." Some insurance companies offer policy advantages to boaters whose craft have passed a CME.

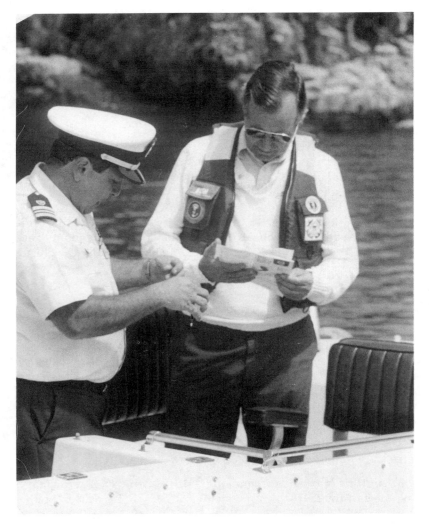

Figure 2-7. Coast Guard Auxiliary officers perform courtesy marine examinations for "all" boat owners.

Public Education

Each year, thousands of people enroll in boating safety courses taught by the Auxiliary. Auxiliarists teach courses to people of all ages, kindergarten to senior citizens—sailors or power boaters. The attempt is to reach boaters, particularly novices, with such life-protecting information as piloting, boat handling, rules of the road, weather, and aids to navigation.

Operations

Auxiliary operations are broad and nonmilitary, covering a wide variety of Coast Guard support missions. Auxiliarists receive training to qualify as boat crew members, operators, and coxswains. In addition, an Auxiliarist may qualify as a communication watchstander and augment a Coast Guard station or group. Auxiliary pilots fly search-and-rescue and pollution patrols and transport Coast Guard and Auxiliary personnel.

Fellowship

This activity is the glue that brings it all together. Auxiliarists exchanging knowledge and swapping "sea stories" develop mutual respect, spark new ideas, enjoy social activities, and establish friendships.

Auxiliarists visit marine dealers and boat and marine trade shows to promote safe boating, particularly during National Safe Boating Week. They assist the Coast Guard's recruiting effort through the Academy Introduction Mission and the Recruiting Assistance Program where young men and women are introduced to the Coast Guard.

Uniforms

Auxiliarists are authorized to wear a uniform similar to the Coast Guard officer's uniform. Distinctive emblems, buttons, insignias, and ribbons are employed to identify the wearers as members of the Auxiliary.

CHAPTER 3

Cutters and Aircraft

Cutters and aircraft are the primary platforms used in the performance of the Coast Guard's many missions. In this chapter we describe the basic characteristics of cutters and aircraft operated and maintained by active-duty and reserve personnel of the Coast Guard.

CUTTERS

A *cutter* is defined as any Coast Guard vessel 65 feet in length or more, having adequate accommodations for the crew to live on board. There are many factors that must be considered when a cutter is being designed to make sure that it can perform its intended missions. It is not practical for the Coast Guard to design cutters that can perform every type of mission. For example, a cutter designed for high stability is rigid and rolls too rapidly for comfort. Designing for speed might require too much space for propulsion equipment, thus lessening crew comfort. (It might also consume fuel at a rate that would drastically reduce its cruising range.) A cutter with a broad beam (that is, very wide in relation to its length) may have more maneuverability, but generally has a reduced speed and shorter cruising range. Therefore, each cutter must be designed with a compromise in which the most desirable features are retained at the sacrifice of other, perhaps less desirable, features.

A multimission Coast Guard requires its cutters to remain at sea

Figure 3-1. Aerial delivery operations extend the range of Coast Guard resources.

for extended periods of time and to travel long distances. There are several things to consider when determining how far a ship can travel and how long it can remain at sea. Among these are the ship's fuel capacity and its rate of fuel consumption. As with a car, the fuel consumed per mile by a ship varies with its speed. Obviously, the most economical speed is that at which the ship travels the greatest distance for the least fuel consumed. Normally when the cruising range of a ship is given, it is at her most economical speed. Factors that affect the speed and therefore the cruising range of a ship are engine efficiency, hull design, and hull cleanliness.

The ability of a ship to sustain high speeds is also very important, since it may mean the difference between success or failure in a rescue operation or in the pursuit of a vessel suspected of a violation of the law.

High-Endurance Cutters (WHEC)

Twelve 378-foot cutters make up the Coast Guard's high-endurance *Hamilton* class. All these cutters will have completed a Fleet Renovation and Modernization (FRAM) program by 1992 to keep them mission capable during the second half of their service lives. Some of the upgraded features include: officer and crew berthing, damage-control systems, communication systems, weapons systems, and engi-

Figure 3-2. High-endurance cutter (WHEC) of the *Hamilton* class.

neering and aviation capabilities. Their primary missions include law enforcement, search and rescue, and defense readiness.

	Hamilton Class
Total crew	180
Length	378 feet
Beam	43 feet
Displacement	3,250 tons
Power plant	two diesel engines
	two gas-turbine engines
Speed	29 knots
Armament	one Mk 75 76-mm gun (anti-air capable)
	two 20-mm machine guns
	two triple torpedo tubes
	eight Harpoon missiles
	one 20-mm Phalanx, Close-In Weapon System (CIWS)

They are equipped with a helicopter landing deck, retractable hangar, and the facilities to support helicopter deployments.

Medium-Endurance Cutters (WMEC)

There are 29 medium-endurance cutters in two major classes, the "Famous" class and the *Reliance* class.

Figure 3-3. Medium-endurance cutter (WMEC) of the "Famous" class.

Thirteen 270-foot, medium-endurance cutters make up the Coast Guard's Famous class. Each is named for a cutter prominent in Coast Guard history. Their primary missions include law enforcement, search and rescue, and defense readiness.

	Famous Class
Total crew	98
Length	270 feet
Beam	38 feet
Displacement	1,820 tons
Power plant	two diesel engines
Speed	19.5 knots
Armament	one Mk 38-25-mm gun
	two .50-caliber machine guns

They are equipped with a helicopter landing deck, retractable hangar, and the facilities to support helicopter deployments.

The Famous class is equipped with a sophisticated computerized shipboard system called COMDAC (for Command, Display, and Control), which provides for maximum operational effectiveness with reduced crews. COMDAC can be used for tracking, plotting,

Figure 3-4. Medium-endurance cutter (WMEC) of the *Reliance* class.

maneuvering, navigation, search-and-rescue patterns, and internal communications.

The 16 cutters of the *Reliance* class are older than those in the Famous class and are currently undergoing a Major Maintenance Availability (MMA) rehabilitation program. The purpose of the MMA is to improve machinery and equipment and to keep the cutters mission capable during the second half of their service lives. Their primary missions include law enforcement, search and rescue, and defense readiness.

	Reliance Class
Total crew	70
Length	210 feet
Beam	34 feet
Displacement	1,000 tons
Power plant	two diesel engines
Speed	18 knots
Armament	one 3″/76-caliber gun
	two .50-caliber machine guns

They are equipped with a helicopter landing deck and the facilities to support helicopter deployments, but have no hangar.

Other Medium-Endurance Cutters

The Coast Guard operates three other classes of medium-endurance cutters, all built in the 1940s: the 180-foot class, the 205-foot class, and the 213-foot class. As old as these cutters are, they are still capable of performing their primary missions of law enforcement and search and rescue.

Icebreakers (WAGB)

The largest cutters operated by the Coast Guard are the icebreakers. These cutters, specifically designed for open-water icebreaking, have reinforced hulls, special icebreaking bows, and a system that allows a rapid shifting of ballast to increase the effectiveness of their icebreaking capabilities. The two Polar-class breakers, the *Polar Star* and *Polar Sea*, were built in the mid-1970s. The remaining breaker, the *Mackinaw*, was built in 1944.

The Polar-class cutters perform their icebreaking duties on the oceans and do much of their work in the earth's polar regions. They

Figure 3-5. Icebreaker (WAGB) of the Polar class.

are capable of breaking ice six feet thick at a speed of three knots, and at a slower speed they can break much thicker ice.

The *Mackinaw* was designed and configured to perform its missions specifically on the Great Lakes where it keeps the shipping lanes open through as much of the winter as possible.

	Polar Class	*Mackinaw*
Total crew	163	75
Length	399 feet	290 feet
Beam	86 feet	74 feet
Displacement	12,000 tons	5,000 tons
Speed	18 knots	18 knots
Power plant	three gas turbine engines five diesel engines	six diesel engines
Armament	two .50-caliber machine guns	small arms
Helicopters	two HH-65As	none

Figure 3-6. Icebreaking tug (WTGB) of the Bay class.

Icebreaking Tugs (WTGB)

Nine 140-foot icebreaking tugs make up the Coast Guard's Bay class. In addition to icebreaking, they are used for search and rescue, enforcement of laws and treaties, deployment of marine environmental-protection equipment, and support for aids-to-navigation activities.

	Bay Class
Total crew	17
Length	140 feet
Beam	37.5 feet
Displacement	662 tons
Power plant	two diesel engines
Speed	14.7 knots
Armament	two M60 machine guns
Icebreaking capability	18–20 inches

The Bay class uses a low-pressure-air hull lubrication or *bubbler* system that forces air and water between the hull and ice. This system improves icebreaking capabilities by reducing resistance against the hull, thereby reducing horsepower requirements.

Figure 3-7. Patrol boat (WPB) of the Island class.

Figure 3-8. Patrol boat (WPB) of the Point class.

Patrol Boats (WPB)

Throughout the history of the Coast Guard, there has always been a need for fast, sturdy, highly maneuverable boats capable of operating in heavy seas. Our duties in search and rescue and the increasing requirement for maritime law enforcement in the interdiction of illegal drugs point out this fact.

There are now two classes of patrol boats in service that have proven to be efficient and seaworthy vessels: the 82-foot Point class (built in the 1960s); and the 110-foot Island class (built in the late 1980s and equipped with advanced electronic equipment). Patrol boat missions include law enforcement, search and rescue, and port security (the Island class is also designed for defense operations).

	Point Class	*Island Class*
Total crew	10	16
Length	82 feet	110 feet
Beam	17 feet	21 feet
Displacement	67.5 tons	185 tons
Power plant	two diesel engines	two diesel engines
Speed	20 knots	26-plus knots
Armament	two .50-caliber machine guns	one 20-mm and two M60 machine guns

Seagoing Buoy Tenders (WLB)

The 27 Coast Guard cutters of the *Cactus*, *Iris*, and *Mesquite* classes are over 40 years old and have all been modernized at least once. A Service Life Extension Program (SLEP) is under way to extend their lives even further. As old as these cutters are, they continue to be highly versatile, durable, and reliable and capable of performing a variety of missions at sea. Eleven have been configured for icebreaking missions. Five are armed with 20-mm machine guns. Their primary missions include tending aids to navigation, law enforcement, and search and rescue.

Figure 3-9. Buoy tender at work.

	Seagoing Buoy Tenders (WLB)
Total crew	53
Length	180 feet
Beam	37 feet
Displacement	1,025 tons
Power plant	two diesel engines
Speed	13 knots

Other Buoy Tenders

The Coast Guard also operates several other classes of buoy tenders: the Coastal class (WLM), 133-175 feet, the Inland class (WLI), 65-100 feet, and the River class (WLR), 65-115 feet. Their primary missions include construction and maintenance of aids to navigation, and search and rescue. Some tenders are also designed for icebreaking. If not outfitted with a crane, these cutters push a barge that is equipped with a crane.

Construction Tenders (WLIC)

The Coast Guard operates 16 Inland-class construction tenders. Their primary missions include the construction and maintenance of many kinds of navigational structures, and search and rescue. These cutters range in length from 75 to 160 feet. If not outfitted with a crane and pile driver, the cutters push a construction barge that is equipped with them.

Surface Effect Ships (WSES)

The three Coast Guard surface effect ships make up the Sea Bird class and are representatives of a new concept in patrol craft. These rigid-side-wall hovercrafts' primary missions include the enforcement of laws and treaties, and search and rescue.

Figure 3-10. Surface Effect Ships (WSES) of the Sea Bird class.

	Surface Effect Ships
Total crew	18
Length	110 feet
Beam	39 feet
Displacement	152 tons
Power plant	two diesel engines (main propulsion)
	two diesel engines (lift fans)
Speed	30-plus knots
Armament	two .50-caliber and
	two M60 machine guns

The lift engines drive fans that create a pressurized air cushion under the cutter and lift it off the surface of the water, reducing drag and draft. The two solid side walls pierce the water's surface, forming a catamaran-like hull with the air cushions sealed by flexible rubberized skirts at the bow and stern. This design makes the SES's highly maneuverable even at low speeds.

Training Cutter (WIX)

The Coast Guard barque *Eagle* bears a name that goes back to the early history of the United States's oldest continuous seagoing service.

The first *Eagle* was commissioned in 1792, just two years after the formation of the Revenue Marine, forerunner of today's Coast Guard.

Today's *Eagle*, the seventh in a long line of proud cutters to bear the name, was built in 1936 by the Blohm & Voss Shipyard, Hamburg, Germany, as a training vessel for German naval cadets. It was commissioned *Horst Wessel*, and following World War II was taken as a war prize by the United States. On 15 May 1946, the barque was commissioned into U.S. Coast Guard service as the *Eagle* and sailed from Bremerhaven to New London, Connecticut.

The *Eagle* serves as a seagoing classroom for approximately 175 cadets and instructors from the U.S. Coast Guard Academy, located in New London, Connecticut. It is on the decks and in the rigging of the *Eagle* that the young men and women of the Coast Guard Academy get their first taste of salt air and life at sea. From this experience they develop a respect for the elements that will be with them throughout their lives.

Sailing in the *Eagle*, cadets handle more than 20,000 square feet of sail and 20 miles of rigging. Over 200 lines must be coordinated

Figure 3-11. Training cutter (WIX) *Eagle.*

during a major ship maneuver, so the cadets must learn the name and function of each line.

The ship readily takes to the task for which it was designed. The *Eagle*'s hull is built of steel four-tenths of an inch thick. It has two full-length steel decks with a platform deck below and a raised forecastle and quarterdeck. The weather decks are three-inch-thick teak over steel.

COAST GUARD YARD

Ships of the Coast Guard fleet must be readily available and have the capability to respond to mission requirements promptly. At the same time they must provide crew safety, comfort, and the assurance that the equipment will continue to operate under adverse conditions.

To ensure that these requirements are met, the ships must be maintained in a seaworthy, dependable condition, with spare-parts support provided for repairs and routine maintenance. Many of these vital functions are performed at the Coast Guard Yard, located at Curtis Bay, Maryland. Ships go there for dry dock, repairs, modification, and modernization. Some Coast Guard ships, patrol boats, and other small craft are built there.

The yard is also the host command to the newly formed Supply

Center, Curtis Bay (SCCB). The Supply Center will act as a central purchasing and supply point for many of the parts needed to support ships throughout the country.

COAST GUARD AVIATION

Coast Guard aviation began officially from an Act of Congress dated 29 August 1916 that authorized the Treasury Department to establish ten Coast Guard air stations along the coasts of the United States.

Provisions were soon made to train pilots and develop rescue procedures for using airplanes in search-and-patrol duties. Also, the Coast Guard became active early in the evolution of helicopters. The Coast Guard developed rescue techniques and equipment to pioneer the use of helicopters as rescue craft. In addition to search-and-rescue duties, Coast Guard helicopters today are used for a variety of missions and are deployed on many of the Coast Guard's cutters.

Coast Guard aircraft types vary and have changed through the years to meet mission requirements. Some of the aircraft and their designs were obtained from other Department of Defense organizations, while others were designed specifically to Coast Guard specifications.

The capabilities that Coast Guard aircraft must have are dictated by the tasks they are called upon to perform. These requirements might include the ability to carry a large amount of cargo for a long distance. Or they might require the ability to become airborne quickly and proceed on a mission at high speed. The ability to land on water, to operate at low speed, to have long endurance, or some combination of these or other specific characteristics, could also be required. No one type of Coast Guard aircraft has all these capabilities, although most have several.

Aircraft Types

It takes more than one type of aircraft to effectively accomplish the varied missions of Coast Guard aviation. There are presently six types of fixed- and rotary-wing (helicopter) aircraft in a Coast Guard fleet of more than 220.

Aircraft Markings

Aircraft operated by the Coast Guard are readily identifiable by their paint schemes and markings. Fixed-wing aircraft are painted with an overall glossy white, solar-reflective finish. The wing tips, tail, and nose of the airplanes are painted red, and there are red and blue Coast Guard emblem stripes on the fuselages. Helicopters have the same basic paint scheme except for those that frequently deploy to the Arctic or Antarctic on ships. These are painted red to contrast with the sea and the frozen background.

Designations

The Coast Guard uses the standard Department of Defense system to designate aircraft. A typical example follows:

HC-130H

H	C	130	H
Modified mission symbol	Basic Mission symbol	Model Number	Modification

Search-and-Rescue Equipment

Coast Guard aircraft are equipped with a variety of search-and-rescue equipment necessary to accomplish their missions plus what is necessary for their crew's protection. For example, in addition to the life rafts carried for crew survival, additional rafts, ready to be dropped to survivors at sea who may need them, are also carried.

These rafts inflate during their descent and can be entered as soon as they reach the water. Attached to the raft, in packets, is a small amount of survival equipment. Additional equipment can be delivered by droppable kits that contain radios, flares, smoke signals, emergency rations, and medicine. Dewatering pumps can also be dropped to assist in pumping out vessels that are taking on water.

Air Stations

Most Coast Guard aircraft operate from bases called air stations. The mission of an air station is to operate and provide maintenance support for the aircraft assigned. This may include providing crews and maintenance support for helicopters assigned to Coast Guard ships. Air stations have facilities such as hangars, maintenance shops, and medical facilities. Most of them have living quarters and dining facilities for officers and enlisted personnel.

Figure 3-12. HC-130H Hercules.

HC-130H Hercules

The HC-130H is a long-range surveillance and transport aircraft that effectively serves the Coast Guard missions of search and rescue, enforcement of laws and treaties (including illegal drug interdiction), marine environmental protection, and International Ice Patrol over the North Atlantic, as well as cargo and personnel transport and military readiness.

The HC-130Hs can exceed 2,600 nautical miles in low-altitude flight with a mission endurance of up to 14 hours. Inertial Navigation Systems, Omega, Loran-C, and radar are guidance aids that enhance the HC-130's effectiveness during long-range maritime patrols. The aircraft are also equipped with scanner windows and a ten-tube flare-launch system.

The Hercules is manufactured by Lockheed-Georgia Company in Marietta, Georgia.

The Coast Guard plans to use HC-130s beyond the year 2000. They meet International Civil Aviation requirements for search and rescue and sea, land, or air surveillance. "Any time—Any where" Coast Guard flight crews have flown early HC-130 models since 1959.

HU-25A Guardian

Forty-one HU-25As, medium-range surveillance fan jets, replaced the HU-16E Albatross and the C-131A Samaritan, prop-driven aircraft, in the Coast Guard fleet. The Guardian's modern technology and design enhance its performance as the service's first multimission jet. It is twice as fast as other aircraft in the service and can get to the scene quickly to perform its role.

The HU-25A can operate from sea level to an altitude of 42,000 feet at dash speed, an important capability for the Coast Guard missions of search and rescue, and enforcement of laws and treaties, including illegal drug interdiction, marine environmental protection, and military readiness. The airframes were assembled in Little

Figure 3-13. HU-25A Guardian.

Rock, Arkansas, at Falcon Jet Corporation, a subsidiary of Dassault-Breguet Aviation.

The Guardian has a surveillance-system operator's (SSO) console that includes radar with a 160-mile range. Through SSO communications gear, radar, VHF, Omnidirectional Rangefinder/Distance Measurement Equipment (VOR/DME), Loran-C and CRT readouts, a Guardian aircraft commander can control search-and-rescue or drug-interdiction operations.

Nine of the HU-25As have been converted to the Night Stalker (HU-25C) version. Each HU-25A was modified to include an AN/APG-66 radar and a WR-360 forward-looking infrared radar (FLIR). Additionally, encrypted radios were installed to increase the aircraft's secure communications capability. The Night Stalker's sensor system combines radar and infrared detection performance to provide all-weather day/night detection, classification, and tracking of ground, maritime, and airborne targets.

HH-65A Dolphin

Ninety-six short-range HH-65A helicopters replaced the aging HH-52A Sikorsky Sea Guard. These twin-engine Dolphins operate up to 150 miles offshore and will fly comfortably at 150 knots for three hours.

Though normally stationed ashore, the Dolphins can be carried on board medium- and high-endurance Coast Guard cutters. They assist in the missions of search and rescue, enforcement of laws and treaties including drug interdiction, polar icebreaking, marine environmental protection including pollution control, and military readiness. Helicopters stationed aboard icebreakers are the ship's eyes in finding thinner and more navigable ice channels. They fly reconnaissance and airlift supplies to ships and to villages isolated by winter ice.

The HH-65A's minimum equipment requirements exceed anything previously packaged into one helicopter weighing less than 10,000 pounds. HH-65As are made of corrosion-resistant, composite materials. The shrouded tail rotor is unique to the Dolphin.

Also a unique feature of the Dolphin is its computerized flight management system, which integrates state-of-the-art communication and navigation equipment. This system provides automatic flight control. At the pilot's direction, the system will bring the aircraft to a stable hover 50 feet above a selected object. This is an

Figure 3-14. HH-65A Dolphin.

important safety feature in darkness or inclement weather. Selected search patterns can be flown automatically, freeing the pilot and copilot to concentrate on sighting the search target.

The Dolphin is manufactured by Aerospatiale Helicopter Corporation in Grand Prairie, Texas.

HH-3F Pelican

The HH-3F, also known as the Pelican, was designed to meet the Coast Guard's requirement for a medium-range search-and-rescue helicopter. In addition to search and rescue (SAR), the H-3 has proven itself very reliable and versatile in the roles of logistic support, reconnaissance, and general utility.

The H-3 is an all-weather aircraft. It has a wide range of navigation systems that include Loran and in some areas Omega. With its boat hull, it is just as at home on the water as on the runway.

With the H-3's two turbine engines, mounted above the cabin, turning the five main and five tail rotor blades, it can travel at 142 knots and lift 22,050 lbs. Since the aircraft has the capability of remaining airborne for over six hours, an automatic flight control

Figure 3-15. HH-3F Pelican.

system (AFCS) was incorporated into its design to reduce pilot fatigue.

The four-man crew consists of pilot, copilot, flight mechanic, and avionicsman. The flight mechanic is responsible for maintaining the aircraft and operating the hoist during rescue. The avionicsman maintains communications with a shore-based unit and assists the flight mechanic during hoisting operations.

HH-60J Jayhawk

The United States Coast Guard is adding 32 new medium-range Sikorsky HH-60J Jayhawk helicopters to its fleet of aircraft. Jayhawks are replacing the Sikorsky HH-3F Pelican helicopters that the Coast Guard has used for over 20 years.

The Jayhawk's state-of-the-art radar, radio, and navigational equipment enables the helicopter to carry out the Coast Guard's

Figure 3-16. HH-60J Jayhawk.

search and rescue, law enforcement, military readiness, and marine environmental protection missions.

The Jayhawk uses the NAVSTAR Global Positioning System as its primary long range navigational aid. On board the Jayhawk, the Collins RCVR-3A radio simultaneously receives information from four of the system's 18 worldwide satellites and converts it into latitude and longitude fixes, pinpointing the helicopter's position.

With its two T700-GE-401C engines, the Jayhawk can fly 300 miles offshore, remain on scene 45 minutes, hoist six people on board, and return to its point of origin with a safe fuel reserve. Normal cruising speeds of 135 knots can be increased to a "dash" speed of 180 knots when necessary.

RG-8A Condor

The RG-8A Condor is a modified Schweitzer motor glider that was introduced into the Coast Guard fleet in 1988. Equipped with a

Figure 3-17. RG-8A Condor.

high-resolution Texas Instruments AN/AAQ-15 forward-looking infrared radar, a night vision goggle–compatible cockpit, and an extensive secure communications and navigation suite, the aircraft is
effective in a variety of Coast Guard missions, including drug interdiction, migrant interdiction, fisheries enforcement, and marine environmental protection. It has a crew of one pilot and one sensor
operator. Two of the aircraft are deployed at the Coast Guard Air
Station in Miami, Florida.

COAST GUARD AIRCRAFT REPAIR AND SUPPLY CENTER

Like Coast Guard ships, Coast Guard aircraft also must have a place
to receive major repairs and modifications. To ensure the prompt
availability, dependable mission capability, crew safety, and equipment longevity, aircraft are flown to the Aircraft Repair and Supply
Center (AR&SC), the primary support facility for the aviation fleet,
located at Elizabeth City, N.C.

Operating units perform regular inspections, preventive maintenance, and some repairs on the aircraft assigned to their unit. Then
the planes go to AR&SC for overhaul at scheduled intervals. They

also go there for some modifications, necessary major repairs, and to be painted. Also, many of the aircraft components are repaired, reconditioned, and tested at Elizabeth City.

The center is also the central purchasing and supply point for much of the spare parts and equipment for the air stations. They are supplied as needed, and arrangements are made for refurbishing the old parts that are turned in.

New aircraft-related equipment and modifications are tested and evaluated at the center, and modification kits are assembled. Because the center's size and facilities do not permit all necessary aircraft work to be performed there, some must be sent to outside contractors, which include other military services.

CHAPTER 4

Uniforms and Awards

The uniform identifies you as being a professional—a member of a military service that is over two-hundred years old. It shows at a glance that you are a member of the United States Coast Guard.

The Coast Guard is unique in its missions when compared to the other armed forces. Because our missions require close contact with the general public, it is important that the public have faith, confidence, and respect for the Coast Guard. Presenting a proper appearance is a critical but easy way of developing that attitude in the public.

The *Uniform Regulations Manual*, COMDTINST M1020.6 (series), can answer just about any question you may have about uniforms, grooming, and insignia.

Common Types of Uniforms

Working blue. The working blue uniform is worn when you are engaged in work that would soil your dress uniform. This uniform is not a liberty uniform but is authorized for wear when traveling between work and your residence. It may also be worn to service-type facilities on base, such as commissaries, exchanges, snack bars, and dispensaries during working hours.

Undress blue. A good way to think of undress blue is as a neat-looking work uniform. It is worn as a work uniform, but it is worn

Figure 4-1. Revenue Cutter Service uniform.

Figure 4-2. Working uniform (male enlisted).

when you are not expecting to get excessively dirty or soiled. The undress blue is not a liberty uniform. However, it is neat enough that you can wear it while traveling in a private vehicle between work and your residence. It may be worn to service-type facilities on the base.

Service dress blue bravo. Service dress blue bravo is the basic dress uniform for all officers and enlisted personnel. It is appropriate any time and in any season when a dress uniform is required. It is an authorized liberty uniform.

Tropical blue. Tropical blue is a warm-weather dress uniform. It

Figure 4-3. Service dress blue uniform (male officer).

is an authorized liberty uniform. In areas that have seasons, commanding officers will distribute a notice stating when you can shift into or out of this uniform.

Winter dress blue. Winter dress blue is an optional cold-weather dress uniform. It is not normally worn as a liberty uniform. In areas that have seasons, commanding officers will distribute a notice stating when you can shift into or out of this uniform.

Maternity uniform. The maternity uniform is worn when the regular Coast Guard uniforms no longer fit. The maternity uniform is actually an Air Force maternity uniform.

Figure 4-4. Service dress blue "Bravo" (male enlisted).

Other Uniforms

The Coast Guard also has service dress blue alpha, full dress, formal dress, and dinner dress uniforms. These are prescribed for special occasions such as changes of command, ceremonial visits, and formal evening functions. Refer to the *Uniform Regulations Manual* for a listing of the items that are worn with these uniforms.

Marking and Tailoring

Ownership markings and tailoring take place when you enter the service. A complete description of markings and tailoring requirements are found in the *Uniform Regulations Manual*.

Figure 4-5. Tropical blue long (female officer).

Organizational Clothing

Local commands can authorize and/or issue clothing, such as foul-weather jackets, flotation coats, and law-enforcement coveralls if a need exists. Local directives will dictate when these items are to be worn.

Civilian Clothing

Officers and enlisted personnel are permitted to have civilian clothing in their possession aboard ship and at units ashore. Civilian clothing may be worn while leaving or returning to ships or stations,

Figure 4-6. Winter dress blue (optional uniform, male enlisted).

while on leave or liberty, or in any off-duty status ashore. Civilian clothing should be appropriate for the occasion and in good taste so as not to bring discredit upon the Coast Guard, and it should not conflict with accepted attire in the geographic area.

Restrictions

There are several restrictions on the wearing of your uniform:

- Do not wear the uniform if your actions in uniform would bring discredit upon the Coast Guard.
- Do not wear the uniform if wearing it indicates that the Coast

Guard approves of an action or a product. This includes political activities and civilian employment.

• Women may not wear skirts when serving as crew members on cutters, boats, or aircraft except for certain official ceremonies.

• As a general rule, do not wear uniform items with civilian clothing. Some uniform items that do not present a distinctive Coast Guard appearance, such as raincoats, gloves, and shoes may, however, be worn with civilian clothes.

Replacing Uniforms

Use Coast Guard-approved items when it is time to replace uniforms. Do not substitute items with similar civilian material. Uniforms have met certain exacting standards for safety. For example, shirts and trousers meet fire retardancy standards, and the steel in safety shoes meets specific impact-resistance standards.

After six months of active duty, enlisted members will receive a clothing maintenance allowance. This is a monetary allowance to replace and maintain uniform items.

If your unit does not have access to a uniform store, you may mail-order items from the Uniform Distribution Center in Cape May. Your unit's personnel or supply office can provide you with information and forms for ordering.

Appearance

The wearing of the Coast Guard uniform must be a matter of personal pride. Members of the Coast Guard are representatives of the United States, and their dress must reflect credit upon themselves, the Coast Guard, and our nation.

Uniforms must be kept clean and pressed. Refer to the labels in the uniform items for instructions on cleaning and pressing.

Shoes are shined, brass is polished. Caps are worn square on the head. Jackets are buttoned or zippered two-thirds of the way up. Items may be carried *in* the pockets, but must not be exposed. Hands are kept out of pockets.

Jewelry may be worn if it is in good taste and appropriate for the occasion and does not create a safety hazard. Necklaces must not be visible.

Sunglasses may be worn if they present a neat, clean military appearance and are appropriate for the occasion. The same goes for umbrellas, cameras, briefcases, gym bags, and luggage. Umbrellas must be black, with a straight handle.

Men's Grooming

Hair should present a neat, clean, military appearance, tapered from the lower hairline upward. It should not touch the ears. Its length (distance from the scalp) should not exceed one and one-half inches. The style should not interfere with the wearing of a cap or safety device.

Sideburns must be straight, end in a horizontal line, and not extend below the lowest part of the external ear opening.

Moustaches are permitted if they present a neat, clean, military appearance. They must be kept off the lip, above the corners of the mouth, and no more than one-quarter inch horizontally past the corners. Beards are not authorized.

Women's Grooming

Hair should present a neat, clean, military appearance. It may touch but not extend below the lower edge of the collar. The style should not interfere with the wearing of a cap or safety device. Hair ornaments such as pins and barrettes should be functional rather than decorative and approximate the color of the hair. Cosmetics should be conservative in color and amount. Gold, silver, or pearl ball earrings (1/4 inch or less in diameter) may be worn, one per ear.

Identification of Personnel

Awards, devices, insignia, and emblems are displayed on the uniform to identify the rate, rank, rating, and experience of each individual.

Cap Insignia

Nonrated members and petty officers (E-1 through E-6) wear a Coast Guard emblem on their caps. The chin strap is black.

Chief petty officers (E-7 through E-9) wear a device consisting of an anchor and shield. E-8s and E-9s also wear one or two stars. The chin strap is black.

Warrant officers and commissioned officers wear a device that is predominantly an eagle. The chin strap is gold. Senior and flag officers (0–5 through 0–10) wear acorns and oak leaves on the brim.

Dress Jacket Sleeve Insignia

Nonrated members (E-1 through E-3) wear a left-arm sleeve insignia, consisting of red, green, or white stripes, that designates their rate.

Petty officers (E-4 through E-6) wear left-arm sleeve insignia consisting of an eagle and red chevrons.

Chief petty officers (E-7 through E-9) wear left-arm sleeve insignia consisting of an eagle, gold chevrons, and a gold rocker. E-8s wear one star above the eagle and E-9s wear two stars.

Warrant officers and commissioned officers wear gold/blue or gold stripes around the lower part of both sleeves. Warrant officers wear a gold insignia designating their specialty. Commissioned officers have a gold shield above the stripe(s).

Figure 4-7. Coast Guard sleeve insignia.

Figure 4-8. Officers' insignia.

NAVY	MARINE CORPS	COAST GUARD	ARMY	AIR FORCE
CAPTAIN	COLONEL	CAPTAIN	COLONEL	COLONEL
REAR ADMIRAL (LOWER HALF)	BRIGADIER GENERAL	REAR ADMIRAL (LOWER HALF)	BRIGADIER GENERAL	BRIGADIER GENERAL
REAR ADMIRAL	MAJOR GENERAL	REAR ADMIRAL	MAJOR GENERAL	MAJOR GENERAL
VICE ADMIRAL	LIEUTENANT GENERAL	VICE ADMIRAL	LIEUTENANT GENERAL	LIEUTENANT GENERAL
ADMIRAL	GENERAL	ADMIRAL	GENERAL	GENERAL
FLEET ADMIRAL	NONE	NONE	GENERAL OF THE ARMY	GENERAL OF THE AIR FORCE
NONE	NONE	NONE	AS PRESCRIBED BY INCUMBENT GENERAL OF THE ARMIES	NONE

Aviation Electrician's Mate

 Aviation Electronics Technician

 Aviation Machinist's Mate

 Aviation Structural Mechanic

 Aviation Survivalman

 Boatswain's Mate

 Damage Controlman

 Electrician's Mate

 Electronic's Technician

Fire Control Technician

Gunner's Mate

Health Services Technician

Investigator

 Machinery Technician

 Marine Science Technician

 Musician

Public Affairs Specialist

 Port Securityman

 Quartermaster

Radarman

 Radioman

 Storekeeper

Subsistance Specialist

 Telephone Technician

Yeoman

Figure 4-9. Coast Guard rating badge specialty marks.

NAVY	MARINES	ARMY	AIR FORCE	
MASTER CHIEF P O	SGT MAJOR / MASTER GUNNERY SGT	STAFF SGT MAJOR / COMMAND SGT MAJOR / SPEC 9	CHIEF MASTER SGT / CHIEF MASTER SGT OF THE AF	E-9
SENIOR CHIEF P O	1ST SGT / MASTER SGT	1ST SGT / MASTER SGT / SPEC 8	SENIOR MASTER SGT	E-8
CHIEF P O	GUNNERY SGT	SGT 1ST CLASS / SPEC 7	MASTER SGT	E-7
P O 1ST CLASS	STAFF SGT	STAFF SGT / SPEC 6	TECHNICAL SGT	E-6
P O 2ND CLASS	SGT	SGT / SPEC 5	STAFF SGT	E-5
P.O 3RD CLASS	CORPORAL	CORPORAL / SPEC 4	SENIOR AIRMAN	E-4
SEAMAN	LANCE CORPORAL	PRIVATE 1ST CLASS	AIRMAN 1ST CLASS	E-3
SEAMAN APPRENTICE	PRIVATE 1ST CLASS	PRIVATE	AIRMAN	E-2
SEAMAN RECRUIT	PRIVATE	PRIVATE	BASIC AIRMAN	E-1

Figure 4-10. Enlisted ratings and paygrades—all five military services.

Enlisted Service Stripes

For every four years of service, enlisted members wear a service stripe on the lower left sleeve of the dress jacket: nonrated members and petty officers (E-1 through E-6), red stripes; chief petty officers (E-7 through E-9), gold.

Shoulder Boards

Warrant officers and commissioned officers wear shoulder boards on certain uniforms. The stripes are similar to the sleeve insignia.

Collar Devices

Nonrated members (E-1 through E-3) do not wear collar devices.

Petty officers (E-4 through E-6) wear collar devices consisting of a Coast Guard shield and chevrons.

Chief petty officers (E-7 through E-9) wear collar devices consisting of an anchor and shield, and the appropriate number of stars.

Warrant officers and commissioned officers wear collar devices appropriate to their rank. Warrant officers wear a device indicating their specialty.

Enlisted Specialty Marks

Enlisted specialty marks are located on the dress-jacket sleeve insignia between the eagle and chevrons. These marks identify the member's rating (job specialty).

Awards

Awards are displayed on the uniform as ribbons or medals. Awards have an order of rank to them. That order can be found in the *Medals and Awards Manual*, COMDTINST M1650.25 (series). This manual lists awards earned in other armed forces that are authorized on the Coast Guard uniform.

Ribbons are centered 1/4 inch above the left pocket on a dress uniform. Ribbons are displayed in order from top to bottom, from center out. In other words, they would be displayed as if someone else was reading lines of print on your chest.

Medals are displayed in a similar fashion.

Appendix C shows the color and design of some of the more common awards in the Coast Guard.

Breast Insignia

Breast insignia is worn to indicate a special qualification or designation such as coxswain, cutterman, or aircrewman. When ribbons or medals are worn, the insignia is worn centered 1/4 inch above the ribbons or medals. On uniforms without ribbons or medals, the insignia is worn centered 1/4 inch above the left pocket.

CHAPTER 5

Customs, Traditions, and Ceremonies

The customs, traditions, courtesies, and ceremonies observed in the Coast Guard have developed over many years. Some are common to all military services, and some are naval in nature, because the Coast Guard is essentially a seagoing service. Coast Guard personnel should learn and observe all the customs, traditions, and ceremonies of the service and take pride in carrying them out properly. Like wearing the uniform, they are a mark of the select group of citizens who have taken a special oath to support and defend their country.

In one sense, service etiquette is simply the Coast Guard way of observing the rules of good manners, which prevail in some form everywhere. To reduce these rules to their essence, well-mannered people always show respect and politeness toward each other, and it is always the duty of the junior to take the initiative. But the senior is equally obligated to respond.

Coast Guard personnel have a special reason for observing the rules of courtesy: Their uniform makes them representatives of the United States and their service, wherever they are.

Customs and ceremonies of the armed forces show courtesies of several kinds. Some of the most important are:

Respect toward the emblems of our nation and toward its officials.
Courteous behavior aboard a ship of the Coast Guard or Navy.

Figure 5-1. Customs and ceremonies are a tradition of every military service.

Mutual respect and courtesy between enlisted personnel and officers.

Respect and courtesy toward the flags, ships, officials, and other personnel of friendly nations.

Honors and ceremonies are prescribed in *Coast Guard Regulations.*

National Ensign and Anthem

The national ensign—the Stars and Stripes—is the flag of the United States. The national anthem is the song "The Star-Spangled Banner." These symbols represent the nation, and are always treated with great respect. Similarly, the anthems and flags of countries whose governments are formally recognized by the United States (and not at war with the United States) are treated with respect. You render the same salutes for other national flags and anthems as are described here for our own. Our national flag is called "ensign" when displayed on a vessel or facility, "colors" when carried by foot, and "standard" when displayed on a vehicle or aircraft.

Colors

Every Coast Guard shore command and every ship *not under way* performs the ceremony of *colors* twice a day—at 0800 and at sunset. This ceremony consists of paying honor to the national ensign as it is hoisted at 0800 and lowered at sunset.

At five minutes before 0800, and five minutes before sunset, "First call" is sounded on the bugle (if the ship or station has a bugler), or a recording of first call is played. If not, the boatswain's mate pipes and passes the word, "First call to colors." PREP is hoisted close-up.

At 0800, "Attention" is sounded on the bugle. Commands without buglers or records will pass the word, "Attention to colors," over their loudspeakers, or the quartermaster will blow a blast with a whistle. PREP is executed.

The national ensign is hoisted smartly to the top of the flagstaff. While it is being hoisted, the band, if there is one, plays the national anthem. If there is no band, but a bugler, the bugler plays "To the colors." Everyone within sight or hearing renders honors as follows:

- If in ranks, you will be called to attention or to present arms.
- If you are in uniform but not in ranks, you stop whatever you are doing, face the colors and salute until "Carry on" is sounded.

- If you are in a vehicle and traffic safety permits, you stop and sit at attention, but do not salute. If conditions permit, the senior person in the vehicle gets out and salutes. The driver remains seated.
- If you are a passenger in a boat, you remain at attention, seated or standing. The boat officer or coxswain salutes for the boat.
- If you are in civilian or athletic gear at colors, stop and face the colors at attention. If you have a hat, hold it in your right hand, over your heart. If you have no hat, salute by holding your right

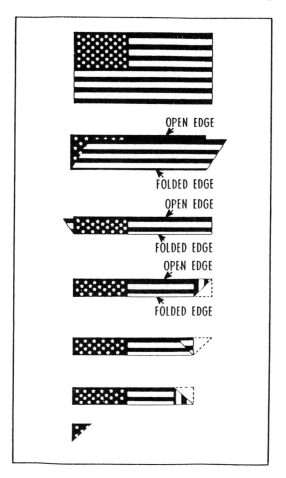

Figure 5-2. Folding the ensign.

hand over your heart. A woman in civilian clothes, with or without a hat, stands at attention and places her right hand over her heart.

At sunset a similar ceremony takes place. Five minutes before sunset, "First call" is sounded. At sunset, "Attention" is sounded and the band, if there is one, plays the national anthem. The flag is lowered slowly, so that it reaches the bottom and is balled up within the field of blue on the last note of the music. If there is no band, but a bugler, then the bugler plays "Retreat."

Your behavior during evening colors is the same as that for morning colors. You face the ensign at attention and hold your salute until "Carry on" is sounded.

Commissioned vessels not under way also hoist and lower the jack at morning and evening colors. This is a square flag with white stars on a blue background, the same as the small square in the national ensign. It is hoisted on the jackstaff, a small flagpole at the bow of a ship.

Ships that are under way do not hold morning or evening colors. They hoist the national ensign at the gaff as they get under way, but the jack is not flown.

Folding the Ensign

The ensign is folded in half the long way so that the crease parallels the red and white stripes. It is folded in half again so that the new crease parallels the red and white stripes and the blue field is to the outside. The fly end (away from the blue field) is folded up to the top so that the single edge lies perpendicular to the stripes. By repeatedly folding the thick triangle thus formed about the inboard edge of the triangle, the ensign is folded into the shape of a cocked hat.

Shifting Colors

On unmooring, the instant the last mooring line leaves the pier or the anchor is aweigh, the quartermaster will blow a long whistle blast over the 1MC and pass the word "Shift colors." The jack and ensign, if flying, will be hauled down smartly. At the same instance the "steaming" ensign will be hoisted on the gaff and the ship's call sign and other signal flags will be hoisted or broken. The jack is not flown. On mooring, the instant the anchor is let go or the first mooring line is made fast on the pier, the quartermaster passes the same

Figure 5-3. Folding the ensign.

word as for unmooring, the ship's call sign and the "steaming" ensign are hauled down smartly, and the jack and ensign are hoisted.

Half-Staffing the Ensign

The ensign is half-staffed as a tribute to the dead. Whenever the ensign is to be half-staffed, it first is closed up and then is lowered to the half-staff position. The same procedure is used when lowering the ensign; it first must be closed up and then lowered.

On Memorial Day, the ensign is half-staffed from 0800 until completion of the 21-gun salute at 1200, or until 1220 if no salute is fired.

During burial at sea, the ensign is at half-staff from the beginning of the funeral service until the body is committed to the deep.

The senior officer present afloat (SOPA) may prescribe a longer period for displaying the ensign at half-staff, depending on circumstances, and after the death of a nationally known figure, all ships and stations may be directed to half-staff the ensign for a stated period.

Dipping the Ensign

Merchant ships salute naval ships by dipping their ensign. They seldom fly an ensign at sea, so this will normally occur in or near a port.

A merchant ship of any nation formally recognized by the United States salutes a ship of the U.S. Navy or Coast Guard by lowering its national colors to half-staff. The Navy ship, at its closest point of approach, will lower the ensign to half-mast for a few seconds, then close it up, after which the merchant ship raises its own colors. If the salute is made when the ensign is not displayed, the Navy ship will hoist her colors, dip for the salute, close them up again, and then haul them down after a suitable interval. Coast Guard and Navy vessels dip the ensign only to answer a salute; they never salute first.

Coast Guard Ensign

The initial job of the first revenue cutters was to guarantee that the maritime public was not evading taxes. Import taxes were the life-blood of the new nation. Smuggling had become a patriotic duty during the revolution. If the new nation under the Constitution were to survive, this activity needed to be stopped.

Working within a limited budget, cutters needed some symbol of authority. Neither officers nor crew members had uniforms. How could a revenue cutter come alongside a merchant ship during an age of pirates and privateers and order it to heave to?

The solution was to create an ensign unique to the revenue cutter to fly in place of the national flag while in American waters.

Nine years after the establishment of the Revenue Cutter Service, Congress, in the Act of 2 March 1799, provided that cutters and boats employed in the service of the revenue should be distinguished from other vessels by a unique ensign and pennant.

On 1 August 1799, Secretary of the Treasury Oliver Wolcott issued an order announcing that in pursuance of authority from the president, the distinguishing ensign and pennant would consist of, "16 perpendicular stripes, alternate red and white, the union of the ensign to be the arms of the United States in a dark blue on a white field."

The ensign was poignant with historical detail, inasmuch as in the canton of the flag, there are 13 stars, 13 leaves to the olive branch, 13 arrows, and 13 bars to the shield. All corresponded to the number of states constituting the union at the time the nation was established. The 16 vertical stripes in the body are symbolic of the number of states in the Union when this ensign was officially adopted.

This ensign soon became very familiar in American waters and served as the sign of authority for the Revenue Cutter Service until the early twentieth century.

Figure 5-4. Coast Guard ensign.

The ensign was intended to be flown only on revenue cutters and boats connected with the Customs Service. But over the years it was found flying atop customshouses as well. However, President William Howard Taft issued an executive order on 7 June 1910, adding an emblem to the ensign flown by the revenue cutters to distinguish it from the ensign flown from the customshouses, which read: "By virtue of the authority vested in me under the provisions of Section 2764 of the revised Statues, I hereby prescribe that the distinguishing flag now used by vessels of the Revenue Cutter Service be marked by the distinctive emblem of that service, in blue and white, placed on a line with the lower edge of the union, and over the center of the seventh vertical red stripe from the mast of said flag, the emblem to cover a horizontal space of three stripes. This change to be made as soon as practicable."

At about this time, cutters began flying the United States flag as their naval ensign, and the revenue ensign became the service's distinctive flag.

When the service adopted the name Coast Guard in 1915, the Revenue Cutter Service's ensign became the distinctive flag on all Coast Guard cutters as it had been for the revenue cutters.

The colors used in the Coast Guard ensign today, as in the Revenue Cutter Service, are all symbolic. The color red stands for our youth and sacrifice of blood for liberty's sake. The color blue not only stands for justice, but also for our covenant against oppression. The white symbolizes our desire for light and purity.

As it was intended in 1799, the ensign is displayed as a mark of authority for boardings, examinations, and seizures of vessels for the purpose of enforcing the laws of the United States. The ensign is never carried as a parade or ceremony standard.

Folding the Coast Guard Ensign

There is no set procedure on how to fold the Coast Guard ensign, and one unit may vary from another. If your unit doesn't have a specific folding procedure, you should fold the ensign neatly and store it with care.

The Standard

The origins of the Coast Guard standard are very obscure. It may have evolved from an early jack. At least one contemporary painting supports this theory. In the 1840 painting pictured above, the revenue cutter *Alexander Hamilton* flies a flag very similar to today's Coast Guard standard as a jack. This flag, like the union jack, which is the upper corner of the United States flag, appears to be the canton or upper corner of the revenue cutter ensign.

An illustration in 1917 shows the Coast Guard standard as a white flag with a blue eagle and 13 stars in a semicircle surrounding it. At a later date, the words "United States Coast Guard—Semper Paratus" were added.

After 1950, the semicircle of stars was changed to the circle containing 13 stars.

The Coast Guard standard is used during parades and ceremonies and is adorned by our battle streamers. We are the only service to have two official flags, the Coast Guard standard and the Coast Guard ensign.

The Battle Streamers

There is no doubt that the Coast Guard cherishes its many peacetime activities. But it is also proud of its services in the wars of the United States. The "system of cutters" was only seven years old when several

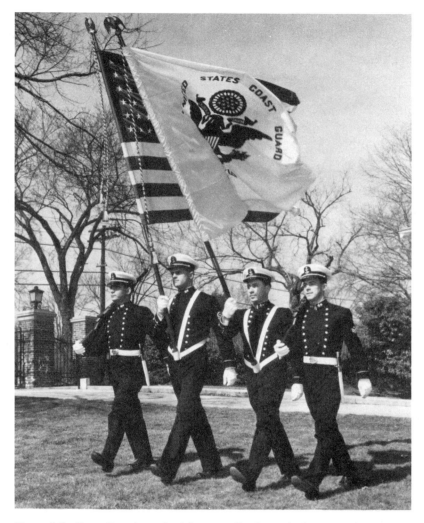

Figure 5-5. Coast Guard standard flies proudly alongside the national ensign.

of its fleet fought in the Quasi-War with France. In this war and the War of 1812, these small, lightly armed cutters proved their worth against experienced European warships.

Embroidering the names of battles on flags may be traced to the early days of the republic. By the end of the nineteenth century, embroidery was discontinued in favor of inscribed silver bands around the color staffs. This too was changed in World War I in favor of small ribbons bearing battle names. The Coast Guard adopted battle streamers in 1968 following the practice established by the United States Marine Corps.

Streamers are attached to the Coast Guard standard, replacing cords and tassels. They are carried in all ceremonies representing heroic actions in all naval encounters from 1798 to the Vietnam War and beyond. Only major headquarters commands may display a complete set of battle streamers. Individual units may only display those they have earned. The Coast Guard has authorized a total of 31 battle streamers for the following campaigns:

French Naval War	Philippine Liberation
War of 1812	Presidential Unit Citation
Indian War	Philippine Independence
Mexican War	Philippine Presidential Unit Citation
Civil War	World War II Victory
Spanish campaign	Navy Occupation Service
World War I Victory	Korean Service
China Service	Navy Unit Commendation
Yangtze Service	National Defense Service
American Defense Service	Armed Forces Expeditionary
American Campaign	Vietnam Service
Asiatic-Pacific Campaign	Philippine Defense

European-African-Middle Eastern Campaign
Meritorious Unit Commendation (Army, Saigon)
Croix De Guerre, French, World War II
Navy Meritorious Unit Commendation
RVN Armed Forces Meritorious Unit Citation,
    Gallantry Cross with Palm
RVN Meritorious Unit Citation,
    Civil Actions Medal First Class Color, with Palm
Operation Desert Storm

The Jack

During its early years, the Revenue Cutter Service flew the canton (the upper corner of the flag nearest the staff) of the revenue cutter ensign as its jack. This practice persisted at least into the 1830s. Prior to the Civil War, the Revenue Cutter Service adopted as its new jack the canton of the United States flag (the union jack), and this continues to this day.

Now the jack is flown from the jackstaff only while at anchor. During the early years of the service it was frequently flown on special occasions either at the jackstaff or atop the mainmast while under way as well as when at anchor.

The Commission Pennant

The Coast Guard commission pennant was created in 1799 at the same time as the ensign. The original commission pennant bore the same style American eagle as the ensign, 16 vertical red-and-white stripes, and a white-over-red vertical tail.

Prior to the Civil War, the Revenue Cutter Service adopted a commission pennant that had 13 blue stars on a white field, 13 vertical red-and-white stripes, and a red swallowtail.

Sometime after the war, the service adopted the same commission pennant as the United States Navy. This pennant has 13 white stars on a blue field, 13 vertical red-and-white stripes, and a red swallowtail. The pennant is flown from the top of the mainmast.

Seals and Emblems

The creation of an official Coast Guard seal confirmed the existence of a symbol that had evolved over the decades. The Revenue Cutter Service, the Life-Saving Service, and the Lighthouse Service all had their own unique distinguishing devices. The Bureau of Marine Inspection and Navigation used drawings of ships and marine equipment on licenses and stationery. But it wasn't until 1927, after Treasury Secretary Andrew W. Mellon approved a design, that the Coast Guard had its first official seal/emblem. At that time, the seal and emblem were the same. This seal/emblem was designed by civilian Coast Guard draftsman Oscar H. Kee.

Over the years, the seal and emblem became two different devices. The emblem, a simplification of the seal, began to appear throughout the service. Consequently, in 1957 Assistant Treasury Secretary David W. Kendall signed an order prescribing the distinctive emblem of the Coast Guard. This order specified that the emblem be used on the Coast Guard ensign, but did not indicate any additional use.

Apparently the emblem continued in wide use. In 1967, Commandant Instruction 5030.6 defined the use of the Coast Guard seal and the Coast Guard emblem.

The seal is used for official documents and records of the Coast Guard. It may also be used for jewelry, stationery, etc., at the discretion of the commandant. The official seal is also used on invitations, programs, certificates, diplomas, and greetings.

The Coast Guard emblem, a simplified version of the seal, was created as a visual identifier for the Coast Guard. It not only appears on the Coast Guard ensign, but also inside the distinctive slash on the sides of our cutters, craft, aircraft, and at our units. It is also used on medals and plaques where space is limited.

The Slash

Our familiar and distinctive red slash or "racing stripe" did not appear on our cutters, boats, and aircraft until relatively late in our history.

In the early sixties, America's visual image had been neglected both inside as well as outside the United States. Since image building played an important role in the election of President John F. Kennedy, the industrial design firm of Raymond Loewy/William Snaith, Inc., was hired to redesign the exterior and interior of the presidential plane. Kennedy was so pleased with the new design that he approved their proposal for improving the worldwide visual identification of the United States government.

In 1964, the firm recommended that the Coast Guard adopt a symbol or mark that would be easily distinguished from other government agencies and easily applied to ships, boats, aircraft, stations, vehicles, signs, and printed forms.

Their design was a wide red bar to the right of a narrow blue bar, both canted at 64 degrees. Centered on the red bar was a new emblem.

Studies were done with experimental markings for their impact on the public, as well as for their long-run compatibility with the Coast Guard's mission and traditions. The reaction was overwhelmingly favorable. Three years later, on 6 April 1967, the now-famous slash appeared throughout the Coast Guard.

In the final design, only the emblem changed. The traditional Coast Guard emblem was selected for centering on the red stripe over the new design.

Semper Paratus

No one seems to know exactly how Semper Paratus was chosen as the

Coast Guard's motto. But there is no doubt as to who put the famous motto to words and music.

Captain Francis Saltus Van Boskerck wrote the words in 1922 in the cabin of the cutter *Yamacraw* in Savannah, Georgia. He wrote the music five years later on a beat-up old piano in Unalaska, Alaska. At that time it was probably the only piano in the whole long chain of Aleutian Islands.

Van Boskerck received his commission in the Revenue Cutter Service on 20 May 1891. In 1917 he was captain of the port in Philadelphia and an aide for the fourth naval district at the American routing office in Philadelphia. He was also censor for the district, and was the first Coast Guard officer to report a German submarine on the Atlantic coast. After the war, Van Boskerck transferred to the Puget Sound Navy Yard to supervise repairs on the famous cutter *Bear*. He commanded *Bear* on the 1920 summer cruise to the Bering Sea and Arctic Ocean.

In 1922, as commander of *Yamacraw*, Van Boskerck was stationed at Savannah and chased rum-runners off the coast of the Carolinas and Florida. In 1923 he went to the Naval War College at Newport, Rhode Island, and in 1924 became district commander of the Great Lakes District. Van Boskerck was commissioned captain in 1925.

"Captain Van," as he was known to his many friends, was next ordered to Seattle as assistant inspector of the Northwest District. In 1925 and 1926 he was commander of the Bering Sea Forces, headquartered at the remote port of Unalaska. It was here that he found time to fit the words of his song to music with the help of two Public Health dentists, Alf E. Nannestad and Joseph O. Fournier. Mrs. Albert C. Clara Goss, the wife of a fur trader, let them use the old piano on which the song was written.

For probably as long as Captain Van could remember, Semper Paratus had been a Revenue Cutter Service and Coast Guard watchword. The words themselves—always ready or ever ready—date back to ancient times.

No official recognition was given to the Coast Guard motto until it appeared in 1910 on the ensign. Captain Van hoped to give it as much recognition as "Semper Fidelis" of the Marines and "Anchor's Aweigh" of the Navy.

Personal Flags and Other Flags and Pennants

The ship carrying an officer of flag rank who commands a fleet or a unit of a fleet flies his personal flag from the main truck at all times

unless he is absent for more than 72 hours. This is a blue flag, carrying five white stars for a fleet admiral, four for admiral, three for
vice admiral, two for rear admiral (upper half), and one for rear
admiral (lower half).

An officer below flag rank, when in command of a force, flotilla,
squadron, carrier division, or aircraft wing, flies a broad command
pennant, white with blue stripes top and bottom.

An official in command of any other division, such as a mine
division or destroyer division, flies a burgee command pennant,
white with red stripes top and bottom.

Absence Indicators

When the commanding officer, or any flag officer, is absent from the
command, for less than 72 hours in port, an "absentee pennant" is
flown as follows:

First Substitute (starboard yardarm). Flown when the admiral or
unit commander whose personal flag or pennant is flying is absent.

Second Substitute (port yardarm). Flown when the chief of staff is
absent.

Third Substitute (port yardarm). When the commanding officer is
on an official absence of more than 72 hours, the executive officer,
serving as acting commanding officer, is accorded the use of this
pennant as if the executive officer were the commanding officer.

Fourth Substitute (starboard yardarm). When the civil or military
official whose flag is flying (such as the Secretary of Defense) is
absent.

Church Pennant

The church pennant is the only flag ever flown over the national
ensign at the same point of hoist, when divine services are conducted
afloat by a chaplain. When divine services are conducted ashore by a
chaplain, the church pennant may be flown from the same halyard
as a personal flag would be flown. If a personal flag is already flying,
it is moved to the halyard one down in precedence.

Red Cross Flag

Hospital ships in wartime fly the Red Cross flag instead of the commission pennant. Boats engaged in sanitary service and landing parties from hospital boats fly the Red Cross flag from a staff in the bow.

Other Flags and Pennants

Both in port and at sea, ships fly many single flags or pennants with special meanings. The senior officer present afloat (SOPA) may prescribe certain flag hoists for local use, such as a request for a garbage or trash lighter, or a water barge. At anchor, ships awarded the Presidential Unit Citation (PUC), Coast Guard Unit Commendation, Navy Unit Commendation (NUC), or Coast Guard Meritorious Unit Commendation should fly the pennant at the fore truck from sunrise to sunset.

Other Honors to the Flag and Anthem

There are many occasions other than colors when you will render honors to the ensign or national anthem. The usual rule is, face the flag if it is displayed; face the music if the flag is not displayed. Hold your salute until the anthem ends or, if there is no anthem, until the flag has been hoisted or lowered, or has passed your position.

Anthem Played Outdoors, Flag Not Displayed

Men and women not in formation stand at attention and face the music. If in uniform render a hand salute; if armed, present arms. In civilian attire, face the music and render the civilian salute. Hold the salute until the last note of music is played. Formations are brought to a halt and the officer in charge faces the music and renders the salute, the ranks remaining at attention facing the direction they were in at the halt.

Anthem Played Outdoors and Flag in View

The salutes are the same, except that the officer in charge of a formation faces the flag instead of the music and salutes; the ranks remain at attention facing in the direction they were in at the halt.

Flag Ceremony Inside a Building

If the anthem is played during a ceremony inside a building in which the flag is brought forward and presented to the audience, or is then retired, the procedures are:

- All personnel face the flag.
- Personnel in civilian attire stand, face the flag, and render the

right-hand-over-heart salute from the first note of the anthem to the last.
- Uncovered military personnel stand at attention with hands at sides.
- Personnel with rifles present arms.
- Personnel covered or with side arms, in uniform, render the hand salute.
- Military formations stand at attention; their officers in charge render the salutes.
- If the audience is all or almost all military, the officer in charge will call "Attention." The officer may order all to salute, or the officer may salute for the audience.
- Salutes are held until the flag is placed and its bearer steps aside.

Anthem Played Inside a Building, Flag Not Displayed

All persons stand and face the music. Men and women in uniform, if covered, render the hand salute; if not covered, stand at attention. Men and women in civilian clothes render civilian salutes.

Personnel in Boats

During the playing of the national anthem, only the boat officer (or coxswain, if there is no boat officer) stands and salutes. Crew and passengers remain standing or seated at attention. If in civilian clothing, remain at attention and do not salute. This is an exception to the general rule.

Passing in Parades

If you are in a formation, obey orders. Your officer in charge will render the salute for the formation. If you are not in formation and the flag is hoisted, or lowered, or passes in a parade, obey the following procedures:

- If seated, rise, come to attention, face the flag, and salute.
- If standing, come to attention, face the flag, and salute.
- If walking, halt at attention, face the flag, and salute.
- If riding in a vehicle, remain seated at attention.

The rules for saluting the anthem apply only if it is played or broadcast as a part of a public ceremony. If you hear it in private or as you walk past a radio, you need not stop or salute.

Pledge of Allegiance

Coast Guard personnel in uniform but uncovered or in civilian clothes render the pledge of allegiance to the flag by facing the flag and standing at attention with the right hand over the heart. Personnel in uniform and covered render the military salute and repeat the pledge.

Hail to the Chief

The song "Hail to the Chief" is played when the President of the United States is being honored. When "Hail to the Chief" is so played, render the same honor given during the playing of the national anthem.

Boarding and Leaving Ship

The officer of the deck (OOD) or a representative—who may be an officer or enlisted—will always be on duty to greet persons leaving or boarding the ship.

The procedure for *boarding your own ship* is as follows: At the gangway, if the national ensign is flying, turn aft and salute the ensign. Then turn to the OOD or a representative, salute and say, "I report my return aboard sir/ma'am." The OOD will return your salute and say, "Very well," or "Very good."

The procedure for *leaving your own ship* is as follows: Step to the OOD, salute, and request, "Permission to leave the ship, sir/ma'am?" or "I request permission to go on the pier to check the after mooring lines, sir/ma'am."

After the OOD has said, "Very well," or "Permission granted," and has returned your salute, drop your salute and step to the gangway. If the ensign is flying, salute in its direction and leave.

When you go aboard a ship other than your own, you must obtain permission from that ship's OOD. Stand at the gangway and salute the ensign, if it is flying, turn to the OOD or a representative, salute, and say, "I request permission to come aboard, sir/ma'am."

On leaving the ship you have been visiting, turn to the OOD or a representative, and say, "With your permission, sir/ma'am, I shall leave the ship." After the OOD has said, "Very well," or "Permission granted," and has returned your salute, step to the gangway, and, if the ensign is flying, salute in its direction and leave.

If you are in a work party, only the person in charge makes the requests to the OOD to board and leave the ship. However, each member salutes the ensign, if flying, and the OOD as they file by, both coming and going. If you are making many trips bringing stores aboard, then you salute only the first and last times over the gangway.

Shipboard Customs

Quarterdeck Customs

The quarterdeck is not a specified deck like the forecastle deck or the poop deck. It is an area designated by the commanding officer to serve for official and ceremonial functions. Therefore, the quarterdeck is treated as the "sacred" part of a ship, and you must obey the following rules:

- Do not be loud or sloppy in its vicinity.
- Never appear on the quarterdeck unless wearing the uniform of the day or as a member of a working party.
- Never smoke on the quarterdeck.
- Never cross or walk on the quarterdeck except when really necessary.
- Do not lounge on or in the vicinity of the quarterdeck.

Sickbay Customs

In the old days, medical and sanitary conditions were so bad that sickbay usually meant a place for dying rather than for getting well—particularly after a battle. Accordingly, it became customary to remove one's cap when entering sickbay, out of respect for the dying and the dead. Nowadays, medicine is so highly developed that we less commonly think of death in connection with sickbay. However, the custom of removing one's cap remains. And, of course, you maintain quiet, and smoking is prohibited.

Messdecks and Living Areas

The messdeck is where enlisted personnel eat; the wardroom is where officers eat. If you enter any of these areas while a meal is in progress, uncover. Even if you are on watch and wearing the duty belt, uncover while a meal is in progress.

Officers' country is the part of a ship where the officers' staterooms and the wardroom are. CPO berthing is where the chief petty officers have their living spaces and mess. Enter these areas only on official business. Never use their passageways as thoroughfares or shortcuts. If you enter the wardroom, or any compartment or office of an officer or CPO, remove your cap. If you are on watch and wearing the duty belt or sidearms, remain covered—unless divine services or a meal is in progress in one of the spaces. Always knock before entering any officer's or chief petty officer's stateroom.

Divine Services

When divine services are in progress, the ship flies the church pennant above the national ensign and the word is passed, "Divine services are in progress (in such and such a space). Maintain quiet about the decks during divine services."

If you enter the area where divine services are in progress, uncover. Even if you are wearing the duty belt and sidearms, uncover. There is one exception: for a Jewish ceremony, remain covered.

The Salute

The military custom you will learn first and use most is the hand salute. This is a courtesy that has been observed for centuries by military personnel of every nationality. It exists by more than force of custom; the occasions and methods of saluting are specified by detailed orders in the *U.S. Coast Guard Regulations*.

Whom To Salute

All uniformed members of the armed forces recognize and greet each other. However, military organization custom requires that this recognition take the form of the official hand salute or rifle salute to any of the following:

Commissioned and warrant officers of the Coast Guard, Navy, Marine Corps, Air Force, and Army.

Officers of foreign armed services whose governments are recognized by the United States. (In practice this means all foreign officers, unless we are actually at war with the country in question.)

Officers of the National Oceanic and Atmospheric Administration (NOAA) and the Public Health Service when they are serving with the armed forces of the United States.

Figure 5-6. Follow all saluting rules in meetings with senior officers; if uncertain as to the rule, salute.

If in doubt, salute. It is better to be overcourteous than to not salute when you should have. Always hold your salute until it is returned or acknowledged (figure 5-6).

Saluting Rules

The hand salute is given with the right hand (figures 5-7 and 5-8). If you have an injury that makes this impossible, or if you are using a boatswain's pipe, salute with the left hand. Personnel in the Coast Guard, Navy, and Marine Corps render the left-hand salute *when necessary*; personnel in the Air Force and Army do not.

Accompany your salute with a cheerful, respectful greeting. "Good morning, sir/ma'am," "Good afternoon, Commander," "Good evening, Miss White," as appropriate. When meeting two or more officers, direct your greeting toward the most senior officer. "Sir/ma'am" should not be made plural.

Always come to attention. If on the double, slow to a walk when saluting a passing officer. You need not stop walking, but hold your-

Figure 5-7. A sharp salute is a sign of respect for both individuals.

self erect. Don't bow your head; don't stare off in the distance; look directly at the officer as you salute. If both hands are occupied and you are unable to salute, face the officer as though you were saluting and greet him as described above. Don't salute with pipe, cigar, or cigarette in your mouth.

If you are accompanying a commissioned officer, do not salute another officer until the officer with you salutes. Then salute at the same time your officer does.

If you are accompanying a commissioned officer who is saluted by an enlisted person, return the salute at the same time your officer does.

Salute an officer even if the officer's hands are engaged (holding packages or a lady's arm) and the salute cannot be returned. The officer will acknowledge your salute by saying either, "Good morning," "Good afternoon," or "Good evening." Salute officers who are in civilian or athletic dress, and salute when introduced to ladies who are not officers. Do not remove your hat. Prisoners do not salute.

Distances for Saluting

Since the salute is basically a courtesy, it should be used in a manner similar to civilian greetings: An officer should be recognized and saluted at about the same distance and at about the same time as one would recognize and greet a civilian acquaintance—six paces away is a good general rule. Remember—an officer must pass near enough to be identified as rating a salute, and the person giving the salute should start while far enough away for the officer to have time to see and return it.

Salutes in Civilian Dress

When outdoors in uniform, Coast Guard personnel use the military salute when recognizing officers in civilian or athletic dress.

If you have occasion to salute the flag while in civilian clothes, remove your hat with your right hand and hold it over your chest, with your hand over your heart.

If you are not wearing a hat, place your right hand over your heart. Women in civilian dress salute in this manner, except they do not remove their hat but just place the right hand over the heart.

Etiquette for Boats, Vehicles, and Passageways

The basic rule in service etiquette as in civilian etiquette is to make way for a senior quickly, quietly, naturally, and without fuss.

Thus, the rule for entering boats and vehicles is, seniors *in* last and *out* first. The idea is that the captain should not have to wait in a boat for a seaman to amble down the accommodation ladder. When reaching a destination, seniors are allowed to get out first because normally their business is more important and more pressing than that of subordinates.

Remember, juniors *enter* a boat or vehicle *first*; that is, they don't make last-minute dashes to reach the boat, but get in a minute or so before the boat gong, or as soon as the OOD says the boat is ready. Similarly, they are ahead of time and *enter* buses, cars, and other vehicles well in advance of the arrival of a senior. When the boat docks or the vehicle arrives at its destination, the juniors wait until their seniors have disembarked before disembarking themselves.

Generally, seniors take the seats farthest aft. If officers are present, do not sit in the stern seats unless invited to do so. Also, enlisted personnel maintain silence while officers are in the boat. (For reasons of safety, never become noisy and boisterous in a boat, regardless of the hour, condition of sea, or who is present.)

If boats with officers on board pass within view, the senior officer and the coxswain of each boat render salutes. Other crew members and passengers remain seated at attention. The coxswain stands and salutes all officers entering or leaving the boat.

Personnel seated in boats in which there is no officer, petty officer, or acting petty officer in charge, rise and salute all officers passing near. When an officer, PO, or acting PO is in charge of a boat, that person alone renders the salute.

Enlisted personnel seated well forward in a large boat do not rise and salute when officers enter or leave the stern seats. However, passengers in the after section of a boat always rise and salute when a commissioned officer enters or leaves.

A boat takes rank according to the rank of the highest grade of officer embarked. A barge with an ensign is junior to a motor whaleboat with a lieutenant. When junior boats pass seniors, the junior boats salute first. The coxswain and senior officer in each boat render the hand salute. Other members of the crew not concealed by canopies stand at attention, facing the senior boat. Passengers sit at attention. Boats passing U.S. or foreign men-of-war during "colors" must lay to, and their crews stand, face the colors, and salute.

For entering and leaving through doors, the rule is to let the senior go *first*. If possible, hold the door for the senior. If, however, the junior is a woman, and the senior motions her to go first, she should do so.

On meeting a senior in a passageway, step aside and let the senior pass. If the senior is an officer and other enlisted personnel or junior officers are present, call, "Gangway," so the others can make way.

Do not overtake and pass an officer without permission. When necessary to walk past, overtake *on the officer's left side*, salute when you are abreast, and ask, "By your leave, sir/ma'am?" After the officer returns the salute and has said, "Very well," or "Permission granted," drop your salute and continue past.

When walking with a senior, always walk *on the left*. That is, you put the senior on *your* right. This rule also applies when seated in an automobile.

Addressing Officers

Senior officers—admirals, captains, and commanders (who wear gold oak leaves or "scrambled eggs" on their cap visors)—are always addressed and referred to by their titles of rank, "Admiral," "Captain," or "Commander." If several officers of the same rank are seated or working together, it is proper to use both rank and name, as "Admiral Taylor," or "Captain Smith," to avoid confusion.

Junior officers—lieutenant commanders, lieutenants, lieutenants (junior grade), and ensigns—are addressed and referred to by "Mister" or "Miss" and their last name, as "Mister Taylor," or "Miss Smith." In speaking to a junior officer whose name is not known, use "sir" or "ma'am." Warrant officers, midshipmen, and aviation cadets are treated in the same manner as junior officers.

By tradition, the commanding officer of any ship or station, regardless of rank, is addressed and referred to as "Captain." Other captains or commanders in the same command should be addressed by rank and name.

Officers in the Medical and Dental Corps are addressed and referred to by rank or as "Doctor," if they are commanders and above; if of junior officer rank, they are addressed as "Doctor" instead of "Mister" or "Miss." A chaplain may be called "Chaplain," regardless of rank.

Officers of the Army, Air Force, and Marine Corps of and above the rank of captain are addressed and referred to by rank, as "General," "Colonel Howes," "Major," and "Captain Farrow"; others are addressed and introduced as "Mister" or "Miss," unless circumstances make it advisable to use the rank to inform other persons present of their status.

When replying to an order, the only correct reply is "Aye, aye, sir/ma'am." This means you heard the order, you understand it, and you will carry it out to the best of your ability.

"Ma'am" or "sir" is a military expression, always used with "Yes" or "No" in addressing officers. Also use "sir" or "ma'am" in addressing enlisted personnel when they are performing a military duty, such as junior officer of the deck or in reporting a muster to a chief petty officer. At such times, you also exchange salutes.

Addressing Enlisted Personnel

A chief petty officer is addressed as "Chief Petty Officer Smith" or more informally as "Chief Smith" or as "Chief" if you do not know the chief's name. Master chief petty officers and senior chief petty officers are customarily addressed and referred to as "Master Chief Smith," or "Senior Chief Smith." CPOs are introduced by rate, rating, and last name: "Chief Radioman Price." Introduce POs by stating the rate and rating first, followed by the last name; "Machinists's Mate First Johnson" or "Petty Officer Johnson."

Introduce "nonrated" personnel by rate and name: "Seaman Wells" or "Fireman Clifton."

When introducing first-, second-, and third-class petty officers to civilians, use the term petty officer: "This is Petty Officer Brown."

Civilians generally address enlisted people as "Mr.," "Miss," or "Mrs."

Seniors may call juniors by first name, but juniors never address seniors by first name. If a petty officer tells you to use his or her first name, do so only in privacy or on liberty. While on duty in the presence of others, use only the last name with the appropriate rank.

In civilian life, it is customary to introduce men to women and youth to age.

The same general rules are followed in military life, except that in most cases, rank establishes the order of introduction: introduce the junior to the senior, whether male or female, except that everyone, no matter the rank or sex, is introduced to a chaplain. If one person is civilian, follow the civilian rules. In making introductions, name the honored or higher-ranking person first, then the name of the person being introduced or presented: "Admiral Jones, this is Ensign Smith," or "Mrs. Jones, this is Master Chief Williams."

There may be times when unofficial letters are exchanged between officers and enlisted personnel; a coxswain might write to a former skipper to congratulate him on promotion. The salutation would be "My Dear Commander Meader," and the complimentary closing should always be "Very respectfully." An officer would not address an enlisted person in writing as "Dear Smith," but as "Dear Chief Petty Officer Smith."

All officers should be addressed by their title of rank, except that officers in the Medical, Dental, Nurse, and Medical Service Corps with doctoral degrees may be addressed as Doctor. Modifiers may be dropped: Address a lieutenant commander as "Commander," a lieutenant (junior grade) as "Lieutenant." When a captain or lieutenant is not in uniform, he would be introduced as "of the Coast Guard" or "of the Navy," in order to avoid confusion with Army, Air Force, or Marine Corps ranks.

Honors

Gun Salutes

In olden days, it took as much as 20 minutes to load and fire a gun, so a ship that fired her guns first did so as a friendly gesture, making herself powerless for the duration of the salute.

Gun salutes prescribed by regulations are fired only by such ships and stations as are designated. A national salute of 21 guns is fired on Independence Day and on Memorial Day, and to honor the President of the United States and heads of foreign nations. Salutes for naval officers are as follows: fleet admiral, 17 guns; admiral, 17 guns; vice admiral, 15 guns; rear admiral (upper half), 13 guns; rear admiral (lower half), 11 guns. Salutes are fired at intervals of five seconds, and always in odd numbers.

Manning the Rail

This custom evolved from that of "manning the yards," which is hundreds of years old. In sailing ships men stood evenly spaced on all the yards and gave three cheers to honor a distinguished person. Now the crew is stationed along the rails and superstructure of a ship when honors are rendered to the president, the head of a foreign nation, or a member of a reigning royal family. Personnel so stationed do not salute.

Dressing and Full-Dressing Ship

Commissioned ships are *full-dressed* on Presidents' Day and Independence Day and *dressed* on other national holidays.

When dressing ship, the national ensign is flown from the flagstaff and, usually, from each masthead. The Coast Guard ensign is flown from the outboard starboard yard arm. When a ship is full-dressed, in addition to the ensigns, a "rainbow" of signal flags is displayed from bow to stern over the mastheads, or as nearly so as the construction of the ship permits. Ships not under way are dressed from 0800 to sunset; ships under way do not dress until they come to anchor during that period.

Side Boys

Side boys are a part of the quarterdeck ceremonies when an important person or officer boards or leaves a ship (figure 5-9). The custom of having side boys originated centuries ago in the Royal Navy when officers were hoisted aboard in a sort of basket, and since senior officers usually weighed more than juniors, more boys were needed on the line. When the side is piped by the boatswain's mate of the watch, from two to eight side boys (men or women), depending on the rank of the officer, will form a passageway at the gangway. They salute on the first note of the pipe and finish together on the last note.

Side boys must be particularly smart in appearance and grooming, with polished shoes and immaculate uniforms.

Arrival and Departure Honors

On board any Coast Guard vessel capable of doing so, the arrival or departure of visiting officers, commander and above, is normally announced. Commanding officers below commander (0–5), are announced if their identity is known to the OOD. High-ranking civilian officials are announced in this manner. Accompanying the announcement of the arrival or departure is the toning of the bell.

Figure 5-8. Side boys salute as officer comes aboard ship. Note that the boatswain is saluting left-handed.

The number of "bongs" should be determined from the list below. For comparison, the number is the same as the number of side boys that the person would rate when receiving official honors. The bongs are sounded in pairs, in the same manner as done to denote the passing of time.

Officer	Number of Bongs
VADM (0–9 and above)	8
RADM (0–8 or 0–7)	6
CAPT (0–6)	4
CDR (0–5)	4
Other officers (OOD's discretion)	2

Senior officers are normally announced aboard using the name of their command or title, as in the following examples:

CO of USCG barque Eagle	"EAGLE"
CO of Coast Guard District One	"FIRST DISTRICT"
Superintendent of USCGA	"COAST GUARD ACADEMY"
Commandant, USCG	"COAST GUARD"
Commander of USCG Group Portland	"GROUP PORTLAND"
Senators	"SENATOR, STATE OF _____"
Representatives	"REPRESENTATIVE, (#) DISTRICT, STATE OF _____"

The following procedure should be adhered to: As the person approaches the bow or begins up the accommodation ladder, the correct number of bongs is sounded in pairs and the announcement is passed. For example, if the captain is returning, the announcement is "Bong, Bong . . . Bong, Bong . . . EAGLE (half pause) ARRIVING." *Only* in the case of the captain or an officer whose pennant is flown aboard the ship is a final "bong" sounded as the person steps aboard or ashore. No other voice announcement is made.

Passing Honors

When ships pass each other, all hands who are topside or who are visible from outboard and are free to do so, should face the ship being passed, stand at attention, and salute on signal, whether in ranks or not.

Coast Guard and Navy ships use the following whistle signals when exchanging passing honors:

Attention—2 blasts
Ship is passing to starboard—1 blast
Ship is passing to port—2 blasts
Salute—1 blast
End salute—2 blasts
Carry on—3 blasts.

Ceremonies

Change of Command

When a new commanding officer takes over any ship or station, all hands fall in at quarters in dress uniform. The captain reads the detachment orders, and the new captain reads the orders to take over the command. Both officers then inspect the crew and the ship.

Christenings and Commissionings

The tradition of christening and commissioning a ship started well before the first ten revenue cutters entered the service. The practice dates back to ancient times when the Greeks, Romans, Egyptians, and Vikings called upon the gods to protect their ships and crew from the perilous sea. Religion played an important role in these ceremonies. In fact, christenings originated as a way to appease the gods of the elements.

Christening gives a ship its identity. Over the years, different cultures and people changed and shaped the way ceremonies were performed, and some of these traditions were carried over into modern times.

A ship is traditionally christened or given its name at the time it is launched into the water. When a ship is christened, it is tradition to break a bottle across the ship's bow. This practice began in Britain in the late seventeenth century. Previously, an official would sip wine from a "standing cup," a large loving cup made of precious metal, then pour out the remaining wine onto the deck or over the ship's bow. The cup was then tossed overboard. This practice soon became too costly, and a net was used to catch the cup so that it could be re-used at other launchings. Wine was the traditional liquid used to christen a ship, although other liquids were used such as whiskey, brandy, and water. At the close of the nineteenth century, champagne became the popular liquid. However, during prohibition ships were christened with water.

Ships' sponsors were generally royalty or senior naval officers. In the nineteenth century, women became ship sponsors for the first time. Women sponsored ships more and more frequently, although it was not the rule.

The actual physical process of launching a new ship from a building site to the water involves three principal methods. The oldest, most familiar, and most widely used is the "end-on" launch in which the vessel slides, usually stern first, down an inclined shipway. The "side launch," whereby the ship enters the water broadside, came into nineteenth-century use on inland waters, rivers, and lakes. It was given major impetus by the World War II building program. Another method involves ships built in basins or graving docks. When ready, ships constructed in this manner are floated by admitting water into the dock.

The commissioning ceremony completes the cycle from christening and launching to full status as a cutter in the United States Coast Guard.

Unlike the christening/launching ceremony, commissionings were attended by no ceremony in early American maritime history. They were not public affairs, and no accounts of them are found in contemporary newspapers. In recent years however, commissionings have come to be public occasions.

Dining-In and Mess Night

The tradition of Dining-In, or Mess Night, can be traced to the days when the Roman Legions held great banquets to celebrate their victories or paraded the prizes of their conquests. The Vikings had a tradition of celebrating great battles and feats by formal ceremony. It is from these customs of celebrating special events that we have formal dinners today.

The Dining-In is a formal dinner function for the officers of a military organization or unit. Originally, such functions provided an excellent setting to recognize both individual and unit achievements, as well as to bid farewell to departing officers and welcome new ones. Today, they are primarily occasions to gather socially at a formal function. But the protocol and traditional amenities remain intact.

The Chief Petty Officer Academy continues the tradition, calling it "Chiefs' Mess Night." Chiefs' Mess Night is a formal military function, like the Dining-In, but the mess members are chiefs and guests. It provides an occasion for chiefs to meet socially and give recognition to a dignitary, individual, or unit. It also may simply be a pleasant way for individuals to become better acquainted.

In early eighteenth century Europe, various regiments of the established monarchies would gather for an evening of good food, drinking, and fellowship to honor individuals and organizations. More recently this custom can be traced to the "messes" of the Royal Navy and regimental "messes" of the British Army. Our early leaders gained background and training from either British regulars or colonial militia in the French and Indian Wars. It is most likely that they became indoctrinated in the formal aspects of military life as practiced by the men of that period.

Prior to World War II, Mess Night had reached its greatest prominence. While the occasion became less of a celebration for individual achievements, the protocol became more formalized. The uniforms prescribed were evening dress with medals.

Figure 5-9. Chiefs' Mess Night provides an opportunity for individuals to become acquainted.

Dining-In and Mess-In are strictly for military people, while Mess-Out and Dining-Out are for military as well as invited guests.

Decommissioning Ceremony

When a ship is taken out of service, either to go into "mothballs" or to be transferred to a foreign navy, the ceremony is smaller and simpler. The commanding officer reads the decommissioning orders to officers and crew at quarters, and the ensign, jack, and commission pennant are hauled down. By tradition, the captain keeps the commission pennant.

Crossing the Line

When a ship crosses the equator, all "pollywogs"—those who have never crossed—are initiated into the "Ancient Order of the Deep," and become shellbacks. All hands are issued a certificate and a wallet-sized card with the name of the ship, date, and longitude. On large ships, shellbacks may spend days planning an elaborate "Neptune party" in which King Neptune, Davy Jones, and a group of "royal" police, judges, surgeons, barbers, bears, and other characters initiate the pollywogs. A Neptune party is an all-hands affair during which the shellbacks take over the ship to a certain extent and initiate all pollywogs, whether they are seamen or admirals.

Golden Dragons

When a ship crosses the 180th meridian—the International Date Line—going west, it enters "The Realm of the Golden Dragon," and all hands are issued a card to mark the occasion.

Blue-Nose Polar Bear

When a ship crosses the Arctic Circle, all hands are issued a wallet-sized card, similar to the shellback card, stating the circumstances, and naming them "Blue-Nose Polar Bears."

New Year's Log

It is traditional that the log for the first mid-watch of the new year— 1 January—must be written in verse. In recent years, some such log entries have been published, especially in the weekly *Navy Times*.

Ship's Bell

On some ships, the oldest member of the crew strikes the old year out with eight bells, and the youngest member of the crew strikes the new year in with eight bells.

Homeward-Bound Pennant

No ship carries this flag; it is made up only when needed. It is flown by a ship that has been overseas for nine months or more when she gets under way to return to the United States. The homeward-bound pennant flies until sunset of the day of arrival in a U.S. port.

The pennant next to the hoist is blue and has one white star for the first nine months overseas and an additional star for each six months. The rest is divided lengthwise; the upper section is red, the lower is white. The pennant is one foot long for each person on board who has been outside the United States for at least nine months, but is never longer than the length of the ship.

After being hauled down, the pennant is cut up. The blue part goes to the commanding officer. The remainder is divided equally among all hands.

Burial at Sea

During combat, or at other times when operations prevent holding a body for services ashore, the dead are buried at sea. When schedules permit, retired persons may be buried at sea. The ceremony may be very simple in combat or more elaborate when time permits. The body is covered by a U.S. flag, which is removed as the body is committed to the deep and is presented to the next of kin.

CHAPTER 6

Military Drill Fundamentals

There are a multitude of reasons for military drill: to teach the fundamentals of military bearing; to provide experience in giving and following commands; to prepare for military operations on land; to facilitate movements of companies from one place to another; and to promote teamwork (figure 6-1). The primary reference document for this chapter is the *U.S. Marine Corps Drill and Ceremonies Manual*.

DRILL COMMANDS

Preparatory commands are indicated in this chapter by SMALL CAPITAL LETTERS and those of execution by LARGE CAPITAL LETTERS.

A military drill command has two parts:

1. The preparatory command, such as HAND, which indicates the movement that is to be executed.

2. The command of execution, such as SALUTE, HALT, or ARMS, which causes the desired movement, or halt, or element of the manual to be executed.

When appropriate, the preparatory command includes the name or title of the group concerned, as, FIRST DIVISION, HAND SALUTE.

In certain commands, the preparatory command and the com-

Figure 6-1. A smart appearance at ceremonies requires each person to be well grounded in basic military fundamentals.

113

mand of execution are combined, as for example: FALL IN, AT EASE, and REST.

To call back or revoke a command or to begin again a movement that started wrong, the command AS YOU WERE is given, at which the movement stops and the former position is taken.

THE POSITIONS

Position of Attention

Command: AT-TEN-SHUN or FALL-IN. Heels close together, feet turned out to form an angle of 45 degrees, knees straight, hips level, body erect, with the weight resting equally on the heels and balls of the feet. Shoulders squared, chest arched, arms hanging down without stiffness so that thumbs are along the seams of the trousers, palms and fingers relaxed. Head erect, chin drawn in, and eyes straight to the front. In coming to attention, the heels are brought together smartly and audibly.

The Rests

Commands: FALL OUT; REST; AT EASE; and 1. PARADE, 2. REST.

FALL OUT. Personnel break rank but remain nearby. Personnel return to places and come to attention at the command FALL IN.

REST. Right foot is kept in place. Personnel may talk and move.

AT EASE. Right foot is kept in place. Personnel keep silent, but may move about.

1. PARADE, 2. REST. Move the left foot smartly 12 inches to the left from the right foot; at the same time, clasp the hands behind the back, palms to the rear, the right hand clasping the left thumb, arms hanging naturally. Keep silent and motionless.

To resume attention from any rest other than FALL OUT the command is, for example: 1. DETAIL, 2. ATTENTION.

Eyes Right or Left

Commands: 1. EYES, 2. RIGHT (or LEFT), 3. READY, 4. FRONT. At the command RIGHT, each person turns his head and eyes smartly 45 degrees to the right. The personnel on the extreme right file keep the head and eyes to the front. At the command FRONT, the head and eyes are turned smartly to the front. The opposite is carried out for EYES LEFT.

Hand Salute

Command: 1. HAND, 2. SALUTE, 3. TWO. The command TWO is used only when saluting by command. At the command SALUTE, salute smartly, looking toward the person saluted.

At the command TWO, drop the arm to its normal position by the side in one movement and turn the head and eyes to the front. In passing in review, execute the hand salute in the same way. During a review the salute is held until six paces beyond the person saluted. Under other circumstances the salute is dropped when returned or upon passing.

FACINGS

Right or Left Face

Command: 1. RIGHT (LEFT), 2. FACE. At the command FACE, slightly raise the left heel and right toe; face to the right, turning on the right heel, putting pressure on the ball of the left foot. Hold the left leg straight. Then place the left foot smartly beside the right.

About Face

Command: 1. right (or left), 2. FACE. At the command, place the toe of the right foot about a half-foot length to the rear and slightly to the left of the left heel without moving the left foot. Put the weight of the body mainly on the heel of the left foot, right leg straight. Then turn to the rear, moving to the right on the left heel and on the ball of the right foot. Place the right heel beside the left to complete the movement.

STEPS AND MARCH COMMANDS

All movements executed from the halt, except right step, begin with the left foot. FORWARD, HALF STEP, HALT, and MARK TIME may be executed one from the other in quick or double time.

The following table prescribes the length in inches and the cadence in steps per minute of steps in marching.

Step	Time	Length	Cadence
Full	Quick	30	120
Full	Double	36	180
Full	Slow	30	—*
Half	Quick	15	120
Half	Double	18	180
Side	Quick	12	120
Back	Quick	15	120

*This is a special step executed only as a funeral escort is approaching the place of interment. The cadence, in accordance with that set by the band, varies with different airs that may be played.

All commands of execution are given on the foot, right or left, in the direction the movement is going. For example, if the march is to be to the right, as 1. BY THE RIGHT FLANK, 2. MARCH, the command MARCH is given on the right foot.

Quick Time

All steps and movements are executed in quick time, which is what most people understand as normal marching pace, unless the unit is marching double time, or unless DOUBLE TIME is added to the command. Example: 1. SQUAD RIGHT, DOUBLE TIME, 2. MARCH.

Marching

At halt, to march forward to quick time, the commands are: 1. FORWARD, 2. MARCH. At the command FORWARD, shift the weight of the body to the right leg. At the command MARCH, step off smartly with the left foot and continue the march with 30-inch steps taken straight forward without stiffness or exaggeration of movements. Swing the arms easily in their natural arcs six inches straight to the front and three inches to the rear of the body.

Double Time

To march in double time, the commands are: 1. DOUBLE TIME, 2. MARCH.

1. If at halt, at the command DOUBLE TIME, shift the weight of the body to the right leg. At the command MARCH, raise the forearms,

fingers closed, knuckles out, to a horizontal position along the waist-line and take up an easy run with the step and cadence of double time, allowing the arms to take a natural swinging motion across the front of the body. Keep the forearms horizontal.

2. If marching in quick time, at the command: 1. DOUBLE TIME, 2. MARCH, given as either foot strikes the ground, take one more step in quick time and then step off in double time.

3. To resume the quick time from double time, the commands are: 1. QUICK TIME, 2. MARCH. At the command MARCH, given as either foot strikes the ground, advance and plant the other foot in double time; resume the quick time, dropping the hands by the sides.

Halt

Commands: 1. SQUAD (PLATOON, COMPANY), 2. HALT.

1. When marching in quick time, at the command HALT, given as either foot strikes the ground, execute the halt in two counts; advance and plant the other foot, then bring up the rear foot.

2. When marching in double time, first bring the squad (platoon, company) to quick time, then halt as above.

3. When executing right step or left step, at the command HALT, given as the heels are together, plant the foot next in cadence and come to the halt when the heels are next brought together.

Mark Time

Commands: 1. MARK TIME, 2. MARCH.

1. Being in march, at the command MARCH, given as either foot strikes the ground, advance and plant the other foot; then bring up the rear foot, placing it so that both heels are on line, and continue the cadence by alternately raising and planting each foot. When raised, the ball of the foot is two inches above the ground.

2. Being at a halt, at the command MARCH, raise and plant first the left foot, then the right as described above.

3. Mark time may be executed in either quick-time cadence or double-time cadence. While marking time, any errors in alignment should be corrected.

4. The halt is executed from mark time, as from quick time or double time. Forward march, halt, and mark time may be executed one from the other in quick time or double time.

Half Step

Commands: 1. HALF STEP, 2. MARCH.

1. Being in march, at the command MARCH, take steps of 15 inches in quick time instead of the normal 30 inches. The half step is executed in quick time only.

2. To resume the full step from half step, the commands are: 1. FORWARD, 2. MARCH.

Right Step

Commands: 1. RIGHT STEP, 2. MARCH.

At the command MARCH, carry the right foot 12 inches to the right; then place the left foot beside the right, left knee straight. Continue in the cadence of quick time. The right step is executed in quick time from a halt for short distances only.

Left Step

Commands: 1. LEFT STEP, 2. MARCH.

At the command MARCH, carry the left foot 12 inches to the left; then place the right foot beside the left, right knee straight. Continue in the cadence of quick time. The left step is executed in quick time from a halt for short distances only.

Back Step

Commands: 1. BACKWARD, 2. MARCH.

At the command MARCH, take steps of 15 inches straight to the rear. The back step is executed in quick time for short distances only.

To Face to the Right (or Left) in Marching

Commands: 1. BY THE RIGHT (or LEFT) FLANK, 2. MARCH.

1. To face to the right (left) in marching and advance from a halt, at the command MARCH, turn to the right (left) on the ball of the right (left) foot; at the same time, step off with the left (right) foot in the new direction with a half or full step in quick time or double time as the case may be.

2. To face to the right (left) in marching and advance, being in march, at the command MARCH, given as the right (left) foot strikes the ground, advance and plant the left (right) foot; then face to the right (left) in marching, and step off with the right (left) foot in the

new direction with a half or full step in quick or double time as the case may be.

To Face to the Rear in Marching

Commands: 1. TO THE REAR, 2. MARCH.

1. Being in march at quick time, at the command MARCH, given as the right foot strikes the ground, advance and plant the left foot; then turn to the right all the way about on the balls of both feet, and immediately step off with the left foot.

2. Being in march at double time, at the command MARCH, given as the right foot strikes the ground, advance two steps in the original direction; turn to the right all the way about while taking four steps in place, keeping the cadence, and step off.

To Change Step

Commands: 1. CHANGE STEP, 2. MARCH.

1. Being in march in quick time, at the command MARCH, given as the right foot strikes the ground, advance and plant the left foot; then plant the toe of the right foot near the heel of the left, and step off with the left foot.

2. The same movement may be executed on the right foot by giving the command MARCH as the left foot strikes the ground and planting the right foot; then plant the toe of the left foot near the heel of the right and step off with the right foot.

To March at Ease

Commands: 1. AT EASE, 2. MARCH.

At the command MARCH, adopt an easy natural stride, without any requirement to keep step or a regular cadence. Keep silent.

To March at Route Step

Commands: 1. ROUTE STEP, 2. MARCH.

At the command MARCH, adopt an easy natural stride, without any requirement to keep step or a regular cadence, or to maintain silence.

MANUAL OF ARMS

The manual of arms described here is performed with the M16 rifle. For instruction purposes, it may be taught by the numbers. When marching at quick time, the only movements that may be executed are Right Shoulder Arms and Port Arms. The cadence of all motions is quick time. Recruits learning the manual of arms should concentrate their attention on the details of the motion; the cadence will be acquired as they become accustomed to handling their rifles. The instructor may require them to count aloud in cadence with the motions.

GENERAL

FALL IN is executed with the rifle at Order Arms. When troops are formed, rifles are immediately inspected. (See commands for Inspection Arms, following.) Prior to executing any movements with the rifle, the magazine is removed and the sling is positioned on the left side of the rifle, drawn tight, the keeper lying flat and on top of the pistol grip just below the selector lever. Before starting any movement from the halted position, except for movements requiring the position of Trail Arms, rifles will be at Right Shoulder Arms, Port Arms, or Sling Arms. While at a position other than Sling Arms, the rifle is brought to Port Arms for marching at Double Time.

Position of Order Arms

This is the basic rifle position. (See figure 6-2.) The rifle butt rests on deck, with the toe of the rifle in line with the toe of the right shoe. The left side of the stock is along the outer edge of the right shoe. The magazine well is to the front and the barrel is in a vertical position. The rifle is held with the fingers extended and joined, the junction of the front sight assembly and the barrel rests in the "V" formed by thumb and fingers of the right hand. The right thumb is on the trouser seam and the entire right arm is behind the rifle (this may cause a slight bend in the arm). The body is at the position of Attention, as it is executed without arms.

Trail Arms from Order Arms

Commands: 1. TRAIL, 2. ARMS.

This command is given at the position of Order Arms only. At the command of execution, raise the rifle vertically three inches off the deck. Do not change the grasp of the right hand, keep the right thumb on the trouser seam and the right arm behind the rifle, keep the left hand in position.

Figure 6-2. Order arms.

Order Arms from Trail Arms

Commands: 1. ORDER, 2. ARMS.

At the command, lower the butt of the rifle to the deck and assume the position of Order Arms.

The rifle is kept at Trail Arms during any movement of Back Step, Extending, or Closing ranks; the position of Order Arms is assumed automatically on halting.

Port Arms from Order Arms

Commands: 1. PORT, 2. ARMS.

At the command of execution, slide the right hand to the barrel with fingers joined and wrapped around it, raise and carry the rifle diagonally across in front of and slightly to the left of your face. The right wrist and forearm are straight, elbow held down without strain. The right arm does not need to be parallel to the deck. Rifle muzzle is up, bisecting the angle formed by neck and shoulder, with magazine well to the left, butt in front of right hip. At the same time, smartly grasp the handguard, fingers joined and wrapped around it, little finger above the slip ring, thumb inboard, centered on the chest. Left wrist and forearm are straight, elbow against the body.

TWO. Release grasp of right hand on the barrel and regrasp the small of the stock. Fingers are joined, wrapped around the small of the stock, parallel to the deck, elbow against the body, upper arm in line with the back. The rifle should be four inches from the belt. (See figure 6-3.)

Order Arms from Port Arms

Commands: 1. ORDER, 2. ARMS.

At the command of execution, release the grasp of the right hand from the stock and smartly regrasp the barrel. Fingers are joined, wrapped around the barrel, palm to the rear, little finger just above the bayonet stud. The right wrist and forearm are straight, elbow held down without strain. The right arm does not need to be parallel to the deck.

Figure 6-3. From order arms to port arms.

TWO. Release the grasp of the left hand from the handguard. With the right hand, lower the rifle to the deck, magazine in front, muzzle in a vertical position. At the same time, guide the weapon into the right side with left hand until thumb is on the trouser seam, left fingers extended and joined, thumb along the forefinger. The first joint of the forefinger should touch the metal below the flash suppressor. The left wrist and forearm are straight, elbow against the body.

THREE. Smartly return the left hand to the left side in the position of Attention, and gently lower the rifle to the deck with the right hand, with the toe of the rifle in line with the toe of the right shoe. The magazine is to the front and in a vertical position. The position is the same as described for Order Arms, above. (See figure 6-4.)

Present Arms from Order Arms

This is used as a salute to persons and colors during parades and ceremonies, and by sentries. Commands: 1. PRESENT, 2. ARMS. On the first count, raise and carry the rifle to a vertical position centered

Figure 6-4. From port arms to order arms.

on the body, magazine well to the front. The fingers of the right hand are joined and wrapped around the barrel, thumb on the left side. At the same time, smartly grasp the rifle at the handguard with the left hand, fingers joined and wrapped around the handguard, thumb just above the slip ring, which should be four inches from the body. The left wrist and forearm are straight, parallel to the deck, elbow against the side and upper arm in line with the back.

TWO. Release the grasp of the right hand from the barrel and regrasp the small of the stock, fingers extended and joined, and the charging handle resting in the "V" of thumb and forefinger. Wrist and forearm are straight, forming a straight line from fingertips to elbow, which is held against the body. (See figure 6-5.)

Order Arms from Present Arms

Commands: 1. ORDER, 2. ARMS. On the command of execution, release the grasp of the right hand from the small of the stock and smartly regrasp the barrel; fingers joined and wrapped around the barrel, palm facing left. Right wrist and forearm are straight, elbow

Figure 6-5. Present arms.

held down without strain. The right arm does not need to be parallel to the deck.

TWO. Release the grasp of the left hand from the handguard and lower the weapon to the right side until the rifle butt is about three inches from the deck, muzzle in front and in a vertical position, magazine well to the front. At the same time, guide the weapon into the right side with the left hand until the thumb is on the trouser seam. Fingers are extended and joined, thumb along the forefinger, palm to the rear, first joint of the forefinger touching the metal just below the flash suppressor. The left wrist and forearm are straight, elbow held against the body. The entire right arm is behind the rifle.

THREE. Smartly, in the most direct manner, return the left hand to the left side in the position of Attention. At the same time, lower the rifle to the deck with the right hand so the toe of the rifle is in line with the toe of the right shoe; the magazine should be well to the front, the muzzle in a vertical position. With the butt of the rifle on deck, the right hand takes the position described earlier for Order Arms. (See figure 6-6.)

Figure 6-6. From present arms to order arms.

Right Shoulder Arms from Order Arms

Commands: 1. RIGHT SHOULDER, 2. ARMS.

At the command of execution, slide the right hand to the muzzle, fingers joined and wrapped around it, and in continuous motion raise and carry the rifle diagonally across the front of the body until the right hand is in front of and slightly left of the face. The right wrist and forearm are straight and slightly to the left of the face. The muzzle is up, bisecting the angle formed by the neck and left shoulder, magazine well to the left, butt of the rifle in front of the right hip. At the same time, smartly grasp the handguard with the left hand, fingers joined and wrapped around the handguard. The little finger is just above the slip ring, thumb on the inboard side and centered above the chest. The left wrist and forearm are straight and the elbow is against the body.

TWO. Release the grasp on the muzzle, regrasp the butt of the rifle, thumb and forefinger joined on the comb of the stock, remaining fingers joined and wrapped around the butt. The right arm is almost extended; the elbow is against the right side of the body.

THREE. Relax the left-hand grip on the handguard, and with the right hand carry the rifle to the right side. At the same time, rotate the rifle so the magazine is well to the rear, and place it on the right shoulder with the pistol grip in the right armpit. Guide the rifle into the right shoulder with the left hand by sliding it down the rifle until the first joint of the left index finger touches metal at the base of the charging handle. The left fingers should be extended and joined with the thumb along the forefinger, palm to the rear. The left wrist and forearm are straight, the elbow held down without strain. The right hand grasp remains unchanged. The right wrist and forearm are straight, parallel to the deck, elbow against the body, and upper arm in line with the back.

FOUR. Return the left hand, in the most direct manner, to the left side at the position of Attention. (See figure 6-7.)

Port Arms from Right Shoulder Arms

Commands: 1. PORT, 2. ARMS.

From the position of Halt, at the command of execution, press the rifle butt down quickly with the right hand so the rifle comes off the right shoulder. At the same time, rotate the rifle with the right hand a quarter of a turn so the magazine is well to the left, and let the rifle fall diagonally across the front of the body. Bring the left hand up,

Figure 6-7. From order arms to right shoulder arms.

grasp the handguard, left fingers joined and wrapped around it; the little finger is just above the slip ring, thumb on the inboard side and centered on the chest. The left arm and wrist are straight, elbow held against the body. Rifle muzzle is up, bisecting the angle formed by the neck and left shoulder; rifle butt is in front of the right hip. The right hand grasp is unchanged; the right arm is nearly extended, but held against the body.

TWO. Release the grasp of the right hand, regrasp the small of the stock with fingers joined, thumb on the inboard side of the rifle. Right wrist and forearm are straight, parallel to the deck, elbow in and upper arm in line with the back. The rifle should be about four inches from the belt.

When the command PORT, ARMS is given while troops are marching at Right Shoulder Arms, it will be given as the left foot strikes the deck. On the next step, the first count of the movement is carried out as if done at a halt. With each following step, another count is executed until the movement is complete. The movement is executed in cadence. Troops continue marching in this position until another command is given.

Order Arms from Right Shoulder Arms

Commands: 1. ORDER, 2. ARMS.

On the command of execution, press the rifle butt down quickly with the right hand so the rifle comes off the right shoulder. At the same time, rotate the rifle a quarter turn with the right hand so the magazine well is to the left, and let the rifle fall diagonally across the front of the body. Bring the left hand up and grasp the handguard; the fingers of the left hand are joined and wrapped around the guard, the little finger just above the slip ring. The left wrist and forearm are held straight and against the body, as is the elbow. The rifle muzzle is up, bisecting the angle formed by the neck and left shoulder. The grasp of the right hand remains unchanged. The right arm is extended, with elbow against the body.

TWO. Release the grasp of the right hand, regrasp the rifle with the palm to the rear, fingers joined and wrapped around the muzzle, thumb inboard. The wrist and forearm are straight, held down without strain.

THREE. Release the grasp of the left hand from the handguard and lower the rifle with the right hand on the right-hand side of the body until the butt is three inches from the deck, magazine to the front and the rifle in a vertical position. At the same time, guide the rifle to the right side with the left hand until the right thumb is on the trouser seam. Left fingers are joined, thumb along the forefinger. The first joint of that finger touches the metal just below the flash suppressor. The left palm faces the rear; the left wrist and forearm are straight, the elbow against the body. The entire right arm is behind the rifle.

FOUR. Return the left hand to the left side in a direct manner and assume the position of Attention. Then lower the rifle to the deck, gently, so the toe of the rifle is in line with the toe of the right shoe, magazine well to the front and rifle in a vertical position. When the butt is on deck, slide the right hand down the barrel so that the front sight assembly and barrel will rest in the "V" formed by the thumb and fingers of the right hand. The fingers of the right hand are joined and extended diagonally across the rifle, right thumb on the trouser seam; the entire right arm is behind the rifle. (See figure 6-8.)

Right Shoulder Arms from Port Arms

Commands: 1. RIGHT SHOULDER, 2. ARMS.

At the commands of execution release the right-hand grasp on the stock and smartly regrasp the butt of the rifle, thumb and forefinger joined and wrapped around the comb of the stock and the remaining three fingers joined and wrapped around the butt. The heel of the butt will be visible between the forefinger and middle finger. The right arm is nearly extended; the right elbow is against the body.

TWO. Relax the grasp of the left hand on the handguard, and with the right hand carry the rifle to the right side. At the same time, rotate the rifle a quarter turn so the magazine is well to the rear, and place the pistol grip in the right armpit; guide the rifle into the right shoulder with the left hand by sliding it down the rifle until the first joint of the index finger touches the base of the charging handle. The left fingers should be joined with the thumb along the forefinger, palm to the rear. The left wrist and forearm are straight, the elbow held down without strain. The right-hand grasp remains unchanged; the right wrist and forearm are straight and parallel to the deck, elbow against the body, upper arm in line with the back.

THREE. Return the left hand to the side in the most direct way and come to the position of Attention.

Note: This command can be executed while marching at quick time, in the same manner as Port Arms from Right Shoulder Arms.

Figure 6-8. From right shoulder arms to order arms.

Order Arms from Left Shoulder Arms

Commands: 1. ORDER, 2. ARMS.

On the command of execution, bring the right hand across the body in the most direct manner and grasp the small of the stock. The fingers are joined and wrapped around the small of the stock, thumb inboard; right wrist and forearm straight, elbow held down without strain.

TWO. Release the grasp of the left hand on the butt of the rifle, and with the right hand bring the rifle from the shoulder to a position diagonally across the front of the body, rotating it a quarter turn so the magazine is well toward the left. At the same time, smartly regrasp the handguard with the left hand; the fingers should be joined and wrapped around the handguard, the little finger just above the slip ring and the thumb inboard and centered on the chest. The left wrist and forearm are straight, elbow against the body; right wrist and forearm straight, elbow in and in line with the back. The rifle muzzle is up, bisecting the angle formed by the neck and left shoulder, the butt in front of the right hip.

THREE. Release the right-hand grasp on the stock and smartly regrasp the barrel, fingers joined, wrapped around the barrel, palm to the rear and little finger just above the bayonet stud. The right wrist and forearm are straight, elbow held down without strain.

FOUR. Release the grasp of the left hand from the handguard, and with your right hand lower the rifle to the right side until the butt is three inches from the deck. The magazine should face the front, rifle in a vertical position. At the same time, guide the rifle into the right side with the left hand until the right thumb is on the trouser seam. The left fingers are extended and joined, thumb along the forefinger, first joint of the forefinger touching the metal of the flash suppressor. The left palm faces the rear; left wrist and forearm are straight, elbow against the body. The right arm is behind the rifle.

FIVE. Return the left hand to the left side and assume the position of Attention. At the same time, lower the rifle to the deck so the toe of the rifle is in line with the toe of the right shoe with the magazine to the front and the rifle in a vertical position. As the rifle touches the deck, slide the right hand to the front sight assembly; fingers joined and extended diagonally across the front of the barrel. The right arm is behind the rifle.

Left Shoulder Arms from Right Shoulder Arms

This movement can be made while at Right Shoulder Arms, Marching at Quick Time, or at a Halt. Commands: 1. LEFT SHOULDER, 2.
ARMS. On the command of execution, press the rifle butt down
quickly with the right hand so the rifle comes off the right shoulder;
rotate the right hand so the rifle comes off the right shoulder; rotate
the rifle a quarter turn with the right hand so that the magazine well
is to the left, and let the rifle fall diagonally across the front of the
body. At the same time bring the left hand up and smartly grasp the
handguard with left fingers joined and wrapped around it, little
finger just above the slip ring, thumb inboard and centered on the
chest. The left wrist and forearm are straight; elbow against the
body. The right-hand grasp is unchanged; the right arm is nearly
extended, the right elbow against the body. The rifle muzzle is up
and bisecting the angle formed by the neck and left shoulder, the butt
behind the right hip, and the rifle four inches in front of the body.

TWO. Release the grasp of the right hand from the butt and
smartly regrasp the small of the stock, fingers joined and wrapped
around it, thumb inboard. The right wrist and forearm are straight,
elbow against the body, upper arm in line with the back.

THREE. Release the grasp of the left hand from the handguard,
and with the right hand carry the rifle to the left side, rotating it a
quarter turn so the magazine is well to the rear; place the pistol grip
in the left armpit. The right wrist and forearm are straight, elbow
held down without strain. At the same time, regrasp the butt with
the left hand; thumb and forefinger joined on the comb of the stock,
remaining three fingers joined and wrapped around the butt. The
heel of the butt will be visible between the forefinger and middle
finger.

FOUR. Release the grasp of the right hand from the small of the
stock and return it across to the right side in a direct manner for the
position of Attention.

Note: This command can be executed while marching at Quick
Time, in the same manner as Port Arms from Right Shoulder Arms.

Movements of Rest

Rest movements are used to give troops a change from the position of
Attention and still maintain an orderly formation. Parade Rest, At
Ease, and At Rest consist of a single count, that of execution. Fall
Out has no count at all.

Parade Rest

When the preparatory command PARADE is given, shift the weight from the left leg to the right without any body movement. When the command of execution, REST, is given, move the left foot smartly 12 inches to the left of the right foot—measured from inside the heels. Heels should be on the same line, legs straight but not stiff, body weight equal on both legs.

The left hand is placed in the small of the back, just below the belt, fingers extended and joined, thumb along the forefinger, palm to the rear and elbow in line with the body.

The butt of the rifle is kept on deck, in line with the feet, and against the right foot. When the left foot is first moved, relax the grasp of the right hand and move it to a point just below the flash suppressor. The fingers are joined and curled with the forefinger touching the thumb. At the same time, straighten the right arm directly to the front so the rifle muzzle points upward.

While at Parade Rest, maintain silence. The only command given to troops in this position is Attention. When that command is given, bring the left foot smartly back against the right foot, lower the left arm back to the side, move the rifle to the position of Order Arms and regrasp the rifle for that position. (See figure 6-9.)

At Ease

In this position the right foot remains stationary, and the rifle butt remains on deck. The rifle is held as in Parade Rest, but the grip and body stance may be more relaxed. Equipment may be adjusted, but silence must be maintained. The only command given while in this position is Attention, the movement for which is described above.

Rest

This is exactly the same as At Ease, except that troops may talk in conversational tones. The only command given to troops in this position is Attention. On the preparatory command, come to Parade Rest. On the command of execution, come to Attention and Order Arms.

Fall Out

When this order is given, troops may leave the present position and go to a designated area or remain in the general vicinity. The only

Figure 6-9. Parade rest, front and side views.

command that can be given after Fall Out is Fall In, at which troops assume the position of Order Arms.

Rifle Salutes

Troops in formation, or individuals who find themselves in a saluting situation, may execute the rifle salute. Salutes are made from Order Arms, Trail Arms, Right Shoulder Arms, or Left Shoulder Arms.

At Order Arms

Commands: 1. RIFLE, 2. SALUTE.

Carry the left hand across the body in the most direct manner until the first joint of the forefinger touches the metal just below the flash suppressor, left fingers extended and joined, thumb along the forefinger, palm down. The wrist and forearm are straight, elbow against the body.

READY, TWO. Smartly return the left hand to the left side and assume the position of Order Arms. (See figure 6-10.)

Figure 6-10. Hand salute at order arms.

At Trail Arms

On the command of execution, carry the left hand across the body in the most direct manner until the first joint of the forefinger touches the metal at the base of the flash suppressor. Left fingers extended and joined, palm down, wrist and forearm straight, elbow against the body.

READY, TWO. Smartly bring the left hand to the side and assume the position of Order Arms.

At Right Shoulder Arms

Smartly carry the left hand across the body until the first joint of the left forefinger touches the metal at the charging handle. The left fingers are extended and joined, palm down, arm parallel to the deck.

READY TWO. Smartly return the left hand to the side and assume the position of Order Arms. (See figure 6-11.)

Figure 6-11. Hand salute at right shoulder arms.

At Left Shoulder Arms

On the command of execution, smartly carry the right hand across
the body until the first joint of the forefinger is touching the base of
the charging handle. Fingers of the right hand are extended and
joined, with thumb along the forefinger, palm down, arm parallel to
the deck.

TWO. Smartly return the right hand to the side and assume the
position of Order Arms.

Inspection Arms (Without Magazine)

Commands: 1. INSPECTION, 2. ARMS.

On the command of execution, slide the right hand to the muzzle,
fingers wrapped around the barrel. Raise and carry the rifle diagonally across the front of the body until the right hand is in front of
and slightly to the left of the face. The right wrist and forearm are
straight and held down without strain. The rifle muzzle is up and
bisecting the angle formed by the neck and left shoulder, magazine

well to the left, butt in front of the right hip. Smartly grasp the handguard with the left hand, little finger just above the slip ring, thumb centered on the chest. Left wrist and forearm are straight, elbow against the body.

TWO. Release the grasp of the right hand on the barrel, regrasp the small of the stock with the thumb wrapped around the inboard portion. Right wrist and forearm are straight and parallel to the deck; elbow against the body, upper arm in line with the back. The rifle should be four inches from the body.

THREE. Release the grasp of the left hand from the handguard and regrasp the rifle at the pistol grip. The thumb of the left hand is over the lower portion of the bolt catch.

FOUR. Release the grasp of the right hand from the stock and use the thumb and forefinger to unlock the charging handle; at the same time pull it sharply to the rear, apply pressure on the bolt catch, and lock the bolt to the rear.

FIVE. With the thumb and forefinger of the right hand, push the charging handle until it is locked in the forward position. Regrasp the small of the stock with the right hand.

SIX. Elevate the rifle to the left with both hands until the rear sight is in line with the left shoulder. At the same time, rotate it a quarter turn clockwise so the chamber is visible, and turn the head and eyes toward the ejector port to inspect the chamber.

SEVEN. After seeing the chamber clear, or clearing it, turn head and eyes back to the front and lower the rifle to the position of Port Arms. As it is lowered, release the grasp on the pistol grip and re-grasp the handguard as in Port Arms. (See figure 6-12.)

Port Arms from Inspection Arms (Without Magazine)

Commands: 1. PORT, 2. ARMS.

At the preliminary command of PORT, release the grasp of the left hand and regrasp the rifle at the magazine well and trigger guard, fingers extended and joined, thumb inboard, thumb and forefinger forming a "V" at the magazine well and trigger guard. At the same time, press the bolt catch and allow the bolt to slide forward. With the fingertips of the left hand, push forward and close the ejection cover, then slide the left hand toward the pistol grip and place the thumb on the trigger.

At the command, ARMS, push down on the trigger with the left thumb and uncock the hammer. Then release the grasp of the left

Figure 6-12. Inspection arms.

hand and regrasp the rifle at the handguard, fingers extended and joined, little finger just above the slip ring, thumb inboard. Left wrist and forearm are straight, elbow against the body.

CLOSE-ORDER DRILL

A group of personnel in uniform and bearing arms must be under the direct control of a senior officer in order for them to move in an orderly fashion. Close-order drill will accomplish this. Such drill also serves to teach discipline by instilling habits of automatic and precise response to orders, developing better morale through team spirit, and making it possible for a Coast Guard unit to make a favorable appearance in a parade or other public ceremony.

The basic unit in a military formation is the squad, a group of eight to twelve people organized as a team.

The squad is usually kept intact. Its normal formation is a single rank or file. This permits variation in the number of personnel in the squad. The original formation is always in line.

The squad marches in line only for minor changes of position.

The squad leader, when in ranks, is posted as the right person of the squad in line or as the leading person in column.

To Form the Squad

The command is: FALL IN.

At the command, the squad forms in line. Each person, except the one on the extreme left, extends the left arm to the side at shoulder height, palm down, fingers extended and joined. Each person, except the one on the extreme right, turns the head and eyes to the right and moves enough in line so that the right shoulder touches the tips of the fingers of the person on the right. As soon as proper intervals have been obtained, each person drops the arm and turns the head smartly to the front.

To Form at Close Interval

Commands: 1. AT CLOSE INTERVAL, 2. FALL IN.

At the command, the personnel fall in as above, except that close intervals are obtained by placing the left hand on the hip, fingers extended downward and joined, thumb along the forefingers, heel of the hand resting along the hip bone, elbow extended to the side.

If the squad is under arms, rifles are inspected.

The squad executes the positions, movements, and manual of arms with all personnel executing the movements together.

To Dismiss the Squad

Commands: 1. INSPECTION, 2. ARMS, 3. PORT, 4. ARMS, 5. DISMISSED.

If the squad is not under arms, the single command DISMISSED is used (the squad, of course, being at attention or having been brought to attention).

To Count Off

Commands: 1. COUNT, 2. OFF.

At the command OFF, each person except the one on the right flank, turns their head and eyes to the right. The right flank person calls out "One." Each person in succession calls out "Two," "Three," etc., turning the head and eyes to the front as the number is given.

To Align the Squad

In line, commands: 1. DRESS RIGHT (or LEFT), or 1. AT CLOSE INTERVAL, DRESS RIGHT (LEFT), 2. DRESS, 3. READY, 4. FRONT.

At the command DRESS, each person except the one on the left, extends the left arm (or if at close intervals, places the left hand upon the hip), and all dress to the right. The squad leader is on the right flank, one pace from and on the line of the squad. From this position the squad leader checks alignment, ordering individuals forward or backward as necessary. Having checked alignment, the squad leader faces to the right in marching, and moves three spaces forward, halts, faces to the left and commands: 1. READY, 2. FRONT. At the command FRONT, arms are dropped quietly and smartly to the side, and heads turned to the front.

In column, command: COVER.

At the command COVER, personnel cover from front to rear with 40-inch intervals between them.

To Obtain Close Interval

Commands: 1. CLOSE, 2. MARCH.

At the command MARCH, all personnel, except the right flank person, face to the right in marching and form at close interval.

To Extend to Normal Interval

Commands: 1. EXTEND, 2. MARCH.

At the command MARCH, all personnel, except the right flank person, face to the left in marching and form at normal interval.

To March to the Flank

Commands: 1. RIGHT (or LEFT), 2. FACE, 3. FORWARD, 4. MARCH. These movements are executed with all personnel stepping off together.

To March to the Oblique

Commands: 1. RIGHT (or LEFT) OBLIQUE, 2. MARCH. (The word *oblique* is pronounced to rhyme with *strike*.)

At the command MARCH, given as the right foot strikes the ground, each person advances, plants the left foot, faces half right, and steps off in a direction of 45 degrees to the right. Each remains in relative place, shoulders parallel to those of the guide, steps regulated so that the ranks stay parallel to the original front.

The command HALT is given on the left foot when halting from the right oblique march, and on the right foot when halting from left oblique march.

At the command HALT (from left oblique march), given as the left foot strikes the ground, each person advances, planting the right foot, turns to the front on the ball of the right foot, and brings the left foot to the side of the right. The opposite is done from right oblique march so that in either case the personnel end facing front.

To stop temporarily the execution of the movement for the correction of errors, the commands are: 1. IN PLACE, 2. HALT.

All halt in place without facing to the front and stand fast. To resume the movement the commands are: 1. RESUME, 2. MARCH.

If at half step or mark time while obliquing, the full step is resumed by the command: 1. RESUME, 2. MARCH.

To resume original direction, the commands are: 1. FORWARD, 2. MARCH.

At the command MARCH, each person faces half left in marching and moves straight to the front. If at half step or marking time while in oblique march, the full step is resumed by the command: 1. OBLIQUE, 2. MARCH.

To March Toward the Flank

Commands: 1. BY THE RIGHT (LEFT) FLANK, 2. MARCH.

At the command MARCH, each person simultaneously executes the movements as described above.

In Column, to Change Direction

Commands: 1. COLUMN RIGHT (or LEFT), (HALF RIGHT), (HALF LEFT), 2. MARCH.

At the command MARCH, the leading person executes the movement immediately; the others in succession as they reach the pivot point.

In Line, to Take Double-arm Interval and Assemble

Commands: 1. TAKE INTERVAL TO THE LEFT (OR RIGHT), 2. MARCH.

At the command MARCH, the right flank person stands fast, extends the left arm at shoulder height, palm down, fingers extended and joined, until the person on the left obtains the proper interval, then drops the arm. Other personnel face to the left in marching and step out until they have an interval of two arms's length from the person on the right, then halt and face to the front. Each person, except the one on the left who raises the right arm only, extends both arms laterally at shoulder height. Each person, except the one on the right flank, then turns the head and eyes to the right and moves enough for alignment so that the fingertips of the right hand touch those of the left hand of the person on the right. As soon as each person is aligned at two arms' length, they drop the right arm to the side and turn the head and eyes to the front. Each drops the left arm when the person on the left has obtained the proper interval.

To assemble, the commands: 1. ASSEMBLE TO THE RIGHT (or LEFT), 2. MARCH.

At the command MARCH, the right-flank person stands fast; all other personnel face to the right in marching and form at normal interval.

Column of Twos

When marching small groups, not at drill, the group may be marched in column of twos by forming it in two ranks and giving the commands: 1. RIGHT (or LEFT), 2. FACE.

To Form Column of Twos from Single File and Re-form

The squad being in column, at halt, to form a column of twos the commands are: 1. FORM COLUMN OF TWOS TO THE RIGHT (LEFT), 2. MARCH.

At the command MARCH, the leading person stands fast; the second person in the squad moves by the oblique to the left of and abreast of the squad leader with normal interval, and halts. The third person moves forward until behind the squad leader at normal interval, and halts. The fourth person moves by the oblique to the left of and abreast of the third person at normal interval, and halts; and so on.

To Form Single File from Column of Twos

Being in column of twos, in marching, to re-form single file the squad is first halted. Commands: 1. COLUMN OF FILES FROM THE RIGHT, 2. MARCH.

At the command MARCH, the leading person of the right column moves forward. The leading person of the left column steps off to the right oblique, and then executes left oblique so as to follow the right file at normal interval. The remaining twos follow successively in the same way.

All military drill is based upon the squad. Two or more squads make up a platoon, which is the basic drill unit. Two or more platoons make up a company. Two or more companies make up a battalion, although it is customary to assign four companies to a battalion when possible. When a formation is large enough to form a battalion, orders may be given by bugle or by signal. A regiment consists of two or more battalions; at a minimum it could be made up of sixteen squads, although usually it would be far larger. Complete instructions for handling platoons and larger formations are contained in the *U.S. Marine Corps Drill and Ceremonies Manual.*

II.
Your Coast Guard Career—Personal Development

CHAPTER 7

Training and Education

Enlistment in the Coast Guard offers you a choice of many career opportunities, many of which are very marketable in the private sector. The option you finally select will depend, in part, on the training you receive, your own aptitudes, and the needs of the service. This chapter will describe some of the training opportunities available to you and will point out how you can start on a Coast Guard career. Remember that the amount of responsibility and self-discipline you display in your work will have a great effect on your duty assignments and promotion potential.

RECRUIT TRAINING

For any one of a number of reasons you have decided to enlist in the Coast Guard. Having been accepted and sworn in, you have been ordered to report to Recruit Training Center, Cape May, New Jersey. Your career in the Coast Guard has begun. Here, in a few short weeks, you must learn to make the difficult change from school and home life to a strict military routine. You will probably be upset and confused at first, but so will almost everyone else. Your instructors have all been through the mill before and are there to help you get organized and learn to do things the Coast Guard way.

Figure 7-1. Coast Guard Training Centers are large and well equipped to support training of Coast Guard personnel to meet the many and varied demands of their missions.

One of the biggest problems the average recruit has, on entering any military service, is learning how to live with a large group of people and become a team member. Recruit training is designed to assist you in solving those problems, but it cannot do it alone. You must help yourself by being tolerant of other people's peculiarities. You probably have some of your own.

While you are in recruit training, you will learn many things. Some of them are taught in formal classes, others you gradually absorb in your daily work. Recruit training is an entry-level instructional program designed to provide you with fundamental skills and knowledge so that you can be productive in a military environment. You will learn the various skills required in the Coast Guard: boatmanship, visual signaling, military drill, personal hygiene, traditions, care of the uniform, seamanship, fire fighting, safety, and many others. You will also learn the main essential of good citizenship—getting along with others.

Basic Tests

Prior to coming into the Coast Guard, you took a series of exams called the Armed Services Vocational Aptitude Battery (ASVAB) tests. The ASVAB is a Department of Defense test that is used by the Coast Guard for enlistment screening and to measure your basic aptitudes—in other words, to find out what things come naturally to you.

The ASVAB consists of the following ten subtests:

General science (GS). This test measures your basic factual knowledge of biology, medicine, chemistry, and physics.

Arithmetic reasoning (AR). Often called "word problems," this test measures your ability to use arithmetic skills to solve problems described by short paragraphs.

Word knowledge (WK). Essentially a vocabulary test.

Paragraph comprehension (PC). This test measures how well you get information from written passages.

Numerical operations (NO). This test covers basic arithmetic operations, which you solve as quickly as possible.

Coding speed (CS). Like numerical operations, this test emphasizes speed and accuracy by comparing code numbers for certain words in a key with those on the answer sheet.

Auto and shop information (AS). This test measures your knowledge of tools and terms associated with vehicle repair and maintenance.

Figure 7-2. First liberty at Cape May.

Mathematics knowledge (MK). This test measures your knowledge of high school algebra, geometry, and trigonometry.

Electronics information (EI). This test measures your familiarity with electrical equipment and terminology.

On your test results printout, you will also see a score for *VE— Verbal Ability.* This score is a composite of the Work Knowledge (WK) and Paragraph Comprehension (PC) subtests. It gives an indication of your overall verbal ability.

Testing is of the utmost importance in determining your aptitude for assignment to petty officer schools. Do your best the first time. Although you may retake any of the subtests a second time, the most recent retest score, *even if it is lower than the original score,* is official and cancels previous test scores.

These tests are important, but they are not the only factor considered; your own determination and ability will determine your success in the Coast Guard.

FIRST DUTY ASSIGNMENTS

Upon completion of recruit training, each graduate is permitted to take up to 12 days regular leave. This "recruit" leave provides you

Figure 7-3. Tests will become an important way to help you advance in your chosen field.

time to visit your family and friends back home for a few days. They may base their entire opinion of the Coast Guard on what you do and how you act and display the training you have received. So make sure you leave them with a good impression.

First duty assignments may be either to sea duty or shore duty. Sea duty could mean a cutter, icebreaker, buoy tender, patrol boat, or any of many other vessels. Shore duty could be at a base, group, or station. Wherever you go, you will find new friends and exciting experiences.

Training

Training consists of basic (Class "A") schools and specialized (Class "C") schools.

Class "A" schools provide the minimum essential rating training designed to provide the basic technical knowledge and skills required for job-entry-level performance for the respective rating. The Class "A" school graduate is an apprentice who will initially require addi-

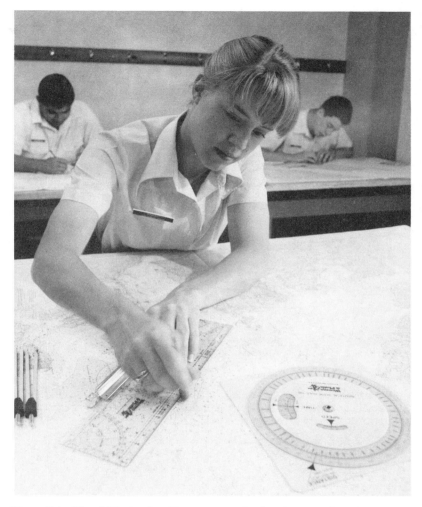

Figure 7-4. Class "A" schools will prepare you for duty in a specific rating.

tional on-the-job training under close supervision to carry out the assigned duties.

Class "C" school is short-term training designed to provide advanced/specialized knowledge and skills to perform a task, or group of tasks, required by a specific billet.

Assignment to Class "A" school may be made upon completion of recruit training. Most personnel gain assignment to Class "A" schools after serving in a ship or at a station for a specific amount of time.

The Coast Guard conducts the following Class "A" schools:

Aviation Technical Training Center, Elizabeth City, North Carolina

Aviation Electrician's Mate (AE)
Aviation Electronics Technician (AT)
Aviation Machinist's Mate (AD)
Aviation Structural Mechanic (AM)
Aviation Survivalman (ASM)

Training Center, Petaluma, California

Electronics Technician (ET)
Telephone Technician (TT)
Health Services Technician (HS)
Radioman (RM)
Storekeeper (SK)
Subsistence Specialist (SS)
Yeoman (YN)

Reserve Training Center, Yorktown, Virginia

Boatswain's Mate (BM)
Damage Controlman (DC)
Electrician's Mate (EM)
Gunner's Mate (GM)
Machinery Technician (MK)
Marine Science Technician (MST)
Quartermaster (QM)
Radarman (RD)

The Coast Guard uses Department of Defense schools for training in the following ratings:

Fire Control Technician (FT)—Navy
Public Affairs Specialist (PA)—Army

Selection for Training

In order to attend an advanced school, you must have attained minimum scores in your classification tests, must have a good-conduct record, and must be recommended by your commanding officer. Your commanding officer's recommendation will be based on observation of your work and attitude by the CO, the executive officer, and your division and petty officers.

Graduates of Class "A" schools may be promoted to petty officer third class if there is a vacancy in that rating, and if they have passed the military requirements course for E-4, have demonstrated leadership abilities, and have the required six-months' service in pay grade E-3. Those not advanced on graduation will be given a school-assigned designator. This allows them to work in their new rating. They will be promoted when the above requirements have been satisfied and they are recommended by their commanding officer.

Some of the knowledge you need can be gained only by experience. The rest comes by studying various publications, including this manual. Remember that knowledge alone will not ensure promotion. You must have a record of satisfactory performance in your present assignment, your conduct record must be satisfactory, you must be reliable, and you must be recommended by your commanding officer. The officers and petty officers of your unit must be able to depend upon you.

Ratings Qualifications

After reaching pay grade E-3, you should decide what rating you prefer to enter. Most ratings are covered by Class "A" schools, but for some you can make your own preparations by "striking for rating."

In addition to the actual knowledge requirements for advancement in rate, you must serve a certain minimum time in the lower rate, be recommended for advancement, and have completed the practical factors for the rating. The *Enlisted Ratings Qualifications Manual* gives details on practical factors.

Correspondence Courses

The Coast Guard Institute furnishes correspondence courses covering the requirements for advancement in practically all ratings. These courses enable you to study for a rating at your own unit. Completion of one of them is required for advancement. Class "A" school graduates do not have to complete the rating correspondence course for advancement to pay grade E-4, but they do have to pass the Military Requirements E-4 (MRN-E4) course for advancement to pay grade E-4. *Note*: Some ratings require Class "A" school attendance. Check with your educational services office.

Figure 7-5. Training never stops.

On-the-Job Training

On-the-job training goes hand in hand with correspondence courses. What you learn in your courses in theory, you can practice in your daily work. In many of the ratings, experience is an absolute necessity. For instance, a boatswain's mate must have experience as a leading seaman. Here, while serving an apprenticeship, you actually learn while doing, under an experienced petty officer. Whether you train on the job or in a formal school, both theoretical knowledge and practical experience are necessary.

Leadership

You need more than knowledge and experience to hold a rating in the Coast Guard. The device on the petty officer badges means more than that they are specialists—the eagle indicates petty officer, a leader. A petty officer is both a *specialist* and a *military leader*. Military duties and responsibilities as a petty officer take precedence over skill in rating. Leadership is a quality that few people are born with. The acquisition of leadership requires study and practice. Some of the study can come from a book or formal course. Much of it must come from observation and emulation of good leaders. In your daily life, you will come in contact with many leaders. Watch them, note the qualities that make them good leaders, and copy them.

A good leader must have a good conduct record. Conduct itself is an integral part of leadership. You cannot expect a higher standard of conduct from your subordinates than you yourself display.

Information and Education Program

It is possible to study almost any subject in your off-duty time through the Coast Guard's educational program. The principal sources of off-duty education are the U.S. Coast Guard Institute (USCGI) and various educational and commercial institutions.

The Coast Guard Institute

The Coast Guard Institute and courses produced there have been reviewed by the National Home Study Council (NHSC) and by the American Council on Education (ACE). The NHSC has approved accreditation of the USCG Institute, and the ACE has recommended educational credit for many Coast Guard correspondence courses. This accreditation makes it easier for students to obtain college or vocational credit for their correspondence course work. In general, the Institute provides correspondence courses and servicewide examinations for enlisted advancements. Most of the courses are directly related to the knowledge and skills that Coast Guard personnel in the various ratings and pay grades must possess. As a general rule, Coast Guard personnel must complete an Institute correspondence course before competing for advancement.

The unit's educational services officer (ESO) has a copy of the Institute's *Correspondence Course Manual*, which contains the rules and procedures of the program and a list of the courses available. The ESO will take care of the details for your enrollment, keep track of your progress, and give instruction and guidance if you have any problems while you are completing the course. You are eligible for enrollment in any course offered by the Institute. Enrollment is usually limited to three courses at a time.

In addition to enlisted rating courses, the Coast Guard Institute offers a number of special courses, among which are oceanography, meteorology, boating safety, and search and rescue. All courses are furnished without cost, and you may keep most of the materials for reference. Satisfactory course completion is recorded in your service record.

Coast Guard Tuition Assistance Program

This program covers courses taken during off-duty hours at accredited colleges, universities, junior colleges, high schools, and commercial schools, but not correspondence courses. (See Veterans Administration Tuition Assistance concerning these.) In order to qualify for

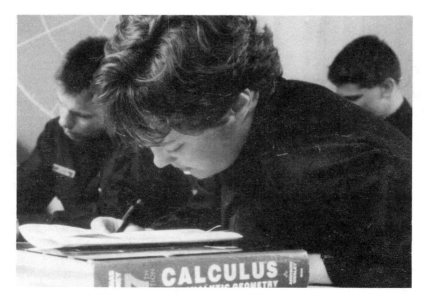

Figure 7-6. Academy cadets complete a rigorous four-year program designed to prepare them as officers.

assistance, the desired course must be one that would broaden your technical and academic background and increase your usefulness to the service. Generally, any course that will increase your chances for promotion—management for a yeoman, accounting for a store-keeper—will meet this requirement. However, funds must be available, and your attendance at the course must not interfere with your assigned duties. Duty comes first.

Education Benefits

Your education is good for you and the Coast Guard. Your increased knowledge will be reflected by improved skills and performance. Therefore, the Coast Guard is ready to help you attain your educational goal, whether it's a high school equivalency or a college degree. Depending on your unit and your job, you could be eligible for off-duty tuition assistance. You'll also be able to take correspondence courses through the Coast Guard Institute and DANTES (see below). Your educational services officer can help you order CLEP and DANTES tests that you can use for college credit.

There are several educational benefits programs that apply to veterans, depending upon when you entered the service. For an explanation of the Montgomery G.I. Bill and the Veterans Educational Assistance Program, check with your unit's educational services office.

Defense Activity for Non-Traditional Education Support (DANTES)

The Defense Activity for Non-Traditional Education Support (DANTES) offers a number of programs through your local educational services officer (ESO) or from various military installation education centers. The DANTES program can help you get credit for what you've learned outside the classroom. You develop and expand your skills and knowledge through training courses and programs, self-study activities, volunteer or community work, on-the-job experiences, and through a variety of other learning experiences. These are considered non-traditional education experiences because they do not normally take place in a traditional classroom setting. Non-traditional education programs are practical for many Coast Guard members who cannot participate in formal education programs due to their work schedules, education levels, duty-station assignments, or for personal reasons. The DANTES program offers high school equivalency credential (such as the GED), college admission exam-

inations (ACT and SAT), military evaluation programs (which are explained in detail under the ACE program), college credit by examination, independent study, experiential learning assessment, and college external degree programs. To receive a free booklet from DANTES, which outlines some of their many programs available, write: DANTES
Code 33
Pensacola, FL 32509-7400

College Level Examination Program (CLEP)

The College Level Examination Program (CLEP) can give you a good start on your road to college. By taking CLEP exams you can receive college credit that will save you time and money during your college career. CLEP credit can even help you satisfy college requirements for Officer Candidate School (OCS). The CLEP consists of a series of examinations that test college-level knowledge you many have gained through military classes or technical assignments, or through your own reading, travel, and intellectual curiosity. About two-thirds of the colleges and universities in the United States give

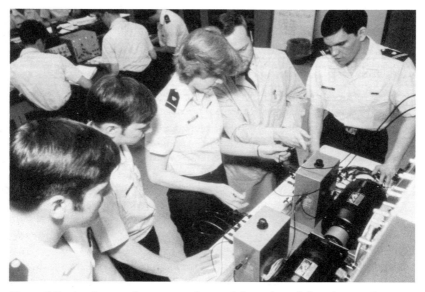

Figure 7-7. Academy cadets must understand the technical disciplines and state-of-the-art equipment.

credit for CLEP exams, but each institution has its own policy for acceptable test scores. Your educational service officer (ESO) or the Coast Guard Institute can provide you with more details.

American Council on Education (ACE)

Today's Coast Guard members are trained to operate the most technologically advanced equipment anywhere in the world. They are continuously and expertly trained, and many have acquired knowledge equivalent to that of college students. The American Council on Education (ACE) recognizes that some military learning experiences can be equated to college course work and encourages college and university personnel to award academic credit for military learning experiences.

For nearly forty-five years, the *ACE Guide to the Evaluation of Educational Experiences in the Armed Services* has been the standard reference work for recognizing learning acquired in military life. ACE has worked cooperatively with the Coast Guard and the other armed services in assisting hundreds of thousands of service men and women to achieve recognition for their learning. Collectively, over 300 Coast Guard resident (Class "A" and "C") and correspondence courses, Coast Guard enlisted ratings, and warrant officer specialties have been granted recommendation for college credit through ACE evaluations.

Servicemembers Opportunity Colleges (SOC)

The Servicemembers Opportunity Colleges (SOC), a consortium of national higher education associations of more than 550 institution members, function in cooperation with the Department of Defense (DoD), the military services, and the Coast Guard to help meet the voluntary higher education needs of military members and their dependents.

Hundreds of Coast Guard members and their family members enroll annually in college-level programs. Many of these programs make it possible for a Coast Guard member to earn a college degree with little or no residency requirement. Over 95 percent of the SOC institutions will accept the ACE recommended college credits, CLEP, and DANTES tests, to apply towards your degree program.

For more information on the SOC and ACE program, see your educational services officer (ESO).

CHAPTER 8

Advancement and Promotion

The Coast Guard Enlisted Advancement System is a fully qualified, competitive system. Personnel are advanced to pay grades E-4 through E-9 to fill servicewide vacancies in total Coast Guard allowances. In the proper path for advancement, a seaman may advance into AD, AE, AM, ASM, AT, BM, ET, FT, GM, HS, MST, PA, QM, RD, RM, SK, SS, TT, or YN ratings. A fireman may advance to DC, EM, or MK ratings. Opportunities exist for enlisted personnel to join the commissioned officer ranks. The *Coast Guard Personnel Manual* and the *Reserve Administration and Training Manual* contain complete details.

COMMON CHANNELS OF ADVANCEMENT

There are three common avenues for advancement in the enlisted rates. They are: (1) nonrated, (2) Class "A" school, and (3) competitive advancements.

Nonrated advancements. Recruits are normally advanced to seaman apprentice or fireman apprentice (E-2) upon graduation from basic training. Six months later, they may be advanced to seaman or fireman (E-3) by their commanding officers if they have maintained good conduct, satisfactory performance, and completed the appropriate correspondence courses and performance-based qualifications.

Figure 8-1. A seaman ready to lower the jack.

161

Class "A" school advancements. Graduates of a Class "A" school are placed on an advancement list for promotion to petty officer third class. After meeting various other prerequisites, depending upon the rating, they may be advanced from the list as vacancies occur.

Competitive advancements. Advancement to E-5 and above is achieved through competition in the Servicewide Advancement System.

The Servicewide Advancement System

Candidates become eligible for advancement after they:

complete the rate-related and general military requirements specified for the target rate and pay grade.

complete the required correspondence courses.

meet citizenship or security clearance requirements.

are in the proper path of advancement.

fulfill special requirements for certain ratings.

Figure 8-2. Training at formal schools will help you advance up the ladder rapidly.

serve a specified minimum number of months in the Coast Guard.
serve a specified number of months in their current rate in the Coast Guard.
fulfill sea-duty requirements.
fulfill additional eligibility requirements for personnel in E-7/E-8/E-9 examinations.
earn acceptable enlisted performance evaluations.
are recommended by their commanding officers.

Recommended candidates must compete with all other candidates in the target rate by taking the Servicewide Examination (SWE). Candidates will be rank ordered with other candidates.

The rank order for advancement to each rate is based upon the final multiple. The final multiple is computed from the SWE score, average performance evaluations for a given period of time, time in service (TIS), time in grade (TIG), and points for certain medals and awards.

The number of candidates to be advanced is based upon a forecast of servicewide vacancies made by the Enlisted Personnel Division at Coast Guard Headquarters. The forecast for each rate will vary with each examination cycle.

TIS and TIG must be completed by specified cutoff dates for each advancement cycle.

Completion of performance-based qualifications requires candidates to satisfactorily demonstrate certain tasks. The performance standards must be met before the candidates may be recommended to participate in the servicewide examination.

All eligibility requirements except TIS and TIG in present rating must be met before an individual may be recommended by the commanding officer. TIS and TIG in present rating must be completed on or prior to terminal eligibility dates established.

The commanding officer's recommendation is the last and, by far, the most important prerequisite. Even if all other requirements are met, a candidate cannot compete without the commanding officer's recommendation.

After all prerequisites have been met, the Personnel Reporting Unit (PERSRU) complete the Advancement Recommendation and Examination Request. Upon receipt of this form at the Institute, a servicewide examination will be mailed to the candidate's examining board.

The Servicewide Examination

Each member who wants to take the servicewide exam must personally verify his or her Personnel Data Extract (PDE) prior to taking the exam. The next and final step is participation in the servicewide examination.

The *Enlisted Qualifications Manual*, COMDTINST M1414.8 (series), is the basis for the development of the servicewide examination. This manual prescribes the minimum occupational and military standards (performance-based) for advancement in rate.

The main goal of the SWE is to identify those candidates best qualified for advancement on the basis of rate-related/required standards.

The SWE is a norm-referenced examination. The minimum acceptable score is set by COMDT (G-PE) for each examination series and may be adjusted for selected rates.

The difficulty of the SWE is set so that, in the judgment of the subject matter expert, the minimally competent candidate will score 70 percent or higher on the SWE. Usually, 80 percent of the candidates should be minimally competent; however, the subject matter expert will make that determination after consultation with the program, training, and force (rating) managers. Candidates are then ranked based on their final multiple.

TIG and TIS are calculated through 1 January and 1 July following the SWE examination. Candidates for E-8 must have ten years of cumulative service in one or more components of the armed forces as of 1 January following the SWE. Candidates for E-9 must have 12 years of cumulative service in one or more components of the armed forces as of 1 January following the SWE.

Servicewide Schedule

The SWE administration schedule for active-duty enlisted personnel is as follows:

E-5 through E-6	November and May
E-7 through E-9	May

The Advancement Results

The results are announced eight to ten weeks after the servicewide examination is administered. All candidates who participate in the

SWE will receive a profile letter. The profile letter indicates the overall performance of the candidate as well as performance by sections. Section scores are provided to identify those areas that the candidate may use to study for the next SWE, if applicable.

An advancement eligibility list is published shortly after the profile letters are mailed. This list includes the names of all candidates who are eligible for advancement. Names that fall *above* the cutoff are guaranteed advancement. Names *below* the cutoff *may* be advanced, but should plan to recompete in the next SWE. This is *not* an automatic process; the candidate must remain qualified and be recommended by the commanding officer for each SWE cycle.

Advancement in the Coast Guard Reserve

The regular procedures for advancement of active-duty enlisted personnel in the Coast Guard apply also to the Coast Guard reservists with the following exceptions: an annual SWE for reservists is given in October, and TIG and TIS are calculated through 1 January following the SWE.

Reservists in emergency rates who are on extended active duty may not participate in the regular SWE. They can only compete in the reserve SWE. If they place above the cut, COMDT (G-PE) will determine if the person is to be advanced.

Personnel who passed an active-duty Coast Guard SWE for advancement to E-4, E-5, or E-6 within one year of their separation from active duty, but were not advanced for any reason other than disciplinary, may be advanced without taking a reserve SWE *if*:

the reserve unit CO recommends advancement within one year of the candidate's separation from active duty,

the candidate's advancement multiple was at least as high as the lowest multiple used in advancing a reservist on the same examination, and

no SWE for that rate has been taken by the candidate since passing that SWE.

Promotion to Warrant and Commissioned Grades

Every petty officer rating has a normal path of advancement to warrant officer rank. Selections for warrant officer are made from among first-class and chief petty officers on the eligibility list who apply for this advancement. An applicant must have the required

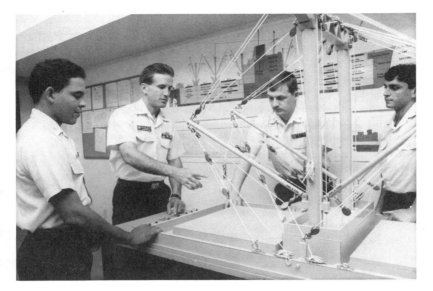

Figure 8-3. "Learning the ropes."

Figure 8-4. OCS personnel practice military fundamentals.

service, must make satisfactory scores on warrant qualification and specialty examinations, and must be recommended by their commanding officers. A selection board of commissioned officers chooses those considered best qualified to fill the vacancies in the various warrant categories. Selected candidates are promoted to W-2 and can later compete for further advancement.

Advancement does not end here. Many warrant and chief warrant officers have been promoted to higher commissioned grades.

Officer Candidate School

Selected enlisted personnel may be ordered to the Officer Candidate School (OCS) at the U.S. Coast Guard Reserve Training Center, Yorktown, Virginia. This training leads to appointments for temporary service as ensigns, providing certain requirements are met. Many such temporary officers eventually receive permanent commissions, after meeting service requirements and after having been selected for promotion to lieutenant. Also, at certain times enlisted personnel with the necessary educational qualifications are given the opportunity to become commissioned officers in the Coast Guard Reserve.

Figure 8-5. Performance yields rewards.

Figure 8-6. Academy Regimental Staff prepares for inspection.

Figure 8-7. Academy cadets being inspected.

Coast Guard Academy Preparatory Program

This ten-month course, delivered at the Naval Academy Preparatory School, Newport, Rhode Island, is designed to provide qualified enlisted and civilian personnel with the educational skills necessary to compete effectively for an appointment to the Coast Guard Academy. NAPS is academically, physically, and mentally demanding. The daily routine strongly emphasizes military leadership and athletic preparation as well as academic study. There are extensive classroom hours devoted to English, reading, math, science, and computers. Graduates may be offered appointments as cadets.

Coast Guard Academy

Enlisted personnel may compete for direct appointments to the Academy. Cadets are selected annually by competitive examination. To qualify for the examination, a candidate must be between the ages of 18 and 22, be of good character, be a United States citizen, and be a high school graduate with school credits in the required subjects. These examinations are open to enlisted people in all the armed forces.

CHAPTER 9

Career Information

As a member of the Coast Guard, you are entitled to many benefits. Upon completing your enlistment, either through discharge or retirement, many of these benefits will still be available to you. This chapter briefly describes some of the most important features of the benefit package.

Pay and Allowances

The pay of all members of the armed services is determined by Congress. Your pay consists of basic pay, basic allowances (one for quarters and one for subsistence or meals), incentive pay or hazardous-duty pay, and miscellaneous pay and allowances.

You will be paid twice a month, generally the first and the fifteenth. The actual amount you receive each pay day is equal to basic pay, plus certain allowances, minus taxes and minus any allotments you may have made. Your basic pay is determined by your rank and your total years of creditable service. Basic pay and basic allowances are computed on a monthly basis.

Direct Deposit

Direct deposit is the Coast Guard's primary pay delivery method. The direct deposit method of payment allows you to have your net

Figure 9-1. Enlistment in the Coast Guard marks the beginning of a career.

pay deposited directly into your savings or checking account at a designated financial institution of your choice. Each regular member enrolled in the direct deposit program will receive a net pay advice statement for the mid-month payday and a Leave and Earnings Statement (LES) for the first-of-the-month payday. Direct deposit provides reliability and convenience and avoids lost or stolen checks. Afloat cashiers aboard vessels deployed outside the continental United States and away from home port more than four days over a payday are authorized to cash personal checks for members on direct deposit. The primary purpose of this check-cashing authority is to provide members on direct deposit with a source of funds to cover incidental expenses, not to provide a cash payroll.

Basic Allowances for Subsistence and Quarters

As a member of the Coast Guard, you are entitled to food and shelter in addition to basic pay. Regardless of your pay grade, you are entitled to certain allowances in cash to provide quarters for your spouse or legal dependents. If you have no legal dependents, you will usually be provided subsistence and quarters "in kind." This means that you will eat in a government mess and will sleep on board ship or in government barracks or quarters. Your food costs you nothing, so you receive no cash allowance for it. There may be times when it is impracticable to furnish you with either subsistence or quarters or both in kind. In that case you will receive a cash allowance in lieu of items not furnished.

Separate Rations

When a regular Coast Guard dining facility is available, but you choose to eat elsewhere, your commanding officer may authorize payment of a daily allowance for this. You may still eat at a dining facility, but you must pay for the meal. The conditions under which "SepRats" may be paid will be explained by your pay officer.

Incentive Pay for Hazardous Duty

For pay purposes the following duties have been designated as hazardous:

Duty involving frequent and regular participation, as a crew member, in aerial flights.

Duty involving frequent and regular participation, not as a crew member, in aerial flights.
Duty involving frequent and regular participation, as a flight-deck tie-down crew member.
Duty involving frequent and regular participation in diving activities.

Assignment to such duties will entitle you to monthly incentive pay that varies, depending on rate and time in service. The directives on hazardous duties and incentive pay change from time to time. Check with your pay office.

Clothing Allowance

Six months after graduation from recruit training you begin receiving a monthly allowance for clothing maintenance. Special clothing, such as arctic clothing, is furnished to you at no cost when you are required to use it.

Proficiency Pay

This was established as an incentive to help fill shortages in certain ratings, or special-duty assignments, and is classified either as Shortage Specialty Pro Pay or Special-Duty Assignment Pro Pay. Each year Coast Guard Headquarters determines which ratings, skills (identified by qualification codes), and special-duty assignments will be authorized Pro Pay.

Family Separation Allowance

This is paid to help offset additional expenses you might have when stationed away from your family. The rate of pay varies, and eligibility is involved. Check with your pay office.

Idea Express Program

The Idea Express program evolved from the first Coast Guard suggestion system. The Coast Guard has saved millions of dollars by gathering and acting upon your ideas. Remember, this program means more than just money to you. It's a way for you to speak out and voice your ideas to top management and actively participate in the future of the Coast Guard. All military, civilian, ready reserve, and retired Coast Guard employees are eligible. Adopted ideas result in two types of savings to the Coast Guard. Tangible savings are measurable. Awards for tangible savings are based on the first year's estimated net savings expected from your idea. You receive 10 percent of what you save the Coast Guard. Intangible savings are those that cannot be specifically identified or measured. Awards for intangible savings are based on the significance of the contribution and the importance of the program affected. Awards for ideas adopted with intangible savings range from $50 to $10,000.

Allotments

You may assign or allot a part of your pay regularly to a spouse, parent, bank, or insurance company. You can also use this method to buy savings bonds. The money you allot is paid each month and is deducted from your pay.

U.S. Savings Bonds

A wise way to save money is by buying U.S. Savings Bonds, preferably by a monthly allotment. Bonds provide savings for family emergencies and for return to civilian life. They may be cashed six months after purchase.

Travel, Transportation, and Per Diem

When traveling under orders, you are entitled to do so at government expense. You may be authorized to travel by automobile, or by government or commercial transportation. In addition, a per diem (daily) allowance may be paid to cover the cost of food, lodging, and other expenses. With the exception of personnel ordered to their first duty station after recruit training, transportation of dependents and household goods at government expense is authorized on a permanent change of station. Orders to a new duty station involve many expenses. The Coast Guard recognizes this and reimburses you through a dislocation allowance, trailer allowance, mileage allowances, dependents' transportation, and shipment of household goods. The rules and regulations covering transportation and travel expenses are complicated and subject to frequent changes. You are only entitled, however, to allowances authorized or directed in the orders.

Work-Life Philosophy

The mission of Work-Life is to create a network of individuals and organizations willing and able to provide support for our members and their families. Through the enhancement of customer service and service delivery, the right information will be in the hands of the right people at the right time.

Building the Partnership

The Coast Guard recognizes that Work-Life issues are critical to individual and organizational success. In response, a *Beneficiary Guide* was developed and distributed to every active-duty Coast Guard member. It introduces the programs and benefits available to you.

Support Service Areas

The *Beneficiary Guide* covers the following support service areas: relocation and housing assistance, dependent resources, individual and family assistance and intervention, health care and wellness, employment and advancement, and specialized services. Each chapter includes important information to help you access services, local points of contact, and toll-free telephone numbers.

Benefits

Veterans Administration Tuition Assistance

The Montgomery G.I. Bill became effective 1 July 1985 and is available to any member who first became a member of the armed forces or first began active duty on or after that date. COMDTINST 1760.6 requires that an allotment authorization be submitted for members who elect to participate in the program. Only the personnel office at Training Center Cape May is authorized to start this allotment, except in the case of a direct-commission officer or a member going through OCS. Detailed information on this program will be provided during recruit training.

Social Security

All service personnel participate in the Social Security program. A portion of your pay is deducted each month for this purpose. The amount of deduction is matched by the Coast Guard. These funds will earn Social Security benefits for you and your dependents.

Insurance Programs

Dependency and Indemnity Compensation (DIC) is a form of insurance payable to the survivors of personnel who die in the line of duty while on active duty. As a member of the Coast Guard you automatically receive this coverage, free.

Servicemen's Group Life Insurance (SGLI). This is a government-sponsored term-insurance program. Upon joining the Coast Guard, you are automatically insured. Part of your pay is deducted each month to pay for this insurance. You may reduce your coverage or cancel it; however, this is seldom done since the cost is so low. This insurance is good only while you are on active duty, or for certain categories of reservists. The Survivors' Benefit Plan (SBP) applies to retired personnel. Under this program you agree to a reduced retirement pay upon retirement, and in return your spouse continues to receive a portion of your retired pay after you die.

Mortgage insurance for servicemen. Some time during your career you may decide to purchase a residence. If you obtain a conventional mortgage loan, you will have to make a down payment of as much as 20 or 30 percent of the purchase price. As a member of the Coast Guard, you are eligible to apply for an FHA in-service loan, or a VA in-service loan, which allows you to purchase a home with a greatly reduced down payment. The Coast Guard does not lend money nor guarantee repayment of the loan. It merely certifies that the service member is eligible for the benefits of the National Housing Act of 1954, and it makes payment to the Federal Housing Administration (FHA) for mortgage insurance premiums on mortgages that have been endorsed by the FHA based on a Certificate of Eligibility issued by the Coast Guard. The service member will find the following advantages in the FHA mortgage insurance system: the mortgage covers a higher percentage of the house valuation, the down payment is lower, there is a limit on the interest the mortgagor can charge, the mortgage limitations are raised for high-cost areas, and the Coast Guard pays the mortgage insurance premiums on FHA loans during the period of ownership by the service member. Detailed information on mortgages and rates of interest can be obtained from any major lending institution. Check chapter 16 of the *Personnel Manual* about additional requirements concerning eligibility.

Medical care. Free medical and dental care is provided all members of the Coast Guard on active duty. This care includes surgery and emergencies, as well as routine immunizations, physical exams, etc. Dependents are eligible for medical care in the facilities of any of the armed services; they pay a small daily charge when they are hospitalized. Another medical care program is CHAMPUS (Civilian Health and Medical Program of the Uniformed Services). Under this program dependents may receive outpatient treatment, and in some instances inpatient care, from civilian facilities. The government pays most of each CHAMPUS bill, but the individual must pay part of it. A dental plan is also available.

Off-duty employment. Personnel on active duty are in a 24-hour duty status, and their military duties take precedence at all times. However, you can hold a part-time job, or work for yourself in off-duty hours. If you do such work, you must remember that even though you are on leave or liberty, you are subject to recall and duty at any time. The Coast Guard *Personnel Manual* covers the conditions under which civilian work or employment is prohibited.

Soldiers' and Sailors' Civil Relief Act

The Soldiers' and Sailors' Civil Relief Act of 1940, as amended, is an act authorizing the civil courts to protect the interest of persons in the armed forces of the United States by temporarily suspending the enforcement of certain civil liabilities if their ability to meet their obligations or to assert their rights is impaired by reason of their military service.

This act does not free a member of the service from obligations. It does, however, contain provisions designed to afford protection to those in service with regard to: debts, leases, evictions, interest rates, taxes, installment purchases, foreclosures, and mortgages, just to name a few. Protection is also provided under certain circumstances to dependents. The interpretation and application of the provisions of the Soldiers' and Sailors' Civil Relief Act is determined by the civil courts of each state, and therefore, each court may rule differently. To find more information on the Soldiers' and Sailors' Civil Relief Act, ask your unit administrative officer or consult the *Personnel Manual*.

Coast Guard Mutual Assistance

This organization provides financial assistance to active-duty and retired personnel in times of need or emergency, in the form of interest-free loans or grants. It is not a loan agency where money may be borrowed as a convenience or for the purchases of automobiles or TV sets. Rather, it is established to assist in cases of real hardship beyond the control of an individual. If you find yourself in such a situation, Coast Guard Mutual Assistance is one of the first activities to go to for help.

Coast Guard Mutual Assistance can help with loans for down payments on homes. Within certain limits, such as the amount of your monthly bills and the cost of the home you desire to purchase, the loan may cover all or a portion of the required down payment.

The American Red Cross

This organization provides several services to Coast Guard units and individuals. Among these are verification of requests for emergency leave or leave extensions based on emergencies, assistance with the unit's blood program, and individual counsel, guidance, and financial assistance in the form of a loan or grant. Any financial assistance given will depend on whether the emergency is real and how serious it is. You should let your family members know about the American Red Cross services. Have them contact a Red Cross chapter if they are unable to reach you directly concerning a family emergency.

Figure 9-2. A proud commanding officer stands on her bridge wing.

Nonappropriated Fund Activities

Many of the larger units have a base or ship's exchange, laundry, tailor shop, barber shop, snack bar, enlisted club, etc. These functions are called nonappropriated fund activities (NAFA), because they are supported by their own profits rather than by government funds. Part of the profits are used by the commanding officer for recreational equipment for the crew, for crew's parties, etc. Part of the profits are distributed to smaller units not having NAF activities in order that they may also benefit. You are entitled to use the exchanges or stores at any Army, Navy, Marine, Air Force, or Coast Guard base.

Legal Assistance

Only the legal officers at Maintenance and Logistics Command Atlantic and Pacific are designated as legal assistance officers. They will interview, advise, and assist members of the Coast Guard and their dependents who have legal problems and, in certain cases, refer them to competent attorneys. All matters are treated confidentially and will not be disclosed without your permission. Legal assistance officers can draw up wills, powers of attorney, affidavits, and a few other documents. They also deal with cases of child adoption.

Duty Tours

In general, you may expect to get the duty or training you desire, unless the needs of the Coast Guard make it impossible. Sometimes you may have to wait, but eventually your requests will be taken care of. It is important to keep up-to-date on changes in rules and regulations, so as to take advantage of all opportunities for either duty or schools.

Sea Service

Sea duty for pay, promotion, and rotation is defined by the commandant. The length of duty tours beyond the continental limits of the United States varies, according to the location, degree of isolation, and the needs of the service.

Shore Duty

After a certain amount of continuous sea duty, or overseas duty, or a combination of both, you become eligible for transfer to shore duty.

The interests of the service come first, but every effort is made to give everyone a fair share of shore duty.

Time Not Creditable for Service

You will not be paid, or credited for time served, if you were not performing duty. In counting time served, days in which you were absent from duty due to misconduct will be deducted from the total. The following count as time not served:

Absence over leave, absence without leave, and desertion.

Absence from duty due to injury, disease, or sickness resulting from intemperate use of drugs or alcohol, or other misconduct.

Absence due to arrest and serving of sentence imposed either by civil or military authorities. If the arrest results in no conviction, the time spent under arrest is not deducted.

Duty Assignments

All enlisted personnel list their personal data and duty preferences on the Assignment Data Form (CG-3698A). Assignments to duty are based on this form, so be sure to have one on file, filled out, and up-to-date.

Petty officer assignments. These are handled by the Central Assignment Control (CAC) program at headquarters. They are based on the billet requirements of each unit, the needs of the service, the enlisted qualification code of certain billets, and billet vacancies.

Nonrated assignments. These are controlled either by headquarters or district personnel officers, in much the same way petty officer assignments are handled.

Mutual Exchange of Station and Unilateral Transfers

On your first duty assignments, it is not always possible to match duty stations with your personal preference; personnel are sent where they are needed most. Later, changes in personnel at various stations make it possible for people to be sent to stations they prefer, but because there is no advantage to the Coast Guard in such a transfer, it must be made at no expense to the government. The person wanting the transfer must find someone at the other station with the same rating and experience who will "mutual" with them—swap duty stations with both paying their own expenses. If a "mutual" exchange cannot be made, a unilateral change of station may be requested. One condition for a unilateral transfer is that the person's unit is in excess of its allowance for the member's rating, or that it has the recommendation of the commanding officer that no immediate replacement will be required if the request is granted. Other restrictions apply; check the *Personnel Manual.*

Humanitarian Assignments

These are special assignments made to help a member handle a hardship of such a nature that it cannot be taken care of by emergency leave. Such transfers are usually for four months, but in special cases a permanent change of station (PCS) will be considered. A PCS humanitarian assignment is at government expense. Details are contained in the *Personnel Manual.*

Discharges

There are six types of discharges for enlisted personnel:

Type of Discharge	Character of Separation	Given by
Honorable	Honorable	Administrative action
General	Under honorable conditions	Administrative action
Undesirable	Conditions other than honorable	Administrative action
Bad Conduct	Conditions other than honorable	Courts-martial
Dishonorable	Dishonorable	General courts-martial
Uncharacterized	Without specific character	Administrative action

The formal reasons for discharge of enlisted personnel are:

Expiration of enlistment	Security
Convenience of the government	Misconduct
Dependency or hardship	Sentence of courts-martial
Minority	Uncharacterized
Disability	Unsuitability

Honorable Discharge

To obtain an honorable discharge, you must fulfill certain conditions described in detail in the *Personnel Manual.* Your record must show high standing in performing the duties of your rate and in conduct.

General Discharge

A general discharge is given for the same reasons as the honorable discharge. If your conduct and performance of duty have been satisfactory, but not high enough to warrant an honorable discharge, you will receive a general discharge.

Discharge Under Other Than Honorable Conditions

This type of discharge is given for reasons of misconduct, security, or for the good of the service.

Bad-Conduct Discharge

A bad-conduct discharge is given, only by approved sentences of special or general courts-martial, for offenses which, although serious, are not sufficiently grave to warrant dishonorable separation.

Dishonorable Discharge

A dishonorable discharge is given only by approved sentences of general courts-martial. It is one of the consequences of serious offenses.

Uncharacterized Discharge

An uncharacterized discharge by its own connotation is separation without characterization of service.

Importance and Benefits of an Honorable Discharge

The kind of discharge you receive may affect you for the rest of your life. Eligibility for veterans' preference in federal employment, for payments for service-connected disability, for a pension, and for many other benefits and privileges—state and federal—will depend upon the type of discharge you receive. Civilian employers may refuse to hire a person with the "wrong" kind of discharge. Do all you can to earn a discharge under honorable conditions.

Formal Reasons for Discharge

Expiration of Enlistment

Normally, enlisted personnel are promptly discharged on the date of expiration of their enlistment. However, they may continue on duty for some time after that date if they extend their enlistment, are undergoing medical treatment, or awaiting trial, or are required to make up lost time. They may be held past the discharge date if the ship is at sea, or in time of war or national emergency.

Disability

This discharge is given to personnel who are unable to carry out their duties because of mental or physical disability.

Convenience of the Government

This term covers such reasons as general demobilization or the acceptance of a permanent commission, plus many more reasons.

Dependency or Hardship

Discharges given for reason of dependency or hardship, sometimes called "hardship discharges," are authorized when it is shown 'that undue and general hardship exists at home; that the hardship is not a temporary one; and that the conditions have arisen or worsened since the person joined the Coast Guard. A dependency discharge is not authorized merely for financial or business reasons or for personal convenience. However, a discharge will not be held up because of the Coast Guard's need to keep the billet filled, or because of indebtedness to the government or to an individual.

Minority

Discharge for minority is of interest only to enlisted personnel who are under 18 years of age. Instructions regarding such discharges are in the *Personnel Manual.*

Unsuitability

The commandant may authorize or direct the discharge of personnel for unsuitability. Among the good and sufficient reasons for such a discharge are inaptitude for service life, personality disorders, apathy, defective attitudes, insanitary habits, alcohol abuse, homosexual (Class III) cases, and financial irresponsibility.

Security

A discharge for reasons of security is directed only when it is determined that the enlisted person cannot continue in service without risk to the national interest.

Misconduct

The commandant may direct the discharge of a member for misconduct in any of the following cases: conviction by civil authorities (foreign or domestic), fraudulent enlistment, absenteeism, involvement with drugs, frequent involvement of a discreditable nature with civil or military authorities, sexual perversion, an established pattern of shirking, an established pattern showing dishonorable failure to pay just debts, dishonorable failure to contribute adequate support to dependents, or failure to comply with valid orders, decrees, or judgments of a civil court concerning support of dependents.

Sentence of a Court-Martial

In addition to other punishments, a court-martial can award a discharge from the Coast Guard. Not only does this rid the service of unwanted persons, but it puts—by way of punishment—a black mark of serious consequences forever in the person's record.

Uncharacterized

An uncharacterized discharge will be used for most recruit separations, other than that for disability, or for prior service personnel entering recruit training. Members must have demonstrated poor proficiency, conduct, or aptitude, or unsuitability for further service during the period from enlistment through recruit training, a period of less than 180 days of active service on date of discharge.

Personnel Data Record

Your Personnel Data Record (PDR) is a four-section folder designed to hold only those specific documents necessary to provide for your personal and pay needs. A PDR is maintained on you at each of the following locations: CG Headquarters, PPC Topeka, your local PERSRU, and your unit. In addition, you are required to maintain your own copy of your PDR.

At the end of your service career the National Personnel Records Center, St. Louis, MO, will consolidate all of the above, including your medical PDR, into one PDR.

Your PDR is important during your service career and later in civilian life, so "keep it clean." Even after you're discharged or retired, information from your PDR may be needed for collecting veteran's benefits, for employment, or for school credits.

Identification Card

The green *Armed Forces of the United States Identification Card*—
"ID card" for short—identifies you as an active member of the armed

Figure 9-3. Honor Guard personnel represent the Coast Guard at ceremonies throughout the country.

forces. It shows your name, social security number, rate, photograph, and the date of expiration of your enlistment. It is not a pass, but you should carry it at all times.

"Non-Petty Officer" is typed on the cards of people in pay grades E-1, E-2, and E-3. Cards for those in higher pay grades are marked appropriately. If you lose your ID card, you will have to sign a statement explaining how it was lost. If you were neglectful, disciplinary action will follow. The card is government property; if you alter, damage, or counterfeit it, or use it in an unauthorized manner, you will be subject to disciplinary action. The same warning applies to lending your card or borrowing another person's card. When you are discharged, your ID card must be turned in. People in an inactive status receive a red ID card; those who are retired receive a blue one.

Special Requests

When people want a transfer to another ship or station, assignment to school, change of rating, permission to bring some piece of personal property on board, or some other consideration, they submit a special request slip, or "request chit." Such slips are submitted in a "chain of command" fashion so that the officer to take final action will know the decision of those immediately above you. If your request is reasonable and valid, and your performance of duty has been good, your request will probably be granted.

Requests Through Channels

Anyone may make a request or an appeal to higher authority (senior to your CO). Appeal from censure or a request for dependency or hardship transfer are possible reasons for "going up the line." The general rule is that these types of requests are usually in letter form and must go through the "chain of command," via your CO, the group commander (if in the chain of command), district, and finally to the commandant. Do not bypass anyone in the chain of command; this is a violation of a basic military principle. You are permitted to make requests; just make them through channels.

Liberty

Authorized absence from duty for periods up to 96 hours is classed as liberty. Most liberties consist of leaving the ship or station around 1630 and returning before 0730 or 0800 the next morning. The normal 48-hour liberty that is granted for weekends may be extended to 72 hours if the period includes a national holiday. A 96-hour liberty must include two consecutive nonwork days and shall not, under any circumstances, extend beyond 96 hours. Various ships and stations will have different types of liberty schedules. For example: "port and starboard liberty" (1-in-2, or liberty every other evening); "three-section liberty" (two liberty nights for each duty night); and even "six-section liberty" (five liberty nights and one duty night).

All liberty is controlled by your commanding officer and is granted as work loads and operating schedules permit. Remember, liberty is a privilege, not a right.

Leave

Leave is the authorized absence of an individual from a place of duty, chargeable against such individual in accordance with applicable law. Leave is earned at the rate of two and one-half days per month of duty, but not for periods of training duty without pay (reservists), any period of less than 30 consecutive days of training duty (reservists), while confined as sentence of court-martial, or while in an unauthorized absent status for 24 hours or more.

Earned Leave

This is the amount of leave you have credited "on the books" at any given date. If you have taken more leave than you were entitled to, then you have *minus leave* on the books. Any minus leave over that which you would normally earn during the rest of your enlistment is treated as *excess leave*. Excess leave is leave over your earned leave and any *advance leave* granted you. Advance leave is leave granted out of the amount of leave you will earn during the rest of your enlistment.

Here is how advance and excess leave works. Say you have ten days' earned leave on the books and four months to go on your enlistment. Because of an emergency you are granted 20 days' leave. Those 20 days are half earned leave and half advance leave. Suppose those 20 days were extended by your commanding officer for ten days. Those last ten days are excess leave.

On a yearly basis, the 30 days you earn are figured from 1 October of one year to 30 September of the next year. As your leave builds up, it is carried over from one fiscal year to the next, to a maximum of 60 days. If you have 67 days on the books on 30 September, you lose seven days and start with just 60 days.

If you are discharged with leave still on the books, you will be paid a lump sum equal to your daily pay for each day on the books. If you are discharged with minus leave on the books—in other words, owing the Coast Guard for leave time—your pay will be reduced by an amount equal to a day's pay for each day's leave you owe.

Your commanding officer has the authority to grant you (on a yearly basis) all your earned leave plus up to 30 days' advance leave. However, you may not have more than 60 days of leave at one time— except for *reenlistment leave.*

Sick Leave

Sick leave is the term used to describe a period of authorized absence granted to persons while under medical care and treatment. It usually follows a period of hospitalization and is not chargeable as leave.

Emergency Leave

In the event of a personal emergency—the death of your father, for example, or the serious illness of your spouse, you will normally be granted emergency leave to take care of important personal matters. Since most family emergencies are highly time-dependent, swift, sensitive action on emergency leave request will be taken.

How Leave Is Counted

The day you depart on leave, whatever the hour, is counted as a day of duty as long as it coincides with the granting of liberty. If you check in to your unit by 0900 on your day of return, it will be counted as a day of duty and will not be charged as leave. If you return after 0900, it will be charged as another day of leave.

Compensatory Absence

This is a form of liberty granted to personnel at isolated units where normal liberty cannot be granted. Compensatory absence is granted insofar as possible for rest and rehabilitation, usually on the basis of seven days' absence for 14 days of duty. There are limits on how much can be accrued. At isolated overseas units, credit is earned at the rate of two and one-half days per month.

Retirement

Retirement means that you are released from active duty but continue to draw a certain fixed pay for the rest of your life. The exact amount of this retired pay depends on many factors. Length of service is the greatest governing factor in most retirements. Degree of disability is the controlling factor in the case of disability retirements. In time of war or national emergency, retired personnel may be called to active duty.

There are several classes of retirement, including compulsory retirement at the age of 62, voluntary retirement after 20 or more years' service, involuntary retirement after 20 or more years' service, and retirement for disabilities incident to service. Retired people are entitled to medical treatment in government facilities and are entitled to use commissary and exchange facilities at any military base.

U.S. Coast Guard Reserve

All personnel, upon original enlistment in the Coast Guard, incur a statutory obligation as described in the Universal Military Training and Service Act. Various enlistment programs require different amounts of active duty, active reserve, or inactive reserve obligations. Regardless of the type or program, all personnel enlisting on or after 1 September 1984 incurred an eight-year period of obligated service.

CHAPTER 10

Enlisted Rates and Ratings

The Career Compensation Act of 1949 established uniform pay grades for officers and enlisted people in all the armed forces. This law requires that the pay in a given grade must be the same in all the services. Coast Guard officer ranks are the same as those in the Navy. Most enlisted ratings are the same as in the Navy, although the Coast Guard does not have all the Navy ratings, and the Coast Guard has some the Navy does not. Those described here are authorized for normal peacetime operations; in times of war or national emergency, there may be a need for other ratings. A more complete listing can be found in the *Enlisted Qualifications Manual* (COMDTINST M1414.8A).

A rating is the name given to an occupation in the Coast Guard that requires basic aptitudes related to the specialty plus training, experience, knowledge, and skills. A person who has a rating is generally a petty officer.

All ratings are equally important. Therefore, no one rating takes precedence over another rating. Among enlisted people present and regularly assigned to the same activity, or among those present in any gathering, the person with the longest period of continuous service in the highest pay grade shall be considered senior regardless of rating.

Figure 10-1. A Port Securityman 2nd class stands guard duty in the Persian Gulf.

A rate is a pay grade that reflects a level of aptitude, training, experience, knowledge, skill, and responsibility. The order of pay grades is as follows:

Rates	*Pay Grade*
Seaman Recruit, Fireman Recruit	E-1
Seaman, Fireman, and Airman Apprentice	E-2
Seaman, Fireman, Airman	E-3
Petty Officer third class (PO3)	E-4
Petty Officer second class (PO2)	E-5
Petty Officer first class (PO1)	E-6
Chief Petty Officer (CPO)	E-7
Senior Chief Petty Officer (SCPO)	E-8
Master Chief Petty Officer (MCPO)	E-9

Duties of the Master Chief Petty Officer of the Coast Guard (MCPOCG)

The senior enlisted member of the Coast Guard is assigned to the office of the commandant for a four-year tour of duty. The MCPOCG is the Coast Guard's only E-10, and he or she advises and assists the commandant on all matters that affect the morale of enlisted personnel.

The master chief petty officer of the Coast Guard makes frequent visits to and corresponds with personnel at field units to ensure that enlisted men and women of the Coast Guard have continued communication with the commandant. This includes direct contact with command enlisted advisors throughout the Coast Guard and with personnel in similar positions in the other armed services.

In this position as the solid communication link between Coast Guard enlisted personnel and the commandant, the MCPOCG serves as a representative of Coast Guard enlisted personnel on many boards, committees, and study groups and at ceremonies, celebrations, and social activities.

Suggestions and concerns of Coast Guard enlisted men and women may be submitted to the master chief petty officer of the Coast Guard where they will be evaluated and forwarded to the commandant with appropriate action recommended.

Duties of Nonrated Personnel (E-1, E-2, E-3)

Recruits (SR, FR). Recruits undergo formal basic training or boot camp at Coast Guard Training Center Cape May.

Apprentices (SA, FA, AA). Apprentices perform the simple duties of seamen, firemen, and airmen while under close supervision.

Seaman (SN). Seamen are nonrated personnel in training for a rating in deck, ordnance, electronics, administrative, and clerical or miscellaneous groups other than engineering. They perform general deck and other detail duties and maintain deck equipment, compartments, lines, rigging, and decks. They perform as members of gun crews, small-boat crews, and security and fire watches.

Fireman (FN). Firemen are nonrated personnel in training for an engineering rating. They operate pumps, motors, and turbines, light off boilers, maintain and clean engineering machinery and compartments, record gauge and instrument readings, and stand security and engineering watches.

Airman (AN). Airmen are nonrated personnel in training for an aviation rating. They assist in the maintenance of aircraft, associated aeronautical equipment, and aircraft ground-support equipment. They service and clean aircraft and assist in aircraft handling. They stand security and fire watches and perform other duties peculiar to the operation of an aviation activity.

Duties of Petty Officer Ratings (E-4–E-9)

The following brief descriptions of duties and responsibilities of ratings in the Coast Guard is based on the rating structure in effect in 1991.

Aviation Group

All initial aviation training for enlisted technicians takes place at the Aviation Technical Training Center, Elizabeth City, North Carolina. While there, students are exposed to the aviation environment and receive basic training in theory of flight, aerodynamics, and aviation rating duties. In addition to their technical responsibilities, personnel in the five aviation ratings are required to perform as members of Coast Guard flight crews. Aircrew duties are taught on the job after completion of technical training.

Aviation machinist's mate (AD). Aviation machinist's mates' ma-

Aviation Machinist's Mate (AD)

jor job responsibilities include maintenance and repair of aircraft engines, including propellers, fuel, ignition, and hydraulic systems, and associated power-plant equipment. Aviation machinist's mates receive 20 weeks of training at the Aviation Technical Training Center, Elizabeth City, North Carolina.

Aviation survivalman (ASM). The aviation survivalmen's primary role is to maintain, rig, and repair all types of parachutes. They operate and work with small arms, aviation munitions, and pyrotechnics. They service and maintain oxygen-breathing equipment, personnel survival equipment, droppable de-watering pumps, and all search-and-rescue life-saving equipment. Aviation survivalmen receive 20 weeks of training at the Aviation Technical Training Center, Elizabeth City, North Carolina, and must complete the U.S. Navy Rescue Swimmer course and be designated as Coast Guard swimmers.

Aviation electronics technician (AT). Aviation electronics technicians are responsible for the maintenance, calibration, and operational condition of airborne radio, radar, and other electrical devices used for navigation, detection of distressed vessels or aircraft, rapid communication, and controlled landing approaches. Aviation elec-

Aviation survivalman (ASM)

Aviation Electronics Technician (AT)

Aviation Electrician's Mate (AE)

Aviation Structural Mechanic (AM)

tronics technicians receive 22 weeks of training at the Aviation Technical Training Center, Elizabeth City, North Carolina.

Aviation electrician's mate (AE). Aviation electrician's mates are taught basic electrical theory, aircraft wiring systems, generator and motor theory, power circuits, direct and alternating currents, and basic electronics. They inspect, maintain, adjust, repair, and replace when necessary, aircraft electrical equipment and instruments. Aviation electrician's mates attend 18 weeks of training at the Aviation Technical Training Center, Elizabeth City, North Carolina.

Aviation structural mechanic (AM). Aviation structural mechanics maintain and repair aircraft surfaces, airframe structures, pneudraulic systems, landing gear, control surfaces, and all associated mechanisms. They work with metal, alloys, plastics, and fabrics, and become expert in welding, fabrication of sheet metal, and operation of basic machine-shop equipment. Aviation structural mechanics receive 18 weeks of training at the Aviation Technical Training Center, Elizabeth City, North Carolina.

Deck and Ordnance Ratings

Boatswain's mate (BM). Boatswain's mates are master seamen, people skilled in all phases of seamanship and in providing guidance to deck personnel. Because senior boatswain's mates frequently serve as officers in charge of patrol boats, tugs, and small shore units, they must possess strong leadership skills. BMs are capable of performing almost any task associated with the operation of small boats, including navigation, storing cargo, and handling ropes, cables, and lines. Under battle conditions, they are assigned as gun captains, ammunition handlers, or members of damage-control teams. Boatswain's mates generally "strike" at their own unit. Quotas are occasionally available for active-duty personnel at the seven-week boatswain's mate training course located at the Reserve Training Center, Yorktown, Virginia.

Quartermaster (QM). Quartermasters are assigned to all types of ships and serve in the pilothouse, on the bridge, or in the charthouse. Quartermasters perform vitally important roles in the day-to-day precise operation of Coast Guard cutters. Safety at sea depends largely upon skillful navigation, maintaining a careful lookout for other ships and obstacles, and proficient signal exchange with other ships and shore stations. Quartermasters know whistle, bell, and light signals, the Rules of the Road, and visual communication,

Boatswain's Mate (BM)

Quartermaster (QM)

which includes blinker signaling, semaphore, and signal flags. They are proficient at taking bearings and soundings and can plot a course and take turns as a helmsman. Quartermasters receive 11 weeks of training at the Reserve Training Center, Yorktown, Virginia.

Gunner's mate (GM). Gunner's mates are expert in all types of ordnance from small arms to rocket launchers. They operate, maintain, and repair all elements of various weapon systems used and stored aboard cutters and shore stations. They frequently perform as demolition experts. They inspect magazines, test powder, stow ammunition and pyrotechnics, clean and repair small arms, and train personnel in the operation and safe handling of weapons. Gunner's mates receive 10 weeks of training at the Reserve Training Center, Yorktown, Virginia. Some Coast Guard cutters are authorized to conduct "striker" training that can lead to designation as gunner's mate.

Fire-control technician (FT). Fire-control technicians maintain and repair the extremely complicated electronic, hydraulic, and mechanical equipment required to compute and resolve the many factors that influence the accuracy of weapons fire. FTs calculate wind effects, parallax, and ship's movement in solving fire-control prob-

Gunner's Mate (GM)

Fire-control Technician (FT)

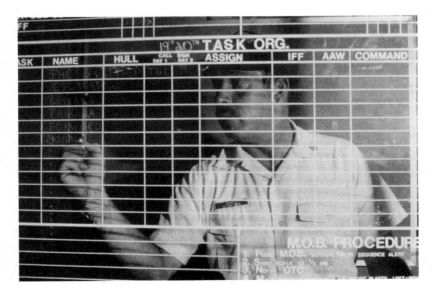

Radarman (RD)

lems. Fire-control technicians receive 34 weeks of training at the U.S. Naval Training Center, Great Lakes, Illinois.

Radarman (RD). Radarmen operate all types of radar, radio, and plotting equipment to search for, locate, and track the movement of ships, aircraft, and other airborne or surface objects. Radarmen are the "eyes" of the ship, especially during bad weather, at night, and in battle conditions. They interpret and plot information received. They perform routine tests, adjustments, and repairs to equipment. Radarman receive 12 weeks of training at the Reserve Training Center, Yorktown, Virginia.

Engineering and Hull Group

Damage controlman (DC). Damage controlmen understand the theory, techniques, and skills of fire-fighting, chemical warfare, carpentry, painting, welding, plumbing, and general damage control aboard ships, and have extensive knowledge and understanding of the associated equipment. They maintain and repair damage-control equipment and perform all types of carpentry work. Damage con-

Damage Controlman (DC)

trolmen receive 13 weeks of training at the Reserve Training Center, Yorktown, Virginia.

Machinery technician (MK). Personnel assigned as machinery technicians operate, maintain, and repair internal combustion engines, steam turbines, and main propulsion power transmission equipment. They perform similar functions on refrigeration, air-conditioning, fuel systems, pneumatic systems, and machine shop equipment. Machinery technicians participate in damage-control parties, perform engineering-related administration functions, and read blueprints. Senior MKs organize and lead damage-control parties. Machinery technicians receive 12 weeks of training at the Reserve Training Center, Yorktown, Virginia.

Electronics technician (ET). Electronics technicians install, operate, maintain, modify, and remove electronic equipment and systems used for all types of electronic communication, electronic detection and tracking (Radar), navigation receiving (Loran, Omega, NAVSAT), radionavigation transmitting (Loran, Omega, radiobea-

Machinery Technician (MK)

cons, racons), and several types of computer systems. Electronics technicians serve aboard ship and at shore stations from Japan to Turkey and Alaska to Puerto Rico. Electronics technicians receive 18 weeks of training at the Coast Guard Training Center, Petaluma, California.

Telephone technician (TT). Telephone technicians design, plan, install, remove, operate, maintain, and repair all types of communication equipment and systems, including telephone (PBX and key); data communications; microwave radio and multiplex carrier systems; antennas and towers; pole lines; underground, overhead, and underwater cables; and public-address systems. TTs serve both ashore and afloat and are required to climb poles. Telephone technicians receive 20 weeks of training at the Training Center, Petaluma, California.

Electronics Technician (ET)

Telephone Technician (TT)

Electrician's Mate (EM)

Electrician's mate (EM). Electrician's mates know the fundamentals of electricity, alternating and direct currents, circuits, switchboards, searchlights, and other electrical instruments. They operate and repair a ship's or station's electrical power plant and electrical equipment. They maintain and care for the electrical propulsion equipment, the gyrocompass and related equipment, and ships' internal communication equipment and systems. Electrician's mates receive 14 weeks of training at the Reserve Training Center, Yorktown, Virginia, or "strike" on the job.

Administrative and Scientific Group

Marine science technician (MST). Marine science technicians observe, collect, analyze, and disseminate meteorological and oceanographic data. They make both visual and instrumental weather and oceanographic observations, and they conduct routine chemical analyses. The MSTs' analysis and interpretation of weather and sea conditions furnish advice used in search-and-rescue operations. The

Marine Science Technician (MST)

Yeoman (YN)

information helps in the direction of merchant, pleasure, and military vessels and provides for the protection of the environment. Marine science technicians receive six weeks of training at the Reserve Training Center, Yorktown, Virginia.

Yeoman (YN). Yeomen perform personnel, clerical, and administrative duties. They prepare, route, and file correspondence, forms, and reports. They maintain directives and publications, and Personnel Data Records by preparing forms for pay, advancement, transfer, separation, and other personnel matters. They determine and correct pay problems. They act in administrative capacities for courts-martial and investigations. They may use typewriters, but a large portion of their duties is accomplished by using computers for word processing, data-base management, and personnel management. Yeomen act as career information counselors providing general information on ratings and service benefits. Yeomen in higher pay grades act as personnel administrators and office supervisors or managers. Yeoman "A" school is a nine-week course at the Coast Guard Training Center, Petaluma, California. Personnel may also "strike" for the yeoman rating at most large units.

Storekeeper (SK). All shore activities and most ships require store-

Storekeeper (SK)

keepers. Storekeepers procure, stow, preserve, package, and issue clothing, spare parts, provisions, technical items, and all other supplies needed. Storekeepers keep inventories, prepare requisitions, and check incoming supplies. Storekeepers handle the disbursal of funds for logistics. Storekeepers know the principles of the Coast Guard accounting system, which prepares financial accounts and reports. Storekeepers operate equipment ranging from typewriters to computers and forklifts. Storekeeper "A" school is a nine-week course at the Coast Guard Training Center, Petaluma, California. Large units allow personnel to "strike" for this rating.

Radioman (RM). Radiomen serve aboard ships, at communications stations, group offices, marine safety offices, and various other units operating radios, computers, radioteletype terminals, and facsimile equipment. They transmit and receive messages on radiotelephone (voice), radioteletype (RATT), radiotelegraph (International Morse Code), and computer network circuits (DISTNET), and maintain all required logs. Radiomen make adjustments and perform system-troubleshooting of telecommunication equipment. In the higher pay grades, radiomen serve as system managers for communication and data networks, providing quality control for Coast

Radioman (RM)

Public Affairs Specialist (PA)

Guard communication circuits. Radiomen receive 18 weeks of training at the Coast Guard Training Center, Petaluma, California.

Public affairs specialist (PA). Public affairs specialists keep the public informed on how well the Coast Guard is doing its job. They do this by working with print and electronic media personnel on a daily basis. They write news releases and television and radio scripts, produce video tapes, and take and process photographs, and frequently are recognized as the "authority" on the subject of the Coast Guard. They help maintain high morale by getting news to their shipmates and the general public about the Coast Guard's developments, accomplishments, and policies. Public affairs specialists receive ten weeks of training at the joint service Defense Information School (DINFOS) at Fort Benjamin Harrison, Indiana.

Subsistence specialist (SS). Subsistence specialists work in the food service areas of afloat and ashore Coast Guard dining facilities. Subsistence specialists know food preparation; the operation of utensils and food service equipment, sanitation, and safety; procurement procedures of food items, equipment, and utensils; receiving and storing subsistence items; menu-planning; inventory management;

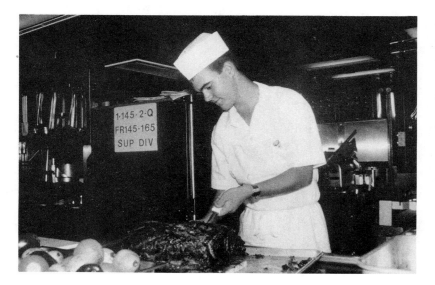

Subsistence Specialist (SS)

paperwork management, and overall knowledge of food service operations. Subsistence specialists receive 12 weeks of training at the Coast Guard Training Center, Petaluma, California.

Health services technician (HS). Health services technicians assist in treating sick and injured personnel, in the prevention and control of disease, and the administration of health services departments ashore and afloat; they perform emergency care, clinical sick call, dental care, and physical examinations; they inspect, investigate, recommend, and supervise all matters pertaining to sanitation, including the sanitary aspects of food and food handling, water, sewage and waste disposal, housing, and other environmental elements that affect health; they perform disease vector surveys and give required immunizations; they prescribe and dispense medications, perform clinical laboratory procedures, and assist in the procurement, storage, and issue of medical supplies; they instruct and counsel in health maintenance and prepare and maintain medical records and reports. Health Services technicians receive 20 weeks of training at the Coast Guard Training Center, Petaluma, California.

Health Services Technician (HS)

Port Securityman (PS)

Port securityman (PS). The port securityman rating is open only to members of the Coast Guard Reserve. Port securitymen supervise and control the safe handling, transportation, and storage of explosives and other dangerous cargo. They are experts in fire prevention and fire fighting and understand the rules and regulations about the security of vessels, harbors, and waterfront facilities. Port securitymen receive ten weeks of training at the Reserve Training Center, Yorktown, Virginia.

CHAPTER 11

Leadership, Discipline, and Moral Responsibility

A complex organization such as the Coast Guard doesn't just "run." It requires people who decide what must be done, how and when it will be done, and who will do it. These people may be petty officers, department heads, or commanding officers, but they all have one common responsibility—to provide leadership.

LEADERSHIP

In a short time, you will be put in charge of a group of people, so it is important that you understand some basic principles about leadership. You do not become a leader by reading a book; however, the following brief discussion about leadership can help start you on your way to becoming a good leader.

The Coast Guard places strong emphasis on leadership. It considers it the most important criterion for advancement in all pay grades. Leadership makes the difference between a good ship, unit, or organization and a poor one. A well-led unit, over the long term, is characterized by commitment to the leader's vision, teamwork, pride, high morale, and motivated workers. Successful leaders do two things well: They get the job done and at the same time develop their subordinates by allowing them to contribute, grow, and be involved.

Figure 11-1. Work on a buoy deck is hard and dangerous. Each person has a role—good leadership and discipline are critical.

Any time you attempt to influence the behavior of others to accomplish a task, you are using leadership. Good leaders have high expectations of performance, both of themselves and of their followers. They communicate to their followers what they want to accomplish, their goal—for example, to be the best SAR boat crew in the district. Leaders constantly monitor the progress toward that goal and use their leadership skills to inspire their followers to attain it. Subordinates are more motivated to give their best effort if they are committed to and believe in the goal, share a part in it, and are allowed to use their talents fully to achieve it.

You'll find that you learn the most about leadership from your own experiences (both as a follower and a leader), by observing role models (both good and bad), and lastly, from formal classroom leadership training. This formal training, provided by the Coast Guard Leadership and Management School, gives you the opportunity to reflect and answer the question, "What did I learn from my experiences, and how can I become a better leader?"

Figure 11-2. Future leaders of the Coast Guard need to learn to follow orders before they can give them.

Because you will learn the most about leadership from your own experiences, it follows that you will not become a good leader overnight. Developing a leader is a complex process that takes time. The Coast Guard begins this developmental process by having you be a follower first. (See figure 11-2.) As you advance, you will be put in positions of responsibility and be given leadership opportunities. Remember that today's master chiefs used to be seaman recruits. Leadership and learning go hand in hand. Good leaders are always trying to learn how to become better leaders.

Your success as a leader can be measured in two ways. One way deals with the job. Was the job done on time and with high-quality work? The second way deals with your people. Did you effectively utilize their talents and, if they were given the choice, would they like to work for you again? This measure of leadership has to do with how the people were treated while they were performing the task. As you advance, you can develop your people into leaders by letting them take the lead, make decisions, and learn from their mistakes while you coach them. Coaching involves spending time with your people daily, talking with them about your goals, listening to their ideas, and providing them with feedback on their efforts and performance. Good leaders usually have followers who enjoy working for them. As a leader, you should strive to get the job done and at the same time properly develop your people.

Leaders influence their subordinates to perform tasks by using power. There are two types of this power. One is position power, which is given to you by the organization, based on the pay grade or job position you hold. Position power allows you to make people comply with your orders because you have the authority to do so. Your followers perform the task because they have to. The other type of power is personal power. Personal power is gained from your subordinates and is based on their respect for you as a person. Personal power encourages your people to give you their commitment and trust because of your personal behavior toward them. Personal power encourages your followers to perform tasks not because they have to but because they want to. Good leaders learn the appropriate use of both personal power and position power to get the job done and to develop their subordinates.

Effective leaders understand and use recognition as a powerful tool to enhance their subordinates' performances and develop them as leaders. There are few, if any, more basic needs than to be noticed, recognized, and appreciated for one's efforts. You can do this by setting a series of high but achievable work goals and by recognizing your followers' efforts to achieve them. Positive recognition is appropriate when your subordinate performed the desired task in the proper manner. Positive recognition can be as simple as saying "Thank you" or "Good job." Negative recognition is appropriate when subordinates do a job incorrectly. It simply means pointing out the improper performance, telling them the proper way, and letting them try again. Recognition is most meaningful when it is timely, specific, and sincere. Positive recognition should be done in public, and negative recognition should be done in private.

Leaders bring about change. Think back to the people in your life whom you looked up to as leaders. They were leaders because they were not content to maintain the status quo. Good leaders are always trying to do things better, seeking to be the best in what they do, and bringing out the best in their people.

The most difficult part about leadership is living it. Followers watch their leaders closely to see what they do, much like you watch your boss. The three following personal leadership principles are good ones for anyone in a leadership position to adhere to:

Lead by example. Actions speak louder than words. Through your

Figure 11-3. There is time in every busy day for reflection and rejuvenation.

personal actions you communicate to your followers what you think is important.

Treat others the way you would like to be treated. The Golden Rule has withstood the test of time. Good leaders still use it today. *Care about your people.* Good leadership requires that you truly care about the people in your charge. Just as we can all think of ways to be better friends, parents, or spouses, we can be better leaders. We must, however, be willing to give of ourselves in dealing with others. True leadership is more about service to our people than anything else.

Finally, leadership deals with human behavior and therefore is not an exact science. You learn about leadership by actually leading people. You will make mistakes, as all leaders do, but the important thing is to learn from your mistakes so that you don't repeat them. Leadership is a journey, not a destination. You can always improve yourself as a leader. When you are doing your job as a leader, the mutual flow of trust and respect between you and the people you are leading is one of the best feelings in the world.

DIVERSITY

Managing diversity is a leadership challenge: to seek ways to maximize the potential of our human resources in order to increase productivity and more effectively accomplish our missions. The focus of total quality is raising levels of productivity through continuous improvement and better service to our diverse customer base. Therefore, incorporating diversity management into the Coast Guard is not only the right thing to do but, as a bottom-line business decision, the practical thing to do. The process of achieving, valuing, and managing diversity in our work force is vital to positioning the Coast Guard to serve its customers while attracting and retaining the best and brightest people from an increasingly diverse labor pool. This commitment to diversity management is essential for the Coast Guard to remain an employer of choice. The Coast Guard is moving beyond affirmative action and issues of race and gender through a process of inclusion in which the value of everyone's differences is celebrated in an environment where all people have the opportunity to reach their maximum potential.

MORAL RESPONSIBILITY

This is a term you must understand. It has many meanings. It means doing your job honestly, the best you know how. It means living up to the rules and regulations that were made for good reasons, not just to annoy people. It means acting in a responsible manner when you go ashore, and showing pride and self-respect. It means thinking of other people, not just of yourself. There are really only two kinds of people. One kind, the majority, understands moral responsibility. They do their job when on duty and keep out of trouble on duty and off. The others—and fortunately there are not many—are the ones who haven't got the word. They are the ones who will goof off on the job and get into trouble no matter where they are.

Your behavior ashore is important, and especially so in any foreign port. There, you not only represent your ship and the Coast Guard, you also represent the United States. People recognize you as an American and base their ideas of America on how you act. The least show of rowdiness or drunkenness can bring severe criticism of Americans and the United States, and will provide anti-American propaganda for subversive elements. Always keep this in mind—your behavior ashore in any foreign land must be perfect, because you represent the United States.

DISCIPLINE

Like moral responsibility, *discipline* is another word with more than one meaning. Sometimes discipline is used to mean punishment. But the real meaning of discipline can best be described by the words *right attitude*. Well-disciplined people have the right attitudes. They are willing to follow orders because they believe in what they are doing, they respect their leaders, and believe they are getting a square deal from them. They behave in a military manner, wear the right uniforms, take pride in their division, their ship, or their station, and are ready to fight bravely in defense of their country.

When discipline fails—that is, when some people do not have the right attitude—then punishment may be necessary for those who refuse to observe rules and regulations. In the Coast Guard, as in civilian life, laws, orders, and regulations must be obeyed, and persons who do not are subject to trial by court-martial, which can punish them according to the laws.

Masters-at-Arms

Masters-at-Arms (MAA) are assigned to maintain order and discipline on ships or stations and are the assistants to the executive officer. Large ships may have a chief master-at-arms (CMAA) with several assistants. Coast Guard members may be assigned to the MAA force for several months or longer. While acting as MAAs, they are relieved of most of their normal watches and duties.

Shore Patrol

The *shore patrol* (SP) is the military police patrol of the Coast Guard and Navy. It consists of officers and petty officers assigned to maintain order among naval personnel off the ship or station. They are identified by armbands with the letters SP.

The Army and Marines have their military police (MP), and the Air Force has its air police (AP). You must obey the MPs and the APs as well as the SPs. In some areas, a combined or unified Armed Services Police Detachment (ASPD) is organized. It consists of members from all the services—SP, MP, AP—under one command and wearing the same armbands.

Uniform Code of Military Justice

Discipline in all the military services is based on the Uniform Code of Military Justice, "UCMJ," which became law 5 May 1950 under an act of Congress. UCMJ is the basis for the *Manual for Courts-Martial*. Before that time, the various services all had different disciplinary systems. The only variations that now exist among the services are those that result from the fact that each governmental department, under which a service operates, issues regulations based upon the differences in the structures of the services. The principles are the same for all.

The manual recognizes the military authority of persons of one service over those of another; it even specifies that personnel can be tried by courts-martial composed of members of other services. Thus, it is evident that Coast Guard personnel are subject to the orders of the Navy shore patrol and the Armed Forces Police. Likewise, Coast Guard shore patrols enforce the UCMJ upon members of the other armed services.

Necessity for the Disciplinary System

All of the armed services, including the Coast Guard, were established to accomplish objectives determined by Congress. The missions of the five services, both in war and peace, involve personal risk. A well-trained, closely knit, disciplined group of people can carry out a mission with a minimum loss of life, but in order to do so, the leaders who direct their operations must have the necessary authority.

Value of the Disciplinary System

The courts and laws of the nation exist to protect all people against criminal acts, and to prevent invasions of, or loss of, the rights of individuals. The disciplinary system of the Coast Guard protects all members of the service. The regulations of the Coast Guard and the Uniform Code of Military Justice protect loyal, law-abiding military personnel from being victimized by criminal or lawless actions.

The disciplinary system also protects conscientious, hard-working members of the service from being unfairly burdened with people who refuse to do their share of the work. If such people get out of doing assigned work, those with a sense of responsibility must do it. The system sets up penalties for nonperformance of assigned duties. It also prohibits compulsory self-incrimination (you cannot be forced to testify against yourself—Article 31); it prohibits cruel or unusual punishment (Article 55); it specifies that parts of the UCMJ be explained to you (Article 137); and it provides a way to make complaints if you are treated unfairly (Article 138). So it works both ways.

Protection of the Accused

Like the laws of our country, the laws of military justice protect those accused of offenses, even convicted lawbreakers. Accused personnel have the right to be informed about the charges against them, to reply to the charges, and to confront and question their accusers. They have the right to legal counsel of their own choosing, if possible under the existing military conditions. There are limitations on the questioning of prisoners, and rules requiring humane treatment. Trials must be conducted fairly. Punishments are limited in accordance with the seriousness of the offense; cruel and inhuman punishments are prohibited. Finally, there is an elaborate system of reviews to ensure that all these provisions for protecting the rights of the accused have been observed and that the court's decision is just.

Mistaken Loyalty

A mistaken concept of loyalty to shipmates sometimes causes otherwise well-intentioned persons to refrain from reporting crimes. Talebearers who constantly run to officers with reports of minor derelictions of duty by other crew members are a nuisance, but you should be able to distinguish between tale-bearing and giving information about a serious offense. If an act or a neglect constituting a legal offense has been committed—or you have serious reason to believe one has been committed—*it is your duty to report this to someone in authority. If you do not, you are punishable under the UCMJ.* In permitting an offender to escape punishment, you weaken the disciplinary system that protects you and your shipmates. *You owe loyalty to those who keep the laws, not to those who break them.*

Offenses Under Military Law

The disciplinary laws of the Coast Guard are stated in the *Uniform Code of Military Justice,* in *United States Coast Guard Regulations,* and in *Coast Guard Reserve Regulations.* Articles 77 to 134 of the UCMJ cover punitive or punishable offenses.

It is your responsibility to acquaint yourself with these laws. The oath you took on entering service obligates you to observe them. As in civilian life, ignorance of the law is no excuse for breaking it.

The UCMJ was explained to you when you entered the Coast Guard. Copies of it are posted where you can read it for yourself. You should note especially the listing of offenses and their definitions. To assist you, certain legal terms are discussed here.

Differences Between Military and Civilian Offenses

In general, acts that would constitute offenses against civilian laws are also offenses under military law, but some acts are military offenses that would not be cause for arrest in civilian life.

Civilians who don't show up for work, or walk off the job will probably lose their jobs, but that is all that will happen. In a military organization, the same act would be unauthorized absence and perhaps neglect of duty or disobedience to an order. Civilians who quarrel violently with the boss will not be arrested as long as they don't harm the boss or threaten harm. In the service, a person would be charged with insubordination and possibly other offenses. Coming to work late, refusal to obey orders, drinking on the job—all of these would probably be cause for discipline by a civilian employer, but not cause for arrest. Yet in a military service each can send a person before a court-martial.

The nature of military duty and the conditions of military life account for the difference. Your military duties are necessary for the Coast Guard to carry out its mission—the defense of the nation, the enforcement of national and international law, and the safety of life at sea. You cannot quit your job, be absent or late without permission, or refuse to do your work without endangering the mission.

People who rebel against lawful authority and stir up trouble are a menace to the teamwork that is necessary for their own safety and that of their shipmates, as well as for the accomplishment of the unit's assigned mission.

Principals and Accessories

A person who commits a crime or who aids in its commission is a *principal*. If a person advises, orders, or persuades someone to commit an offense, and that person does commit the crime, both are principals. After a crime has been committed, anyone who knows the person who committed it, and who helps the offender to escape trial or punishment, is an *accessory after the fact*. Principals and accessories are both punished according to the table of maximum punishment.

Lesser Included Offenses

If, during a trial, a person is charged with desertion and it develops that the defendant was absent without leave but did not intend to abandon the service permanently, the court may convict that person of unauthorized absence and punish accordingly. This is a lesser included offense within the more serious one of desertion originally charged. Punishment for a lesser included offense may occur under other charges. Housebreaking, for example, might be a lesser offense under a charge of burglary.

Attempt. An attempt to commit an offense is a violation even though the crime is not consummated. An attempt to commit a particular crime is always a potential lesser included offense when a perpetrator is tried for the crime.

Conspiracy. When two or more persons agree to violate the UCMJ by concerted action, and any one of them performs any action seeking to accomplish the agreed objective, all of the parties to the agreement are guilty of conspiracy.

Offenses Related to War

Certain offenses become much more serious if committed when the United States is at war. Others are particularly related to wartime situations. Among those that become more serious are desertion and assaulting or disobeying an officer. For each of the offenses listed below, the death penalty may be imposed in time of war:

- Misbehavior before the enemy
- Subordinate compelling surrender
- Forcing a safeguard
- Improper handling of captured or abandoned property
- Aiding the enemy
- Misconduct as a prisoner of war
- Spying

General Article

Article 134, the last of the punitive articles, makes it an offense to commit acts or to neglect duties that result in creating disorders, which are to the prejudice of good order and discipline, or which bring discredit upon the Coast Guard. Such offenses are subject to trial by court-martial.

Liability Under Civil Laws

What about civil laws? For example, suppose you do not pay your debts or that you run off with another person's spouse. Can you be given military punishment for such nonmilitary offenses? Yes, you can. In the first place, of course, you are liable to civil lawsuits and the actions of the civil courts and police. But military courts can also try you for conduct casting discredit on the Coast Guard, and can award you various types of punishment.

Suppose you are arrested for speeding, for drunkenness, or for being criminally involved with drugs, and are held in jail until you are absent without leave. You not only will have to pay your fine and suffer your imprisonment, but you may also have to appear before a captain's mast and perhaps a court-martial for your AWOL (Absent Without Leave) time and for any discredit you have cast upon the Coast Guard. If you refuse to pay just debts, you will be warned by your commanding officer (CO). You may lose your advancement opportunity, because the Coast Guard does not promote people who are not honest. Finally, if you continue to run up unpaid debts, you could be administratively discharged or even receive an undesirable or bad-conduct discharge. (On the other hand, if you are being gouged by unscrupulous dealers, see your executive officer or legal officer. They can help you in many ways.)

Purpose of Punishment

The punishment used by the Coast Guard—such as extra instruction, loss of liberty, loss of pay, and confinement—has three purposes:

- To deter you from breaking the rules;
- To encourage you to do your duty; and
- To provide an example to others.

The smart person learns from the mistakes of others. When others are being punished for being late, out of uniform, or careless in their attitude, smart people make sure that they are on time, in proper uniform, and attentive to duty.

If you receive punishment in the Coast Guard, remember, you brought it on yourself by your behavior. Take it like an adult; don't grouse, and don't feel sorry for yourself.

Learn your lesson. Avoid the habits, attitudes, and companions that led you wrong.

Don't hold grudges. The people who punished you are simply doing their duty—which they wouldn't have had to do if you had done yours.

Nonjudicial Punishment—Courts-Martial

Pretrial Procedure

Any Coast Guard member who knows an offense has been committed can prefer charges. Ordinarily, the facts are reported to the supervisor, who relays them to the commanding officer or officer in charge, who then takes the necessary action. No physical contact is necessary to apprehend, but the person must clearly be notified of being taken into custody. *Arrest* is moral restraint limiting a person's liberty pending disposition of charges. If there is reason to believe that people will not observe their military obligation to obey the order of arrest, they may be placed in *confinement*. This is forcible detention, but is not for punishment, and they must be so advised.

Preliminary Inquiry

The commanding officer orders a preliminary investigation to develop information to permit intelligent disposition of the case. The accused are informed of the charge and are permitted, but not required, to make a statement. The accused are advised that any statement made may be used against them. After the investigating officer has developed the facts, a full report is made to the commanding officer. If an offense has been committed, the commanding officer may sign the charge sheet. If the offense is within the jurisdiction of the commanding officer, a court-martial or other appropriate action may follow. If the offense requires a general court-martial, the full report is forwarded to the district commander or other officer exercising general court-martial supervision over the unit. If a general court-martial is to be held, it must be preceded by a formal investigation.

Nonjudicial Punishment (Mast)

If you break a rule or are negligent, careless, or unmilitary in your conduct, you may be *placed on report* by a petty officer or commissioned officer. This means that you must appear before the captain at a specified time for a hearing and possible punishment. That is, you must appear at *captain's mast.*

Captain's mast gets its name from the old sailing days when the setting for this form of naval justice was on the weather deck, at the foot of the ship's mainmast.

The commanding officer is authorized to assign certain punishments for minor offenses. Cases are tried and punishments given at captain's mast. At mast the commanding officer may give the following punishments:

Type of Punishment	CO (LCDR or Above)	CO (LT or Below)	Officer in Charge
Admonition or reprimand	Yes (written)	Yes (written)	No
Correctional custody (E-5 and below)	30 days	7 days	No
Extra duties	45 days	14 days	14 days
Restriction	60 days	14 days	14 days
Forfeiture of pay	$1/2$ of one month's pay for 2 months	7 days pay	3 days pay
Reduction to next inferior grade (E-6 and below)	Yes	Yes	No

Mast is not always held for disciplinary purposes. A *meritorious mast* is held by the captain to give awards or commendations to people who have earned them.

On many ships and stations, a certain time of the day is set aside by the executive officer to hear requests from members of the crew. This practice is called *request and complaint mast.*

Types of Courts-Martial

Summary Court-Martial

An officer who is designated as a commanding officer may convene a summary court-martial. It is composed of one officer, preferably a lieutenant or higher, and has authority to try any noncapital offense. The court has jurisdiction only over enlisted personnel, and such personnel have the right to refuse trial by it; in the latter case, the trial will be held by special or general court-martial.

A summary court is authorized to award punishment up to the maximum allowed under the *Manual For Courts-Martial*, except the punishments of death, punitive discharge, confinement over one month, hard labor over 45 days, or forfeiture of pay in excess of two-thirds pay for one month.

Special Court-Martial

An officer who is designated as a commanding officer may convene a special court-martial. It is composed of three or more persons, one third of whom must be enlisted if the accused is enlisted and so requests. It has authority to try any member of the service for any offense not carrying the death penalty. In special cases, the district commander may direct a special court to try cases on charges for which the death penalty is allowed. Prosecution and defense counsels of equal qualifications are appointed by the convening authority.

The court may award any punishment up to the maximum allowed by the *Manual* except death, dishonorable discharge, dismissal, confinement over six months, hard labor over three months, or forfeiture of pay exceeding two-thirds pay per month for longer than six months.

General Court-Martial

The commandant or a district commander may convene general courts-martial. They are composed of five or more members, one third of whom must be enlisted if the accused is enlisted and so requests. Prosecution and defense counsels of equal qualifications are appointed by the convening authority.

A general court-martial has the power to try any member of the Coast Guard for any offense, and to award any punishment up to the maximum allowed under the *Manual For Courts-Martial*.

Figure 11-4. Leadership and discipline are vital to safety in many dangerous shipboard operations, such as lowering away the small boat.

CHAPTER 12

Personal Standards

The Coast Guard will train you to perform your military and professional duties, but your ability to perform them quickly and efficiently will depend upon the state of your health, both mental and physical. Good health habits and a positive attitude will make your job easier and improve relations with people. No one can order you to be healthy and cheerful, that's entirely up to you. The following pages offer some suggestions.

PERSONAL CARE

As a member of the Coast Guard, you will have the facilities and the opportunity to maintain a good standard of living and health. Even the smallest unit has facilities to provide nourishing meals, comfortable berthing, and all the amenities necessary to live in a comfortable and productive fashion. It is important that you take advantage of the healthful environment provided by the service and adopt good personal habits and standards.

Hygiene

Good hygiene and good health run hand in hand. Simply being careful about keeping clean can help you avoid many common health problems. Afflictions such as athlete's foot, ringworm, "jock-

Figure 12-1. A petty officer in the Coast Guard Honor Guard in full ceremonial dress.

itch," or "jungle rot" all can be prevented by habitual good hygiene. It's not always easy to keep clean when it's hot, when you're doing dirty work, or when the water supply is limited, but it's well worth the effort. Shower with soap daily in warm weather or when you're sweating heavily. In cool weather, once every other day should be enough, but wash your hands and face well before every meal. Wash your hair at least twice a week. Use talc or an antifungal powder on your feet and, if necessary, around your crotch, to prevent itching. Habitual good hygiene will help you feel, look, and smell better, all of which will make you happier, more productive, and more pleasant to be around.

Care of Teeth

The three most common dental diseases are tooth decay (caries), inflammation of the gum (gingivitis), and disease of the gum and bone surrounding the teeth (pyorrhea). They cause needless loss of teeth, for they all can be prevented or controlled. All Coast Guard personnel should have an annual dental exam. This is essential for timely detection of tooth decay as well as any other type of mouth disease.

Caries

There is no sure-fire way to prevent tooth decay, but it can be cut down greatly by regular, correct brushing and by reducing the amount of sweets you eat. At the first sign of tooth decay, see a dentist. Untreated cavities can have serious long-term health consequences.

Gingivitis

Normal and healthy gums are pale pink and firm in texture. If they are swollen or puffy, hang loosely about the teeth and bleed easily, you have gingivitis.

Pyorrhea

If gingivitis goes untreated, you may notice pockets or crevices between the tooth and gum. This is an indication of pyorrhea (sometimes called periodontitis). More teeth are lost from these two disease than from tooth decay. Most dental diseases result from poor mouth hygiene combined with the *misuse* of the toothbrush and lack of flossing.

Toothbrushes

Proper use of the toothbrush is most effective in control or prevention of dental diseases. Keep at least two brushes, so you can always use a dry one. When the bristles become soft or flattened, throw the brush away.

Brush your teeth regularly, after each meal if you can. Use dental floss at least once a day. The proper toothbrushing technique will clean the teeth and gums, stimulate circulation in the gum tissues, and toughen the gums by the friction of the bristles, but not injure the teeth or gums. Brush with the mouth barely open, the muscles relaxed, permitting easier access to hard-to-get-at areas.

Diet

The Coast Guard takes great care to serve good-tasting and well-balanced meals, but they will do you little good unless you observe certain rules in your diet. Don't concentrate too much on one food group, such as meat or potatoes or especially desserts! Do yourself, your strength and stamina, your general health, and your teeth and gums a favor; eat a balanced diet. The basic foods, with suggested daily amounts of each, are listed below.

Green, leafy, yellow vegetables and fruits	1 or more servings
Citrus fruits, tomatoes, or berries	1 or more servings
Other vegetables and fruits	2 or more servings
Milk, ice cream, cheese, yogurt	2 cups
Meat or fish, shell fish, poultry, eggs, dried beans and peas, nuts	4 ounces or 1 serving
Bread, flour, and cereals	4–6 slices or the equivalent

Don't eat to excess. Regulate the amount you eat and watch your weight.

Dysentery

Dysentery is common in the tropics, and can occur in the United States. The major symptom is diarrhea, although nausea, stomach cramps, and vomiting may also occur. Dysentery is most often spread by food handlers or through produce fertilized with human waste. Water and flies are also factors. Ashore, in countries where dysentery is known to exist, avoid uncooked food, particularly lettuce, celery, cabbage, and radishes. If you must eat ashore, eat in reputable restaurants, avoid establishments that appear to have less than the highest standards of cleanliness. In areas where dysentery might exist, water should be boiled for at least five minutes and then stowed in sterile containers for use. If in doubt, drink bottled water and order your beverages without ice.

Drug Abuse

The word *drugs* as used here refers to barbiturates, narcotics, various hallucinogenic compounds, and other substances taken for nonmedical purposes.

Drugs are classified as *hallucinogens, stimulants, depressants and tranquilizers, narcotics (opiates),* and *inhalants.*

Hallucinogens include LSD, mescaline, psilocybin, DMT, and THC (the active ingredient in marijuana and hashish). Hallu-

Figure 12-2. Coast Guard personnel fully understand the negative effects of illegal drugs.

cinogens, or psychedelics, are drugs that affect a person's perceptions, sensations, thinking, self-awareness and emotions. The effects of psychedelics are unpredictable. The physical effects include dilated pupils, higher body temperature, increased heart rate and blood pressure, loss of appetite, sleeplessness, dry mouth, and tremors. Sensations may seem to "cross over"—sometimes resulting in trauma, personality change, or psychosis. Marijuana is a controlled substance and has clinically the same effects as hallucinogens, though usually to a lesser degree. Regular use of marijuana does three things to your body:

The tars in marijuana smoke are far more likely to cause cancer of the lungs than those in tobacco smoke.

The THC crystals in the smoke affect the chromosomes in the female ova, distort the male sperm, and will endanger a fetus.

The THC crystals collect in the nerve endings in the brain, ultimately affecting memory, physical activity, and learning ability.

Stimulants make the entire body "run fast." People abusing stimulants may appear to comprehend, but display poor judgment; also they might seem extremely nervous and hyperactive and fatigued at the same time. Abusers may experience damage to the liver and kidneys and hemorrhages in brain tissue. The two most prevalent stimulants are nicotine in tobacco products and caffeine, the active ingredient in coffee, tea, and some bottled beverages.

Depressants (tranquilizers) have an effect resembling alcohol intoxication (keep in mind that alcohol is a sedative). A person may be confused and disorganized and exhibit a loss of judgment. Pupils become constricted, speech is slurred, thick, and incoherent at times. Some users and abusers develop allergic reactions that are sometimes fatal. A common occurrence among abusers is called synergism, that is, combining a depressant drug with alcohol; the result is to multiply rather than add the cumulative effects of the drugs. Synergism often results in a fatal overdose.

Among the most addictive drugs are the *opiates*. Included in this group are codeine, morphine, and heroin. All of the opiates and their synthetic derivatives are addictive. Opiates briefly stimulate the higher centers of the brain, then depress activity of the central nervous system. Users may appear drowsy, nodding; they are able to understand and answer questions, but are mentally dull. Their pupils are constricted, with little reaction to light; eyelids are droopy. Chronic users become psychologically and/or physically dependent on opiates. In recovery from addiction (abstinence), some bodily functions do not return to normal for as long as six months. Sudden withdrawal by heavily dependent users who are in poor health has occasionally been fatal.

Cocaine is a local anesthetic. It is also a stimulant of the central nervous system. Chronic cocaine use eventually leads to a depressed, low-energy state characterized by flattened emotions, lack of interest in sex, and listlessness. The speed and probability of getting addicted is different for different people, but definitely higher in people with drinking problems. *Crack* is cocaine that is sold in the form of small, cream-colored chunks resembling rock salt. It is smoked. This leads to a reaction in less than ten seconds, lasting from five to ten minutes. *Cocaine* damages nasal membranes, causes bronchitis, and affects cardiac irregularities often resulting in heart attacks. It can be instantly fatal.

Inhalants are breathable chemicals that produce psychoactive (mind-altering) vapors. Nearly all of the abused inhalants produce effects similar to anesthetics. Initial effects include nausea, sneezing, coughing, nosebleeds, feeling and looking tired, bad breath, lack of coordination, and a loss of appetite. Solvents and aerosols decrease the heart and breathing rate and affect judgment. Sniffing highly concentrated amounts of solvents or aerosol spray can produce heart failure and instant death. Repeated sniffing of concentrated vapors can cause permanent damage to the nervous system.

Do not use illegal drugs, or prescription drugs for nonmedical reasons. Not only is it dangerous and illegal, drug abuse can get you discharged.

As a law enforcement agency, the Coast Guard works to stop drugs from being smuggled into the country. Since the money that buys drugs supports smuggling, the use of drugs by Coast Guardsmen is counter to the efforts of the Coast Guard. Drug use impairs the users' abilities. Every Coast Guardsman has a critical job that requires absolute attention. If you stand an improper lookout or cannot do your job on a repair party, lives may be lost. If your senses are impaired, you endanger more lives than just your own; you are a threat to everyone on board your ship.

The Coast Guard's drug policy is clear: drug abuse undermines and jeopardizes morale, mission performance, and safety, and will not be tolerated. Service members who have had a drug incident are processed for discharge. To eliminate drug use, commands randomly select members to submit urine samples, which are tested for evidence of drug use. Positive results from a confirmed urinalysis test constitute a drug incident, and the member will be processed for discharge. There is no second chance.

Alcohol Abuse

Alcoholic beverages are an accepted part of American life, and "social drinking" is considered normal behavior. The Coast Guard is a representative of our society. Since alcohol is the most abused drug in our society, the Coast Guard has a "drinking problem." A person doesn't have to be an "out and out bum" in order to have an alcohol problem. A person has an alcohol problem when drinking creates problem situations; the Coast Guard has a problem when alcohol problems cost the service time lost through absence, sickness, administration, and performance. A person drinking sensibly is usually not a problem. Think of the word "sense," and use good sense by keeping all your senses alert and limiting yourself accordingly. Don't drink on an empty stomach, or when you are fatigued, or when you are taking medication, or when you have to drive or operate machinery.

If a man or woman develops an alcohol problem, that person should be encouraged to get professional help. Alcohol abuse training is not intended for "down and outers" only, but for less affected people. A person need not "hit bottom" in order to get help with an alcohol problem. That's why the Coast Guard offers help to its members. Some Navy training programs even offer college credits to their participants.

The Coast Guard considers alcohol abuse a serious threat to job performance and safety. If you have an alcohol incident, your command will normally provide counseling for you. If there is a second alcohol incident, you will normally be processed for discharge. An alcohol incident is defined as alcohol abuse that has an outward detrimental effect on the abuser or others, such as involvement in any injury, loss of duty status, inability at any required time to properly perform duties due to alcohol consumption, damage or loss of property, or violation of the UCMJ, or federal, state, or local laws.

Sexually Transmitted Diseases (STD)

STD or venereal diseases were for many years "swept under the rug" and not mentioned in polite society. "Nice people" didn't even know what to call the various types of infections, although that didn't prevent everybody from royalty to riff-raff from getting them. VD is no longer treated in a hush-hush fashion. It is a matter of concern for everyone because it is on the increase despite advances in medicine to treat it.

VD is an infectious disease that can be transmitted only by contact between two people. Anyone who is sexually active can catch VD. The frequency of contact and number of sexual partners determine a person's risk of contracting VD. Prostitutes, or anyone else who has frequent sexual contact with different partners, are at high risk of contracting VD and passing it on to others.

There are five general types of VD: *syphilis* (syph, pox, old Joe); *gonorrhea* (clap, dose, the drip, GC); *chancroid* (bubo, haircut); *granuloma inguinale*, and *lymphogranuloma venereum*. All can be transmitted from an infected person, man or woman, to an uninfected person, man or woman, through sexual intercourse. Syphilis can also be transmitted by a kiss if an infected person has an open sore on the lips. A woman can transmit syphilis to her unborn child, or gonorrhea to her child at birth.

The incubation period—the time from contact until the first symptoms appear—varies; 10 days to 10 weeks for syphilis; 2 to 10 days for gonorrhea and chancroid; longer times for others. Some types of gonorrhea, particularly in women, have no symptoms. A person who has become infected can transmit the disease to another *before* signs of infection appear. There is *no* way to tell that a person is not infected. Latent syphilis, the state in which clinical signs and symptoms of infection are absent, may appear as early as four years or as late as 20 years after infection. Among the infinite variety of results to be expected are destructive ulcers, disease of the heart or blood vessels, blindness, and insanity. Other kinds of VD have other kinds of results, none of them pleasant.

Venereal disease control is a worldwide effort, but it all depends upon the individual. Medical department personnel will emphasize that individual abstinence from sexual intercourse other than marital relations is the one sure way to avoid VD. Medical department personnel can also instruct in the effective use of condoms as a preventive measure.

There is no military punishment for contracting VD, but it is misconduct to conceal an infection. It is important that you conduct your social life so as to avoid contracting VD and to report for medical attention promptly at the first sign of infection. This is necessary for two reasons: to commence treatment to cure the infection, and to make certain that the person from whom the infection was received is identified and treated. Remember—VD doesn't just happen. It can usually be cured, but prevention is a lot less trouble and pain.

Homosexuality

The armed forces of the United States have long held that, as a general rule, homosexuality is incompatible with military service because it interferes with the factors critical to combat effectiveness, including unit morale, unit cohesion, and individual privacy.

Nevertheless, the armed forces also recognize that individuals with a homosexual orientation have served with distinction in the military. Therefore, it is the policy of the Departments of Defense and Transportation to judge the suitability of persons to serve in the armed forces on the basis of their conduct.

Homosexual conduct will be grounds for separation from the military services. Homosexual conduct is defined as a homosexual act, a statement by the service member that demonstrates a propensity or intent to engage in homosexual acts, or a homosexual marriage or attempted marriage.

Sexual orientation is considered a personal and private matter, and homosexual orientation is not a bar to service entry or continued service unless manifested by homosexual conduct.

Acquired Immune Deficiency Syndrome (AIDS)

Acquired Immune Deficiency Syndrome is a deadly disease that breaks down the body's resistance. The cause of the disease is the human immune deficiency virus. The H-IV is transmitted through exposure to the blood, blood products, or semen, of a previously exposed person. Means of exposure include sex, blood transfusions, and hypodermic needles. Not everyone who is exposed to the virus develops immunological deficiency or clinical illness, but the virus remains in the body for life. An individual who is exposed but who does not develop any illness can still transmit the virus to others. Once an individual develops immunological deficiencies, that person is prone to opportunistic illness, such as pneumonia and cancer. Victims die from these secondary illnesses rather than from the virus itself.

Exposure to the virus can be prevented. The majority of those with AIDS fall into one of the following groups: gay or bisexual men, I.V. drug users, Haitians, and hemophiliacs. Sexual partners of people in one of these categories stand the next highest chance of contracting the virus. If you have specific questions about exposure to the AIDS virus, ask your health service technician.

The Coast Guard recognizes the severity of this illness and has initiated a testing program to detect exposure to the H-IV virus. Applicants for regular or reserve service, officer or enlisted, or for the Coast Guard Academy who test H-IV positive will be rejected from Coast Guard service. Members of the Coast Guard and Coast Guard Reserve who test positive will be considered not fit for duty and evaluated by a medical review board. Members who test positive but do not demonstrate immunological deficiencies or clinical illnesses may be retained on active duty but will not be assigned to certain duty, including sea duty, isolated duty, aircrew duty, or small-boat crew duty. The Coast Guard constantly reviews its policy on AIDS as more is learned about the disease.

HUMAN RELATIONS

In the Coast Guard, you will interact with people from various socio-economic, racial, ethnic, and religious backgrounds. Your day-to-

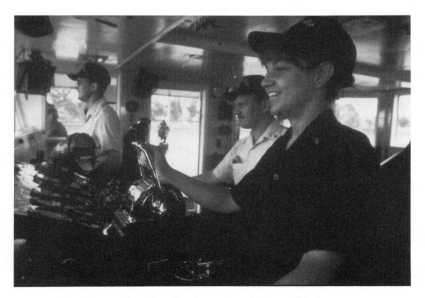

Figure 12-3. Teamwork makes the Coast Guard the world-class organization it is.

day interactions are crucial to maintaining a healthy and professional environment. The first requirement in creating this environment is to have respect, tolerance, and consideration for others. Each person brings a diversity to the Coast Guard that should be valued and that enhances the organization. Every member plays an integral part in the accomplishment of Coast Guard missions.

Civil Rights

Civil rights are rights each person has just by virtue of being a citizen or a member of a civil society. These rights include fair treatment and equal opportunity regardless of race, color, religion, national origin, or sex. Treating members unfairly based on these factors can lead to illegal forms of discrimination that cannot be tolerated in the Coast Guard.

Discrimination

Illegal forms of discrimination include any actions, omissions, or use of language that deprives an individual or group of their rights because of race, color, religion, national origin, or sex. Whether the discriminatory action taken is intentional or not, it is unproductive behavior that negatively affects the working and living environment. All members must have the opportunity to work to their full potential without feeling that they are being treated differently because of these nonmerit factors.

Sexual Harassment

Sexual harassment is a form of sex discrimination that is characterized by sexually oriented communication, comments, gestures, or physical contact that is unsolicited and unwelcomed. It includes offers or threats to influence or alter conditions of service in order to secure sexual favors. Examples of sexual harassment are repeated requests for dates or promises of good duty assignments by a superior if the subordinate will go along with the sexual requests. Both men and women can harass or be victims of harassment. Acts of sexual harassment are inappropriate, diminish self-esteem, and undermine the professionalism of the Coast Guard. Put simply, sexual harassment is illegal behavior and will not be tolerated.

Positive human relations are the key to the growth and development of each individual in the Coast Guard. You have the responsibility to ensure that your conduct supports Coast Guard policy and fosters a positive human relations environment. You must ensure that you treat your shipmates and coworkers with the same respect and dignity that you expect from them.

Fraternization

Fraternization is defined as an inappropriate relationship between junior and senior personnel. This relationship could be between an officer and an enlisted, senior and junior enlisted, or with civilian employees. Even though you may feel your actions do not constitute fraternizing, others may. It is this perception by others that weighs heavily in determining whether an inappropriate relationship exists. It is important that you ensure that neither you nor your shipmates engage in any practices that might be considered fraternizing. Not only can it lead to disciplinary action and loss of personal credibility, but it is also a significant detriment to military good order and discipline.

Relations with the Public

As Coast Guard personnel, you are evaluated by your supervisors on how well you "represent the Coast Guard." You are an ambassador of the service, both on the job and off duty. Most often, you will be in direct, personal contact with the public, but you may also have the opportunity to tell the Coast Guard story through the media. In either case, your unit commander establishes policy on how to deal with the public. A good guideline when talking to both the press and the public is never to say anything you wouldn't like to read on the front page of the next day's newspaper.

Foreigners

As a U.S. citizen, you regard people from other countries as foreigners. Bear in mind that when you are a visitor in any country in the world, it is *you* who are the foreigner. The customs of other people may seem strange to you, but it's their way of doing things, and they like it. Don't make fun of anyone or anything in another country; at best it's impolite, and at worst such thoughtlessness can result in serious trouble.

III.
Nautical and
Military Skills

CHAPTER 13

Seamanship

Seamanship is the oldest of all technical seagoing skills. Long before navigation, gunnery, and steam power were developed, men had learned the elements of seamanship. Knotting and splicing, rigging, boathandling, and anchoring and mooring began thousands of years ago. Along with other aspects of going to sea, modern Coast Guard personnel also must learn to be good seamen. They must begin with the basic subjects in this chapter.

MARLINSPIKE SEAMANSHIP

Marlinspike seamanship is one of the oldest and most basic of all seagoing skills. It includes knot tying and the handling of ropes and lines.

Ropemaking

Ropemaking is essentially a series of three twisting operations. Fiber is first twisted from left to right to spin the yarn. The yarn is then twisted from right to left to form the strand. Strands are then twisted from left to right to lay the rope. This is the standard procedure, and the result is known as "right-laid" rope. When the process is reversed, a "left-laid" rope is produced. (See figure 13-2.)

Opposite twists give a rope stability. Rope must be kept twisted in

Figure 13-1. Crew member on board the cutter *Harriet Lane* properly stows a hawser.

244   SEAMANSHIP

the same way in which it was made if the rope is to stay in good condition.

Size of fiber line. The length of fiber line is given in fathoms. One fathom equals six feet. The size is specified by the circumference in inches. Thus a 100-fathom coil of eight-inch nylon would be a piece of line 600 feet long and 2.50 inches in diameter.

The smaller sizes of cordage are known as *small stuff*—³/₄-inch, 1-inch, 1 ¹/₈-inch, 1 ¹/₄-inch, and 1 ¹/₂-inch lines—are frequently called 6-, 9-, 12-, 15-, and 21-thread stuff. Sizes larger than 21-thread are termed *line*, and those five inches or more in circumference are called *hawsers*. Other terms for small stuff, depending on specific usage, are *ratline stuff*, *seizing stuff*, and *marline*.

Rope and Line

After rope has been acquired, but before it has been made up for a specific use, it is called *line*. When placed into use, each *line* takes its

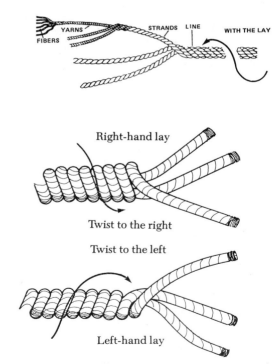

Figure 13-2. Lay of natural line.

name from the purpose it serves. Some examples are *mooring line*, *manrope*, *seizing stuff*, and *sea painter*.

Synthetic Fiber Line

Synthetic fiber line is made from inorganic material (man-made). The four most common types of synthetic line are nylon, poly-propylene, polyethylene, and polyester. The types most commonly used in the Coast Guard are nylon and polyethylene.

Nylon, which has replaced manila for the most part, is almost three times as strong as manila of the same size. Nylon comes in twisted, braided, and plaited construction. It can be used for almost any purpose except for lashings, highlines, and other purposes where its stretch and slippery surface are dangerous.

Nylon differs from other fiber ropes in that it stretches (elongates) under load, yet recovers to its normal size when tension is removed (elasticity). Depending on the type of nylon line used, it can be stretched up to 40 percent of its original length before it reaches a critical point. Elongation may, at times, be a disadvantage, but you can halve it by doubling the lines. Doubling the line will reduce elongation, but it can cause an excessive strain on the deck fittings. Nylon rope can stand repeated stretching with no serious effect, but as it becomes older, the critical point is reduced.

Polyethylene is only half as strong as nylon, size for size. It is lighter than nylon, will float in water, and is usually brightly col-ored. It is used mainly for heaving lines and trail lines on life-ring buoys.

Dacron has characteristics similar to nylon but it will not stretch quite as much. It is becoming very popular since it wears well and handles quite well.

Cotton line is used for such things as the taffrail log, lead lines, heaving lines, and signal halyards. These lines are usually braided instead of laid.

Wire Rope

Wire rope is made in much the same way as fiber rope. It is used extensively for heavy lifts because it is much stronger than natural or synthetic fiber line. A four-inch manila hawser has a breaking point of 15,000 pounds, whereas a one-inch wire, which is approximately the same size, has a breaking point of 46,000 pounds. *Always wear heavy gloves when handling wire rope.*

Line Handling

For convenience, the parts of a line are named in accordance with the way the line is laying or hanging. In taking turns around a bitt, take enough so you can hold the line. It is much easier to throw one turn off than to try an extra turn when you find that you cannot hold the line. Always stay out of the bight of a line.

Learning to handle line well is important, since rescue operations, logistics, small-boat, and aids-to-navigation work all involve the use of line or rope in some critical part of the operation.

Opening New Coil of Line

When opening a new coil of fiber line, look inside the center tunnel of the coil and locate the line end. Then position the coil so that the inside line end is at the bottom of the center tunnel. Start uncoiling the line by drawing the *inside end up through the top of the tunnel*. (See figure 13-3.)

Once a line has been removed from the manufacturer's coil, it may be made up for storage or for ready use, either by winding on a reel or in one of the following three ways:

Coiling down. This simply means laying it down in circles, roughly one on top of the other. Remember, right-laid line is *always* coiled down right-handed, or clockwise. When a line has been coiled

Figure 13-3. Uncoiling new line.

down, one end is ready to run off. This is the end that went down *last* and that is now on *top*. If you try to walk away with the bottom end, a foul-up will result. If for some reason the bottom end must go out first, turn your entire coil upside down to free it for running.

Faking down. This means laying it down in the same manner, except that it is laid out in long, flat bights, one forward of the other, instead of in round coils. With a long line, this saves the space a large coil might occupy, and faking down a heavy line is much easier than coiling it down.

Flemishing down. This means to coil it down first, and then wind it tight from the bottom end so that it forms a close mat. Slack ends of boat painters, boat falls, boat-boom guys, or any other short lines about the decks that are not in continuous use should be flemished down for neatness.

Securing ends. Never leave the end of a line dangling loose without a *whipping.* It will begin to unlay of its own accord. Use tape to whip nylon line ends.

A temporary plain whipping can be put on with anything, even rope yarn. Lay the end of the whipping along the line and bind it down with a couple of turns. Then lay the other end on the opposite way, bind it down with a couple of turns from the bight of the whipping, and pull the end tight. (See figure 13-5.)

Care of Line

Lines can be weakened to the breaking point by neglect or mistreatment. Here are a few pointers on keeping them in good condition.

- Always make up line neatly and in the correct direction, otherwise it will kink. This also prevents fouling.
- Work kinks and turns out of a line. Avoid removing kinks by putting a strain on the line; the kink may disappear, but the line may have been seriously weakened.
- Always make sure that the line is dry before you stow it. Wet line can develop mildew and rot.
- Avoid dragging line over sharp objects. Some of the fibers will surely be damaged.
- Do not allow dirt or sand to work into the strands; it cuts the fibers.
- Don't use frozen line. Line that freezes after becoming wet is easily broken and cannot be trusted. Thaw it out and dry it thoroughly before using it again.

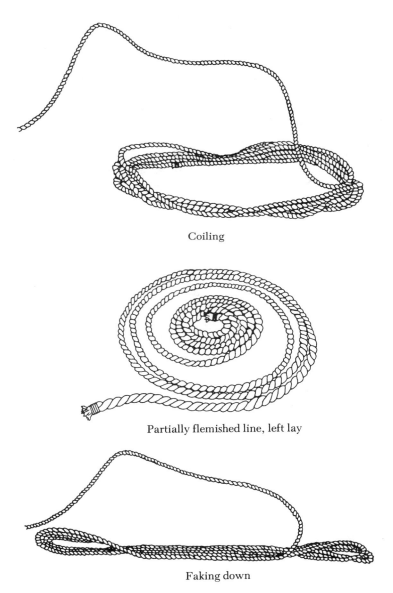

Coiling

Partially flemished line, left lay

Faking down

Figure 13-4. Three essentials in line handling: coiling, flemishing, and faking.

Handling Nylon Line

When new nylon hawsers are used and strained, sharp, cracking noises will be heard. This is normal and does not mean the nylon will part unless the line is stretched too much (more than one third of its length).

When wet nylon is strained, it gives off water vapor that looks like steam. This is a normal, not dangerous, effect.

If nylon line is parted by too much strain, it will first have stretched nearly one half its length. When this stretched line parts, the ends whip back with great force and can easily injure any bystander. Stand clear!

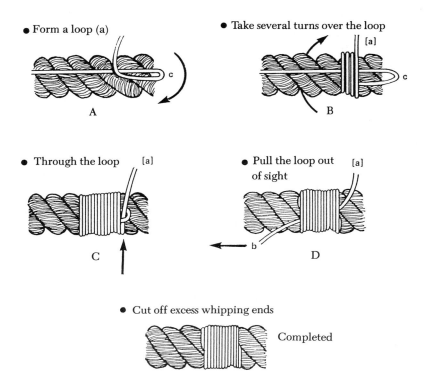

- Form a loop (a)

A

- Take several turns over the loop   [a]

B

- Through the loop   [a]

C

- Pull the loop out of sight   [a]

D

- Cut off excess whipping ends   Completed

Figure 13-5. Temporary whipping.

Knots, Bends, and Hitches

Splicing

Splicing is a method of permanently joining the ends of two lines or of bending a line back on itself so as to form a permanent loop or eye. If properly done, splicing does not weaken the line, and a splice between two lines runs over a sheave or through a pulley much easier than a knot does.

There are various forms of splices: long splice, short splice, and eye splice.

MOORING

Mooring a ship to a pier, buoy, or another ship, and unmooring, are the most basic jobs of the deck department. These involve skillful use of mooring lines (called line handling), capstans, and such fittings as cleats, bitts, bollards, and chocks. Quick, efficient line handling, when coming alongside or getting under way, is one of the marks of a smart ship and well-trained deck force.

Mooring Lines

Ships are moored to piers by a system of mooring lines that varies according to the size and character of the ship. In all of the systems,

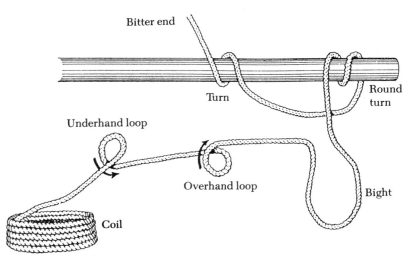

Figure 13-6. Elements of knots, bends, and hitches.

the lines are classified in accordance with their employment, such as *breast lines* or *spring lines*. A breast line leads nearly perpendicular to the keel of the ship and controls the distance of that part of the ship from the pier. A spring line leads obliquely but nearly parallel to the keel and controls the fore-and-aft position of the ship with respect to her berth. "Springing" is a term applied to the use of spring lines to move the ship in toward the pier by surging forward or aft against a line that leads obliquely to the pier.

Deck Fittings

A *cleat* consists of a pair of projecting horns used for belaying a line. *Bitts* are cylindrical shapes of cast iron or steel, arranged in pairs on deck, forward and aft of each chock. A *chock* is a fitting through which mooring lines are led; the lines run from bitts on deck through chocks to bollards on the dock. Chocks are of three types: open,

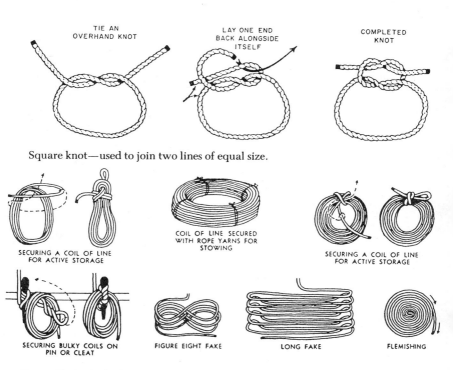

Square knot—used to join two lines of equal size.

Figure 13-7. Coils, fakes, and flemishes.

A

• Make a loop

B

• Up through and around back

Figure 13-8. Bowline—used to place a temporary eye in the end of a line.

● BACK DOWN THROUGH

C

● PULLED TAUT

D

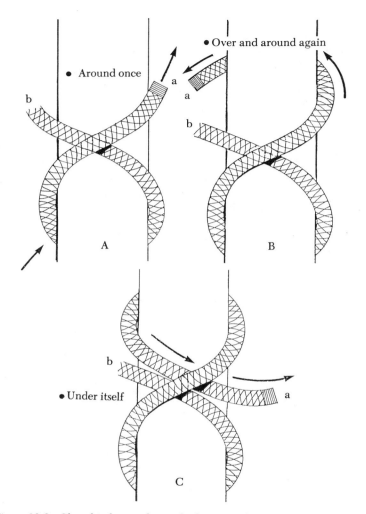

- Around once
- Over and around again
- Under itself

A

B

C

Figure 13-9. Clove hitch—used to make fast (tie) a line to a piling or railing.

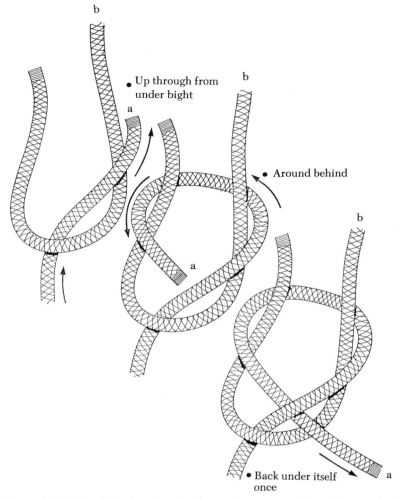

Figure 13-10. Single becket/sheet bend—used to join two lines of unequal circumference together.

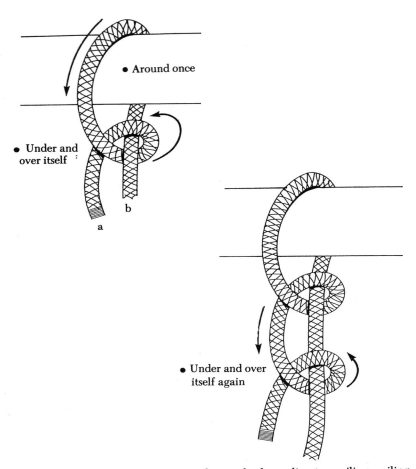

• Around once

• Under and
over itself

a

b

• Under and over
itself again

Figure 13-11. Two half hitches—used to make fast a line to a piling, railing, ring, or anchor.

Figure 13-12. Figure eight—used as a stop knot for block and tackle.

closed, and roller. A *bollard* looks somewhat like half a bitt, but larger; it is on the pier, and the bight of a line is placed over it.

Mooring may often involve putting out fenders, handling camels, and placing rat guards. *Fenders* are shock absorbers of various types placed between ships or between a ship and a pier; they are dropped over the side and tended from the deck. *Camels* are floats used to keep a ship away from a pier or wharf so that overhanging structures will not strike objects on the pier. *Rat guards* are circular metal discs lashed onto mooring lines to keep rats from coming aboard.

In mooring, the messenger (a light line) is first sent over to the pier by heaving line, and then is hauled in with the attached mooring line by a person on the pier. A *heaving line* is a light line with a weight, called a monkey fist, on one end. (See figure 13-13.)

After the ship is secured, the mooring lines are normally *doubled up*; a bight of line is passed to the pier or other ship, giving two parts

Monkey fist

Figure 13-13. Heaving line.

of line each taking an equal strain, instead of only one part. The size of mooring line used depends on the type of line and type of ship.

Commands to Line Handlers

Commands to line handlers are listed here, with the exact meaning following each command.

"Stand by your lines."—Man the lines, ready to cast off or let go.

"Let go," or "Let go all lines."—Slack off smartly to permit those tending lines on the pier or another ship to cast off.

"Send the lines over."—Pass the lines to the pier, place the eye over the appropriate bollard, but take no strain.

"Take ——— to the capstan."—Lead the end of the designated line to the capstan, take the slack out of the line, but *take no strain.*

"Heave around on ———."—Apply tension on the line with the capstan.

"Avast heaving."—Stop the capstan.

"Hold what you've got."—Hold the line as it is.

"Hold."—Do not allow any more line to go out. Caution: this risks parting the line.

"Check."—Hold heavy tension on line, but render it (let it slip) as necessary to prevent parting the line.

"Surge."—Hold moderate tension on the line, but render it enough to permit movement of the ship (used when moving along the pier to adjust position).

"Double up."—Pass an additional bight on all mooring lines from the ship to the shore so that there are three parts of each mooring line fastened to the pier instead of only one part of each line.

"Single up."—Take in all bights and extra lines so that there remains only a single part of each of the normal mooring lines.

"Take in all lines."—Used when secured with your *own* lines. Have the ends of all lines cast off from the pier and brought on board.

"Cast off all lines."—Used when secured with *another* ship's lines in a nest. Cast off the ends of the lines and allow the other ship to retrieve her lines.

"Shift."—Used when moving a line along a pier. Followed by a designation of which line and where it is to go: "Shift number three from the bollard to the cleat."

If auxiliary deck machinery is to be used to haul in on a line, the command is given, "Take one (number one) to the winch (capstan)." This may be followed by, "Heave around on one (number one)" and then, "Avast heaving on one (number one)."

CHAPTER 14

Coast Guard Boats

All Coast Guard boats, whether assigned to a cutter or not, have *service numbers* of five digits. The first two digits give the length of the boat and the last three its individual number.

Cutter boats are numbered in accordance with their location on the ship. The lower numbers indicate forward stowage, with odd numbers being on the starboard side and even numbers on the port side.

Classes

The Coast Guard uses a wide range of boats, ranging from dinghies and outboard motorboats to amphibious craft. Only a few of them are briefly described and shown in this chapter.

Motor Lifeboats (MLBs)

Motor lifeboats are the standard workhorses of the rescue stations. They are built to withstand the most severe conditions at sea and are capable of effecting a rescue at sea even under the most difficult circumstances. They are self-bailing, self-righting, and almost unsinkable, and have an extraordinarily long cruising radius for their size. The standard motor lifeboats in use today are the 52- , 47- , and

Figure 14-1. The Coast Guard's Surf Rescue Boat heading out a coastal inlet on a rough day.

44-foot models. The modern 44-foot MLB has great power and carries electronics equipment (figure 14-2).

Motor Self-bailing Surfboats

These 25-foot boats are standard equipment on large cutters. They are not as heavily constructed as the motor lifeboat, but are self-bailing and rugged. They are designed for all-around assistance work in operations requiring a high degree of maneuverability (figure 14-3).

Motor Buoy Boats

These boats are beamy, heavily constructed, roundbottom boats built for buoy work in rivers, harbors, and shallow water. Standard buoy boats are 55 feet, 46 feet, and 45 feet in length. Some new boats are jet-propelled.

Utility Boats

Utility boats are well adapted for such work as patrol, boarding, crashboat service, and rescue missions. Although not capable of withstanding extreme sea conditions, these high-speed craft are adequate for operations in moderate seas. They are 32 feet and 41 feet in length (figure 14-4).

Figure 14-2. MLBs are rugged and dependable.

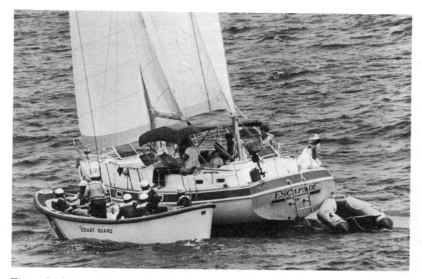

Figure 14-3. Boarding parties find these boats extremely reliable.

Rigid Hull Inflatable (RHI)

Rigid hull inflatable boats are deep-V glass-reinforced plastic hulls to which a multicompartment buoyancy tube is attached. They are powered by either a gasoline outboard motor or an inboard/outboard diesel engine. The RHI can be easily deployed from a cutter with a four-point bridle used for davit lifting and lowering (figure 14-5).

Outboard Motorboats

Several types of outboards and out-drive motorboats, mostly under 20 feet in length, are in use for boarding, light rescue, and minor aids-to-navigation work. These may be hauled on trailers to the scene of operations.

Surf Rescue Boats

These 30-foot double-ended boats are replacing the 25-foot motor surfboats and 22-foot motor rescue boats (MRSBs) at rescue stations. The 30-footer is extremely seaworthy and can handle many of the tasks in surf performed by the 44-foot motor lifeboats.

Figure 14-4. A 41-foot utility boat on patrol.

Figure 14-5. One of the many rigid-hull inflatable boats the Coast Guard currently operates. It's capable of speeds in excess of 30 knots.

Boat Equipment and Gear

The equipment supplied with each boat varies with the conditions under which it must operate. Each class of Coast Guard boat comes equipped with certain gear and parts that are standard issue (i.e., spare parts, tools, bilge pump, binoculars, navigational equipment, etc.). *Boat Outfit Lists* itemize the articles of equipment recommended for each standard service boat. At shore stations, conditions of use may require modification of the list, and this may be accomplished by the commanding officer or officer in charge of the unit. Checks are made at frequent intervals to ensure that all equipment required for the proper operation of the boat is aboard. Lives may depend on this.

Lifeboats

While at sea, cutters always have one boat designated as the ready lifeboat. This boat is equipped for rescue work and can be launched immediately. The people that crew lifeboats, as well as the boat-lowering crew, must be thoroughly familiar with their duties and ready to take their stations immediately.

Lowering Lifeboats at Sea

The crew mans the boat and dons lifejackets. Personnel on deck, who man the falls, frapping lines, sea painter, fenders, etc., take their stations. When all is ready, the gripes are tripped and cleared away and fenders lowered. Personnel in the boat *must* grasp the knotted lifelines firmly until the boat is waterborne, so that they will not be lost overboard if the boat drops out from under them. Frapping lines are passed around the falls and tended on deck. (Frapping lines prevent the boat from swinging while being lowered.) Members of the boat's crew stand by the releasing hooks of the falls fore and aft to release them at the command of the coxswain. One member of the boat's crew stands by the sea painter, ready to release it.

At the command "Lower away together," crew members manning the falls lower away smartly so that the boat will be dropped onto the crest of a wave. When the boat is waterborne, the coxswain orders the *after* falls released first, and then the *forward* falls. At this point the boat is sheered away from the ship's side by use of the sea painter and steering sweep.

Once the boat is clear of the ship's side, the sea painter is released and the boat proceeds on its mission.

Hoisting Lifeboats at Sea

This procedure is practically a repeat of the lowering procedure, *in reverse*. The sea painter is passed from the ship to the boat and secured in the boat. The coxswain veers the boat under the falls, using the sea painter and rudder. The *forward* fall is hooked first, then the *after* fall. When the falls are hooked and secured, the slack is taken up, and at the command "Hoist away," the deck crew hoists the boat with the utmost speed possible.

Prior to the boat's return to the ship, the deck crew makes full preparations to hoist in without delay; frapping lines are passed, fenders manned, sea painter made ready to pass to the boat, falls led out and all hoisting stations manned.

Keep your hands off the gunwales. If the boat hits the side of the ship you can lose part or all of your hand.

Fuel

Most Coast Guard motorboats are powered by diesel engines. However, many gasoline outboard engines are also in use. Gasoline is a highly inflammable, volatile liquid that must be handled with great caution. Diesel fuel, though not as inflammable or as volatile as gasoline, is still dangerous, and you must never develop a false sense of security just because a boat is diesel-powered.

Motorboat Handling

The following factors should be considered in handling motorboats:

Normal effect of the rudder. When the steering wheel is turned to the right, or the tiller moved to the left, the boat's head is swung to the right if the boat is moving ahead.

Screw current. With the screw turning ahead, the normal rudder effect is greatly increased due to increased pressure exerted by the water expelled from the screw. When the screw is turning astern, the water expelled moves in the reverse direction; hence the result is to slightly lessen the effectiveness of the rudder if the boat is still going ahead.

Sidewise pressure of screw blades. As the blades turn, they tend to push the stern in the opposite direction from that in which they are moving. Fortunately, upper and lower blades exert this force in opposite directions. However, there is a difference in water pressure at the top and the bottom of the screw equal roughly to a half-pound for each foot of the diameter of the screw. The lower blades are moving in greater water pressure and therefore exert more sidewise thrust. For this reason, when standard service boats are going ahead, the stern tends to swing to starboard. The reverse effect is noted when going astern. The effect of the sidewise pressure of the blades is hardly noticeable when going ahead. Going astern, there is a strong tendency for the stern to swing to port. For this reason single-screw boats should always make portside landings if possible.

Effect of wind. The wind has a decided effect on a boat, especially at slow speed. If the bow is high out of the water, it will be difficult to turn into the wind, as the sail area of the bow will have a "wind rudder" effect opposite to that of the rudder. This situation can be helped by increasing the bow weight—a process called "trimming." Despite trim, if the wind is strong and the boat is going astern, her stern will come up into the wind in spite of anything you can do.

Effect of current. If stopped, the boat will float with the current like a cork. When running, the course made good is a resultant of this motion and the motion imparted to the boat by the effects of screw, rudder, and wind.

Figure 14-6. It takes training and experience to handle modern boats.

CHAPTER 15

Navigation

There are three kinds of navigation: marine navigation, air navigation, and space navigation. Only marine navigation, which includes four methods of determining position—*piloting, dead reckoning, electronic navigation,* and *celestial navigation*—will be discussed here. Even though you are not a navigator, you should understand the elements of navigation.

All navigational methods depend on exact measurements of distance, speed, direction, and time. Marine navigation sometimes requires the measurements of the depth of water, called *soundings*. The final result, in any method, is a position or location, usually called a "fix."

The location anywhere on earth is determined by latitude—the distance north or south of the equator—and longitude—the distance east or west of the prime meridian, which runs from the North Pole to the South Pole through Greenwich, England. Latitude is measured in degrees north or south of the equator, with 0 degrees at the equator and 90 degrees at each pole. Longitude is measured in degrees from Greenwich, 180 degrees east and 180 degrees west. The place where 180 degrees east and 180 degrees west meet, halfway around the world from Greenwich, is called the International Date Line. The location of a ship at sea is established on a chart.

Charts. Charts, which show ocean areas and shorelines, and

Figure 15-1. Navigation is a skill that can be learned only through study and practice.

maps, which show landmasses, are marked off in parallels of latitude—degrees north or south—and meridians of longitude—degrees east or west. Each degree (°) is divided into 60 minutes (′) or nautical miles. A nautical mile measured along the equator or a meridian is 6076.11549 feet, or roughly 2,000 yards. Any position at sea or place ashore is stated in degrees and minutes north or south and east or west; Cleveland, Ohio, is 41°30′N and 81°45′W, the island of Funafuti in the South Pacific is 8°30′S and 178°30′E.

Distance. Distance at sea is measured in nautical miles. A nautical mile is one minute, or one sixtieth of a degree. Speed is measured in *knots*, a seaman's term meaning nautical miles *per hour*. A ship makes 27 knots, but never 27 knots per hour. In electronic navigation, distance measured by radar is called *range*.

Direction. This is determined by a compass, either magnetic or gyrocompass, which will be described later. The four cardinal directions are north, east, south, and west. All directions are measured from north on a system of 360 degrees, in which east is 090 degrees, south is 180 degrees, west is 270 degrees, and north is either 360 or 000 degrees.

Time. There are two kinds of time predominantly used at sea: local apparent time as determined by the passage of the sun across the sky, and Greenwich mean time (GMT), which is mean time (time based on the sun) at the prime meridian in Greenwich, England, from which all meridians of longitude east and west are measured. All standard time is also measured from that meridian (see *Zone Time*, chapter 11). GMT is used for observations in celestial navigation and is shown by chronometers (highly accurate clocks).

The world is divided into 24 standard time zones, each covering 15 degrees of longitude, or 900 miles at the equator. Each standard time zone bears a number, a plus (+) or minus (−) sign, and a letter. The number refers to the difference in time between that zone and the Greenwich zone. The sign tells whether the time is earlier (+) or later (−) than the Greenwich zone time; the sign shows how to find Greenwich time from the standard time in any zone. If a ship is in zone + 4, and the clock showed the time to be 1300 aboard the ship, it would be 1300 + 4 or 1700 in the Greenwich zone. In radio traffic, when the time of origin of a dispatch is expressed in GMT, it is indicated by ZULU after the date-time group.

In recent years a new basis of timekeeping has been developed, required by the exacting needs of modern science, electronics, and navigation. Called *Universal Coordinated Time (UTC)*, it is based on the frequency of vibration of a radioactive element, usually cesium. Because UTC is based upon an unchanging atomic time standard, and because GMT can be affected by small variations in the motion of the earth, there can be as much as a .9-second difference between the two. However, the two systems are kept in close agreement by the periodic insertion of a "leap second" by international time authorities, so that the actual difference rarely approaches this maximum and can be disregarded for most normal navigational purposes. Most *radio time signals* broadcast by various maritime nations by which navigators check their chronometers use UTC.

Soundings. Soundings are made with an electronic device, usually an echo sounder. A ship is said to be "on soundings" when she is in water shallow enough that a lead line can be used to determine depth. Deep-sea soundings show when a ship crosses a submarine canyon, sea mount, or other bottom feature, and when a chart shows bottom contours, soundings may be used to establish the ship's position by an actual fix.

METHODS OF DETERMINING POSITION

Piloting

This is the oldest method of navigation, used before man ventured out of sight of land and across the seas. It is a method of directing the movements of a ship by referring to landmarks, navigational aids such as lighthouses or lightships, or soundings. Piloting is generally used when entering or leaving port and in navigating along the coast and may be used at sea when the bottom contour makes the establishment of a fix possible.

Navigational aids used in piloting include the *compass*, to determine the ship's heading; the *bearing circle*, to determine direction of objects on land, buoys, ships, etc.; *charts*, which depict the outlines of the shore, as well as the positions of landmarks and seamarks and the standard depths of water at many locations; *buoys; navigational lights;* the *echo sounder*, which determines the depth of water under the ship's keel by measuring the time it takes a sound signal to reach the bottom and return to the ship; and the *lead line*, which determines the depth of the water by actual measurement. *Coast Pilot* and *Sailing Directions* are books containing detailed information on coastal waters, harbor facilities, etc., for use in conjunction with the chart of the area. *Tide Tables* predict the times and heights of the tide, and *Current Tables* predict the times, direction of flow, and velocity of tidal currents in harbors, bays, and inlets.

Bearing, range, fixes. In clear-weather piloting, the ship's position is usually determined by taking simultaneous gyrocompass bearings on three objects of fixed position. In addition, radar is used to obtain ranges and bearings to landmarks and seamarks.

A ship's position can be fixed by simultaneous visual bearings of two known objects, and also by a radar bearing and *range* on a single object, both of which are *plotted* or drawn on the chart. (See figure 15-2.) The lighthouse bears 035° from the ship, so the navigator draws a *line of position (LOP)* in the reverse direction, or 215° (180° + 35°) from the lighthouse in the direction of the ship. A factory bears 121°; a line of position 301° is similarly drawn *from* the factory. Each line is labeled with the bearing, 035° and 121°, below the line as shown.

The intersection of these two lines represents the actual position of the ship on the chart. A position that has been accurately established is called a *fix*, and is so labeled, together with the time that it was established. The symbol used to represent a fix is a small circle, placed over the intersection of the LOPs.

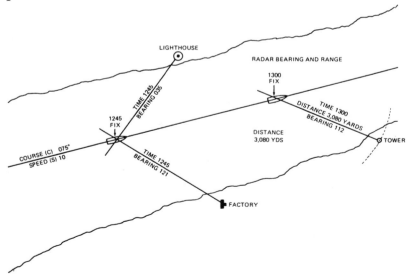

Figure 15-2. Fixes established by gyrocompass (1245 fix) and by radar bearing and range (1300 fix).

A line drawn from the fix in the direction in which the ship is steaming is called a *course line*. The direction, or *course*, is labeled above the line; speed in knots is labeled below the line.

The manner of obtaining a fix by radar bearing and range or distance is shown below. Radar gives a bearing of 112° on a prominent tower and a range of 3,080 yards. The navigator plots a line from the tower, uses dividers to measure 3,080 yards on the chart scale, then puts one leg of the dividers on the tower location on the chart and marks the bearing line with the other end. This establishes the fix by bearing and range.

Good piloting permits almost continuous position fixing to a high order of accuracy but demands great care and judgment.

These examples demonstrate general principles. It should be noted that two LOPs are known as an estimated position while three LOPs are necessary for a fix.

Dead Reckoning (DR)

This is a method in which the position of a ship is calculated by plotting the course steamed and distance covered by the ship from the last well-determined position. DR gets it name from "deduced (abbreviated "de'd") reckoning," used in the old days when navigators "deduced" a new position mathematically rather than determining it graphically, as is the modern practice. Today, the navigator determines the DR position on a chart by plotting courses and distances run from the last known position.

When celestial navigation or piloting is used, dead reckoning provides a check and helps uncover errors. If other means of navigation fail, the navigator must rely solely upon dead reckoning.

Figure 15-3 shows the DR *plot* on the chart. The 1200 fix is plotted and labeled. A course line is drawn from the fix on the ship's course of 073°. Course is labeled above the line and speed of 15 knots below the line. At 15 knots, in one hour the ship will cover one-quarter degree, or 15 minutes on the chart. To determine the 1300 position, the navigator uses dividers to measure 15 minutes of *latitude* on the vertical latitude scale printed on each side of the chart. (One degree of latitude equals 60 nautical miles; one minute of latitude equals one mile.) This distance is marked off from the fix along the course line, and the resulting spot is labeled "1330 DR," as shown.

The captain orders the OOD to put the ship on a new course, 117° at 1330. Using his dividers, the navigator marks a spot seven and one-half miles from the 1300 DR position along the direction in which the

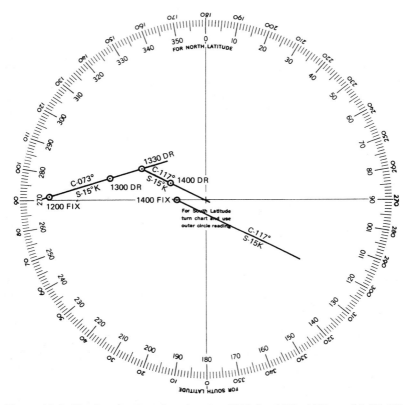

Figure 15-3. Dead reckoning plot, showing 1200 fix, 1300, 1330, and 1400 DR position. At 1400 a new fix is taken, and ship's position on the chart is changed accordingly.

ship is steaming, labels it "1330 DR," and draws in a new course line in the direction 117°.

When properly maintained, the DR plot permits the ship's approximate position to be quickly determined.

Electronic Navigation

This division of navigation will be further developed during the coming years. As far as basic techniques are concerned, it is analogous in many respects to piloting, differing primarily in the methods by which the data are collected. *Radar, Satellite, Omega,* and *Loran* are examples of electronic navigation equipment.

Increasing use is being made of satellite-based electronic navigation systems for mid-ocean navigation. Two systems are in widespread use: the Transit or NAVSAT system, consisting of seven operational satellites in polar orbits that yield periodic fixes as the satellites pass overhead, and the Global Positioning System (GPS), which in the future will consist of 24 satellites in synchronous orbits capable of furnishing continuous fix information worldwide.

Celestial Navigation

This is the determination of position by the observation of celestial bodies (sun, moon, planets, and stars) and is still the most widely used offshore navigation method, though electronic and satellite-based navigation are fast becoming predominant. Observations, made with a sextant, involve measuring the altitude above the horizon of navigational stars or other bodies and are called *sights*. When the navigator and quartermaster take a sight, they usually say they are "shooting a star."

Many of the navigational aids used in piloting are used in celestial navigation, but additional equipment, such as chronometers and sextants, is required. A DR plot is always maintained. On some ships this is done automatically by a Dead Reckoning Tracer (DRT).

NAVIGATIONAL INSTRUMENTS AND EQUIPMENT

Sextant. The sextant is a precision instrument that can measure angles in degrees, minutes, and seconds. Through a system of mirrors, the image of a star is brought down to the horizon; then, very exact scales allow the navigator to read the angle between the actual star and the horizon. This angle is called the *altitude* and is the basis of all celestial navigation.

In establishing a position by star sight, several observations are taken. Each one is *reduced* or worked out by means of the *Nautical Almanac* and the reduction tables, and results in a single *line of position*, a line passing through the ship's position. The ship's location is represented by the point at which the various lines of position intersect on the chart. This is the ship's location at the time of the observation and is marked "2000 posit," "0530 posit," etc.

Stadimeter. The stadimeter measures the distance of an object of known height, such as a masthead light, between heights of 50 to 200 feet at distances of 200 to 10,000 yards. Like a sextant, the stadimeter operates on the principle of measuring an angle. The height of an object is set on a scale, and then the reflecting image is brought into coincidence with the actual direct image and the distance is read off another scale.

Azimuth circle and bearing circle. An azimuth circle is a metal ring that fits over a compass bowl and measures bearings of objects on the surface of the earth and *azimuths* (or bearings) of celestial bodies.

Plotting equipment. Position plotting on a chart is usually done with a universal drafting machine, also called a parallel motion protractor (PMP), which is clamped to a chart table and allows both distance and bearing to be plotted at once. Sometimes a simple plastic protractor and straight edge are used.

Chronometer. This is a highly accurate clock, mounted in a brass case, which is supported in gimbals in a wooden case, so as to eliminate much of the ship's motion. Chronometers are kept in a cabinet in the chartroom, usually on the centerline of the ship, where they are protected against shock and temperature changes. Chronometers are set to show GMT; they are wound every day at exactly the same time, and this fact is always reported to the captain with the noon reports. Once a chronometer is started, it is never allowed to stop, and it is not reset while aboard ship. A record is kept of whether it is running fast or slow, but a good chronometer will never deviate more than a hundredth of a second from its average daily rate. Chronometers are checked against radio time signals, which are broadcast all over the world. To do this, a quartermaster uses a comparing watch, or hack watch, and calls the process "getting a time tick." The exact GMT time, as determined by radio, is *never* used to change the chronometer, but only to show whether it is running fast or slow.

Exact time, as indicated by the chronometer, is necessary because all celestial navigation is based on tables using Greenwich mean time. The time of a celestial observation, anywhere in the world, must be converted to GMT before the navigator works out the position.

COMPASSES, COURSES, AND BEARINGS
Compass

A *compass* is a device for determining direction on the surface of the earth. There are two main types of compasses: *magnetic* and *gyroscopic*. In each is a *compass card* from which the directions can be read (figure 15-4).

Figure 15-4. A modern compass, this one is installed aboard the cutter *Active*. The card is marked in 360 degrees, with North at 0°, South at 180°.

Magnetic Compass

Magnetic compasses have the following general characteristics. The magnetized compass needles align themselves with the earth's magnetic field and are fastened to either a disk or a cylinder marked with the cardinal points of the compass: north, east, south, and west. North, on a magnetic compass, points to the magnetic North Pole, which is several hundred miles from the geographic North Pole.

The card and needles are supported on a pivot. No matter how the ship, aircraft, or boat swings, the card is free to rotate until it has realigned itself to magnetic north.

The moving parts are contained in a bowl or housing provided with a window through which the compass card may be seen. Ship's compasses usually have a flat glass top for all-around visibility and for taking bearings.

The *lubber's line*, a mark in the window of the compass, or on the compass bowl, indicates the fore-and-aft line of the ship or boat. The compass direction under the lubber's line tells the ship's heading.

A *deviation card* is attached to the binnacle (the stand in which the compass is housed) or near it. The card gives the deviation for various headings in this form:

000°(360°)	14°W	120°	15°E	240°	4°E
015°	10°W	135°	16°E	255°	1°W
030°	5°W	150°	12°E	270°	7°W
045°	1°W	165°	12°E	285°	12°W
060°	2°E	180°	13°E	300°	15°W
075°	5°E	195°	14°E	315°	19°W
090°	7°E	210°	12°E	330°	19°W
105°	9°E	225°	9°E	345°	17°W

Compass error. The magnetic North Pole and the true, or geographic, North Pole are not at the same location, so the magnetic compass does not point directly north in most places. Usually there is a difference of several degrees, known as *compass error*, which is made up of variation and deviation. The *variation* of a compass is caused by changes in the magnetic field of the earth from place to place; hence, the needle follows the magnetic field and "varies" from the real north. The *deviation* of a compass is caused by the presence of metal objects around the compass, such as the iron and steel of the ship and her equipment. Even a knife in the pocket of the helmsman can cause the compass to deviate. Never bring a metal object near a compass.

Variation. This is the difference between geographic north and magnetic north (figure 15-5). Variation for any given locality, together with the amount of yearly increase or decrease, is shown on the *compass rose* of the chart for that particular locality. Variation remains the same for any heading of the ship at a given locality.

Deviation. This error is caused by the magnetic effect of any metal near the compass. It is different for different headings of the ship.

Every so often, the navigator and quartermaster go through an operation called "swinging ship." The ship steams in a complete circle from 0° to 360°, and the amount of her compass deviation is noted at every 15°. The results are compiled in a deviation table that is kept near the compass. There is a similar table near the magnetic compass in every aircraft. Compass error for any compass is the final effect of the variation of the locality and the deviation of the ship's heading. In some cases these must be added; in other cases one is subtracted from the other, as explained below.

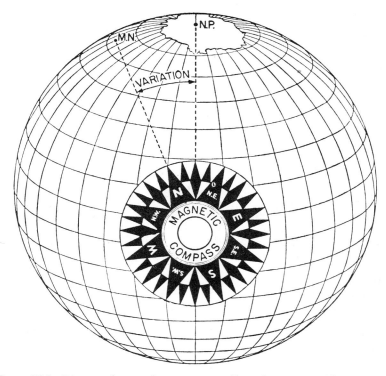

Figure 15-5. Diagram showing how variation affects the compass. The magnetic needle points to the magnetic pole (MN) instead of the geographic north pole (NP).

True course. This is the heading of the ship or boat in degrees measured clockwise from true north.

Magnetic course. This is the heading of the ship or boat in degrees measured clockwise from magnetic north.

Compass course. The reading of a particular magnetic compass, that is, the course the compass actually indicates, is called the compass course.

Correcting for Compass Error

Variation and deviation combined give what is known as magnetic *compass error.* The course on which the ship is to head is the *true course,* worked out from the chart, on which only true courses and bearings are given. Given the true course, it is necessary to find the *compass course* that you must steer to make good the true course. Do this by applying variation and deviation to the true course. This is done by a simple rule, remembered as a nonsense statement: *Can Dead Men Vote Twice?*

In order to change from true to compass course, or vice versa, set up the columns as follows:

Can	Compass
Dead	Deviation
Men	Magnetic
Vote	Variation
Twice	True

Going *up*, or changing from true to compass, is called *uncorrecting*. Coming down, or changing from compass to true, is called *correcting*. Just remember this rule:

When *correcting, add* easterly and *subtract* westerly error.
When *uncorrecting, subtract* easterly and *add* westerly error.

All compass errors are either easterly or westerly. (There are no northerly or southerly errors.) To correct a compass course of 270° to the true course, first correct for deviation, and then correct for variation. An example is given below. The deviation table described earlier shows that the deviation for 270° is 7° west. Assume that the chart shows the variation to be 12° east. Make a table as follows:

Compass	270°	Compass	270°
Deviation	7°W	Deviation	7°W
Magnetic		Magnetic	263°
Variation	12°E	Variation	12°E
True		True	275°
Total error		Total error	5°E

To find *true course*, the 7°W deviation is subtracted from the compass course of 270°, (column two), which gives a magnetic course of 263°. The variation, 12°E, is then added to the magnetic course, giving the true course of 275°. The total compass error is 5°E, which is the difference between 7°W and 12°E.

But how do you decide whether to add or subtract the deviation or variation? Remember: when *correcting*—going from compass course to true course—*add easterly errors and subtract westerly errors.*

Note that *true* differs from *magnetic* by the amount of *variation*, and that *magnetic* differs from *compass* by the amount of *deviation*.

Uncorrecting

The process of finding the *compass course* from the *true course* is called *uncorrecting*. Suppose that the given true course is 180° and variation is 10°W.

Apply variation	Compass	
	Deviation	
	Magnetic	190°
	Variation	10°W
	True	180°
	Total error	
to true course	Compass	176°
	Deviation	14°E
	Magnetic	190°
	Variation	10°W
	True	180°
	Total error	4°E

This is *uncorrecting*, so reverse the rule and *add* westerly variation, giving a *magnetic course* of 190°.

Refer to the deviation table previously discussed. Take the deviation nearest the heading you are on. In this case the nearest deviation is 14°E, or that shown for 195°. Remember: when *uncorrecting*—going from *true to compass*—add westerly errors and *subtract* easterly errors.

Gyrocompass (Gyro)

The gyrocompass is essentially a heavy fly wheel driven at high speed by an electric motor and mounted on gimbals so that it is free to move in all directions. It is usually located in a well-protected place below deck. *Repeaters*—compass cards electrically connected to the gyrocompass and placed on the bridge and in other parts of the ship—show the same readings as the master gyrocompass.

Gyro error. The gyrocompass is not affected by either variation or deviation. The motion of the earth will cause the rotor to move so that its axis lies in a north-south direction. For mechanical reasons and because of the vibrations of the ship, even the best gyrocompass will vary from time to time from true north. This *gyro error* is rarely more than a few degrees, and normally it is constant over a long period of time and on any heading of the ship.

Correcting for gyro error. Gyro error is determined by taking an azimuth, or bearing, on a celestial body where the exact bearing can be determined. This error is applied every time the compass is used, and the rule for the magnetic compass is followed: when *correcting*, *add* easterly errors and *subtract* westerly errors.

Bearings

Bearings are lines drawn, pointed, or sighted from one object to another. For accurate navigation, a system of true and relative bearings has been worked out so that all directions at sea are given in bearings that are measured in degrees (figure 15-6).

Relative bearings are based on a circle drawn around the ship itself, with the bow as 000°, the starboard beam as 090°, the stern as 180°, and the port beam as 270°. Thus, if a ship is on a course true north (000°), another ship sighted dead ahead would bear 000° *true* and 000° *relative*. But if the ship were on a course true east and sighted a ship dead ahead, it would bear 090° *true* but would still be dead ahead or 000° *relative*. Relative bearings are used wherever there is no compass. Lookouts cannot have accurate compasses at hand, nor can they be expected to know the course of the ship and the true directions that lie about it. They need a way to point out where objects lie, and this method must be fast, accurate, and unmistakable. By using the Navy system of relative bearings measured in degrees from the bow of the ship, a crew member can soon learn to report objects in such a way that anyone can locate them immediately.

True Bearings

True bearings can be obtained directly from a gyro repeater, from a magnetic compass situated so as to make bearings on outside objects possible and with the appropriate corrections applied, or by calculation from a *relative* bearing.

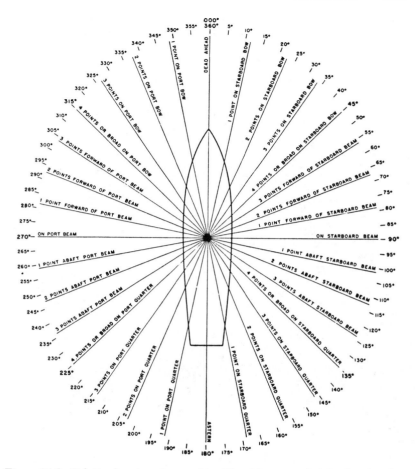

Figure 15-6. Relative bearings from a ship. The old system of giving bearings by the 32 "points" of the compass is indicated, but no longer used.

Pelorus. This is a flat, nonmagnetic metal ring mounted on a vertical stand about five feet high (figure 15-7). The inner edge of the ring is graduated in degrees from 0° at the ship's head clockwise through 360°. This ring encloses a gyro repeater. Upon the ring is mounted a pair of sighting vanes. These vanes are sighted through on an object much like the sights on a rifle.

Gyro bearings. Since the gyrocompass, and therefore the gyro re-

Figure 15-7. A pelorus.

peater in the pelorus, are already closely lined up with the true geographic directions, taking a true bearing over the gyro card is the easiest and most common method. Merely line the vane sights of the bearing circle on the object, steady the compass bowl in its gimbals (rings that compensate for the roll of the ship) until the leveler bubble shows that the vanes are level, and then read off the bearing in degrees on the compass card.

TIDES

Tides are very important in many shiphandling operations. In some harbors, deep-draft ships may be able to enter only at high tide. Large ships are usually launched, or dry-docked, at high tide. Ships going alongside piers in channels subject to strong tidal currents will usually wait for slack water, when the tide is neither ebbing nor flooding. Every Coast Guard person concerned with the handling of a vessel, from the largest cutter to a motor whaleboat, must understand what causes *tides* and the meaning of the names given to different tidal conditions.

The term *tide* describes the regular rise and fall of the water level along a seacoast or in an ocean port. Gravitational attraction of the moon is the primary cause of tides (figure 15-8). It exerts a very considerable pull on the sea, piling the water up on that part of the earth nearest the moon. There is an almost equal *bulge* of water on the opposite side of the earth, because the centrifugal force of the earth piles the water up where the pull of the moon is weakest.

Because the moon orbits the earth every 24 hours and 50 minutes, there are two low and two high tides at any place during that period. The low and high tides each are 12 hours and 25 minutes apart. The sun also affects the tide, but it is so much farther away than the moon that its pull is not nearly so great. A tide rising or moving from low to high water is said to be *flooding*; when the tide is falling, after high tide, it is said to be *ebbing*.

The difference in water depth between a high and the next low tide is considerable in many harbors; areas that are safe for a powerboat at high tide may be completely dry at low water.

CURRENTS

In most harbors and inlets, the tides are the chief causes of currents; however, if the port is on a large river, the river's flow may have a

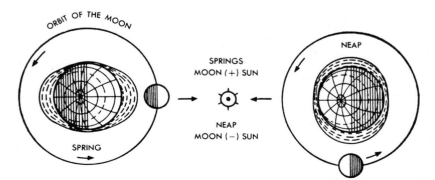

Figure 15-8. Relations of positions of the sun and moon to height of tides.

marked effect on the tidal currents. The flow of such a river will prolong the duration of the ebb current compared to that of the flood, and the velocity of the ebb current will be considerably greater than that of the flood.

Where the currents are chiefly caused by the rise and fall of the tide, their direction and speed are largely governed by the shape of the shorelines and the contour of the bottom. Where there is a long *reach*, or straight section of the waterway, the current will tend to flow most rapidly in the center and considerably slower in the shoal water near each shore. If your boat goes with the current, you should generally want to stay near the center of the waterway; if the boat goes against the current, you should stay as near shore as the prevailing water depth will allow.

In many wide inlets, near the time of *slack water*, when the current is at the end of the ebb or flood, the current may actually reverse itself in part of the inlet; while the ebb is still moving out in the main channel, a gentle flood current may start near one shore. This condition, where it exists, can be very helpful to a small-boat operator.

Where there is a bend in the channel, the current will flow strongest on the outside of the bend. This effect is very marked, particularly with a strong current.

In some areas, a strong current can create areas of very rough water, called *tide rips*. These are usually shown on charts and should be avoided.

Every vessel, regardless of size, must make some allowance for the set and drift of the current, or this will affect the course to steer.

One more thing to bear in mind about currents is that only on the seacoast does the time of the turn of the current agree with the turn of the tide; that is, only on the seacoast does the current *flood* until the time of high water and *ebb* until the time of low water. Owing to the effect of the shape of the land on the water flow, at many ports there may be a very considerable difference between the time of high or low water and the time that the current starts to ebb or flood.

A strong wind, blowing for a considerable period of time, will increase the speed of the current if they are both moving in the same direction. A wind will also prolong somewhat the duration of that current. Similarly, a strong wind may blow so much water out of a harbor that the water level will be considerably lower than its predicted depth for that time.

Effect of Wind and Currents on a Life Raft

For the greatest part, the movement of a raft will be governed by prevailing winds and currents. These, of course, cannot be altered, but they sometimes can be intelligently utilized if you know the direction in which you want to go.

Wind and current do not necessarily move in the same direction in a given area. One may be favorable, the other unfavorable.

The lower the raft rides in the water and the lower its occupants remain, the greater will be the effect of current. This effect can be increased by the use of a sea anchor or drag (or drogue) if the current is setting toward land.

On the other hand, if the wind should be favorable, the raft should be lightened as much as practicable. Survivors should sit erect to offer wind resistance. Any sort of makeshift sail would be of help.

To use wind or current advantageously, two things are required:

Knowledge of the direction you wish to go.
Knowledge of the direction of wind and current.

NAVIGATION AIDS IN THE HEAVENS

The Sun

The sun rises in the east and sets in the west. If you are north of latitude 23°27'N, the sun will invariably pass to the south of you on its daily trip across the sky.

Latitude 23°27'N is an imaginary line passing approximately through Marcus Island, Taiwan, the tip of Lower California, along the northern shore of Cuba, and through the northern part of the Arabian Sea (figure 15-9).

The sun follows the upper path at about the 21st of June each year before starting slowly south.

If you are south of latitude 23°27'S, the sun will *always* pass to the north of you on its daily trip from east to west. Latitude 23°27'S passes roughly through Noumea, Rio de Janeiro, and the southern part of Madagascar. These imaginary lines represent the Tropic of Cancer (north) and the Tropic of Capricorn.

Planets

Planets such as Mars, Jupiter, and Venus resemble stars—except that they do not twinkle. Planets are known as wanderers, since they

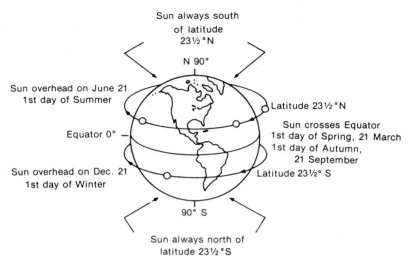

Sun always south
of latitude
23½°N

N 90°

Sun overhead on June 21
1st day of Summer

Latitude 23½°N

Equator 0°

Sun crosses Equator
1st day of Spring, 21 March
1st day of Autumn,
21 September
Latitude 23½° S

Sun overhead on Dec. 21
1st day of Winter

90° S

Sun always north of
latitude 23½°S

Figure 15-9. Diagram showing the sun's apparent path around the earth.

move about among the stars, and are not much help in determining direction. If possible, learn something about the planets and how and where they usually appear, so that when a planet appears in some constellation you will not think that you have mistaken the order of the stars and therefore of the constellation.

Stars

Like the sun, the stars move across the sky from east to west. Their position relative to one another remains fixed. Once you learn the relationship of stars and groups of stars to one another, this is a convenience in locating them. Upon locating one or more stars or constellations, you can use them as markers that tell you where to look for others.

You won't find the same stars in the same part of the sky every night. This is because the sun moves westward around the earth at a slightly greater speed than do the stars.

Consequently, stars that may be just appearing over the horizon at midnight in one month may be high in the sky at midnight another month. Or they may not appear at all. The latter happens when they travel across the sky within a few hours of the sun, which, of course, would be during daylight—for the stars travel across the sky in daylight just as they do at night.

Groups of stars are known as constellations. Some of the most prominent and easily identifiable constellations and single stars are described in the following pages. Train yourself to recognize them.

Orion

The constellation of Orion (figure 15-10) always rises true east, sets true west, and follows a path directly over the equator. Notice how the three stars forming the belt are almost parallel to the equator. The two brightest stars of the constellation, Betelgeuse and Rigel, lie approximately the same distance north and south of the line, respectively. Orion can be seen from any position on earth.

On a clear night around Christmas, Orion is visible for almost the entire night, rising around 1800 and setting about 0600. Each month thereafter, it is visible for shorter periods of time, appearing at dusk in a progressively higher position until March when it first appears near its zenith (highest position in relation to you). From then until June it is in a lower position to the west of you. In June, Orion is not visible at all as it makes its passage during daylight hours. Then in July it once more makes its appearance in the east, around 0400, and each month thereafter appears about two hours earlier.

Figure 15-10. The constellation Orion is the biggest and brightest in the Northern Hemisphere; it includes several navigational stars.

The Big Dipper (Ursa Major)

The Dipper is a distinctive constellation containing seven stars. If you are in northern latitudes, it will be the most important and useful constellation for navigational purposes.

Polaris (the North Star)

As the Big Dipper is the most important constellation in northern latitudes, Polaris is the most important star. Since it is almost directly over the North Pole, for practical purposes it can be considered to be due north of you wherever you may be.

Polaris is not very bright and is sometimes hard to see when the sky is hazy. Without the Dipper it would be very hard to find. But the two "pointers" of the Dipper, whatever its position, "point" to Polaris. *The number of degrees Polaris is above your horizon will always be nearly equal to your latitude.*

This means that if Polaris is 30° above the horizon, you are in latitude 30°N; if it is 50° above the horizon, you are in 50°N. It is directly overhead at the North Pole.

To estimate the angular distance of Polaris above the horizon you must first estimate the point in the sky that is exactly overhead (the zenith). From the horizon to that point is 90°. Halfway from the horizon to the zenith is 45°; one-sixth (or one-third of halfway) is 15°, and so on.

Southern Cross

In the Southern Hemisphere, Polaris is not visible. There, the Southern Cross is the most distinctive constellation. As you go south, the Southern Cross appears shortly before Polaris drops from sight astern. An imaginary line through the long axis of the Southern Cross points toward the South Pole. The Southern Cross should not be confused with a larger cross nearby, known as the False Cross. The latter, though the stars are more widely spaced, is less bright. It has a star in the center, making five stars in all; the Southern Cross has only four, two of which are among the brightest stars in the sky.

There is no star at the South Pole to correspond to Polaris at the North Pole. In fact, the point where such a star would be, if one existed, lies in a region devoid of stars. This point is so dark in comparison with the rest of the sky that it is known as the Coal Sack.

To find the South Pole, extend an imaginary line southward along the long axis of the Cross. Join the two bright stars to the east of the Cross with an imaginary line. Bisect this line with one at right angles. Where this east line intersects the one through the Cross is (approximately) the point above the South Pole.

This point can be used to estimate latitude in the same manner as is Polaris in northern latitudes—by its height above the horizon.

Orientation

It is possible to determine north, east, south, and west by day or night. If you can determine any of the cardinal directions, you can easily determine the others.

Well out to sea the prevailing winds from about latitude 8°–10°N to about latitude 40°N are from the northeast—blowing toward the southwest. They are called the northeast trades and will carry you in a southwesterly direction.

North of 40°N and south of 40°S the winds are usually from the west and will tend to carry you eastward.

These are only general rules. There are many local and some seasonal exceptions. Learn as much as you can by observation and questions about the winds and sea currents in the areas in which you operate.

Learn to pick out the stars that have been mentioned and many more. Learn where to look for them in the sky. This is how the first navigators found their way, and, without navigational instruments, it is still the best method.

NAVIGATIONAL PUBLICATIONS

The principles of all methods of navigation can be learned, but much detailed information necessary in working navigational problems must be obtained from complicated charts and tables. One of these is the *Nautical Almanac*, which enables the navigator to determine the exact location in the sky of the planets, sun, moon, and major stars for any second of GMT. *Tide Tables* show the predicted times and height of high and low tides. This publication also shows the exact time of sunrise and sunset. *Tidal Current Tables* list the predicted times of slack water and the predicted times and velocities of maximum flood and ebb currents, as well as the flood and ebb current directions. A ship will carry a large number of charts, and an important duty of the quartermaster is to keep them corrected and up-to-date.

CHAPTER 16

Rules of the Road and Buoyage Systems

Just as an automobile driver must know traffic signals and the laws governing speed, parking, and passing on curves, so people who handle ships and boats must know the signals, lights, laws, buoyage systems, and other matters governing traffic on the high seas, their connecting waters, and in crowded harbors. The rules are not just for big ships; they apply to boats and ships of all sizes.

SEAGOING TRAFFIC RULES

The nautical traffic laws are embodied in a set of rules, termed collectively the Rules of the Road. On the high seas and in the navigable inland waters of countries without special local rules of their own, ships are governed by a set of laws established by agreement among maritime nations, known as the *International Rules*. Along the coasts and in adjacent rivers and harbors of the United States, its territories, and possessions, however, ships are subject to local regulations known as *Inland Rules*.

Content of the Rules

The Rules of the Road are hard to think of in terms of automobile operation, because cars and trucks are mostly limited to roadways. Roadways can have lanes marked with paint, have signs for directions and warnings, be controlled by signal lights, and be illuminated

Figure 16-1. Coast Guard cutters and boats must also obey the rules of the road.

by street lights. Except in harbors with marked channels for deep-draft vessels, navigating a ship or boat on open water is a lot like driving a car around a large, mostly empty parking lot. The nautical Rules of the Road, to be useful, must provide for both day and night situations, and when vessels can see each other and when, because of poor visibility, they cannot. The rules should let one vessel know something about the other, what it is doing, where it's going, its size, whether or not it can maneuver, and, on congested waters, its intentions. Information like this may not be important to a driver on a roadway, but in a large, nearly empty parking lot—if you think about it—that information might be very useful.

The Rules of the Road apply to a vessel when it is "under way," meaning it is not at anchor, made fast to the shore, or aground, and they apply when it is at anchor or aground. They do not apply when it is moored to the shore.

There are rules that are mostly common sense, such as keeping a lookout, being cautious, going at a safe speed, using the equipment you have to minimize risk, avoiding dangerous situations before they happen, considering the need for other vessels to move in narrow waterways because of their draft and not blocking them or embarrassing them, keeping to the right in narrow channels, and obeying special navigation rules and regulations. There are rules that govern power-driven vessels, sailing vessels, and other vessels that have limited maneuverability when they are in sight of one another. Certain rules describe which vessels have the right-of-way. The vessel with the right-of-way is called the *stand-on vessel*, and the one that has to keep out of the way of the other is called the *give-way vessel*. Then, there are rules for vessels in restricted visibility, rules for lights and shapes, rules for sound and light signals, and rules for distress signals.

The Basic Rule of Safety

The basic rule of safety for ships and boats is practically the same as that for automobiles: safety first, keep to the right, and proceed cautiously when in doubt. And while doing this, report immediately to the officer in charge of the ship or boat all lights, sounds, and signals of any sort.

Application and Scope of the Rules

For many years, the International Rules of the Road and the Inland Rules were quite different. In 1981, a new set of Inland Rules, very similar to the International Rules of the Road, came into effect. Although there are a few areas in United States waters where some parts of the old rules still apply, most navigators of oceangoing vessels will not be faced with the confusion of the past. Some important differences still do exist, however, such as the use of maneuvering signals, which mean "intent" on inland waters, but which mean an actual maneuver is taking place on international waters. And there are some towing light differences and minimal vessel length requirements.

It is important that persons who navigate vessels have a full and complete understanding of the Rules of the Road. But you should also realize the purposes of the rules, and being aware of their importance, take an intelligent and active interest in your duties as lookout, crew member, or passenger in a boat. You *must* realize that all lights and sounds at sea have meaning, and that no light or sound signal should ever be overlooked. This chapter gives an idea of the importance of the rules and some details as to their application to small boats. A section on buoys is included. Although not actually part of the Rules of the Road, the buoyage system (the traffic lights and signals of harbors and channels) also governs water traffic.

Navigation Lights

At the same time that the new mariner learns the meaning of the words "port" and "starboard," the colors red and green pop up. Red for port and green for starboard are two of the four colors used in navigation lights. Sometimes navigation lights are called "running lights." The other two colors are white and yellow. White navigation lights on a vessel are used along with red and green navigation lights to let an observer know in which direction a vessel is going when only its lights can be seen. The yellow light is used in special circumstances such as in towing situations.

Red port and green starboard lights are used to mark the sides of the vessel, and the white lights are usually located on the vessel's centerline. Navigation lights are not used by the navigator to see by, as are the headlights of a car, but rather to allow navigators and lookouts on other vessels to see the vessel. The red and green lights are called "side lights." A white light at or near the stern is called a "stern light," and one, and sometimes two, white lights on the vessel's superstructure, or on masts, are called "masthead lights."

These navigation lights are allowed to show only in certain sectors around the vessel. Using the 360-degree system, each of the two side lights are positioned to show from right ahead to 22.5 degrees abaft the beam on each side for a total of 112.5 (90° + 22.5°) degrees on the horizon on each side. The stern light is positioned to show from right aft to 67.5 degrees on each side of the vessel for a total of 135 (67.5° + 67.5°) degrees on the horizon. Masthead lights are positioned to show from right ahead to 22.5 degrees abaft the beam on both sides or 225 (22.5° + 90.0° + 22.5°) degrees on the horizon. Masthead lights combined with the stern light show at least one white light all around the vessel, (masthead 225° + stern 135° = 360°). When two masthead lights are required, such as on vessels 50 or more meters in length, or when they are optimally installed on vessels of less than 50 meters, the aftermost masthead light is higher than the forward one.

Side lights let you know which side of another vessel you see and in that way, you know in which general direction the other vessel is heading. If you don't see the side lights, then you know you are looking at the stern of the other vessel. When you see both side lights, the other vessel is headed right at you. The use of two masthead lights on larger vessels lets you see changes of heading on the part of the other vessel. If the two white lights get closer together, the ship is changing its heading toward you. If the white lights separate, it is heading away.

A single white light seen on another vessel that is under way is usually the vessel's stern light. That means that you are astern of the other vessel. When a side light is visible, that means that you are nearly abeam of the other vessel or forward of it. The masthead lights and one or both side lights on another vessel should be visible at the same time, and the other vessel's stern light should never be visible to you at the same time as one of its side lights.

A lot of other kinds of lights are shown by vessels at night. Some are used for towing, some for anchoring, and some for a special purpose or situation of the vessel displaying the lights.

Sound Signals

There are two reasons for using sound signals. One is to let a vessel, which is aware of the presence of another, announce the direction of maneuver or intended maneuver. On the Inland Waterways of the United States, and under overtaking situations in international narrow channels and fairways, agreement with the other vessel's intentions is also signaled by sound. Warning signals are used when needed in connection with maneuvering signals. The other reason for sound signals is so that one vessel can let other vessels know of its presence when visibility is restricted. The sound signals are made by blasts of the ship's whistle. A short blast is about one second in duration, a prolonged blast is four to six seconds in duration.

Maneuvering and Warning Signals

On the high seas under the International Rules of the Road one short blast means "I'm altering my course to starboard" and two short blasts means, "I'm altering my course to port." On Inland Waters, the one-short-blast signal means that the vessel *intends* to leave the other on its port side; two short blasts means an intent to leave the other vessel on the starboard side. The direction of the maneuver is the same for both United States Inland and International Waters, but on United States Inland Waters, the vessel being signaled must repeat the signal when in agreement or sound the danger signal of five or more short and rapid blasts.

Three short blasts, both inland and international, means a vessel is operating astern propulsion. The danger signal for both rules is the same: five or more short and rapid blasts.

On international waters in narrow channels or fairways, overtaking signals that include intent signals and agreement signals are exchanged. Intent to overtake on the starboard side is signaled by two prolonged blasts followed by one short blast; on the port side, the signal is two prolonged and two short. The agreement signal is one prolonged, one short, one prolonged and one short (or "Charlie" in Morse Code).

On United States Inland Waters, one prolonged blast is sounded when other vessels may not be observed, such as at a bend of a channel, or behind other obstructions, and when leaving docks.

Lights may be used in conjunction with whistle signals to show the sound signal. The light is flashed for the same duration as the whistle is sounded. The lights used are all-around (360°) lights; International Rules specify the color white of five miles' minimum visibility, and Inland Rules specify white *or* yellow of two miles' visibility.

On United States waters when agreement is reached by bridge-to-bridge radiotelephone (Channel 13 VHF, 156.65 MHz), a vessel in a meeting, crossing, or overtaking situation is not obliged to sound whistle signals but may do so. If agreement is not reached, whistle signals shall be exchanged.

Sound Signals in Restricted Visibility

Whether day or night, in or near an area of restricted visibility, sound signals, often called "fog signals," shall be sounded. A power-driven vessel making way through the water shall sound, at intervals of not more than two minutes, one prolonged blast. If the vessel is under way but stopped and not making way through the water, it shall sound, not more than two minutes apart, two prolonged blasts with a two-second interval between the blasts. These signals are required on both International and United States Inland Waters.

There are additional special signals for vessels at anchor, vessels not under command, fishing vessels, pilot vessels, sailing vessels, towing and towed vessels, and vessels aground. There are some exceptions for vessels of less than 12 meters. Basically, the "fog signals" for both United States Inland and International Waters are the same.

Right of Way

A vessel having the right of way is the *stand-on* vessel. Instead of doing whatever it wishes, the stand-on vessel has a number of obligations. Likewise, the other vessel—the *give-way* vessel—has its own obligations.

Deciding which vessel is stand-on and which is give-way depends upon a number of factors. Manner of propulsion, or lack of it, is one factor; whichever vessel is to the port of the other is another; and sailing vessels approaching one another are governed by the position of the wind. Moreover, narrow channel situations, Vessel Traffic Regulation situations, and overtaking situations create their own requirements. But both United States Inland and International Rules are alike with few exceptions on the matter of determining stand-on and give-way vessels.

The rules involving two sailing vessels are somewhat complicated and may require a detailed explanation. Except where a power-driven vessel is confined to a narrow channel, or is being controlled by a traffic service, or is being overtaken, a sailing vessel is the stand-on vessel in a power-driven—sailing vessel encounter. The power-driven vessel is, thus, the give-way vessel. The give-way vessel must keep out of the way of the stand-on vessel and so far as possible take early and substantial action to keep well clear.

In any overtaking situation, the overtaking vessel must keep out of the way of the overtaken vessel; therefore, the overtaken vessel is the stand-on vessel, the overtaking is the give-way vessel. Overtaking means when one vessel is coming up on another vessel so that at night the vessel coming up would only see the other's sternlight. That would mean it was coming from a direction more than 22.5 degrees abaft the overtaken vessel's beam.

In a head-on situation where two power-driven vessels are meeting on reciprocal or nearly reciprocal courses, each must alter course to starboard so that each shall pass on the port side of the other. There is no give-way nor stand-on vessel in this situation.

Whenever two power-driven vessels are crossing so as to involve risk of collision, the vessel that has the other to starboard becomes the give-way vessel and, hence, shall keep out of the way. If the circumstances of the case allow, the give-way vessel must avoid crossing ahead of the other vessel. On the Great Lakes, United States Western Rivers, or other specified waters, a vessel crossing a river shall keep out of the way of a power-driven vessel ascending (going upstream) or descending (going downstream) the river.

Stand-on vessels must keep their course and speed. Otherwise, the give-way vessel's maneuver to keep clear could result in a collision. A stand-on vessel can take action to avoid a collision by its maneuver alone as soon as it becomes apparent that the give-way vessel is not taking appropriate avoiding action. If it is necessary for the stand-on vessel to take this action, it shall not alter course to port for a vessel on its port side. The stand-on vessel shall take such action to avoid a collision when it is so close that action by the give-way vessel alone would not avoid a collision.

Except in vessel traffic controlled situations, narrow channel situations, and overtaking situations, a power-driven vessel shall keep out of the way of a vessel not under command, a vessel restricted in its ability to maneuver, a vessel engaged in fishing, and a sailing vessel. Sailing vessels under way shall keep out of the way of a vessel not under command, a vessel restricted in its ability to maneuver, and a vessel engaged in fishing. A vessel engaged in fishing when under way shall so far as possible keep out of the way of a vessel not under command and a vessel restricted in its ability to maneuver. Seaplanes on the water shall generally keep out of the way of all vessels and avoid impeding their navigation. When a risk of collision exists between a seaplane and a vessel, the seaplane shall comply with the Rules of the Road.

Figure 16-2. Failure to understand and observe all the rules of the road can result in disaster.

Rule of Good Seamanship

Nothing in the rules shall exonerate any vessel, or the owner, master, or crew thereof, from the consequences of any neglect to comply with the rules or of the neglect of any precaution that may be required by the ordinary practice of seamen, or by the special circumstances of the case.

General Prudential Rule

In construing and complying with the rules, due regard shall be paid to all dangers of navigation and collision and to any special circumstances, including the limitations of the vessels involved, which may make a departure from the rules necessary to avoid immediate danger.

Submarine Distress Signals

A yellow smoke bomb fired into the air indicates a submarine is coming to periscope depth from below periscope depth. A red smoke bomb fired into the air indicates the submarine is in trouble and will surface immediately if able to do so. In any case it requires assistance. Any colored smoke bomb fired into the air at short intervals indicates that a submarine is in trouble and requires assistance.

AIDS TO NAVIGATION IN UNITED STATES WATERS

There are two systems of navigational aids used throughout the world. They are known as IALA A and IALA B. The United States uses IALA B as shown in appendix E and elsewhere in this chapter. The most basic difference between the systems is that the use of red and green is reversed.

Buoys Used in United States Waters

Buoys are plastic, foam, or metal floats of various types. They direct vessel traffic in the same way that road markers direct automobiles on highways. There are seven types of buoys.

Nun buoy. A conical-shaped buoy, used principally to mark the right-hand side of a channel, that is, the right-hand side when facing inland. When speaking of right hand or left hand with regard to buoys, it is understood that the ship or boat in question is approaching land from seaward.

Can buoy. A cylindrical buoy, used principally to mark the left-hand side of the same channel. The nun and can buoys are the only buoys whose shapes have special significance. When a ship is going toward land, the nun buoy should be to starboard, the can buoy to port.

Bell buoy. A float with a flat top surmounted by a framework in which a bell is fixed. The motion of the sea causes the bell to ring.

Gong buoy. Similar to a bell buoy, but has four gongs, each of a different tone.

Whistle buoy. Usually a conical-shaped buoy bearing a whistle. The motion of the sea causes the whistle to sound.

Lighted buoy. A buoy that contains batteries. It is surmounted by a framework supporting a light. Shapes of lighted buoys are not uniform.

Combination buoy. A buoy in which light and sound signals are combined, such as a lighted bell buoy, lighted gong buoy, or lighted whistle buoy. Shapes of combination buoys follow no set pattern.

Purposes of Buoys

Buoys of many shapes and colors are used to mark the sides of channels, junctions of one channel with another, obstructions, anchorages (including quarantine anchorages), areas where fish nets and traps are permitted, and areas where dredging operations are being conducted.

All types of buoys are used for all the purposes listed, except that nun buoys are not found on the left-hand side of a channel and can buoys are not found on the right-hand side of a channel as viewed from seaward.

At night or in fog the nun and can buoys are difficult to see; therefore, other types of buoys may replace them at important points.

Colored Buoys

Buoys are painted in various colors and combinations of colors, according to location and purpose as follows:

Red: Right-hand side of a channel (as seen from seaward).
Green: Left-hand side of the same channel.

Red and green horizontal bands: Obstructions in the channel, or junction where two channels meet. If the top band is red, the better channel is to the left of the buoy, which usually is a nun buoy. If the top band is black, the better channel is to the right of the buoy, which usually is a can buoy. Such marking always means that there is a channel on either side of the buoy. A junction where a secondary channel leads off from the main channel at a right angle usually is not marked by a junction buoy.

Red and white vertical stripes: Middle of the channel. Buoy may be passed on either side.
White: Information and regulatory marks.
Yellow: Special marks.

Numbered Buoys

In addition to being colored, some buoys are numbered, lettered, or marked with combinations of numbers and letters. Red buoys bear even numbers, green buoys odd numbers, with numbers running from seaward toward the shore. If there are more buoys on one side of the channel than on the other, some numbers are omitted so as to keep these buoys numbered in approximate sequence. Numbers are not given to banded or striped buoys, but letters are assigned to some of them for identification purposes.

"Red, Right, Returning"

"Red, right, returning" is a widely used phrase that helps in remembering the significance of the color on channel markers. The *red* buoys should be on the *right* when a ship is *returning* from the sea.

Lighted Buoys

Lighted buoys are used in important locations, particularly where they must be located and identified at night. If the lights are off longer than they are on—that is, if the period of darkness is longer than the period of light—they are called *flashing lights*. If the lights are on more than they are off, they are called *occulting lights*.

Any regularly flashing or occulting lighted buoy on which the light goes on every two or three seconds marks the side of a channel. If it goes on and off regularly but at a much faster rate, it marks a point on the side of a channel where special caution is required, such as a turn. Colors used for such buoy lights are red or white on the right side of the channel, and green or white on the left side of the channel. Note that white may be used for either side, but a red light is used only for the right side, and a green light only for the left side.

Lights that flash rapidly a number of times, pause, and then repeat the flashes are called *interrupted quick-flashing lights*. They are used on lighted obstruction and lighted junction buoys. A white light means there is no preferred channel. If the light is red, the preferred channel will be followed by keeping the buoy to starboard; if green, keep the buoy to port (as viewed from seaward).

Lights that produce groups of short-long flashes, each group appearing at regular intervals, are called *short-long flashing lights*. They are always white and always represent black-and-white vertically striped midchannel buoys.

Fixed Aids

Fixed aids called daymarks are often positioned along United States inland waterways in place of buoys. Sometimes these aids are on pilings over water, sometimes they are on shore. Fixed aids are occasionally placed in line with other fixed aids to form a "range" to mark the center of a channel. Aids, buoys and fixed, use the same system of numbers, lights, and colors.

Temporary Markers

Temporary channel markers usually consist of floats carrying lights, pennants, or lights and pennants. Red pennants mark the right side of the channel and green pennants mark the left side. Red and green vertically striped pennants mark obstructions and channel junctions, and red and white vertically striped pennants mark the midchannel (also called the fairway). If lighted, the right side of the channel will be marked by red lights, the left by white lights, obstructions by blue-over-red combination lights, and fairways by green lights.

Mariners must keep on the alert and not rely solely on these sea markers. Buoys have a way of shifting about; lights burn out, or the blinking mechanism fails; whistles, bells, and gongs fail to sound loudly when the sea is calm. Good navigation practices require the use of "backup" systems.

Storm Warnings

In United States waters, information regarding the weather and the approach of storms is furnished by the National Weather Service by means of bulletins, radio broadcasts, and, in certain seaport towns, by storm warnings signaled by a system of flags, pennants, or lights (see appendix E). The night equivalent of these signals consists of lights in a vertical line.

Small Craft

When conditions dangerous to the operation of small craft are forecast for the area (winds up to 33 knots), a red pennant will be displayed by day, and a red light over a white light will be displayed at night.

Gale

Two red pennants or a white light over a red light indicate that winds ranging from 34 to 48 knots are forecast.

Whole Gale

A square red flag with a black center or two red lights indicate that winds from 48 to 63 knots are forecast.

Hurricane

Two red flags with black centers or three lights (red, white, red), indicate that winds of 64 knots and above are forecast.

CHAPTER 17
Weapons

Coast Guard units are armed with various types of weapons, according to their missions. Law enforcement and military readiness both require the use of weapons, and individuals may be armed, depending on their duty assignments. This chapter offers an introduction to weapons in general use by the Coast Guard.

Terminology

Ordnance. An overall term including everything that makes up a ship's firepower.

Gun. Basically a tube closed at one end from which a projectile is propelled by the burning of gun powder.

Rocket. A weapon containing an explosive section and a propulsion section. A rocket is unable to change its direction of movement after it has been fired.

Missile. A vehicle containing an explosive section, propulsion section, and a guidance section. After it is fired (launched), a missile is able to change its direction of movement to hit the target.

Torpedo. A self-propelled underwater missile used against surface and underwater targets.

Mine. An underwater explosive weapon put into position by surface ships, submarines, or aircraft. A mine explodes only when a target comes near or into contact with it.

Figure 17-1. The Famous-class cutters carry the new Mk 75 mounted guns.

Bomb. Any weapon other than torpedoes, mines, rockets, or missiles, dropped from an aircraft.

Guns

The caliber of a gun is its inside diameter, measured from the tops of the lands. Caliber is expressed in inches and the length of the gun barrel in calibers (divide length by diameter), as 5-inch 54 caliber (5″/54 cal.), a gun 270 (5 × 54) inches long with a bore of 5 inches. Guns are grouped as major (8 inches and larger), intermediate (less than 8 inches and larger than 4 inches), and minor (less than 4 inches in diameter), except small arms. The various types of guns are described hereafter.

Bag guns. These are guns in which the projectile is loaded first, then the powder in silk bags is inserted. U.S. Navy battleships carry nine 16″/50 cal. guns that use this type of ammunition.

Case guns. Except for the bag guns, all modern naval guns are of the case type; the propelling charge of powder is contained in a metal cartridge or case. Ammunition for case guns is either fixed or separated. Fixed ammunition has a propellant powder case and projectile attached as one unit. Small arms and minor-caliber guns use fixed ammunition. Separated ammunition is in two parts, powder case and projectile. All 5-inch guns and larger use separated ammunition.

Automatic guns. These guns use the recoil of the gun to eject the fired case and reload the gun; the 76-millimeter gun is of the automatic type.

Semiautomatic guns. These guns eject the fixed case and leave the breech open in a proper position for hand loading, as in the 3″/50 cal. gun.

Dual-purpose guns (DP). These guns are used against both surface and air targets. The 5″/38 cal. and 3″/50 cal. guns are dual-purpose guns.

Saluting guns. These guns fire gun salutes, normally black powder blanks.

Line-throwing guns. These guns shoot a light line across a space that is too great to throw a heaving line.

Battery. This is a group of guns of the same size, normally controlled from the same point. The main battery of a ship consists of the largest size gun aboard. The secondary battery consists of dual-purpose guns or guns of the next size. An antiaircraft (AA) battery consists of small-caliber guns, and is usually called the machine-gun battery.

Ammunition

Ammunition is either fixed or separated, and consists of the propellant charge (powder), the primer that sets off the propellant charge, and the projectile.

All naval guns use smokeless powder shaped into cylindrical grains. This shape, with holes through the powder grain, ensures complete and predictable burning of the powder to develop propelling pressures.

Ammunition Handling

Ammunition is perfectly safe to handle, as long as it is handled carefully and cautiously. Ammunition safety precautions are posted in handling areas, and strict compliance with them is necessary for safety. These rules are based upon experiences and disasters that resulted in loss of life, ships, and port facilities.

Small Arms

Small arms are defined as all rifles, pistols, revolvers, line-throwing guns, pyro pistols, shot guns, machine guns, and other hand- or shoulder-fired firearms .60 cal. and below.

When a semiautomatic rifle is fired, the bolt is unlocked, the case is extracted from the chamber and ejected out of the receiver, the hammer is cocked, and another round is automatically chambered. The trigger must be released and squeezed again to fire the weapon.

The semiautomatic pistol, upon being fired, has a pressure buildup caused by the expanding gases in the cartridge, which causes the slide and barrel assembly to recoil. The slide extracts and ejects the fired cartridge case, cocks the hammer, and compresses the recoil spring. The slide moves forward under recoil spring pressure, feeding the next round from the magazine into the chamber. The trigger must be released and squeezed again to fire another round.

The double action works the same as with a semiautomatic with one exception: when a round is in the chamber with the safety on and hammer down, double action allows the pistol to fire by placing the safety in the fire position and pulling the trigger.

Automatic weapons follow the same chain of events as semiautomatic weapons, except that as long as the trigger is held in the fire position, the weapon will continue to fire.

The *M16 rifle* is a gas-operated, magazine-fed, air-cooled, lightweight shoulder weapon, capable of either semiautomatic or automatic fire through the use of a selector lever on the left side of the receiver. When the last round is fired from the magazine, the bolt is held open by the bolt catch. The weapon is equipped with a manual safety and a three-position fire-selector lever on the left side of the receiver (safe, semiautomatic, and full automatic). It is classified as safe *only* when the magazine is out, the chamber is empty, the bolt carrier is to the rear, and the selector is on safe.

Figure 17-2. M60 machine guns are important weapons in the war against drugs.

Figure 17-3. Practice at the range improves your skill.

The *machine gun M2 caliber .50* is an air-cooled, belt-fed, recoil-operated weapon fired from stand or tripod.

The *M60 machine gun* is an air-cooled, belt-fed, gas-operated weapon firing the 7.62-mm (NATO) cartridge. The M60 machine gun may have either a bipod or tripod mount.

Marksmanship. The two keys to accurate shooting are correct sight alignment and trigger control. To make them work, proper attitude and discipline must be displayed. Above all, know your weapons and follow all the rules of safety when handling them.

Table 17.1 Small Arms Data

Model	Caliber	Capacity	Weight	Barrel Length	Type of Action
Pistol—Beretta	9 mm	15-round magazine	33.86 oz	8.54 inches	semiautomatic dbl. action
M16 Rifle	5.56 mm	20-round magazine	7¹/₂ lbs	20 inches	semiautomatic/ automatic
Shotgun	12 gauge	5 rounds	7¹/₂ lbs	20 inches various	pump
Machine Gun M2	.50 cal	50- or 300-round belt	84 lbs	45 inches	semiautomatic/ automatic
Machine Gun M60D	7.62 mm	100-round belt	22 lbs	24 inches	automatic
Line-throwing Gun	.30 cal Blank	single shot	N/A	N/A	N/A

Safety Precautions

A weapon is just as safe as the person behind it, regardless of how well built it is or how many safety features it has. Unless the person who handles it regards it as a deadly weapon, it is a source of danger to that person and everyone nearby. Accidents don't just happen; they are usually caused by carelessness. Observe the following firearm safety precautions at all times and insist that those around you do likewise:

- Consider every firearm to be loaded until you examine it and find it to be unloaded. Never trust your memory in this respect.
- *Never* point a weapon at anyone unless you intend to shoot, nor in a direction where an accidental discharge may do harm.
- *Never* fire a weapon until it has been inspected to see that the bore or chamber is clear. Firing a weapon with any obstruction in the bore may burst the barrel, resulting in serious injury to you or your shipmates.
- On the firing line when a weapon is loaded, keep the safety on

until you are ready to shoot, and do not turn around on the line with a loaded weapon in your hands.

- *Never* put your trigger finger within the trigger guard until you intend to fire and the weapon is pointed toward the target.
- On leaving the firing line, remove the magazine, open the chamber, and keep it open.
- *Never* leave a loaded firearm or one with cartridges in the magazine where it can be picked up by somebody else.

When pistols are issued to persons on watch, the following applies:

- The pistol is carried in the holster, loaded with a full magazine, de-cocking lever off.
- On relieving the watch, the relief avoids standing in front of the person armed with the pistol, but stands to one side.
- The previous watchstander points the weapon in a safe, designated area, ensures that the safety is on, removes the magazine, lock slide open, catches the round in the hand, locks the slide to the rear, and inspects the chamber to ensure it is clear. The pistol is then turned over to the relief.
- The relief assumes the raised pistol position, lowers the slide gently after seeing that the chamber is empty, and releases the firing pin.

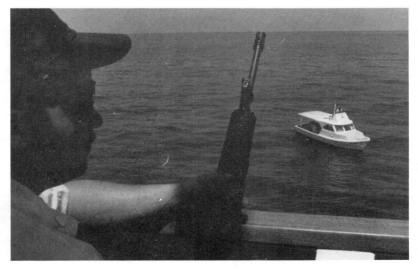

Figure 17-4. Safety is a paramount concern.

- The relief checks the number of rounds in the magazine, reinserts it in the pistol, chambers a round/delocking lever off, and returns the pistol to the holster.
- The pistol must not be removed from the holster during a watch except for the inspection as required above and for actual use.
- Personnel entrusted with pistols may not use them when off watch for any purpose, except when specifically ordered to do so and when adequately supervised.

Torpedoes

The torpedo is a self-propelled, explosive-carrying underwater weapon that carries its own automatic guidance system.

Guidance systems are either preset, wire-guided, or homing. Preset torpedoes follow a set course and depth after they are launched. Wire-guided torpedoes have a thin wire connecting the torpedo and the firing ship through which signals can be transmitted to the torpedo to intercept the target. Homing torpedoes are either active or passive types. Active types depend on the sensing signals generated and returned to the torpedo through a sonar device contained within the torpedo. Passive types listen for the noise generated by the target and home in on it.

MK 92 Fire-Control System

The MK 92 fire-control system provides the ship with a means to detect and track air and surface contacts around the ship. The system's radar provides continuously updated information about the contacts to the computer. The computer analyzes the radar data and other information provided by various ship's systems and develops a tactical display. If desired, the computer determines precisely where to aim the Mk 75 gun, or programs the Harpoon missile. The radar employs various antijamming features, allowing it to operate in any expected combat environment. In addition to weapons control, the system can be used for search and rescue, law enforcement, and navigation.

Close-In Weapons System

The Close-In Weapons System (CIWS) provides a last-effort defense against inbound antiship missiles. The system consists of a radar-mounted Gatling gun and a computer. The radar tracks the inbound missiles, the computer determines where the gun must be pointed to hit the missile, and the gun delivers a hail of bullets (over 3,000 per minute). The radar tracks both the missile and the bullets and corrects the gun's aim to bring them together. If two or more missiles are approaching the ship, the computer analyses the threat of each, and reacts to the bigger threat first.

Mines

Most information on mines is classified, so only a very general discussion can be given here. Mines are of several types and can be described according to the method of actuation (firing), method of planting, and position in the water.

Method of actuation. A contact mine fires when a ship strikes it. Usually it has lead horns containing glass tubes filled with an electrolyte. When the horn is struck, the glass breaks and the electrolyte generates enough current to fire the mine. *Influence* mines may be actuated by the underwater sound generated by a passing ship, by a ship's magnetic field, or by sensitivity to the reduction of water pressure caused by the passing of a ship.

Figure 17-5. Proper equipment is always required.

Method of planting. Mines may be planted by surface craft, submarines, or aircraft. Surface ships planting mines are subject to enemy interception. Submarines can plant mines in secret, but cannot return to plant more mines until those planted have been destroyed or have become inactive. Aircraft can plant mines in shallow waters where submarines and surface craft cannot operate.

Position in the water. Moored mines are anchored in place and float near the surface of the water, where a ship can strike them. They are usually contact types. Bottom mines lie on the bottom, so they can be used only in shallow water; they are usually influence types, set off by sound, magnetism, or pressure.

USE OF FORCE

Coast Guard personnel, both during military operations and peacetime law enforcement, must often resort to the use of weapons. Training in "use of force" policies is a vital part of weapons training, particularly in the area of law enforcement. It is not appropriate to deal with those policies in this manual inasmuch as they are subject to legal interpretations and continuing reevaluation. Before you are given a weapon, you will be trained in all aspects of its use, including *how* and *when* to use it.

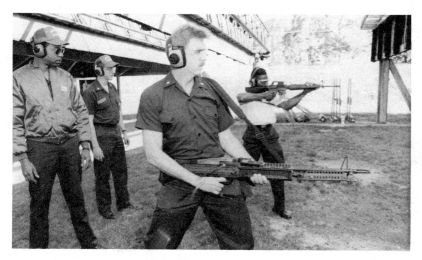

Figure 17-6. Training is vital for all personnel using weapons.

CHAPTER 18

Communications

Communication is defined as an exchange of information. That includes radiomen sending and receiving messages and quartermasters making flaghoists, but it also includes people talking to people. Messages, signals, conversations, and written reports are all communication. The bow lookout using a sound-powered telephone to report to the bridge is communicating, just as the OOD, using bridge-to-bridge communication to advise another ship of a course change, is communicating. The lookout is using *internal* communication, and the OOD is using *external* communication; all communication can be classified as one or the other.

INTERNAL COMMUNICATION

Internal communications are those that take place within a ship or a shore-based unit. They can include everything from "passing the word" over the MC circuits, to using "squawk boxes," the sound-powered telephone system, regular dial phones, bell and buzzer systems, boat gongs, or messengers. Internal communication also includes printed or written material such as the plan of the day, visual display systems such as the rudder-angle indicator and engine-order telegraph on the bridge, the plot in CIC, and even the "On Board-Ashore" display board for officers at the quarterdeck. Everyone must keep tuned in to the internal communication system at all times.

Figure 18-1. Communications—flag hoist, blinder light, and radio antenna—the heart of the cutter's operations.

Passing the Word

Before the PA systems were developed, information or orders for the crew were passed by a boatswain's mate, who first sounded the appropriate call on the pipe and then repeated "the word," fore and aft throughout the ship. Now, on the one MC system, the word is broadcast all over the ship at once. An announcement is usually preceded with "Now hear this," or "Now hear there," unless a boatswain's call is used. When a boatswain's call (or pipe) is used, "All hands" is piped before any word concerning drills and emergencies, and "Attention" before routine words. Common shipboard events are listed here, with the appropriate words following each one:

Air bedding. "All divisions, air bedding." (First pipe "All hands.")

Arrivals and departures. (Title of officer, preceded by proper number of boat gongs.) (First pipe "Attention.")

Boats. "Away, the motor whaleboat (gig, barge), away." (First pipe "Boat.")

Church call. "Divine services are now being held in (location). Maintain quiet about the decks during divine services." (First pipe "Attention." Smoking lamp is out.)

Eight o'clock reports. "On deck all eight o'clock reports." (First pipe "Attention.")

Extra duty men. "Lay up to the quarterdeck for muster, all extra duty men (or other special group)." (First pipe "Attention.")

Fire. "Fire! Fire! (state location, including deck, frame, and side)." (First pipe "Attention.")

Flight quarters. "Flight quarters. Flight quarters. Man all flight quarters stations to launch (recover) aircraft (helicopters)." (First pipe "Attention.")

General quarters. "General quarters! General quarters! All hands man battle stations." (First pipe "All hands.")

Hoist boats. "First division stand by to hoist in (out) number _____ motor launch (gig)." (First pipe "Boat.")

Idlers. "Up all idlers." (At sea. First pipe "Attention.")

Inspection (personnel). "All hands to quarters for captain's personnel inspection." (First pipe "All hands.")

Inspection (material). "Stand by all lower-deck and topside spaces for inspection." (First pipe "Attention.")

Knock off work (before noon meal). "Knock off all ship's work." (First pipe "All hands.")

Knock off work (before evening meal). "Knock off all ship's work. Shift into the uniform of the day." (First pipe "All hands.")

Late bunks. "Up all late bunks." (First pipe "Attention.")

Liberty. "Liberty to commence for the (first) and (third) sections at 1600; to expire on board at (hour, date, month)."

Mail. "Mail call." (First pipe "All hands.")

Meals. "All hands, pipe to breakfast (noon meal or dinner; evening meal or supper)." (First pipe "Mess call.")

Mess gear. "Mess gear (call). Clear the mess decks." (First pipe "Mess call.")

Mistake or error. "Belay that last word." (First pipe "Attention.")

Muster on stations. "All divisions muster on stations." (First pipe "All hands.")

Pay. "The crew is now being paid in the mess hall." (First pipe "All hands.")

Preparations for getting under way. "Make all preparations for getting under way." (First pipe "All hands.")

Quarters for muster. "All hands to quarters for muster." (First pipe "All hands.")

Quarters for muster (inclement weather). "All hands to quarters for muster. Foul-weather parade." (First pipe "All hands.")

Rain squall. "Haul over all hatch hoods and gun covers." (First pipe "Attention.")

Readiness for getting underway reports. "All departments, make readiness for getting underway reports to the officer of the deck on the bridge." (First pipe "Attention.")

Relieving the watch. "Relieve the watch. On deck the _____ section. Lifeboat crew on deck to muster. Relieve the wheel and lookouts." (First pipe "Attention.")

Rescue and assistance. "Away rescue and assistance party, _____ section." (First pipe "Attention.")

Reveille. "Reveille. Reveille, all hands heave out and trice (lash) up." Or "Reveille. Up all hands, trice up all bunks." (First pipe "All hands.")

Shifting the watch. "The officer of the deck is shifting his watch to the bridge (quarterdeck)." (First pipe "Attention.")

Side boys. "Lay up on the quarterdeck, the side boys." (First pipe "The side.")

Smoking. "The smoking lamp is lighted (out)." (Unless the word applies to the whole ship, the location should be specified.) (First pipe "Attention.")

Special sea detail. "Go to (man) your stations, all the special sea detail." Or "Station the special sea detail." (First pipe "Attention.")

Sweepers. "Sweepers, start (man) your brooms. Make a clean sweep down fore and aft." (First pipe "Sweepers.")

Taps. "Taps. Lights out. All hands turn in to your bunks and keep silence about the decks." (First pipe "Pipe down.")

Turn to. "Turn to (Scrub down all weather decks) (Scrub all canvas) (Sweep down compartments) (Dump trash)." (First pipe "Attention.")

Sound-Powered Telephones

These phones are used on all ships. They do not require outside electrical power; the user's voice acts on a carbon-filled cell and diaphragm to generate enough current to power the circuit. All handset phones look much like ordinary desk telephones and are used for routine ship's business; headset phones are somewhat more complicated and are used for drills and exercises. The handset phone has a button on the bar between receiver and mouthpiece that must be depressed to talk or listen. On the headset phone, this button is in the top of the mouthpiece.

The headset phone consists of a headband that holds receivers over the ears, a breastplate supported by a cloth neckstrap, and a yoke that holds the transmitter in front of the mouth. The phone has a lead, which may be up to 50 feet long, ending in a jack that plugs into a jackbox connected to the circuit.

To use the phone, hold the entire unit in the left hand, then unhook the right side of the neckstrap from the breastplate, run it around your neck, and hook it back to the breastplate. Put the headband over your head, adjust the earphones, push the jack into the jackbox, and turn the collar up tight to make a good connection. Adjust the mouthpiece so that it is about one-half inch from your lips. Be careful in all adjustments not to break any cords running into the function block. Remember that with the phones on you can go no farther than the length of the cord. Keep the cord slack so that it lies flat on deck and will not trip anyone; don't get yourself twisted around a piece of equipment.

Testing

Always test the phone immediately; press the mouthpiece button and transmit (for example: "Bridge, fantail, phone check"). If the phone does not work, immediately notify the person in charge of your station; use a spare phone if one is available. Never turn an earphone away from your head; it will pick up and transmit all noise in the area and drown out the circuit. If the mouthpiece is damaged, you can talk through one earphone and listen through the other; if both earphones become damaged, you can talk and listen through the mouthpiece.

Securing

Remove the jack from the jackbox by holding it in one hand and backing off the collar with the other. When the collar is free, pull the jack out. Don't pull on the lead cord or drop or bang the jack or you will have a bad connection the next time you use the phone. Replace the jackbox cover finger-tight, otherwise dust, dirt, and salt-air corrosion will soon short-circuit the jackbox.

To make up the phone, remove the headband and drape it over the yoke, then coil the lead cord beginning from the headset, making ten-inch clockwise loops in one hand. Next, remove the headpiece from the yoke and hold it with the lead cord; hold the mouthpiece in the same hand. Unhook the neckstrap from the breastplate, fold the yoke flat (being careful not to bend the mouthpiece cord), and wrap the strap around the coiled cord and the headband, leaving a short end that hooks to the breastplate again.

The phone should now be in a compact package, ready to hang up or stow in the storage box provided at the station. Be careful not to crowd or jam any cords.

Caution—Remember that the jack must always be unplugged when the phone is not in use, otherwise the phone will transmit any noises through the circuit. Don't lay the phone on deck for the same reason; besides, someone could step on it.

Telephone Circuits

Sound-powered phones are hooked up in circuits, according to their use. Most ships will have these circuits:

JA	Captain's battle control
JC	Ordnance control
JF	Flag Officer
1JG	Aircraft control
JL	Battle lookouts
2JC	Dual-purpose battery control
1JS	Sonar control

1JV	Maneuvering, docking, catapult control
JW	Ship control, navigation
JX	Radio and signals
JZ	Damage control

Every outlet on a circuit will have a number. Some circuits may have auxiliary circuits; these have the same letter designation, prefixed by an X. All circuits feed into main switchboards where more than one can be tied together, or certain stations on a circuit can be cut out.

Telephone Technique

The way you talk in ordinary conversation is not the way to use a telephone. The person on the other end of the line cannot see you, they may not know you, and they may be unfamiliar with the things you say. Telephone talkers must speak clearly, be specific, and act businesslike; they are not on the circuit for social chitchat. Follow these suggestions:

- Use a strong, calm voice. Speak slowly, pronounce words carefully.
- Don't mumble, run things together, or talk with gum or a cigarette in your mouth.
- Use standard terms and phraseology. Avoid slang or "in" words.
- When transmitting numbers and letters, use approved communications procedure. The expression "Item 5C" may sound like "Item 9D," but "FIFE Charlie" will not be mistaken for "Niner Delta."

Circuit Discipline

Circuits are like a "party line"—everyone can talk, and listen, at the same time. To prevent such a confusing state of affairs, strict circuit discipline must be maintained.

- Send only official messages.
- Keep the button on the *off* position except when actually talking.
- Do not leave your station or engage in other work or pastimes without permission.
- Use only standard phraseology.
- Never show anger, impatience, or excitement.

Each phone talker is a key link in the ship's interior communication chain. Unauthorized talking means that the chain is weakened. Don't do it; don't permit it.

Circuit Testing

To find out if stations on the circuit are manned and ready, the control-station talker says:

"All stations, Control, report when manned and ready." Each talker then acknowledges in the assigned order (or sequence). Here's how it would go on a gun circuit:

Gun one—"One, manned and ready."
Gun two—"Two, manned but not ready" (for example).
Gun three—"Three, manned and ready."

Normally each station answers in order, but does not wait more than a few seconds if the station ahead of it does not acknowledge. If you are on gun three, and gun two does not answer, acknowledge for your gun. Gun two then can come in at the end.

The test is not complete until each station has answered and any equipment faults have been checked.

Message Form

Most messages have three parts: the name of the station being called, the name of the station calling, and the information to be sent. This order must always be followed. Call the station the message is for, identify your own station, then transmit the message. Remember this order: *whom to, who from, what about.* If you are on the anchor detail and want to call the bridge, the message is "Bridge (whom to), forecastle (who from), anchor secured (what about)." Forecastle is pronounced fo'c's'le.

Messages are acknowledged when understood by repeating back the entire message. This lets the sender know the message has been received by the station called, and that it is understood. If you don't understand, then transmit "say again."

Sending a Message

First, name the station being called. Next, name the station doing the calling. Then, the message:

"Bridge, forecastle; anchor ready for letting go."

Receiving a Message

First, identify station being called; then, your station; then, acknowledge for the message. If your station is the forecastle, and the bridge has just ordered the anchor "let go," acknowledge with "Bridge, Forecastle, Let go aye, aye."

Sometimes there are three or four steps involved, for example:

"Forecastle, bridge; how many lines are to the pier?" If you don't know, you say, "Bridge, Forecastle, wait."

After getting the desired information, call the bridge:

"Bridge, forecastle; five lines to the pier."

The bridge will acknowledge:

"Forecastle, Bridge, understand, five lines to the pier."

Requesting Repeats

If an incoming message is not clear, the receiving station says, "Say again." After the message is repeated and understood, the receiving station acknowledges by repeating back the message.

Spelling Words

Difficult or little-known words are spelled out, using the phonetic alphabet: "Stand by to receive officer from NASA. I spell NOVEMBER ALFA SIERRA ALFA—NASA."

Securing the Phones

Never secure until you have permission from the control station:

Forecastle—"Bridge, forecastle; permission to secure."
Bridge—"Forecastle, bridge, wait."

The bridge talker learns that the forecastle may secure and responds:

"Forecastle, bridge; you may secure."
"Bridge, forecastle, securing."

Remember to make the phones up properly and stow them before leaving your station.

Squawk Boxes

Intercommunication voice (MC) units, or "squawk boxes," are installed in most important stations of most ships. They are normally used only by officers, and should be limited to emergency use if paralleled by sound-powered telephones. No matter who uses the MC system, circuit discipline and standard phone talker procedure must be observed. A complete list of MC circuits follows.

Circuit Announcing System

One-way system		Two-way system	
1MC	Battle and general	19MC	Readyroom
2MC	Engineers	21MC	Captain's command
4MC	Damage control	22MC	Radio room
6MC	Boat control	23MC	Distribution control
11MC	Turret	24MC	Flag officer's command
16MC	Turret	25MC	Wardroom
17MC	Antiaircraft	26MC	Machinery control
18MC	Bridge	27MC	Sonar control
		29MC	Sonar information
		31MC	Escape trunk

EXTERNAL COMMUNICATIONS

External communications are all those between a ship and another ship, aircraft, or command whether it is afloat or ashore. They may be visual—flaghoist, semaphore, signal searchlight, blinker; sound—whistles, bells, foghorns, or even a gun (for distress signal); physical delivery—guard mail and United States mail; and electrical—CW, voice radio, facsimile (FAX), radioteletype (RATT), and telephone when it is possible to hook into shore circuits, and even hand-held radios.

With ships and aircraft operating 24 hours a day around the world, there must be rapid, reliable communication, not only for tactical and strategic control in wartime, but also for administrative and logistic purposes at all times. No ship or aircraft is ever out of touch with its base of operations or its tactical, type, or administrative commander.

Visual Signals

Visual signals began centuries ago, when flags and pennants were given special meanings. Columbus hoisted a lantern in the rigging to let his ships know land had been sighted. Even with dozens of radios on a ship, visual signals are still used extensively, especially in fleet

operations, for two reasons—speed and security. Radio messages may
be intercepted by anyone with a receiver, perhaps hundreds of miles
away. Visual signals are limited to line-of-sight transmissions—the
receiver and sender have to be where they can see each other—and
do not require complicated equipment.

The three main systems of visual signals are: flashing light, semaphore, and flaghoist.

Flashing Light Signaling

This system uses short and long flashes of light to spell out dot-and-
dash messages. The transmitting signalman sends one word at a
time, with a slight pause between each letter. The receiving signalman flashes a dash after each word, meaning it was received and the
receiver is ready for another.

Directional method. In this system the sender aims the light directly at the receiver. Only people near the receiver can see the light.
The signalman controls the length of the flash by a shutter on the
face of the light. Other types of directional gear are the blinker tube
(or blinker gun) and the multipurpose lamp—both battery operated
with trigger switches to control the light flashes (figure 18-2).

Nondirectional method. Another term for this type of signaling is
"all-around." Most of it is done by yardarm blinkers, lights mounted
high on a mast and controlled by a signal key on the signal bridge.
This method is best for sending a message to several ships at once.

Nancy. Whereas other signal systems use "white" light, Nancy
uses invisible infrared light that can be seen only by those who have a
special Nancy receiver that gathers the infrared rays and converts
them to visible light. Nancy has a range of from 10,000 to 15,000
yards, and can be used only at night. It is a very secure method of
communication.

Semaphore

This requires the least equipment of all—two small hand-held flags.
A good signalman can send or receive 25 five-letter groups a minute.
Only 30 flag positions need to be learned.

Flaghoist

This is the most rapid system of visual signaling, but like semaphore,
it can be used only in the daytime. Usually it is used for tactical

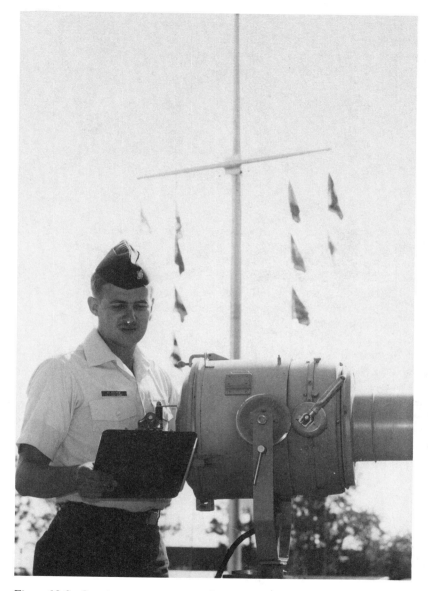

Figure 18-2. Quartermasters are trained in flashing light signals.

Figure 18-3. The semaphore alphabet is easily learned and can be used by anyone.

O   P   Q   R

S   T   U   V

W   X   Y   Z

ERROR   FRONT   NUMERALS   ATTENTION

orders; the meanings of each signal must be looked up in a signal book. There is a signal flag for each letter of the alphabet, one for each numeral from 0 through 9, and others with special uses. A complete set of signal flags will have 68 flags and pennants (see appendix B), and with them, thousands of signals can be sent. Most ships carry only two or three complete sets of flags, and substitutes are used when particular flags are already flying: the *first substitute* repeats the first flag or pennant in the same hoist, the *second substitute* repeats the second flag or pennant, and so on.

The following five flags, and their meanings, should be known to every crew member, whether they stand bridge watch or not:

BRAVO—ship is handling explosives or fuel oil
OSCAR—man overboard
PAPA—all hands return to ship
QUEBEC—all boats return to ship
FIVE FLAG—breakdown.

Absence Indicators

When the commanding officer, or any flag officer, is absent from the command, an "absentee pennant" is flown as follows:

First substitute (starboard yardarm). The admiral or unit commander, whose personal flag or pennant is flying, is absent.

Second substitute (port yardarm). The chief of staff is absent.

Third substitute (port yardarm). The commanding officer is absent. (If the commanding officer is to be gone more than 72 hours, the pennant shows the absence of the executive officer.)

Fourth substitute (starboard yardarm). The civil or military official whose flag is flying is absent.

Other Visual Signaling Systems

Other visual systems involve special methods for special occasions. Here are some of them:

Speed indicators. These are flags and pennants, or red or white lights in combinations of flashes, used to show a ship's speed.

Pyrotechnics. These are colored smoke and flare signals, usually used for distress or emergency purposes.

Panels. Large strips of colored cloth laid out in different designs on the ground or the deck of a ship to signal aircraft.

Procedure Signs

Procedure signs (PROSIGNS) are a form of communication shorthand. They provide, in brief form, orders, requests, instructions, and other types of information used often in communication. Shown below are some of the more common prosigns that may be sent by radiotelegraph (CW), radioteletype (RATT), semaphore, or flashing light.

Prosign	Meaning
AA	Unknown station
AR	Out (End of transmission)
AS	Wait
B	More to follow
BT	Break
DE	This is (from)
EEEEEEEE	Error
F	Do not answer
HM HM HM	Emergency silence
IMI AB	Repeat all before (word)
IMI AA	Repeat all after (word)
IMI WA	Repeat word after (word)
IX	Execute to follow
K	Over (invitation to transmit)
NR	Number
R	Received (also Routine)
T	Relay to (Unit)

The International Morse Code

All radiotelegraph and flashing light signaling use the International Morse Code, a system in which letters and numbers are formed by combinations of dots and dashes, or "dits" and "dahs." A skilled radioman or quartermaster sends code in evenly timed dots and dashes, in which a dot is one unit long, a dash is three units long; there is a one unit interval between dots and dashes in a letter, three units between letters, and seven units between words.

Letter	Code	Letter	Code
A	• __	N	__ •
B	__ • • •	O	__ __ __
C	__ • __ •	P	• __ __ •

D	— · ·	Q	— — · —
E	·	R	· — ·
F	· · — ·	S	· · ·
G	— — ·	T	—
H	· · · ·	U	· · —
I	· ·	V	· · · —
J	· — — —	W	· — —
K	— · —	X	— · · —
L	· — · ·	Y	— · — —
M	— —	Z	— — · ·

Number	Code	Number	Code
1	· — — — —	6	— · · · ·
2	· · — — —	7	— — · · ·
3	· · · — —	8	— — — · ·
4	· · · · —	9	— — — — ·
5	· · · · ·	0	— — — — —

Electronic communication can be made through various methods. Dedicated direct wire circuits, such as district teletype circuits, go directly from the sending unit to the receiving unit. The signals on these circuits cannot be intercepted except by physically cutting into the circuit. Radio communication such as radiotelephone (RT), radioteletype (RATT) radiotelegraph (CW), and facsimile (FAX) use the electromagnetic waves from antennas to broadcast signals through the atmosphere.

Radiotelegraph (CW)

Although this method of communication is slowly being phased out, it is still one of the most reliable means of communication. Messages transmitted by radiotelegraph are sent using the International Morse Code. These transmissions are all in plain language. Anyone can intercept and read them. Important or classified messages that must be sent CW will be encrypted using a code or cipher system known only to the sender and the receiver. An encrypted message may be copied by anyone listening to the circuit, but it cannot be decrypted and read without the code system.

Radiotelegraph messages are sent out in two ways. In the *broadcast method*, one station transmits messages for many ships. Every ship must copy all the messages sent. They do not acknowledge receipt so that an enemy cannot determine how many ships are listening or where they are.

In the *receipt method*, each station acknowledges receipt for messages; this way there is no doubt that it has been received. The disadvantage of this system is that an enemy can locate the receiving stations by using radio-direction-finding equipment.

Radiotelephone (RT)

Radiotelephone, or voice radio, is one of the most useful military communication systems. Because of its directness, convenience, and ease of operation, voice radio is used almost exclusively between ships and aircraft for short-range tactical communication (up to 25 miles). RT transmissions on *VHF* (Very High Frequencies), and *UHF* (Ultra High Frequencies) are good for *line-of-sight* communication. RT transmissions on *MF* (Medium Frequencies) and *HF* (High Frequencies) are used for longer-range communication. Though most RT communication is made in the clear, equipment is installed at most Coast Guard units to allow for covered and secure voice transmissions. Since RT circuits are used by many people, strict circuit discipline is necessary at all times.

Radioteletype (RATT)

Radioteletype is basically an electronic typewriter transmitted over radio to a similar typewriter. RATT is used extensively on ships at sea and at selected shore stations. A keyboard, similar to a typewriter, produces printed letters simultaneously at both the sending and receiving machines, no matter how many receiving machines may be on the circuit. RATT messages are sent over cryptographically covered circuits. Only units with the same cryptographic gear installed will be able to read the messages. Attempts to copy the messages will receive only jumbled characters that do not make sense. RATT messages can be prepared and stored on paper tape, magnetic tape, or computer floppy disks for future transmission.

Facsimile (FAX)

Facsimile is a method of transmitting pictorial and graphic information electronically by wire or radio, reproducing it in its original form at the receiving station. The image to be sent is scanned by a photoelectric cell, and electrical variations, corresponding to light and dark areas being scanned, are transmitted to the receiver that reproduces the picture. The process is similar to television, but is slower and cannot produce a moving picture. FAX signals may be transmitted by wire or radio.

Transmitting Techniques

Because voice radio is used so widely, everyone must understand the basics of circuit discipline (discussed earlier) and transmitting techniques. Because voice radio can be heard by anyone with the proper equipment, the following are strictly prohibited:

Violation of radio silence;
Unofficial conversation or prowords;
Transmitting without permission;
Unauthorized plain language;
Profane, indecent, or obscene language.

The following techniques will ensure good communication:

- Listen before transmitting. Don't break in on a message.
- Speak clearly, distinctly, and slowly, but transmit phrase by phrase, not word by word.
- Use standard pronunciation, use standard terminology, and always use prescribed procedures.

Procedure Words

Procedure words (prowords) are words and phrases used to speed up radio communication. They perform the same functions and are used in the same manner as prosigns. Many prosigns and prowords have the same meaning.

Proword	Meaning
Correction	An error has been made.
I say again	I am repeating transmission or portions indicated.
I spell	I shall spell the next word phonetically.
Out	End of transmission, no receipt required.
Over	Go ahead; or this is end of transmission, reply is necessary.
Roger	I have received your last transmission or message.
Say again	Repeat your last message.
Wilco	I have received your message, understood it, and will comply. *(Used by commanding officer only.)*

Pronouncing Numbers

Always pronounce numbers as follows:

Number	Pronunciation
0	Ze-ro
1	Wun
2	Too
3	Thu-ree
4	Fow-er
5	Fife
6	Six
7	Sev-en
8	Ait
9	Nin-er
44	Fow-er fow-er
90	Nin-er ze-ro
136	Wun thu-ree six
500	Fife ze-ro ze-ro
1478	Wun fow-er sev-en ait
7000	Sev-en tou-sand
16000	Wun six tou-sand
16400	Wun six fow-er ze-ro ze-ro
812681	Ait wun too six ait wun

Decimal is pronounced "day-see-mal."

Ranges and distance given in miles are transmitted as cardinal (whole) numbers, such as "range two thousand." Speeds are given as individual numbers, such as "speed two zero."

Altitude is given in feet (except for weapons orders, which are always in yards) and transmitted in cardinal numbers.

Pronouncing Letters

In all communication, a phonetic alphabet is used to avoid confusion between letters that sound alike, such as C, D, and T. Each letter is designated by a word, as follows:

Letter	Name	Spoken
A	ALFA	*AL*-FAH
B	BRAVO	*BRAH-VOH*
C	CHARLIE	*CHAR*-LEE
D	DELTA	*DEL*-TAH

Letter	Name	Spoken
E	ECHO	*ECK*-OH
F	FOXTROT	*FOKS*-TROT
G	GOLF	GOLF
H	HOTEL	HOH-*TEL*
I	INDIA	*IN*-DEE-AH
J	JULIETT	*JEW*-LEE-*ETT*
K	KILO	*KEY*-LOH
L	LIMA	*LEE*-MAH
M	MIKE	MIKE
N	NOVEMBER	NO-*VEM*-BER
O	OSCAR	*OSS*-CAH
P	PAPA	PAH-*PAH*
Q	QUEBEC	KAY-BECK
R	ROMEO	*ROW*-ME-OH
S	SIERRA	SEE-*AIR*-RAH
T	TANGO	*TANG*-GO
U	UNIFORM	*YOU*-NEE-FORM
V	VICTOR	*VIK*-TAH
W	WHISKEY	*WISS*-KEY
X	XRAY	*ECKS*-RAY
Y	YANKEE	*YANG*-KEY
Z	ZULU	*ZOO*-LOO

Standard Phraseology

Because of the specialized and technical nature of most operations, it is necessary that, in all communication, everyone "talk the same language." There is one correct, proper way to say things, and it must be used to avoid confusion, which in many high-speed operations can easily lead to danger and disaster.

Cryptography

Since all communication may be intercepted by an enemy, messages that contain vital information must be "disguised" so that they cannot be read. This is done by putting messages in codes or ciphers.

Cryptography is the science of enciphering and deciphering messages; *cryptanalysis* is the breaking of enemy ciphers or codes. All ciphers are designed to allow a large volume of traffic, and at the same time to defeat enemy cryptanalysts.

Codes are word-for-word substitutions of letter or number groups, with prearranged meanings for entire phrases (such as are found in signal books). They are used where speed is preferred to security and are changed frequently, since they are subject to compromise.

Ciphers offer letter-for-letter substitutions and greater flexibility and security than codes and are easier to use in rapid communication. Most ciphers are changed periodically. Simple tactical codes and ciphers are changed frequently; those considered more secure may be used for months or years.

Sound Signals

Sound signal devices include the ship's bell, whistle, siren, gong, and sometimes underwater sound devices (sonar). The bell is sounded when the ship is at anchor in fog, mist, snow, or heavy rain. The gong is sounded under certain conditions when the ship is in international waters. The whistle or siren is sounded in fog and whenever required by *Rules of the Road* either as a signal of intent or as a danger signal. Whistles, sirens, and bells are used by ships for transmitting emergency warning signals (such as air raid alerts) and, in wartime, for communication between ships in convoy.

On most small vessels, the voice tube is the primary means of interior communication. The voice tube requires only lung power; its effectiveness decreases according to its length and the number of bends in it. On large ships, voice tube communication is for short distances only, as between an open conning station and the pilothouse.

MAIL

A vast amount of administrative detail concerning personnel, supplies, logistics, and operations is handled by *official mail*, which is carried through the United States postal system. Official mail between ships or stations in the same port is carried by guard mail. Guard mail petty officers are designated in writing. They carry registered-mail log books, and must ensure that all mail is logged and receipted. Classified mail is carried by officer couriers. Personal mail is handled much as it is in a civilian community. Always have your correspondents use the correct zip code.

Censorship

In time of war, all letters written by personnel on ships and at overseas bases must be examined by official censors.

When censorship is in effect, censors must delete such information as follows:

Location, identity, and actual or prospective movements of ships or aircraft;

Information on the forces, weapons, military installations, or plans of the United States or allied forces;

Information regarding the employment of any naval or military unit of the United States or allied forces;

Effects of enemy operations, including casualties to personnel or material of the United States or her allies;

Criticism of equipment or morale of the United States or allied forces.

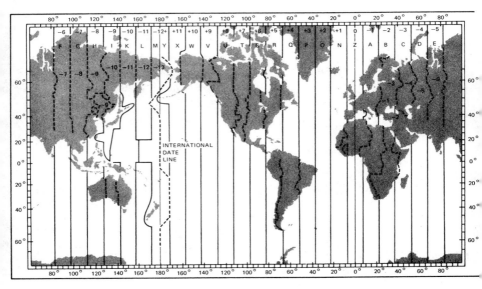

Figure 18-4. Standard time zones, showing latitudes east and west from Greenwich (the prime meridian), time zone numbers (+ and −), and GMT or Zulu time designations used in radio communications.

ZONE TIME

The solar day contains 24 hours, the time it takes the earth to turn once on its axis. The earth is divided into 24 different time zones, so that at any moment of the day there are 24 different times around the world. The United States has four time zones—Eastern, Central, Mountain, and Pacific. When the time is 0800 in Boston it is 0500 in San Francisco, 0600 in Denver, and 0700 in Chicago.

The standard time zones begin at Greenwich, England, the point from which all longitudes east and west are measured. All navigation and most communication is based on Greenwich Mean Time (GMT), the time at the 0, or prime, meridian at Greenwich. Time zones are numbered from 1 to 12, east and west of Greenwich; those west are + and those east are −. (The line between east and west is the 180th meridian, halfway around the world from Greenwich.)

If your ship is in Boston, Zone +5, and you need to know GMT at 0800 Eastern Standard Time, you add 8 and 5 and find that it is 1300 GMT. In Hawaii, which is five zones farther west, the local time is naturally five hours earlier than in Boston, or 0300. To check on this, note that Hawaii is in zone +10, and 0300 plus 10 equals 1300, GMT.

The 180th meridian is also called the *International Date Line.* When it is Saturday east of the line, it is Sunday west of the line. As a ship steaming around the world crosses each time zone, it has its clocks *advanced* one hour if it is steaming *east,* and *set back* one hour if steaming *west.* To compensate for this gain or loss of 24 hours, the date is changed when crossing the date line. A ship steaming west and setting the clocks back an hour for each time zone it crosses will advance the calendar one day when it crosses the International Date Line; a ship going east will set the calendar back and have the same day twice.

This change does not have to be made the instant the ship crosses the date line; it may be delayed for a reasonable period. It would not be desirable to lose a Sunday, nor to have Sunday twice in a row. Usually, a ship will advance the clocks (shorten the day) during the mid-watch, and retard the clocks (lengthen the day) during the second dog-watch.

In the accompanying diagram of world time zones, note that the zones are also lettered. When a date-time group ends in ZULU, the time used is GMT. If your ship is operating out of Hawaii, which is in time zone WHISKEY (+10), you add 10 to the local zone time to find GMT.

CHAPTER 19

Security

Security, as used in most training manuals and publications, refers to the safeguarding of classified information. The security of the United States in general, and of military operations in particular, depends greatly upon the success attained in the safeguarding of classified information. But security takes in more than just classified printed information (i.e., classified or registered publications, manuals, and charts). It may include such forms of communication as radio, visual signals, and mail, and knowledge of ships' movements. Security, in the full sense of the word, has to do with the safeguarding of materials and the physical safety of ships and stations.

It is important that everyone understand what classified information is, its importance, how to safeguard it, how to obtain clearance to work with or have access to it, and the penalties for security violations. Refer to COMDTINST M5500.11A for information.

Security Classifications

Information, oral or written, that is vital to the national security is classified. Three classifications are used to protect this information: top secret, secret and confidential. The term "FOUO," for official

Figure 19-1. A major portion of the Coast Guard's national purpose is law enforcement. That can mean the enforcement of drug laws, safety laws, pollution laws, fisheries laws, and port security laws, such as shown in this photo when demonstrators attempted to interfere with a Navy submarine. Security is a serious matter!

use only, is assigned to sensitive information and is not considered a security classification.

Top Secret

Information of such importance to the national security of the United States that unauthorized disclosure, or loss, would result in *exceptionally grave damage* to the United States or its allies. Examples of exceptionally grave damage include hostilities against the United States or its allies; disruption of foreign relations affecting the national security; and the compromise of vital national defense plans or complex cryptologic and communications systems.

Secret

Information of such importance that unauthorized disclosure could reasonably be expected to cause *serious damage* to national security. Examples of serious damage include disruption of foreign relations, compromise of significant military plans or intelligence operations, and compromise of significant scientific or technological developments relating to national security.

Confidential

Information of such importance that unauthorized disclosure could reasonably be expected to *cause damage* to the national security. Examples of damage include the compromise of information that indicates the strength of ground, air, and naval forces in the United States and overseas; disclosure of technical information used for training, maintenance, and inspection of classified munitions of war, and performance characteristics, test data, design, and production data on munitions of war.

For Official Use Only (FOUO)

The term *For Official Use Only* (FOUO) is assigned to official *unclassified* information that requires protection against uncontrolled release to the public. Examples of information that qualifies for the FOUO designation are the results of investigations, names and locations of informants, servicewide examination questions, bids on contracts, and plans to buy or lease real estate. It is important to remember that FOUO is *not* a classification but is only a designator.

Disciplinary Actions for Security Violations

Anyone responsible for the loss or unauthorized disclosure of classified material, and anyone who violates security regulations, will be subject to disciplinary action under the UCMJ. Disciplinary action may include trial by court-martial.

Security Clearance

Before you can be granted *access* to classified information, you must have a *valid* security clearance. The clearance must be equal to, or higher than, the classification of the information to which you will have access.

Standards for Granting Clearances

All the standards required for the granting of a security clearance are listed in the *Personnel Security Manual* (COMDTINST M5510.16). A security clearance is an administrative determination by competent authority that you are trustworthy and dependable and possess the integrity required for a position of trust. This determination is based upon a security investigation. Once this determination has been made, you may be granted access to classified information up to, and including, the level of your clearance.

Security Investigations

Various types of security investigations are used to grant security clearance. Personnel requiring access to top secret material must have a Background Investigation (BI) completed prior to access. Personnel requiring access to information classified secret and below must have a National Agency Check completed prior to access.

Background Investigation (BI). All of the paperwork requirements for a BI can be found in the *Military Personnel Security Program* (COMDTINST M5510.16). To maintain continuous access to top secret material, BIs must be updated every five years. Neglecting to update the investigation will result in removal of access to top secret material until the investigation has been updated.

National Agency Check (NAC). Every person entering the Coast Guard has an NAC completed. This investigation allows commanding officers to grant access to material classified up to, and including, secret. To maintain continuous access to this material, the NAC must be updated every ten years. Neglecting to update the investigation will result in removal of access to all classified material until the investigation has been updated.

Clearance Requirements

The following requirements must be met before military personnel can be granted access to classified information.

Top Secret. A *Final Top Secret* clearance can only be granted by Coast Guard Headquarters Office of Intelligence, Investigations and Security (G-OIS). This clearance may be granted after a Background Investigation (BI) has been completed along with a review of your personnel and health records.

Secret. A *Final Secret* clearance may be granted by unit commanding officers based upon a National Agency Check by G-OIS and a check of your personnel and health records.

Confidential. A *Final Confidential* clearance can be granted by unit commanding officers based upon a National Agency Check by G-OIS and a check of your personnel and health records.

Interim clearances. Interim clearances are normally granted only for short-term access to classified information during special operations or emergency situations. The granting of interim clearances will be kept to a minimum.

Security investigations remain valid and may serve as the basis for the issuance of future clearances *unless*:

Derogatory information becomes available, indicating a need for further investigation; or

The individual is assigned to a particularly sensitive billet requiring a greater clearance criterion than indicated by the foregoing; or

Continuous active service in the armed forces or civilian employment in the government service is broken by a period longer than one year.

Access

Access to classified information is granted based on a "need to know." If you need to have classified information in order to perform your assigned duties, you will be granted access by your commanding officer or officer-in-charge. Having access does not mean that you will be able to look at all the classified material held by the com-

Figure 19-2. The Coast Guard and Coast Guard Reserve provide security patrols in many major ports in this country.

mand. You will receive only the information you need to perform your job.

All classified material entrusted to you will be clearly marked with its appropriate classification. There is never an excuse for the careless handling of classified material. There may be times when you will be exposed to classified information that you do not have a "need to know." Do not discuss this information with anyone or attempt to pry into the details of this information.

Threats to Security

The compromise of classified information, through loss or disclosure to unauthorized persons, presents a threat to national security. The seriousness of that threat must be determined and measures taken to negate or minimize the adverse effects of the compromise. Any individual becoming aware of a compromise or subjection to compromise of classified material must immediately notify the most readily available command. Take any measures necessary to keep unauthorized persons from viewing the material until someone is sent to take charge.

To keep yourself from getting involved in a compromise, remember the following: *What you do, see, and hear at work stays at work.* Bragging or talking freely about what you know and do may impress your family and friends, but it could jeopardize your safety and the safety of your shipmates. There was a saying during World War II, "Loose lips sink ships." Believe it or not, that saying is as applicable today as it was then.

Coast Guard Investigations

Coast Guard Investigations, or CGI, is a diverse group of special agents, investigations assistants, and support personnel who assist Coast Guard commands in maintaining internal integrity, good order, and discipline. In addition, CGI agents conduct external investigations addressing issues such as drug and alien smuggling, environmental crimes, and crimes against the government generally. These men and women, both military and civilian, serve in much the same capacity as their counterparts in the Naval Investigative Service (NIS), the Air Force Office of Special Investigations (OSI), and the Army Criminal Investigation Command (CIDC).

Intelligence Collection Methods

Unfriendly nations, and drug smugglers, are always interested in classified information on developments, weapons, techniques, materials, and ship and aircraft movements and their operating capabilities. The people who attempt to collect such information will not look or act like spies in TV thrillers. They're just like the people who lived next door when you were growing up. This ability to blend in with the normal populace allows them to be successful in their work. This brings us back to what was discussed in Threats to Security. If you have access to and work with classified material, you should never discuss it with anyone other than those you know have access and a need to know. Intelligence agents collect many odd little bits of information. From these little bits, they piece together a fairly complete picture. Don't make their work easier.

Safeguarding Classified Information

If you accidentally come across some classified matter—a letter, booklet, or a device—that has been left unguarded, misplaced, or not properly secured, do not read or examine it or try to decide what to do with it. Notify the nearest officer or petty officer in charge, and then stand by to keep unauthorized personnel away until a responsible person arrives to take charge.

Restricted Areas

Restricted areas are established at units to provide additional safeguards for material and equipment. These areas will be clearly marked with warning signs. Persons on watch in such areas should not hesitate to ask visitors for identification. No responsible person will object to being stopped politely, but firmly, pending identification.

Three levels of restricted areas meet the security requirements for the protection of the information stored in the space. These areas are as follows.

Exclusion Area

Access to this area constitutes, for all practical purposes, access to classified material or equipment.

Limited Area

An area in which uncontrolled movement would permit access to classified material or equipment.

Controlled Area

The area adjacent to or surrounding an exclusion or limited area.

A complete breakdown of each area can be found in chapter 12 of the *Security Manual* (COMDTINST M5500.11).

Censorship

In time of war or under certain peacetime emergency conditions, censorship of personal mail may be imposed. The main intent of censorship is to avoid security violations that might occur through carelessness or lack of judgment in writing letters.

The use of cameras may also be subject to censorship. Cameras may be barred, or all pictures taken aboard ship may require clearance for release.

External Security

Every person aboard ship, whether on watch or not, must always be security-minded and on the alert for any sign of danger to the ship. A ship in port should be relatively safe, but it can be threatened by many things—hurricane, tidal wave, flooding, fire, explosion, sabotage from within the ship, saboteurs, sneak attack, civil disorder, riot.

Threats to security may originate outside the ship. Strangers who approach the ship should be regarded with suspicion, even though they appear to be ordinary visitors, salesmen, agents, newsboys, or delivery people. All individuals coming on board must be identified by the officer of the deck or designated representative, and packages, parcels, brief cases, tool boxes, etc., should be inspected. Crew members standing gangway or quarterdeck watches assist the OOD in identifying approaching boats, screening visitors, and checking packages.

Sentries and Guards

These crew members, posted for security purposes, are guided by written instructions and must know how to challenge boats in order to identify occupants before they come alongside. All sentries may be armed when the situation demands. An armed guard should be reasonably proficient in the use of the weapon; one who does not know the weapon is useless and a danger to ship and shipmates.

Sneak Attack and Sabotage

Particularly at night, ships moored or at anchor are vulnerable to sneak attack or sabotage. The ship could be approached by swimmers, small boat, midget submarine, or submarine. Boarders may pose as bumboat crews; saboteurs may mingle with the returning liberty party, pose as visitors, or sneak aboard when ships are moored to a pier. Where such dangers of attack exist, the operations officer will organize special watches and issue instructions.

The Signal Bridge

In port, the bridge and signal watches perform the following functions with regard to security:

They report to the OOD any boats approaching the ship, or operating in the vicinity of the ship in a suspicious or aimless manner.

They report to the OOD any unusual disturbances or signs of distress in the harbor, aboard other ships, or ashore.

Internal Security

The safety of a ship may be threatened from within. Sabotage is possible, particularly in times of great international tension. Abrasives in oil, nails driven into multiple conductor cables, or foreign objects placed in turbines or reduction gears can cause great damage. Fire or flooding, accidental or otherwise, is always a danger. All ships maintain watches to help maintain internal security.

Emission Control (EMCON)

This is necessary in wartime because modern science enables an enemy to detect almost any electronic emission. When EMCON is set, personal radios aboard ship may not be used.

Darken Ship

This order demands rigid observance by everyone going topside. On a dark night, the glow of a cigarette can be seen for miles; the loom of light from an improperly shielded hatchway will let a submarine make a successful periscope attack.

Quiet Ship

Observance of this order is most important. Banging or hammering can give away the position of an otherwise perfectly silent vessel.

Trash, Garbage, and Oil Slicks

Orders covering trash disposal and pumping bilges must be carefully observed. A ship littering the ocean with floating debris can be tracked down by an alert enemy. It is also violating both United States and international law.

Keys

The commanding officer is custodian of all keys to all magazines, but he may designate others to have duplicate keys. Heads of departments are responsible for keys to locked spaces under their cognizance. Keys to other spaces are kept in the custody of designated officers or petty officers. Each department head maintains a key locker containing all the keys to spaces in their department. Keys to these key lockers are available to the OOD at all times.

Crew members must provide locks for their personal lockers and should carry their keys at all times. Any other keys with which they may be entrusted should never be carried off the ship.

Shipyard Security

When a ship is in a shipyard, all workmen coming on board must be identified. Compartments containing classified matter must be secured, either by locking or by sentries. Fire watches are normally assigned each welder and burner who comes on board. Special precaution must be taken after each shift to inspect spaces for all fire hazards.

Prisoners of War

Personnel captured by the enemy will be questioned at great length. Enemy interrogators are clever and persistent and every trick will be used to obtain classified information. Article 1223 of *U.S. Navy Regulations* states that any member of the naval service who is captured shall not disclose any information other than name, rate, service number, and date of birth. Since the Coast Guard operates with the Navy in time of war or national emergency, this regulation applies to the Coast Guard.

General Security Measures

Security refers to all measures taken to protect a ship or station against damage by storm or fire, and to guard against theft, sabotage, and other subversive activities. Security involves sentry duty, fire watches, guard duty, and barracks watches. *Sentry duty* is a formal, military duty, governed by specific orders. *Guard duty* may be the same as sentry duty, or, at times, guards may be permitted to relax military bearing so long as they are on the job and ready for action. A *fire watch* may cover an assigned area on foot, or with a vehicle, or simply be an assignment to a certain place for a certain period. A *barracks watch* may sometimes stand a sentry watch, or sometimes merely be available to answer a phone, check people in and out, turn lights off and on, and preserve order and cleanliness.

Sentry Duty

The requirements for standing sentry duty are the same as for all watches: keep alert, attend to duty, report all violations, preserve

Figure 19-3. The Coast Guard maintains security zones for every space shuttle launch.

order, and remain on watch until properly relieved. The rules or orders for sentries form the basic rules for all security watches.

Detail to a sentry watch involves two sets of orders, which follow.

Special Orders

These cover duty as a sentry, with regard to the specific watch in question, and will be passed on and explained to you by the petty officer of the watch or corporal of the guard.

General Orders

These never change. You will always be responsible for carrying out general orders, whether or not anyone explains them to you or reminds you of them. The eleven general orders, with an explanation of each, follow. You must memorize them and be able to recite them whenever called upon to do so.

1. To take charge of this post and all government property in view.

2. To walk my post in a military manner, keeping always on the alert, and observing everything that takes place within sight or hearing.

3. To report all violations of orders I am instructed to enforce.

4. To repeat all calls from posts more distant from the guard house than my own.

5. To quit my post only when properly relieved.

6. To receive, obey, and pass on to the sentry who relieves me all orders from the commanding officer, field officer of the day, officer of the day, and officers and petty officers of the watch.

7. To talk to no one except in line of duty.

8. To give the alarm in case of fire or disorder.

9. To call the petty officer of the watch in any case not covered by instructions.

10. To salute all officers and all colors and standards not cased.

11. To be especially watchful at night, and during the time for challenging, to challenge all persons on or near my post, and to allow no one to pass without proper authority.

Orders 1, 2, and 3 mean that all persons in the service, whatever their rank, are required to respect you in the performance of your duties as a sentinel and a member of the guard.

You report immediately, by telephone or other means, every unusual or suspicious occurrence.

You apprehend and turn over to proper authority all suspicious persons involved in a disorder occurring on or near your post and all parties who try to enter your post at any time without authority. You report violations of orders when you are inspected or relieved. If it is urgent and necessary, apprehend the offender and call the petty officer of the watch.

Order 4 means that you "pass the word" by calling "petty officer of the watch," giving the number of your post, when you need the petty officer of the watch for any reason other than relief, fire, or disorder.

Order 5 means that if you become sick or for any reason must leave your post, you call "petty officer of the watch." You must not leave your post for meals or any other reason unless properly relieved. If your relief is late, telephone or call the petty officer of the watch, but do not leave your post.

Order 6 names the officers whose orders you must obey. However, any officer can investigate apparent violations of regulations when that officer observes them.

You give up possession of your weapon only on receiving a direct order to do so from the person who can lawfully give you orders while on your post. No other person can require a sentinel to hand over a weapon or even require it to be inspected.

When challenging or holding conversation with any person, you take the position of Port Arms if you are armed with a rifle, and take the position of Raise Pistol if you are armed with a pistol.

Order 8 means that, if fire is discovered, you must immediately call, "Fire," then turn in the alarm, or make certain that it has been turned in, and, if possible, extinguish the fire.

Order 10 covers saluting. A sentry salutes as follows:

- If walking post, the sentry halts, and if armed with a rifle, the sentry salutes by presenting arms; if otherwise armed, the sentry renders the hand salute.
- If doing patrol duty, the sentry does not halt, unless spoken to, but renders the rifle salute (at Shoulder Arms); if otherwise armed, the sentry renders the hand salute.
- If in a sentry box, the sentry stands at Attention in the doorway upon the approach of the person or party entitled to the salute, and if armed with the rifle, the sentry salutes by presenting arms; if otherwise armed, the sentry renders the hand salute.

During the hours when a sentry is required to challenge, the sentry salutes an officer as soon as the officer is recognized.

The sentry salutes an officer as the officer comes on the post. If the officer stops to hold a conversation, the sentry assumes the position of Port Arms if armed with a rifle, or the position of Attention throughout the conversation, and salutes again when the officer leaves.

In talking to an officer, the sentry does not interrupt to salute another officer unless the officer being addressed salutes, then the sentry follows this example.

When the flag is raised at morning colors or lowered at evening colors, the sentry stands at Attention at the first note of the national anthem or "To the Colors" and renders the prescribed salute. Those engaged in duties that would hamper them need not salute. One should face the flag while saluting; but if duty requires, it is permissible to face in another direction.

When a person approaches a post during challenging hours, challenge sharply: "Halt! Who is there?" The sentry then takes the best position to pass or apprehend the person, and requires the person to advance, remain halted, or face toward the light, in order to determine whether to pass or turn the person over to the petty officer of the watch.

If a person is in a vehicle, the same procedure is followed. If necessary, the sentry may require drivers and passengers to get out of the vehicle.

A sentry permits only one out of a group of people to approach to be recognized. If the sentry is not satisfied with the identification, the sentry detains a person and calls the petty officer of the watch.

When two or more individuals approach from different directions at the same time, a sentry challenges each in turn and requires them to halt and remain halted until told to proceed.

A sentry must never be taken by surprise or permit two persons to advance at the same time.

A sentry should always say, "Advance one to be recognized." If the party has replied properly, the sentry says, "Advance, friend (officer of the day, etc.)." As soon as recognition is sure, the sentry salutes and permits the person to pass.

Guard duties aboard ships will differ somewhat from those ashore. Some of the variations follow.

Guard duty, if required, is performed by details from the ship's divisions and is known as the *security watch*. The OOD performs the functions of the officer of the day.

The guard of the day is mustered only at morning and evening colors and in the daylight hours in between when honors may have to be rendered.

IV.
Sailors at
Sea and Ashore

CHAPTER 20

Living Aboard Ship

The Coast Guard is first and foremost a seagoing service; therefore, many of you will serve in our fleet of cutters at some time in your careers. Duty aboard a cutter is your opportunity to serve our country in a way rich in challenge, adventure, and tradition.

The sailor's life is unique and demanding, an experience for which you are actually beginning preparation as a recruit, cadet, or officer candidate. The training received in these roles and supplemented by the information in this and other chapters in this manual is intended to help smooth your transition from "landlubber" to "salt"; additional reference reading on much of the information discussed in this chapter is published in *Coast Guard Regulations*.

Welcome aboard!

Ship's Orientation and Indoctrination Program

It has long been recognized that newly reporting enlisted personnel, particularly those who are reporting to their first ship, have a definite need for a complete formal introduction to their new and perhaps initially bewildering world. For this reason, each Coast Guard ship includes just such a program as a part of its training plan and assigns a senior enlisted member to act as *indoctrination petty officer* (IPO). The IPO is responsible for administering the ship's *Orientation and Indoctrination Program* to you, and for monitoring your

Figure 20-1. Duty aboard a Coast Guard cutter is an exciting opportunity.

progress as you take your important place in the ship's company. The IPO will provide you with an Orientation and Indoctrination Sheet, which will be used to document your completion of the various steps of your training. As well as the technical aspects of a ship's operation, the program will provide new "hands" very useful information on many subjects, including:

History and mission of the ship
Ship's routine and regulations
Personnel procedures
Education services
Career benefits
Legal services
Morale and religious services
Minority affairs and human relations
Drug and alcohol abuse
Medical and dental services
Safety
Security
Vehicle regulations

Organization and Regulations Manual/Shipboard Regulations Manual

Aboard ship, order is understandably important, and because of the great need for efficiency in all our operations, Coast Guard regulations prescribe a standard organization to ensure each ship is organized in a way efficient and meaningful to its mission. This organization is detailed for each type of Coast Guard ship in a publication called the *Organization and Regulations Manual*. The specific regulations that support the organization of Coast Guard ships of all types are detailed in another Coast Guard publication, the *Shipboard Regulations Manual*.

The *Organization and Regulations Manual* and the *Shipboard Regulations Manual* provide ship's personnel with a ready source of information about their duties and responsibilities for administering, operating, living in, and fighting the ship. Because commanding officers may modify these regulations to some extent to meet specific needs of the ship, you will be required to familiarize yourself with your ship's particular *Organization and Regulations Manual*. This will normally be accomplished in the initial stage of your orientation and indoctrination. Pay careful attention as you read it, and ask the IPO any questions you may have about the information it contains, for you will be required to sign a form stating that you have read and you *understand* this very important publication.

SHIPBOARD ORGANIZATION

Commanding Officer

The officer ordered to command a ship is always called the "captain," regardless of actual rank. The *commanding officer* is responsible for the operation and efficiency of the ship and the conduct and performance of the crew. The commanding officer enforces all regulations and directives from higher authority. All authority, command direction, and responsibility for the command rests with the commanding officer. In practice, the commanding officer delegates duties for carrying out functions of the ship to the executive officer, department heads, other officers, and certain crew members.

Executive Officer

The officer ordered as assistant to the commanding officer is the *executive officer* ("exec" or "XO"). The executive officer is next in the chain of command below the captain. The XO is in charge of the personnel, routine, and discipline of the ship. Department heads may consult directly with the captain, but the executive officer must be informed of any decisions the captain makes.

Command Enlisted Adviser

The senior enlisted assigned to a unit is the command enlisted adviser (CEA). He or she functions as an adviser to the commanding officer on matters relating to the welfare of enlisted personnel. While the CEA does not replace the chain of command, issues that cannot be resolved in the normal manner should be brought to his or her attention.

Departments and Divisions

Coast Guard ships are organized, under a commanding officer and an executive officer, into at least three *departments*: operations, engineering, and deck or weapons. Depending upon the size and type of ship, there may also be a supply department, medical department, and, if a helicopter detachment is assigned, an aviation department. These departments are subdivided into *divisions*; the smaller the department, the fewer the divisions. Each department is directed by a commissioned, warrant, or petty officer called the *department head*, who is assigned by the commanding officer. Similarly, each division is headed by a *division officer* or petty officer. In small ships, an officer may head two departments, or be a division officer as well as a department head. The department head, assisted by the division officers, represents the commanding officer in all matters pertaining to the department and is responsible to the commanding officer for the general condition of the department. All members in a department make requests to the executive officer through the division officer and the department head.

Operations Department

The officer in charge of the operations department is the *operations officer*. As you might expect, the operations officer is responsible for the operation of the ship at its missions, and for handling operational and combat intelligence. The operations officer may be assisted by division officers such as the *navigator, communications officer, electronics material officer*, and *combat information center officer*.

Figure 20-2. Engineering spaces aboard modern cutters are efficient and well organized.

Navigator

The navigator is responsible to the commanding officer for the safe navigation of the ship. The navigator reports first to the commanding officer and then to the operations officer on all matters having to do with navigation. The navigator is responsible for the proper condition of all charts and instruments and the steering equipment of the ship.

Communications Officer

The communications officer is responsible for all exterior communications, including electronic and visual signals. The communications officer oversees the handling of all official messages to and from the ship, and ensures proper communications security is employed by the ship's communicators.

Electronics Material Officer

The electronics material officer is responsible for the material readiness of all electronic equipment on board.

Combat Information Center (CIC) Officer

The combat information center officer is responsible for the operation and readiness of the CIC. The CIC collects, displays, evaluates, and distributes tactical information, such as surface or air radar contacts.

Engineering Department

The officer in charge of the ship's engineering plant is the engineer officer ("EO"). The engineer is responsible for the propulsion plant, auxiliary machinery, all related systems, hull repairs, and damage control. The engineer officer may be assisted by division officers such as the *main propulsion assistant, auxiliary officer,* and *damage control officer* or *assistant.*

Deck Department

The officer in charge of the deck department is the first lieutenant. The first lieutenant is responsible for all deck and ordnance equipment and for upkeep and cleanliness of parts of the ship not assigned to other departments. The first lieutenant handles ground tackle, mooring lines, rigging, towing gear, and all boats. The first lieutenant may be assisted by a *weapons officer*, who is responsible for armament and ammunition. On high endurance cutters, this function is performed by the *weapons or combat systems department*, of which the deck *division* is normally a part.

Officer of the Deck (Day)

There is much activity aboard a ship even when it is quietly moored in a safe harbor. It is impossible for the captain and the executive officer to stay awake day and night supervising all operations of each watch. Hence it is necessary that there be an officer to act as a central clearing station and keep the daily happenings organized. This officer must have the ability and authority to act immediately in an emergency.

When the ship is under way, it is even more important that all operations be under the control of an officer of the watch. The engineroom watch cannot be expected to know whether the ship should suddenly be stopped, slowed, or speeded up. The lookouts, observing an object in the water, cannot run to the bridge and tell the helmsman which way to turn. There must be an officer constantly on watch to receive the incoming reports, act on some of them immediately, and decide what others should be referred to the captain, executive officer, or other officer. At sea, the officer so in charge of each watch is known as the *officer of the deck* (OOD); in port, this officer is identified as the *officer of the day*.

The OOD is the officer on watch in charge of the ship. The OOD is responsible for the safety of the ship, and every person on board who is subject to the captain's orders, except the executive officer, is likewise subject to the orders of the OOD. Only the captain and the executive officer are superior to the officer carrying out the duties of the OOD.

At sea, the OOD takes station on the bridge. In port, the OOD is stationed on the quarterdeck or at the main gangway, depending on the construction of the ship and the decision of the commanding officer as to the limits of the quarterdeck.

All the ship's company must cooperate fully with the OOD in the performance of that duty, and the OOD's orders must be obeyed quickly and respectfully.

Engineering Officer of the Watch

The *engineering officer of the watch* (EOOW) is the officer on watch in charge of the ship's main propulsion plant and the associated

Figure 20-3. The main propulsion area of a modern cutter.

auxiliaries. The EOOW ensures that the engineering log, the engineer's bell book, and the prescribed operating records are properly kept, and that all orders received from the OOD are promptly and properly executed.

The EOOW may be directed in the duties of the watch by the engineering officer (EO) or the main propulsion assistant (MPA), either of whom may assume charge of the watch if they consider such action necessary. The EOOW reports to the OOD and to the engineering officer any defects of machinery, boiler, or auxiliaries that may affect the proper operation of the ship. The EOOW ensures that frequent inspections of engines, machinery, and boilers are made and that all safety precautions are observed.

Collateral Duties

Some jobs aboard ship are not assigned directly to the executive officer or to department heads. These are known as collateral duties and may be assigned to any individual aboard ship, who then acts as an assistant to the executive officer. Collateral duties may include educational services, commissary and crew's mess, property accounting, and supply.

Boards and Committees

A board or committee is a group of ship's personnel organized under a leader to inspect, deliberate, and evaluate a function, situation, or problem. Officers, and in some cases enlisted personnel, are assigned to boards and committees by the commanding officer or executive officer. Some examples of such groups are

Formal Survey Board
Morale Committee
Planning Board for Training
Exchange Audit Board

Watch Organization and Logkeeping

A ship in commission *always* has personnel up, about, and actively engaged in the operation or oversight of the ship. These many different duties are organized into periods called *watches*. Watches and related logkeeping are discussed in chapter 21.

Shipboard Bills

A commanding officer sets forth detailed written instructions for assigning personnel to duties or stations within the ship for the purpose of executing every specific operational job (*evolution*) or administrative function that carries out or supports the ship's missions. Each such instruction is called a *bill* and systematically describes the "who," "what," "where," "when," and "why" for every evolution and function performed by the ship. The *Organization and Regulations Manual* for each ship describes *administrative bills, operational bills, emergency bills,* and *special bills.* Additionally, two documents devoted to organizing and assigning members of the ship's company that are common to all ships, but not included in the *Organization and Regulations Manual,* are the *battle bills* and the *Watch, Quarter, and Station Bill*; these are individually developed by each command.

Administrative Bills

Administrative bills set forth procedure for the everyday administration of the ship and its company. Examples include:

- Personnel Assignment Bill
- Cleaning, Preservation, and Maintenance Bill
- Damage Control Inspection and Maintenance Bill

- Material Conditions of Readiness Bill
- Berthing and Locker Bill
- Security Bill
- Zone Material Inspection Bill
- Crew Recall Bill

Operational Bills

Operational bills detail procedure and specific assignments of crew members for evolutions of a periodic nature. Such bills may include:

- Boat Bill
- Cold Weather Bill
- Darken Ship Bill
- Aircraft Ditch and Rescue Bill
- Drydocking and Undrydocking Bill
- Fuel Transfer and Loading Bill
- Heavy Weather Bill
- Helicopter Operations Bill
- Hurricane/Typhoon Preparedness Bill
- Law Enforcement Bill
- Navigation Bill and Navigation Standards
- Pollution Control Bill
- Search and Rescue Bill
- Replenishment at Sea Bill
- Rescue of Survivors Bill
- Rescue and Assistance Bill
- Ship's Silencing Bill
- Special Sea and Anchor Detail Bill
- Towing Bill
- Visit and Search, Boarding, and Custody Crew Bill

Emergency Bills

Emergency bills detail procedures and specific assignment of the ship's company to perform a critical evolution where there is danger of injury or loss of life, damage to or loss of important material, or damage to the ship itself:

- General Emergency Bill (e.g., collision, grounding, abandon ship)
- Man Overboard Bill

- Chemical, Biological, and Radiological Defense Bill
- Emergency Destruction of Classified Material Bill

Battle Bills

The battle bills provide the information necessary for all hands to fight the ship efficiently. These bills include:

- Officer Assignments to Battle Stations Bill
- Officer Succession to Command Bill
- Enlisted Assignments to Battle Stations Bill
- Battle Messing Bill
- Casualty Treatment and Collection Stations Bill
- General Degrees of Readiness—Personnel Assignments Bill

Special Bills

Special bills detail procedures and specific assignments of crew members for evolutions of an irregular nature, or for evolutions unique to special or unusual mission assignments for the ship:

- Anti-Sneak/Anti-Swimmer Attack Bill
- Civilian Evacuation Bill
- Prisoners and Prisoners of War Bill

Watch, Quarter, and Station Bill (WQS)

The watch, quarter, and station bill is actually an amplification of the bills discussed above, inasmuch as it displays in one place the duties of each crew member in the emergency and battle bills, and for each watch condition. The WQS also shows each member's duties in some or all of the ship's administrative and operational bills.

Billets and Billet Numbers

The ship's company is organized for bills by assigning each member to a *billet*—a set of duties. Because it would be impossible to place enough crew members aboard ship so that each person could have only one duty supporting one bill, each crew member is assigned a group of duties that provide them a part in most, if not all, of the ship's bills. Every billet is identified by a *billet number*. This number is the same on each bill. A billet number consists of four digits, or a letter followed by three digits. The first digit or letter may, depending upon the size of the ship's company, indicate the member's department or division, the second the section, and the third and fourth the member's seniority within the section. A member whose billet number is OH-103 is in the operations department, and in the first section, and is the third most senior member in the section. The last digit may also indicate port or starboard watch, odd or even, when a two-section watch condition is in effect for the ship. When reporting aboard, you will be provided with a billet slip by your division officer or department head. This slip will list your billet number and duties for the various ship's bills. The skills required of some or all of these duties or stations may be provided you within the scope of the ship's orientation and indoctrination program, or by means of the Personnel Qualification Standard (PQS) system included in the ship's training program. In either case, it is ultimately your responsibility to learn and know your station and duties for each bill *thoroughly*.

Ship's Bell

The passage of time is marked by the striking of the ship's bell at the end of each half hour of the watch period. The bell is struck an increasing number of times, so that it is struck once at the end of the first half hour, twice at the end of the first hour, and so on to eight times at the end of the fourth hour. After eight bells are struck, the sequence starts all over again, with an odd number of bells marking a half hour, and an even number marking an hour. For the relation between time, bells, and watches, see the table below:

midwatch		morning watch		forenoon watch		afternoon watch		evening watch		night watch	
time	bells	time	bells	time	bells	time	bells	time	bells	time	bells
0030	1	0430	1	0830	1	1230	1	1630	1	2030	1
0100	2	0500	2	0900	2	1300	2	1700	2	2100	2
0130	3	0530	3	0930	3	1330	3	1730	3	2130	3
0200	4	0600	4	1000	4	1400	4	1800	4	2200	4
0230	5	0630	5	1030	5	1430	5	1830	5	2230	5
0300	6	0700	6	1100	6	1500	6	1900	6	2300	6
0330	7	0730	7	1130	7	1530	7	1930	7	2330	7
0400	8	0800	8	1200	8	1600	8	2000	8	2400 (0000)	8

Standard Routine

As discussed earlier in this chapter, the *Organization and Regulations Manual* for each ship type provides each captain with a somewhat flexible standard for organizing the ship and its company. The routines provided as examples below may vary *greatly* from those published for many ships, based upon each commanding officer's desires, the specific ship's type and administration, and the local situation:

Time	Daily routine in port
0345	Relieve the midwatch.
0500	Call the galley force.
0530	Call the relief for the two-hour watches.
0545	Call the OOD, master-at-arms (MAA), messcooks, and other early risers.

At five minutes before sunrise—stand by lights.
At sunrise—secure aircraft warning, deck, and in-port standing lights.

Figure 20-4. The daily routine aboard a cutter ensures smooth operations and efficient utilization of time.

0545	Relieve the watch.
0600	Reveille. Up all hands.
	Liberty expires for messcooks.
0615	Scrub down weather decks. Wipe down deckhouses with fresh water. Sweep down compartments.
	MAA report "crew turned out" to the OOD.
0630	Morning meal.
0715	Secure from morning meal.
0745	Liberty expires.
0745	Relieve the watch.
0755	Quarters for muster.
	Report approach of eight o'clock to the captain.
	First call to colors.
0800	Colors (moored or anchored).
	Turn to.
0900	Sick call. OOD is relieved.
1000	Knock off ship's work. Coffee break for the crew. Up all late sleepers.
1015	Secure from coffee break. Turn to ship's work.
1045	Division officers inspect compartments.
1100	Inspection of messcooks and food handlers.
	XO's request and complaint mast.
	Secure the mess deck.
1115	Knock off all hands from work.
	Noon meal for the watch.
1130	Noon meal for crew.
1145	Relieve the watch.
1155	Wind ship's chronometers. Report chronometers wound to the captain; request permission to strike eight bells.
1200	Test the general alarms and whistle.
1230	Secure from noon meal.
1255	Officers' call. All hands fall in for quarters.
1300	Quarters for inspection and drills.
1350	Secure from drills.
1400	Turn to.
1545	Relieve the watch.
1600	Clean sweepdown fore and aft. Empty all trash receptacles.
1630	Liberty for all hands.
1645	Evening meal for all hands.

One hour before sunset—electrician test anchor, gangway, and deck lights, and searchlights.

Five minutes before sunset—first call to colors, stand by ensign and jack, stand by anchor and deck lights.

Sunset—colors (moored or anchored). Energize lights.

1900	Set material condition YOKE about the ship.
1945	Muster eight o'clock reports.
	Muster restricted personnel.
1945	Relieve the watch.
1955	Report the ship secure to the commanding officer.
2000	Strike eight bells.
2200	Taps. Lights out and silence about the decks.
	Start hourly security patrols.
2330	Call the watch relief.
2345	Relieve the watch.

Time	Daily routine at sea
0150	Relieve the wheel and lookout.
0330	Call the relief watch.
0345	Relieve the watch; relieve the wheel and lookout.
0500	Call the galley force.
0545	Call the MAA, messcooks, and other early risers.

Five minutes before sunrise—stand by the running lights.

Sunrise—secure running lights.

0550	Relieve the wheel and lookout.
0600	Reveille, up all hands. Trice up racks.
	Announce weather.
	Boatswain's mate of the watch (BMOW) secures hourly rounds.
0630	Turn to field day. Scrub down weather decks.
	Wipe down deckhouses with fresh water. Sweep down compartments.
	MAA report "crew turned out" to OOD.
0700	Knock off field day.
	Morning meal for all hands.
	Publish uniform of the day.

0745	Relieve the watch. Relieve the wheel and lookout.
	Boat crew of the watch to muster.
0755	Report the approach of eight o'clock to the captain.
	Request permission to strike eight bells.
0800	Turn to ship's work.
0950	Relieve the wheel and lookout.
1000	Up all late sleepers.
	CO's material inspection (Saturday only).
1045	Division officers inspect compartments.
1100	Inspection of messcooks and food handlers.
	Report mast.
	Request and complaint mast.
1115	Knock off the relief watch from work.
	Noon meal for the watch.
	Knock off all hands from work. Clean sweepdown fore and aft.
1130	Noon meal for crew.
1145	Relieve the watch.
	Relieve the wheel and lookout.
	Boat crew of the watch to muster.
1155	Wind ship's chronometers. Report chronometers wound to captain. Request permission to strike eight bells.
1200	Test the general alarms and whistle.
1255	Officers' call. All hands fall in for quarters.
1300	Quarters for inspections and drills.
1330	Secure relief wheel and lookout from drills.
1350	Relieve the wheel and lookout.
	Secure from drills.
1400	Turn to ship's work.
1545	Relieve the watch. Relieve the wheel and lookout.
	Boat crew of the watch to muster.
1600	Knock off ship's work. Clean sweepdown fore and aft.
1630	Evening meal for all hands.
1750	Relieve the wheel and lookout.

One hour before sunset—electrician test the running lights and searchlight.

Five minutes before sunset—stand by running lights.

Thirty minutes after sunset—division officers verify that designated material condition is set.

1945	Eight o'clock reports. Department petty officers report the department areas secure for the night to their department heads, who in turn report the department secure to the executive officer.
1945	Relieve the watch. Relieve the wheel and lookout. Boat crew of the watch to muster.
1955	Executive officer reports the vessel secure for the night to the captain. Report approach of eight o'clock. Obtain permission to strike eight bells.
2000	Movie call.
2150	Relieve the wheel and lookout.
2200	Taps. Lights out and silence about the decks.
2315	Midwatch rations served on the mess deck.
2330	Call the relief watch.
2345	Relieve the watch. Relieve the wheel and lookout. Boat crew of the watch to muster.

Holiday routine

Some variation from the daily ship's routine is employed, when possible, on weekends and designated holidays, and when otherwise authorized by the commanding or executive officer. *Holiday routine* includes a later reveille, extended galley hours, and the cessation of nonessential ship's work for crew members not on watch at sea or in the duty section in port.

Plan of the Day

The executive officer prepares and issues daily a plan of the day, which includes such things as:

The schedule of the routine, and any variations or additions.

The orders of the day, detailing drills, training schedule, duty section, liberty sections, working parties, time and location of movies, etc.

Notices of matters to be brought to the attention of officers and crew.

Reprints of regulations and orders to be brought to the attention of officers and crew.

Copies of the plan of the day are distributed to the OOD, all offices, officers, and division bulletin boards of the ship. *Everyone* is responsible for knowing what is in the plan of the day, as any instruction or direction it provides constitutes an official order.

The plan of the day is carried out by the OOD and the division officers unless modified by the authority of the captain or the executive officer. In case of necessity, the OOD may make immediate changes and report that action later to the executive officer.

Passing the Word

In the case of certain emergency situations, special signals are employed, such as the general alarm for battle, the collision alarm, and the chemical-attack alarm. The main reliance for passing the word is placed on the loudspeaker system, when installed. This system consists of a transmitter on the bridge and others at selected spots. Speakers are located at useful and conventional places throughout the ship. Most ships also have a 21-MC or "Captain's Command" circuit, which consists of several transmitter-receiver units similar to an office intercommunication system. When this system is used, there is always an instrument on the bridge, one in the cabin, and one in the wardroom. There are usually at least three other command circuit transmitter-receiver stations on the ship.

The Boatswain's Pipe

Even though there are loudspeakers and intercommunication systems on modern ships, the boatswain's (pronounced "bosun's") pipe is sometimes used for calling and passing the word. The purpose of these calls is:

Purpose

- To command silence before passing an order or information.
- To call all hands' attention.
- To call away a boat; also to call a division or divisions to quarters.

- To assemble the boatswain's mates; also to rouse quick notice or attention from a working group.
- To announce meals.
- To signal that official personages are coming aboard or departing.

Tattoo and Taps

Tattoo is the signal for all hands to turn in and keep silence about the decks. Taps is sounded five minutes after tattoo except when circumstances warrant a longer delay.

Special Sea Detail

In getting under way or entering port, a ship has a *special sea detail*. This detail consists of the stationing of various ship's personnel at locations necessary throughout the ship to moor and unmoor the ship. The special sea detail is set about one half hour before getting under way, and remains there until the ship clears the harbor; or it may be set before entering port and remain so until the ship is properly docked or anchored. Special sea-detail duty takes precedence over everything else for each member of the detail assigned to it.

Sea Watch

Once the ship has cleared the harbor, the special sea detail is relieved and the *sea watch* is stationed or *set*; that is, the cruising watches begin, and the regular sections of the watch take over their prescribed duties.

Smoking Aboard Ship

Smoking is permitted only on the weather decks as authorized by the commanding officer.

Lights

All lights, except those in the cabin, offices, officers' quarters, and those designated as "standing lights," are extinguished at tattoo.

The lights on the lower decks are reduced in number before tattoo unless they are required for the comfort of the crew. All lights in the

Figure 20-5. Bridge equipment aboard CGC *Bear.*

holds, storerooms, and orlops (lowest decks) and all open lights in the ship, except those in officers' quarters, are, in some ships, extinguished before 1930 or at the time of evening inspection by the executive officer.

During the night, a sufficient number of lights throughout the open part of the ship, generally red in color to preserve night-vision capability, are kept lighted to enable the officers and crew to turn out, to get to the upper decks, or to attend to any duty arising from an emergency. These are knows as "standing lights."

Such lights and fires as the captain may deem dangerous are extinguished when the magazines are opened or when handling or passing powder, explosives, or other combustibles.

In time of war or when necessary to conceal a ship from an enemy, only such lights are used as are deemed advisable by the senior officer present.

Eight O'clock Reports

Each evening, the heads of departments assure themselves as to the condition of security and readiness of their departments. At 1945, the department heads or their representatives muster and report their finding as to the condition of the ship to the executive officer (under way) or the officer of the day (in port). Under way, the executive officer in turn passes these reports to the captain. Thus at the end of each day, the captain, the executive officer, and all department heads are aware of the exact state of the entire ship.

Visitors

There are two types of visitation: routine visiting and general visiting. Routine visiting means the everyday, informal visits of friends. General visiting occurs on days such as Armed Forces Day, when the ship is open to the public.

Routine visiting. Members of the crew may have civilian visitors aboard ship after working hours on weekdays, and on Saturdays, Sundays, and holidays during the hours specified within ship's regulations. A member of the crew who has guests must meet them at the gangway and escort them at all times while they are on board or within the shipyard. The OOD must be advised of the impending presence of all routine visitors. In the event of sickness or accident to any visitor, a report must be made immediately to the OOD. Guests are permitted only in the spaces authorized by the commanding officer, and may be subject to other restrictions as the commanding officer may direct.

General visiting. Each ship lays out a plan for handling visitors—the general public as well as United States and foreign dignitaries who may be expected on days of open ship. Prior to visiting hours the word is passed, such as "Rig ship for general visiting. All hands shift into uniform of the day." While visitors are on board, all officers and crew must remain alert that no visitors be permitted in an unauthorized part of the ship, that no visitors endanger themselves, and that all guests be treated with special courtesy.

Pets

Pets are not generally allowed aboard ship. A pet may be adopted as a ship's mascot only by direct authorization of the commanding officer.

Officers' Quarters and Bridge

Crew members are allowed on the quarterdeck only when on duty. This is also true of officers' country (wardroom and staterooms), and the bridge, wheelhouse, and charthouse. Personnel should uncover entering the cabin or wardroom; conversely, all personnel should remain covered on the bridge.

Prisoners at Large (PAL)

For certain reasons, personnel may be denied liberty or leave. Such members may not leave the ship without specific authority of the executive officer. This group includes those who are:

- Confined to the limits of the ship by sentence of court-martial.
- Awaiting trial by, or approval of, court-martial.
- Awaiting mast for serious cases (designated PAL by the commanding officer).
- Restricted to the ship by punishment assigned at mast.
- On report and awaiting mast for other than serious offenses, but not yet made PAL by order of the commanding officer.
- On the medical restricted list.

Restricted Personnel

These are personnel under restraint according to the Uniform Code of Military Justice (UCMJ). They are either under *restriction* or *under arrest.*

Restriction is a restraint of the same nature as arrest, imposed under similar circumstances and by the same authorities, but it does not involve the suspension of military duties.

Arrest is the moral restraint of a member, by an order, oral or written, to certain specified limits pending disposition of charges against the individual. It is not imposed as punishment, and it relieves the member of all military duties other than normal cleaning and policing.

Liberty

Normally, liberty commences at 1600 or 1630 daily and expires on board at 0745 the following day. Liberty is normally granted to three-quarters or two-thirds of the crew, depending upon circumstances.

Personnel on continuous running watches, such as radiomen aboard some ships, may be granted liberty commencing at 1400 if the head of the department requests it for them.

Special liberty will be granted only for good reasons. A request for such liberty must be made on a form provided, signed by the division officer and the head of the department, and delivered to the executive officer's office prior to 1000. The request, marked "approved" or "disapproved" will be returned to the requesting member.

Liberty may be exchanged in special cases if a member obtains a volunteer relief from someone in the member's division who rate liberty. Such a relief, called a *standby*, must be of similar rating or with similar qualifications. The member desiring liberty submits a written request to the member's division officer. If the division officer approves, the request is delivered to the executive officer for final action.

Liberty may be granted more frequently in commands that have enough personnel to allow it and still maintain security. Remember, liberty is an earned privilege, not a right.

Meritorious liberty. Extra liberty may be granted to personnel for superior conduct, performance of duty, or achievement.

QUARTERS FOR MUSTER AND INSPECTION

Division Parades

Each division is assigned a parade—a space on deck where division personnel assemble for quarters or inspection. The fair-weather parades are on the uncovered decks; the foul-weather parades are on the covered decks and in the living spaces as designated.

Where possible, the departments form with all divisions facing inboard. Divisions that are aligned athwartships face forward if in the forward part of the ship and aft if in the after part.

Mustering the Divisions

At the command *FALL IN*, each section forms in line. Section leaders muster the sections while the division is being formed. When the division is formed, the division leading petty officer commands *REPORT*.

The section leaders in succession from front to rear, without moving from their assigned positions, report, "All present or accounted for," or "All present or accounted for with exception of (identity of absentees)."

The division leading petty officer commands 1. DRESS RIGHT, 2. DRESS. After dressing the division the division petty officer commands 3. READY 4. FRONT. The division leading petty officer posts in front of the division, faces the division officer, salutes, relays the report of the division to the division officer, and, without command, faces about and moves by the most direct route to post on the right flank of the front rank of the division.

The division officer proceeds with the inspection of the division. After the inspection, the division officer leaves the division in charge of the junior division officer and falls in with other division officers to report to the executive officer.

Division Inspections

Ranks are opened for inspection unless the division parade space is too limited. The division officer posts on the right flank of the front rank. Upon the approach of the inspecting officer, the division officer presents the division by executing the hand salute and reporting, "Sir/ma'am, the division is ready for inspection."

The inspecting officer inspects the division rank by rank, in succession, passing from right to the left along the front of each rank, and from the left to right along the rear of each rank.

Preparing for inspection. The command PREPARE FOR IN-SPECTION is issued by the executive officer or department heads. The division officer or the leading petty officer of each division, posting at center and facing the division, commands 1. OPEN RANKS, 2. MARCH. At the command MARCH, the front rank takes two steps forward, halts, and executes dress right; the second rank takes one step forward, halts, and executes dress right; the third rank stands fast and executes dress right, and the fourth rank, if any, takes two back steps, halts, and executes dress right. The officer in charge aligns each rank in succession, moves three paces beyond the right flank of the front rank, halts, faces to the left, and commands 3. READY, 4. FRONT.

To close ranks, the commands are 1. CLOSE RANKS, 2. MARCH. At the command MARCH, the front rank stands fast; the second rank takes one step forward and halts, the third rank takes two steps forward and halts, and the fourth rank, if any, takes three steps forward and halts. Each element covers their file leader.

To form for inspection, where the restricted space of the parade does not permit normal opening of ranks, the command is FORM FOR INSPECTION, CLOSE DISTANCE. The division stands fast and, upon the approach of the inspecting officer, is presented to the inspecting officer in the standard manner.

When the front of the first rank has been inspected from right to left by the inspecting officer, the division officer commands 1. FIRST RANK ONE PACE FORWARD, 2. MARCH. The rear of the first rank is inspected from left to right, followed by the inspection of the front of the second rank from right to left. The same procedure is followed for the second, third, and fourth ranks.

General Muster (All hands aft)

The general muster or dress parade (sometimes called "all hands aft") is a massed formation of the ship's company at a designated place. Dress parade is formed with standard close-order drill commands, though with some variation from ship to ship.

Enlisted Details

Many jobs involving work and responsibilities are not covered by any particular rating description. Such duties may involve responsibility for a division's damage-control fittings and equipment and the orderliness of ship's berthing and messing spaces. Personnel may be detailed to these jobs by a division officer, department head, or the executive officer.

Inspections

Inspections are made on a daily, weekly, monthly, quarterly, semiannual, annual, and as-required basis. They are made to verify the material, administrative, and operational readiness of the ship to perform its missions and related functions.

Daily Inspection

At quarters for muster, division officers check their personnel for general appearance and cleanliness. They also make frequent inspections of the spaces, equipment, and supplies that belong to their division. Heads of departments, either by personal or delegated inspections, ensure that all aspects of their departments are in proper condition or that steps are being taken to make them so.

The executive officer likewise is required to make frequent inspections; usually the XO inspects a different part of the ship each day. Division officers and department heads, or their representatives, are required to inspect all parts of their respective departments each day as far as may be feasible.

Captain's Material Inspection

Captain's material inspection is usually held on Friday in port, and on Saturday mornings when under way, and consists of a formal

Figure 20-6. Sleeping quarters aboard CGC *Bear*.

inspection of the ship by the commanding officer or the commanding officer's delegates.

Personnel Inspection

Normally conducted once a month, personnel inspection is conducted by the commanding officer or the commanding officer's delegates to ensure that all members of the ship's company are in compliance with established uniform and grooming standards.

General Mess

At least once daily, the OOD or assistant inspects the general mess and samples a ration to determine that it is wholesome and properly served.

Messcooks

Messcooks and food handlers are inspected daily by the chief master-at-arms (CMAA) or the OOD, and weekly by the medical officer or the medical officer's assistant.

Locker Inspection

Locker inspection usually is made by the division officer, but may be combined with another inspection. Such an inspection, normally conducted for personnel E-5 and below, is to determine that each has a complete uniform outfit, properly marked, cleaned, and stowed.

Change of Command

When the commanding officer of a ship is to be relieved, the commanding officer makes a thorough inspection of the ship—personnel, material, and administration—in company with the incoming commanding officer.

Customs and Health Inspections

When a ship returns to the United States from foreign waters, the ship is liable to inspection by United States customs and health authorities to ensure that no unauthorized or contraband items are on board and that no contagious or communicable diseases are among the crew. These inspections can be routine, but inspectors can turn a ship "upside down" if they have cause to suspect that anything is being hidden.

CHAPTER 21

Shipboard Watches

For the proper performance of duty, every unit in the Coast Guard—whether a 17-person crew of a 140 foot icebreaking tug or the entire crew of a high-endurance cutter—must be organized. The organization for similar units throughout the service is similar; to make this organization work, routines and duties in similar units are standardized. Even time has been standardized.

In the Coast Guard, as in all military services, routines are based on a 24-hour day. Time is counted in hours—0 to 24—and minutes in each hour—01 to 59. The day begins at midnight, when the time is 0000, and ends with 2359. One minute later, the time is 0000, or midnight, and the next day starts. Aboard ship, the day is also half-hour periods, marked by the ship's bell, and by watches, which regulate the time on and off duty.

Watches

A ship in commission always has part of its crew on watch. Even when she is tied up in port and receiving electricity from the pier or another ship, it is necessary to have crew members on watch for communications, security, and safety. Personnel assigned to watches are called watchstanders. Traditionally, the 24-hour day is divided into seven watches, as follows:

0000–0400—midwatch

Figure 21-1. The basic business of a professional afloat is carrying out the watch routine.

0400–0800—morning watch
0800–1200—forenoon watch
1200–1600—afternoon watch
1600–1800—first dog watch
1800–2000—second dog watch
2000–2400—first watch

The two "dog watches," from 1600 to 1800 and 1800 to 2000, serve to alternate the daily watch routine so that personnel who have the midwatch one night will not have it again on the following night.

Watch may refer to the location of the person on watch, as the *forecastle watch, bridge watch,* or to the section of the ship's crew on duty: "section two has the watch."

Watch Section

Each crew member is assigned to a *section* of the watch. These sections are numbered; small ships usually have three sections, large ships may have four sections. Thus, when the word is passed that the first section (or the second or the third) has the watch, each person in that section immediately reports to his or her assigned watch station. At sea, watches may be either two or four hours in length.

On some ships the divisions may be divided into a *starboard watch* and a *port watch.* Each of these watches is divided into two sections: the odd-numbered sections, 1 and 3, are in the starboard watch; the even-numbered sections, 2 and 4, are in the port watch.

Crew members in a three-section watch are spoken of as having a one-in-three watch; those in a four-section watch have a one-in-four watch, and so on. Thus, a crew member standing a one-in-three is on watch for four hours, off for eight hours, and then back on watch for four more. In all, that person stands eight hours' watch in 24 hours.

Relieving the Watch

Watches must be relieved on time. This does not mean at the exact minute the watch changes, but usually 15 minutes before—in order that the relief can receive information and instructions from the person on watch. Some ships muster the oncoming watch to make sure that each crew member is ready ahead of time.

When reporting directly to the person relieved, an oncoming watchstander says, "I am ready to relieve you." The person on watch passes on any pertinent instruction or information relating to the proper standing of the watch. When relieving watchstanders are sure that they understand conditions and instructions given, they say, "I relieve you." Thereafter they are completely responsible for the watch.

Remember that you must report to the responsible officer (of the deck or engineering watch, for example) that you have been relieved.

Watch Officers

A watch officer is placed in charge of a watch or a portion of a watch. The commanding officer assigns as a watch officer any commissioned or warrant officer who is considered qualified. The CO may, when conditions require, assign a petty officer to such duty. The stations of the officers or petty officers in charge of the watch are where they can best perform their duties and supervise and control the performance of those on watch under them.

Logs

The *deck log* is a complete daily record, by watches, in which are described every circumstance and occurrence of importance or interest that concern the crew and the operation and safety of the ship, or that may be of historical value. The navigator has general responsibility for preparation and care of the deck log. Each OOD, however, is responsible for the proper completion of the log during the OOD's underway or anchor watch or for the entire duty day if in port.

The *quartermaster's* rough log is a record of events occurring during the watch. Entries in this log are made at the time of occurrence or when knowledge of such occurrence is first obtained. The quartermaster's rough log is signed by the quartermaster of the watch on being relieved. It is used in preparing the deck log, also called the smooth log.

Enlisted Watchstanders

The two most interesting aspects of Coast Guard life are what you do and what the unit does. There are literally hundreds of different jobs in a large command, each one important to the mission. Because organization and routine are standardized as much as possible, the jobs you perform are also generally standardized.

A day's work aboard ship, or ashore, involves both professional and military duties. "Turn to ship's work" means that you carry out the professional duties of your rating. During general drills, and when on watch, you may perform both general military assignments and professional duties. The daily routine, at sea, in port, or ashore, also requires crew members on duty at all times as watchstanders.

The following is a listing of the most common enlisted watchstanders, with a brief description of their duties.

Boatswain's Mate of the Watch (BMOW)

The petty officer in charge of the watch is one of the most important enlisted assistants to the OOD. The BMOW's status in these respects is the same regardless of the readiness condition in effect.

At sea, the normal peacetime deck watch for which the boatswain's mate of the watch is responsible consists of the *helmsman, lee helmsman, OOD messenger, lookouts,* and *lifeboat crew of the watch* (also called *ready boat crew*). Besides being a principal enlisted assistant to the OOD, the boatswain's mate of the watch is the watch petty officer. It is the BMOW's responsibility that all deck watch stations are manned, and that all hands in the previous watch are relieved. The BMOW reports to the OOD when the deck watch has been relieved.

Main Engine and Auxiliaries Watches

These watches are stood by qualified personnel in the engineering division, under the supervision of the engineering officer of the watch. These watchstanders ensure that all machinery is properly maintained and operating properly.

Bridge and Signal Watch

When stationed, in addition to their regular duties, bridge and signal watches keep the OOD informed of notable changes in the weather, boats approaching the ship, unusual disturbances or signs of distress in the harbor, and movements of other ships. (See also quartermaster.)

Cold Iron Watch

This watch inspects main machinery spaces that are secured and have no regular watch posted, and reports hourly to the OOD.

Combat Information Center

Watchstanders perform duties under the supervision of the CIC officer and as required by the OOD.

Helmsman

The helmsman steers the ship as directed by the OOD or the conning officer.

Lookouts

Every ship will have at least one lookout. On larger ships, additional lookouts may be stationed, when circumstances demand, on the flying bridge, on the fantail and bow, or elsewhere. Bridge lookouts may report orally to the OOD; others will report via telephone. This is a very important job; it may look to an outsider as if all a lookout has to do is stand around and enjoy the view, but actually it takes considerable skill to stand a good lookout watch, and the safety of the ship may depend on just how well the lookout attends to duties.

The first duty of the lookout is to sight an object and report it. The second duty is to identify it. The report of an object sighted should not be held up until the object is identified. After reporting, the lookout must be certain that the officer of the deck acknowledges the report.

Bridge lookouts. These lookouts, sometimes port and starboard, stand watch in the wings of the bridge or on the flying bridge. They report ships, aircraft, land, or any object sighted, and at night they make half-hourly reports on the ship's running lights.

Forecastle lookout. These lookouts may be stationed during periods of low visibility—fog or snow—and while entering harbor.

Fog lookout. This lookout may be the forecastle lookout. Other fog lookouts may be stationed on the wings of the bridge, to keep watch astern. Their primary job is to listen carefully.

Sky and surface lookouts. On larger ships, when enemy operations are expected, additional lookouts are assigned certain sectors of the sky and surface all around the ship.

Night Lookouts

Crew members regularly assigned to lookout duty will receive special training, but as a preparation they should learn some facts in advance. As is the case with day lookouts, each night lookout should scan the sector slowly and regularly so that no point is skipped. But there are certain differences that must be taken into account. These are based on the fact that a person's eyes work differently at night.

Night vision. Human eyes are adapted to seeing color and distant objects. This is done by light-sensitive nerves in the center of the eye, called cones. Cats and owls, which see well in the dark, cannot see color, but their eyes are sensitive to motion; this is done by nerves around the cones, called rods. Human eyes have rods too, and the way to see at night is not to look directly at an object, because the cones will merely make "spots in front of your eyes," but to look all around an object and give the rods a chance to pick it up.

A simple experiment will help to explain this. Stay in the dark for 15 minutes. Hold your finger up at arm's length, and look steadily at it. It will disappear. Look a little to one side and it will appear again. Keep staring a little to one side and it will be gone again. Move your eyes to the other side and it will reappear. Practice is necessary to learn the trick of seeing things at night without looking directly at them.

Don't sweep the sky or horizon, as you can't see well while your eyes are moving rapidly. Scan the sky or sea slowly, because night eyes are slow in reacting and you may not notice an object until you have looked near it several times.

The eyes can pick up a moving light or object more easily than one that is standing still. When an object appears, move your head from side to side. This will give the object the appearance of movement even though it is barely seen.

It takes practice and care to become a good night lookout. The following rules for using the eyes at night should be followed:

- Don't try working at night until your eyes are dark-adapted. This takes about 20 minutes in darkness or red light.
- Avoid *all* light. If necessary to use a light, use only a dim red light.
- When seeking an object on the horizon at night, always look for it out of the corner of the eye. Practice this constantly.
- Scan the region you are investigating. Be alert for any objects. Practice scanning as much as possible.
- If you must go into a lighted place, either blindfold yourself or wear the red dark-adaptation goggles that are available, which permit you to see without disturbing dark-adaptation.

- Avoid looking at instrument panels that are illuminated, even by red light. Never stare at lighted instruments.
- Use aids, such as night binoculars, as much as possible.
- Keep all your optical equipment clean.
- Don't keep looking at something you've already spotted.
- *Above all,* keep in good physical shape. Fatigue and alcohol seriously hurt night vision.

Anchor and Security Watches

Crew members are assigned to the anchor watch to assist the OOD in such tasks as reporting signs of dragging the anchor, veering chain, or other emergency work. The number of people assigned and their specific duties vary from ship to ship.

A security watch patrols topside and below decks whether at sea or in port. At sea, the BMOW is normally assigned this responsibility. In port, it usually falls upon the messenger, who will make these rounds between taps and reveille.

Messenger

The crew member assigned to the OOD, either on the bridge when under way or on the quarterdeck in port, is commonly called the OOD messenger. The messenger should know the names and locations of the various parts of the ship, department offices, and department heads; names and duties of the various officers and senior enlisted, and where to find various crew members. The messenger must be familiar with standard naval phraseology to understand and repeat messages without error or confusion.

Phone Talker

There may be one or more phone talkers, depending on the ship and the operation. Phone talkers must use correct phone procedure, know all the stations on their circuit, transmit orders to the stations as directed, and inform the OOD of all information received.

Quartermaster of the Watch (In port)

This is one of the most responsible jobs an enlisted person can have.

There should be no confusion as to the official status of these petty officers; they are assistants to the *officers of the deck*, subject only in the performance of their duty to the orders of the commanding officer, executive officer, OOD, and JOOD. The assignment of petty officers as QMOW is made in writing, either in the ship's organization book, in the senior watch officer's watch list, or in the plan of the day. The QMOW (in port) is also called the petty officer of the watch (POOW). This crew member is not necessarily a quartermaster.

Quartermaster of the Watch (Under way)

The *quartermaster of the watch* assists the OOD or conning officer in navigation, supervises the performance of the helmsman, instructs the OOD messenger in calling officers and crew for the watch, reports to the OOD all changes in weather, temperature, and barometer readings, and makes appropriate entries in the ship's log. The QMOW often acts as the JOOD when there are insufficient officers on board.

Radioman of the Watch

This technician maintains required communications in the main radio room, receiving, transmitting, and routing traffic as required.

Sounding and Security Patrol

The sounding and security patrol is a crew member in the engineering department who maintains a continuous patrol of unmanned spaces below decks. The patrol takes periodic soundings of designated tanks and spaces, checks damage-control closures, and is alert for evidence of sabotage, theft, fire, and fire hazards. In addition to making an hourly report to the EOOW or OOD, the patrol frequently relays the report of the *cold iron watch*. Both of these watches are usually manned during nonworking hours at sea and in port.

Late Sleepers

Crew members on watch from 0000 to 0400—the midwatch—have a difficult time getting enough sleep. For this reason, they are permitted to sleep in after "all hands" are called. They are the "late sleepers" referred to in the daily routines.

Standard Commands and Terminology

There is a correct and proper name for everything and a standard form of order or command for everything that is done. Disregard for proper terms or orders may lead to mistakes, confusion, and perhaps disaster.

Commands to the Helmsman

All commands to the helmsman that specify a change in course or heading will refer to the compass by which the helmsman is steering, and will give the new course or heading in degrees: "Come left to course two seven zero," or "Steer zero zero five." The helmsmen repeat most commands that are given to be sure they understand them. Only the following commands are used:

Right (left) standard rudder. Put the rudder over to the right (left) the specified number of degrees necessary for the ship to make its standard tactical diameter.

Right (left) full rudder. Put the rudder over to the right (left) the specified number of degrees necessary for the ship to make its reduced tactical diameter.

Right (left) five (ten, etc.) degrees rudder. Turn the wheel to right (left) until the rudder is placed at the number of degrees ordered. (This command is used in making changes of course. The helmsman would then be ordered to steer the new course by such command as, "Steady on course _____," in time to permit the helmsman to meet it on the new course. The complete command would be, for example, "Right five degrees rudder. Steady on course two seven five.")

Right (left) handsomely. Turn the rudder a small amount. (The command is given when a very slight change of course is desired.)

Increase your rudder to _____ degrees. Increase the rudder angle. (Given with the rudder already over, when it is desired to make the ship turn more rapidly. The command must be followed by the exact number of degrees of rudder desired.)

Ease your rudder to _____ degrees. Decrease the rudder angle. (Given when the ship, turning with right (left) rudder, is turning toward or nearing the heading desired. The command can be given, for example, "Ease to fifteen.")

Meet her. Use rudder as may be necessary to check the ship's turn. (Given when the ship is nearing the desired course.)

Steady, or steady as you go. Steer the course on which the ship is heading when the command is received. (Given when, in changing course, the new course is reached or the ship is heading as desired. The helmsman responds, "Steady as you go. Course ———— , sir/ma'am.")

Rudder amidships. Rudder angle zero. (Given when the ship is turning, and it is desired to make her swing less rapidly.)

Shift your rudder. Change from right to left rudder (or vice versa) an equal amount.

Mind your helm. A warning that the ship is swinging off the course because of bad steering. It is also a command to steer exactly, using less rudder.

Nothing to the left (right) of ————. The helmsman is not to steer to the left (right) of the course ordered.

How is your rudder. A question to the helmsman. The helmsman should reply, "Five (ten, fifteen, etc.) degrees right (left)," or "Full (standard) right (left) rudder, sir/ma'am."

Mark your head. A question. The helmsman should give the ship's head at the time; for example, "Two seven five, sir/ma'am."

Keep her so. A command given when the helmsman reports the ship's heading and it is desired to steady her on that heading.

Very well. Given after a report by the helmsman to let the helmsman know that the OOD understands the situation.

Come right (left) to ————. Put over the rudder right (left) and steady on new course.

Command. Given by the helmsman when the command from the OOD is unclear or misunderstood.

Lookout Reports

The proper way for a lookout to let others know exactly where an object is requires that the lookout give its direction with reference to the bow of the lookout's ship, that is, by means of *relative bearings*. To locate surface objects, only the direction and the range or distance from the ship need be given. To locate aircraft, the direction and the elevation, or height above water, are required. The elevation is known as the *position angle*.

In reporting objects, a strict form of wording is used. First the object is named: "ship," "buoy," "discolored water," "floating log," "periscope wake," "aircraft." If the object cannot be identified, the lookout says "object." Next, the direction is given as explained below. Last, if the object is a surface craft, the range is given; if an aircraft, the elevation, or position angle, is given.

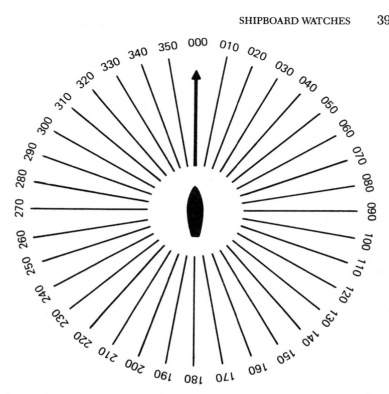

Figure 21-2. Relative bearings, measured clockwise from the ship's head, locate an object in relation to the ship. They have nothing to do with geographical directions.

Thus, a full report on a surface object would go something like this:

"*Buoy*" (the object); "*zero niner zero*" (the bearing); "*fife hundred*" (the range).

How to report relative bearings and ranges. First, say the word "bearing"; then give the degrees of the bearing in three digits. Correct wording is "Bearing three five zero" and "Bearing zero one zero." There are no "ohs" in relative bearings; only "zeros" are used. The word "bearing" may be omitted.

Do not add the word "degrees." Since the bearing comes first and is always in three digits, the hearer knows that degrees are intended and it is not necessary to say so.

The range is always given in yards. In making estimates it might be useful to remember that 2,000 yards equals one nautical mile. When the range is an even hundred or thousand, it is spoken so: "Range eight hundred (800)," "Range twenty thousand (20,000)."

When the range is below 1,000, and not in even 100s, it is spoken in hundreds and the number of digits. Ciphers are pronounced "zero": "Range nine seven zero (970)."

Where the range is above 1,000 and in even 100s, it is spoken in thousands and hundreds: "Range four seven hundred (4,700)"; "Range five zero two hundred (50,200)"; "Range one one zero six hundred (110,600)."

Where the range is above 1,000 and not in even 100s, it is spoken in number of thousands, the balance given as in ranges below a 1,000: "Range three three five zero (3,350)"; "Range three zero two five zero (30,250)."

Distance of Visibility at Sea

Estimating distances at sea takes practice. The table below will be of assistance. As an example, consider that the eyes of a six-foot person standing on a bridge deck 30 feet above sea level are a little more than 35.5 feet above sea level, so the horizon is 6.8 miles away. But objects high enough to be seen above the horizon can be seen more than 6.8 miles away. A lighthouse 65 feet high has a horizon of 9.2 miles; this means that the person could see the light just at the horizon at a distance of 6.8 + 9.2 miles, or 16 miles.

Height (feet)	Nautical miles	Height (feet)	Nautical miles
1	1.1	31	6.4
5	2.5	35	6.8
10	3.6	40	7.2
15	4.4	45	7.7
20	5.1	50	8.1
25	5.7	75	9.9
30	6.3	100	11.5

Position Angle

The position angle is the height in degrees of an aircraft above the horizon (see figure 21-3). The horizon is zero degrees (0°) and di-

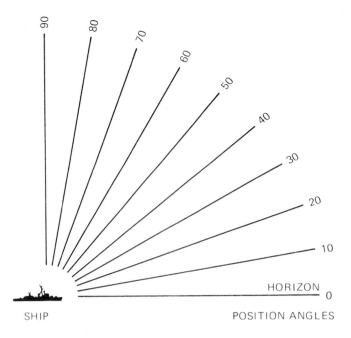

Figure 21-3. Position angles locate an object in the sky. Measure up, not down.

rectly overhead is ninety degrees (90°). For position angles the ordinary way of expressing numbers is used; that is, say "one," "eight," "twenty," "sixty." As with bearings, the word "degrees" is omitted, since the hearer automatically understands that with aircraft, the numerals stated mean degrees of elevation. Examples of reporting position angles are:

08°   "position angle, eight."
10°   "position angle, ten."
30°   "position angle, thirty."

Note that the words "position angle" precede the numerals of the report.

An example of a sighted aircraft report might be:

"Bridge, sky aft, plane, bearing one four five, position angle twenty-five, moving right."

SHIP CONTROL

One of the most important people in a bridge crew is the helmsman, who steers the ship. The helmsman must know the course ordered and the rudder angle required to keep the ship on that course. The helmsman must understand the use of the gyro and magnetic compasses, wheel, and rudder, the principles of steering a ship, and the proper helm commands and responses.

Compass

The magnetic compass consists of a magnetized needle attached to a circular compass card; both are supported on a pivot set in a cast bronze bowl filled with a mixture of alcohol and water. This liquid supports the card and magnet, thus reducing the friction and letting the card turn more easily on the pivot. It also slows the swing of the card and brings it to rest more quickly. The lubber's line marked on the bowl agrees with the fore-and-aft line of the ship. The heading (direction the ship is going) is read from the compass card at the point nearest the lubber's line.

A magnetic compass can be thrown off the correct heading by the attraction of any metal near it. Never go on watch as helmsman carrying a large knife or other metal articles.

Gyrocompass. A gyrocompass is basically a heavy spinning flywheel that, because of the rotation of the earth, will seek a position in which its axis always points true north and south and is unaffected by variation or deviation.

Gyro repeaters. Set to point the same way as the master gyro, these are located in the wheelhouse, steering stations, and on the bridge wings. If the ship has two master gyros, there will be two repeater stands in the steering station, but only one of these will be used. Be certain that you are steering from the repeater in use, and be especially careful not to confuse them.

The course by gyro, when corrected for any slight mechanical error, is always the true course, but the gyro is subject to mechanical and electrical failure. Report to the OOD at once if it stops swinging as the ship's head changes, or if it starts to jump.

Rudder

All ships or boats are steered by one or more rudders at the stern.

When the rudder is moved to one side or the other, the headway of the ship causes water to push against the side of the rudder, creating a force that swings the stern of the ship in the opposite direction. The faster a ship is moving, the greater the pressure against the rudder and the quicker the turning effect. A ship always "answers" its rudder more quickly at high speed than at low speed, and it takes more rudder to turn a slow ship than a fast one. Large rudders are balanced, with part of the rudder forward of the pintle on which it hangs. This is to balance some of the force of the water against the after part, and thus make the rudder easier to turn.

Steering motor. The rudder of a small boat is moved mechanically by rudder ropes (usually of wire) as the wheel turns. Ships have an electric motor that pumps hydraulic fluid through a system that moves the rudder.

Steering sense. Many an inexperienced helmsman gets into trouble when bringing a ship to a new heading, trying to make the compass card turn by turning the ship's wheel. *It won't work!* The compass card floats and is not fast to the compass. The compass stand is fast to the ship; the *lubber's line* moves as the ship moves, and always in the direction the wheel is turned. Remember: turn the wheel the way the bow is to swing; if the wheel turns left, the lubber's line moves left, and the ship turns left; everything moves in the same direction, left, or right, from bow to rudder.

Steering a ship is not as simple as driving an automobile, where control is quick and positive. A ship is heavy, slow to start turning, and sometimes reluctant to stop turning. When it reaches the proper heading, you may have to give it a touch of rudder to finally steady it, and you must get the rudder off it before it starts to swing again.

The most common error is using too much rudder. The new helmsman turns the wheel a few degrees, but nothing happens; it takes a little time before the ship begins to answer the rudder. After a second or two, the helmsman turns the wheel a little more. When the lubber's line reaches the course desired, the helmsman puts the rudder midships, but the ship keeps on going. The helmsman puts on opposite rudder, but has to increase it considerably before the swing stops, and starts again immediately in the other direction with increased speed. Remember, the less rudder you use, the better; much less rudder is required to head off a swing than to stop one that has started.

Have the ship steady on its course before you surrender the wheel to your relief. Don't turn it over in the middle of a swing. Tell your relief the course and which compass or repeater you are steering by. Tell your relief about any steering peculiarity you know of; e.g., "Taking a little right rudder," "Taking mostly left," and so on. Relay any orders you received that still are standing; as, "Nothing to the left," "Steady as you go," etc. Before leaving the steering station, report to the officer of the deck that you have been relieved.

Engine Order Telegraph

Speed orders to the engineroom are handled by an engine order telegraph, which generally has sectors marked AHEAD: FLANK, FULL, STAND (standard) $^2/_3$, $^1/_3$—STOP—BACK: $^1/_3$, $^2/_3$, FULL. A lever, fitted with an indicator, travels over the circular face of the instrument. When moved to the required speed sector, an answering pointer follows to the same sector as soon as the engineroom has complied with the order.

A ship with one engine has a telegraph with a single handle. Two-engine ships generally have a handle on the port side and another on the starboard side of the telegraph. Be sure you grasp the handle for the correct engine. If the answering pointer moves to a line between two sectors, so that you are in doubt about the speed set on the engine, repeat your operation on the lever. Report immediately to the OOD if the pointer does not move as ordered.

Orders to the person operating the engine order telegraph are given in this form: First, the engine to be used, *port* or *starboard*; next, the direction, either *ahead* or *astern*; then the speed, *standard*, *one-third*, etc.

Make sure you have heard an order correctly, and repeat it aloud distinctly before you act, thus: "Starboard engine ahead two-thirds, sir/ma'am." When the answer appears on the pointer from below, sing out "Starboard engine answers ahead two-thirds, sir/ma'am."

Ship Control Console

Ship control consoles provided on new ships have controls for the main engines, the bow-thruster (an athwartships propeller forward to help steer the ship), and the rudder. Indicators are located on the panel to show engine RPMs, direction, and degrees of thrust (on variable-pitch propellers), and rudder angle and direction of the bow-thruster. Commands relating to propeller pitch are given in so many inches or feet of thrust as "zero pitch," twelve inches ahead, twelve astern or any desired pitch. In ships with control consoles, the conning officer usually handles all the controls.

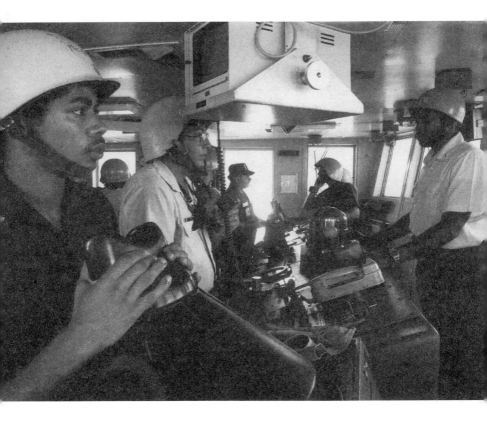

CHAPTER 22

Shipboard Drills and Emergencies

General drills aboard ship are designed to prepare a crew to handle emergencies. At shore stations, drills are based on shipboard practices. By using a standard system of drills throughout the Coast Guard, it is possible for a crew member to move from one ship or unit to another and still know generally what to do in an emergency.

On board ship, a general drill means all hands—everyone. You must know exactly where your station is, and what your job is, for each drill or emergency. This important information is clearly stated on the Watch, Quarter, and Station Bill for each division and is usually posted in the division's living compartment. Your job may be important, or perhaps you may be required only to stand at quarters waiting to be assigned as a relief. No matter what it is, no one is excused from any drill unless permission has been granted by the executive officer through the department head.

General drills develop teamwork so that every crew member in every department, division, and section knows and does exactly what must be done in every emergency. Every job has been assigned for a purpose. By drilling together, the ship's crew develops unity of action and teamwork. For this reason, all hands must participate wholeheartedly in all emergency drills.

All-Hands Drills

All-hands drills are the emergency drills: General Quarters, Fire,

Figure 22-1. *Gallatin*'s OOD discusses simulated battle problems facing the ship with bridge personnel during general quarters.

Man Overboard, Collision, Rescue and Assistance. When the alarm for one of these sounds, go to your station on the double —FORWARD and UP the STARBOARD side, DOWN and AFT the PORT side. Maintain silence; only personnel in charge will speak.

Alarms

General Quarters (GQ)

Sounding of the general alarm plus the words "general quarters" passed twice over the general announcing system. For example, "General quarters! General quarters! All hands man your battle stations."

Fire

Sounding of the general alarm plus the word "Fire" passed twice over the general announcing system, giving class of fire and compartment location. For example, "Fire! Fire! Class Bravo fire in compartment 1-10-3, Paint Locker."

Man Overboard

Word passed twice "Man overboard, man overboard, port (starboard) side," followed by five or more short blasts of the whistle. Do not sound the general alarm as stations for man overboard are normally different from those for GQ.

Collision

Sounding of collision alarm plus words "Collision, port (starboard) side, forward (aft, amidships), all hands brace for collision." After a collision, all hands go to general quarters.

Rescue and Assistance

Word passed over the general announcing system, as appropriate: "Plane crash, port (starboard) side," "Away, the rescue and assistance detail, rescue survivors." Do not sound the GQ alarm.

Emergency Bills

Emergency bills detail procedures and the specific assignment of all hands to perform an evolution on short notice when there is danger of loss of life or of the ship itself.

- General Emergency
- Man Overboard
- Emergency Destruction
- Abandon Ship
- Chemical, Biological, and Radiological Defense

General Emergency

The general emergency bill organizes the crew to handle the effects of a major emergency, such as collision, grounding, explosion, earthquake, storm, or battle damage. It also provides for an orderly process of abandoning ship if necessary, and for salvage of the ship if feasible. It is set up to assign crew members to necessary duties, whether a full crew or partial crew is on board.

The general emergency bill will not give detailed duties for every emergency, because it is impossible to plan for all emergencies. The one thing all hands must remember is that they must carry out all orders from persons in authority with speed and precision. As it is possible that any emergency may result in casualties, all hands must learn the general duties and responsibilities of those senior to them, because they may have to take them over.

Man Overboard

The first necessity when a person goes overboard is prompt action. Anyone who sees someone go overboard should immediately give the alarm "Man overboard, port (starboard) side," drop life rings or life jackets if possible, try to keep the person in sight, and point. If a smoke float and dye marker are available, they should be dropped. Make sure the officer of the deck is informed immediately. Every underway watch is organized to handle this emergency. The OOD will maneuver the ship to reach a recovery position, at the same time having the word passed twice, sounding five or more short blasts on the whistle, hoisting OSCAR by day or showing two pulsating red lights by night. These signals apply to naval task force operations and are practiced by all cutters. The ready-boat crew will stand by to lower away when directed. A helicopter may be launched, if available, as the helicopter can quickly spot people in the water and can pick them up even if they are unable to help themselves. A muster of the crew is held in order to find out who is missing. There is always the possibility that the person overboard may be *you*. If this should happen, keep your head. Don't panic or despair. Hold your breath when you hit the water and the buoyancy of your lungs will bring you to the surface. Don't swim frantically away from the ship; the screws won't suck you under, because they are too deep in the water. Just keep afloat and try to stay right where you went in. The ship will maneuver so as to come right back down its track to you.

Even if no one saw you go over, keep afloat. When a person is missed, ships and aircraft commence a search. People have been found and picked up after several hours in the water. In at least one case, a person was picked up after an entire day.

If a person goes overboard in port, the alarm is sounded as usual, and the OOD uses the best available method of rescue. Boats in the water will assist in any emergency without orders.

Emergency Destruction

Emergency destruction is action, ordered by the commanding officer, to burn or otherwise destroy registered publications and cryptographic material to avoid their falling into enemy hands. Personnel assigned to duties under this bill are given specific and detailed instructions. In shallow water (less than 100 fathoms) papers must be burned; in deep water (more than 100 fathoms) papers may be permitted to go down with the ship.

Abandon Ship

Abandon ship is one emergency in which many senior officers and petty officers may be lost as battle casualties, and full responsibility may fall on the shoulders of very junior personnel.

Abandon-ship stations and duties are noted on the Watch, Quarter, and Station Bill. Additional details are listed in the *Organizational Manual*. Careful planning takes care of who goes into which boat or raft and what emergency equipment is to be supplied and who supplies it. Know your abandon-ship station and duties. Know *all* escape routes from berthing spaces or working spaces below decks to topside, how to inflate a life jacket, how to lower a boat or let go a life raft, how to handle survival gear, and how to do it all in the dark.

Only the commanding officer can order the ship abandoned, and the commanding officer will do so only after all efforts to save the ship prove futile. When the abandon-ship alarm sounds, *act fast*. It's your last chance. Survival at sea depends on knowledge, equipment, training, and self-control; it is your only aim after you do abandon ship, but you have to prepare and train for it before the emergency comes. Disaster can strike suddenly at sea; a ship can go down within three minutes after a collision or explosion. On the other hand, people with very little equipment but plenty of self-control have survived for more than 40 days in an open boat.

Remember that it is a seaman's duty to "maintain hope, perseverance, and obedience." If personnel cooperate in keeping high morale, they will be happier and more comfortable, and most important, they will survive. When you have to abandon ship, that's the name of the game—survive!

THE BATTLE BILL AND WATCH, QUARTER, AND STATION BILL

Two documents devoted to organizing and assigning the crew on a ship that are common to all ships, but not included in the *Organization Manual*, are the *Battle Bill*, or the Ship Manning Document, and the *Watch, Quarter, and Station Bill*.

The Battle Bill

This bill assigns personnel with certain qualifications to specific jobs on a ship while at general quarters, and complements the organization of watches for conditions of lesser readiness when all hands are not at a battle station.

In the battle bill, each station and duty is assigned to an enlisted person by a billet number—a combination of numbers and letters indicating a person's division, section within the division, and seniority within the section. All hands reporting aboard ship, when assigned to a division, will be given a billet slip by the division officer, listing the billet number and duties for the various bills. It is each person's responsibility to know the stations and duties for each bill.

The Watch, Quarter, and Station Bill

This bill displays in one place the duties of each person in each emergency and watch condition. It also shows the duties in the administrative and the operational bills.

The readiness conditions are:

Condition I. General quarters: All hands at battle stations.

Condition II. Modified general quarters: Used only in large ships, it permits some relaxation among personnel.

Condition III. Wartime cruising: Usually only one-third of the crew on watch and only certain stations staffed or partially staffed.

Condition IV. Peacetime cruising: Only necessary personnel on watch, the remainder available for work and training.

Condition V. Peacetime watch in port: Enough personnel on board to get ship under way if necessary or to handle fires and similar emergencies.

Condition VI. Peacetime in port: No armament staffed.

Variations in these conditions include:

Condition 1A. Amphibious battle stations. All hands on station to conduct amphibious operations and limited defense of the ship.

Condition 1AA. All hands at battle stations to counter an air or surface threat.

Condition 1AS. All hands at battle stations to counter a submarine threat.

Condition 1E. Relaxation from general quarters for brief periods of rest and the distribution of food at battle stations.

Condition 1M. All hands at battle stations to take mine countermeasures.

General Quarters

The ship is in Condition of Readiness I, with all hands at battle stations and all equipment ready for instant action; GQ is sounded whenever battle is imminent or when the highest state of readiness to meet an emergency is desired. For example, the OOD should immediately sound the general quarters alarm when a lookout sings out that a periscope has been sighted; when CIC reports that an unidentified plane has been picked up by radar; or for precaution at dawn and dusk, when there is an increased chance of enemy attack.

When personnel reach their stations, they throw off gun covers, break out ammunition, or prepare for action the equipment to which they are assigned. GQ must be set in seconds, not minutes. When each station is manned and ready, the person in charge notifies the control station. When all stations in the control group are ready, the bridge is notified.

When the danger has passed or the drill is over, "Secure from GQ" is announced over the general announcing system and sound-powered telephone circuits. No person leaves a station until "Secure from GQ" is sounded or until permission from a control station has been granted. All gear on hand must be stowed or secured as necessary.

Fire

Alarm for a real fire may be given at any time. For drill purposes, a fire may be assumed to be in a specified place—for example, in an ammunition space.

The crew member who discovers an actual fire must give the alarm. The most important thing is to notify at least one other person who can go for help. Too often a fire has gotten out of control because someone tried to put it out alone without calling for help.

Use any means at hand to spread an alarm. Use the telephone, messenger, or word of mouth to notify the OOD in port, or the OOD or damage-control central when under way.

Once the alarm has sounded, personnel nearby should act promptly to check or extinguish the fire, using the means nearest at hand. All other crew members respond to the alarm in accordance with the Watch, Quarter, and Stations Bill. If you and several others have begun to fight the fire, do not leave the scene until the fire or repair party arrives.

Fire During Condition I

When the ship is in Condition I, the damage-control organization is ready to fight several fires at once, and little assistance will be required from other stations. Damage-control central will direct a repair party to fight the fire and will keep the captain and the OOD informed as to progress.

Fire During Condition II, III, IV, or V (under way or in port)

When the ship is in any of these conditions of readiness with all hands aboard, Condition I is set immediately so that the highly trained damage-control organization may be used most effectively to fight the fire.

In port when Condition IV or V is set, the duty section furnishes the fire party. This fire organization is made up of key people from the regular damage-control parties.

Special steps to be taken when the fire alarm is sounded:

- Main engine control must maintain fire-main pressure. All electrical circuits in the vicinity of the fire are shut off.
- Supply department sends a storekeeper to the scene of the fire, with keys to the supply storerooms in the area.
- Medical department sends a health services technician with first-aid kit to the scene of the fire.
- Air crews stand by their helicopters if any are on board.
- Weapons department stands by all magazine spaces and inspects bulkheads for rise in temperature. The magazine sprinkling-system valves are constantly staffed.

CBR DEFENSE

CBR warfare refers to the use of chemical, biological, or radiological weapons, which are termed mass weapons because they can affect great numbers of people. CBR defense is planned for in the CBR bill, which provides an organization and procedures to follow in case an enemy attacks with any of these weapons or in the event of an accident involving any CBR weapon in use by friendly forces.

The effects of a CBR attack may extend over large areas of land or water. Some effects—air blast, thermal radiation, and ionizing radiation of nuclear weapons—end almost instantly. Other effects—base surge and fallout of nuclear weapons—can contaminate an area for a long time and spread to other areas if carried by wind or water currents. The hazards of biological and chemical agents can also move with the winds. All CBR contamination remaining in an area can affect personnel in the area where it occurs, or those entering the area later.

Chemical Warfare (CW)

This is the military use of any chemical that can produce powerful casualty or harassing effects, and includes screening smokes and incendiaries. With proper protection, such as clothing and gas masks, you have an excellent chance of surviving any chemical attack. Chemical smoke screens are used to hide enemy targets or troop movements, but they might also disguise other types of CW agents. Incendiaries—chemical compounds that burn with terrific heat—may be dropped by aircraft, fired in shells, or used with flame throwers, and include napalm, jellied gasoline, and thermite and magnesium bombs. The most dangerous aspect of chemical warfare is the use of casualty or harassing agents against troops or civilian populaces.

Casualty Agents

These agents can kill or seriously injure large numbers of people. They include nerve agents, blister agents, choking agents, and blood agents.

Harassing Agents

These agents are not as dangerous as casualty agents, but produce effects that harass an enemy by reducing efficiency. Principal types are tear gases and vomiting agents.

Detection of CW Agents

The most important CW agents to detect are the nerve gases, which can kill very quickly. Several chemical agent detector kits are in use, but some of them identify only certain gases, and some do not give warning soon enough for personnel to don protective clothing.

Your best defense is to learn to note clues that might indicate CW agents: the presence of oily liquids after an explosion; drying and browning vegetation; a spray from aircraft; a vaporous cloud that remains close to the ground or water. Any unusual enemy operation that does not involve conventional projectiles and explosives should be treated as possible CW or BW attacks.

Defense against CW attack is much the same as for RW or BW attacks. The main difference will lie in the speed with which nerve and blood agents act. At the first sign of a nerve gas, *hold your breath* until your mask is on and properly adjusted. Any liquid on your skin should be blotted with cloths from a Protective Ointment Kit, or some other cloth. Do not rub; this will only increase skin absorption. Flush exposed skin with water for half a minute and apply the ointment from the kit, but *not near or in the eyes*. If drops of nerve agent get into your eyes, flush with water immediately, even if you have to remove your mask. While unmasked, do not breathe contaminated atmosphere. Symptoms of nerve poisoning are local sweating and muscular twitching of contaminated skin area, or the contraction of the pupils of the eyes. If these are observed, use the atropine syrette in the Protective Ointment Kit, but *not* until you are *sure* that the symptoms are nerve agents.

Biological Warfare (BW)

This is the military use of living organisms or their toxic products to diminish the ability of an enemy to wage war through destruction or contamination of food sources, such as crops and domestic animals, and through infliction of disability or death on the populace by spreading an epidemic. A BW attack is most probably conducted by producing a biological agent that can be spread by an aerosol released into air currents or water supplies; this can be done by aircraft, bombs, long-range missiles, or even by people trained to infiltrate enemy territory, as the quantity of material needed could be very small.

It is nearly impossible to see, smell, or taste any BW agent, and because of their various incubation periods, there may be no immediate effects on people, animals, or crops to indicate that an attack has been made. The only way to detect and identify a BW agent is for trained experts to examine specimens of air, food, water, or human and animal blood and excretions. Most BW agents are not fatal; they will cause illness if taken into the body, but the victims will recover. Depending on their type, BW agents may be absorbed through the skin, taken in with food or water, or inhaled. The best defense against them is to keep yourself and your living areas clean, and report any sickness immediately. Action under known attack is much the same as RW: wear protective clothing and a gas mask, or breathe through a folded cloth. Decontamination and washup procedures are the same as for RW.

Most BW agents will die or lose their effectiveness after a few days of exposure to ordinary weather conditions, but there are some that may remain dormant for a long period. All clothing should be boiled in soapy water or exposed to the sun for a few days before wearing. Food in sealed containers should be safe, but food or water that has been exposed should be avoided until tested. Play it safe; don't assume danger is past after a BW decontamination team has done its work.

Radiological Warfare (RW)

Radiological or nuclear warfare, the use of a weapon armed with a nuclear warhead, may produce these effects:

- *Shock wave*, a blast, as in any explosion, followed by rapid movement of air or water away from the explosion, the force of which can wreck ships, smash buildings, and kill or severely injure people at a considerable distance.

Shock-wave protection is similar to general damage-control precautions against any explosion: keep loose gear secured, be prepared for the effects of heavy shock and blasts, maintain watertight integrity, and make repairs as fast as possible.

- *Thermal radiation*, heat so intense that everything touched by the fireball melts, and buildings at a great distance burst into flame.
- *Radiation (both initial and residual)*, which cannot be seen or felt, is more dangerous than the shock or heat. The radiation is composed of invisible Alpha and Beta particles of energy, neutrons, and Gamma rays. Alpha particles can be stopped by a thin sheet of paper; the other particles travel at the speed of light and therefore are more difficult to stop.

Initial radiation from the detonation of a nuclear weapon consists mostly of neutrons and Gamma rays, both injurious to human tissue. It lasts only one-tenth of a second. Heavy shielding is required as a protection, depending on distance from the burst and the "yield" or size of the bomb.

Residual radiation, the radioactive "fallout" from a nuclear explosion, can contaminate large areas. (Fallout from bomb tests in China can be detected in the United States.) This contamination can be detected and measured only by special instruments; if it is hazardous, the area must be decontaminated (washed clean) before unprotected personnel may enter.

Ships may be exposed to three types of bursts: air burst, in which the fireball does not touch the earth; surface burst, in which the fireball touches the surface; and subsurface, in which the explosion is underground or underwater. An air burst produces blast, heat, intense light, and initial radiation, but no fallout requiring decontamination of ship or personnel. In an air burst, 85 percent of the damage is due to shock, ten percent due to thermal radiation, and five percent due to initial or residual radiation. A surface burst will produce shock, heat, intense light, and initial and residual radiation. The fallout, especially over water, will spread radioactive contamination over a much wider area than the base surge of an underwater (or subsurface) explosion. A subsurface blast normally produces no heat or light and very little initial radiation. The danger in this type of explosion is in the intense underwater shock and heavy residual radiation from the highly contaminated base surge of earth or water created when the column formed by the explosion falls back to the surface.

CBR Attack at Sea

The alarm for a CBR attack is the 1,000-cycle chemical alarm. When it sounds, *take shelter* at once. The actions of all hands on duty, of course, must be determined by circumstances and their orders. The air blast can knock people around like ping pong balls, so *hang on* to something solid to reduce the chance of injury. The same warning goes for personnel below decks, as the shock wave transmitted to the hull by water can smash them against bulkheads and overheads. Never lie flat on the deck, but rest on the balls of your feet and flex your knees. Thermal radiation from an air or surface burst will produce skin burns and eye damage only among those directly exposed. Personnel can reduce the chance of burns by dropping out of direct line of sight of the fireball and covering exposed skin surface.

Attack without alarm is always possible, and the only warning will be a very bright flash or the sky lighting up. When you see the flash, close your eyes, cover your face with your hands, drop to the deck if you can, or crouch and bend down, and after two to five seconds, or after you feel a sudden wave of heat, grasp something solid and *hang on*. Otherwise, the air blast could blow you over the side. You may suffer from flash blindness, but will be able to see perfectly well in 30 minutes.

Radiation Measurement

The effect of nuclear radiation on any living thing depends on the intensity of radiation and the time exposed to it, and can be determined by multiplying one by the other. The result, called *dosage*, is measured in RADs or Roentgens, and is used to determine the treatment required after exposure to radiation. It is important that no one is exposed to a greater radiation dose than the body can absorb without permanent damage. Some individuals have greater resistance to radiation injury than others. Personnel previously exposed may require less radiation to become ill. Radiation injury normally does not become apparent for some time. This delay is called the "latent period." The amount of radiation received affects the degree of injury and the length of the latent period—the larger the radiation dose, the quicker symptoms are noticeable. The latent period is important, because people exposed to a large amount of radiation may still be able to perform their duties for hours and even days. Killing doses of radiation may reduce the period to less than an hour.

Radiation sickness is *not* a communicable disease; you get it only by exposure to radiation. Sometimes, for psychological or other reasons, an individual may develop symptoms that are similar to radiation sickness, such as nausea and vomiting, but that are actually not due to radiation exposure.

Maximum Permissible Exposure

There is a limit on radiation exposure, established by competent authority. Ships will use appropriate maneuvers and countermeasures (washdown, shelter, rotation of personnel between topside and deep shelter stations, etc.) to limit radiation exposure as much as possible.

Detection Equipment

This equipment is designed to be worn by individuals in certain situations, or to be used by monitors. Individuals will use a *pocket dosimeter*, which looks like a fountain pen and records radiation by deflection of a needle on a roentgen scale; a *film badge*, made of lead or cadmium, in which the film records radiation but must be removed and developed to determine the amount; or a *glass dosimeter*, which replaces the film badge. The glass dosimeter is a plastic disc worn on a dog tag chain. The important fact about the dosimeter is that it measures *total dose* received.

Monitoring Equipment

This equipment is usually handled by trained teams, and is used to locate and monitor "hot spots." The purpose in monitoring is to measure the *instantaneous* intensity of radiation; once this is known, it is possible to control the amount of time any person spends in any area so as to keep the total dose below the maximum permissible exposure. Monitoring equipment, generally known as *radiac sets*, has no popular names, but carries "short titles" such as AN/PDR-45 or AN/PDR-56. The various types are designed to measure high-range Gamma radiation, lower-range Gamma and Beta radiation, Alpha radiation, and neutron radiation. A monitoring team consists of a person in charge, called the monitor, who measures intensity of radiation, a recorder who records intensity of readings and time and location, a marker who marks intensity and time of contamination and places warning signs, and a talker or messenger who relays readings to damage-control central.

Shipboard Decontamination

Tactical decontamination takes place immediately at sea, and reduces contamination so that the ship can carry out its mission without subjecting the crew to more than the maximum permissible exposure. Phase one—primary gross decontamination—consists of a saltwater washdown of the entire topside. This will remove 98 percent of contamination if the surface was wet prior to contamination and washdown commences while it is still wet; if the surface has dried, only 50 percent of contamination will be removed. Washdown should be completed within 15 minutes after contamination occurs. Hose squads wear protective clothing and gas masks. Saltwater washdown commences even if the sea is contaminated, in which case it will continue until the ship reaches a clear area.

The second phase—conducted by individual ship departments—involves reducing contamination of equipment vital to the ship's mission, by use of steam lance and detergents, scrubbing paint work, scraping with abrasives, or removing with flame.

Personnel Decontamination

Preliminary decontamination is done immediately; exposed personnel wash down under firehoses or topside showers. Detailed decontamination is done in stations divided into three sections where all possible precautions are taken to prevent contamination spreading from one section to the other. In the undressing area all contaminated clothing is removed; in a washing area, each person scrubs thoroughly with soap and water; in the clean dressing area, uncontaminated clothing is provided. Radiation detection devices at each section ensure that contamination is not spread throughout the center. Decontamination priority is as follows: repair party and damage-control teams, uninjured personnel, injured personnel. Injured personnel are usually handled last because of the extra time required for medical personnel to assist them.

Protective Mask

This important part of CBR defense is designed to protect your face, eyes, nose, throat, and lungs by filtering the air, removing particles of dust and smoke that may be radioactive or contaminated with BW or CW agents, and purifying the air of many poisonous gases. It will not protect against ammonia, carbon monoxide, carbon dioxide (CO_2), cooking gas, sulphur dioxide, and certain other industrial gases or fire-produced fumes. It will not produce oxygen and is useless where there is not enough oxygen to breathe, even after the mask has purified what air there is. In such places the oxygen breathing apparatus (OBA), or air-line hose mask, must be used.

Because of the great importance of the protective mask, it should receive careful attention. Perspiration should be dried out completely, as moisture will cause rotting, corrosion, deterioration of the canisters, and mildew. Only authorized equipment, such as the Protective Ointment Kit, should be stowed in the carrier. The mask should be inspected periodically, tested in a gas chamber, and stored in a cool, dry place away from solvents, such as cleaning fluid, and their vapors.

Protective Clothing

This clothing, provided for monitoring and decontamination teams, must have the best possible care. Tears, holes, broken or missing buttons, broken or jammed zippers, and other such defects might leave you unprotected during an attack.

Special protective clothing made of rubberized cloth is airtight and provides the most complete protection against BW and CW agents. Liquid CW agents will penetrate it after a few hours, so wearers should go through decontamination as soon as possible. Permeable clothing is chemically treated to neutralize blister agents, but provides little protection against nerve gas and only limited protection against any other contamination. Regular stock issue wet-weather clothing and ordinary work clothing will keep some contamination away from the skin, and is easily decontaminated by washing. All contaminated clothing should be removed as soon as possible.

CHAPTER 23

Maritime Law Enforcement

The Coast Guard is the oldest federal law enforcement agency in the United States. Today, the Coast Guard is more deeply involved in law enforcement than at any time in its history. The United States Codes state that: "The Coast Guard shall enforce, or assist in the enforcement of all applicable Federal laws on or under the high seas and waters subject to the jurisdiction of the United States." The Coast Guard currently enforces laws concerning narcotics, pollution, boating safety, fisheries protection, alien interdiction, and other general crimes afloat.

Because of the multimission nature of the Coast Guard, almost every operational unit is involved in law enforcement to some extent. The importance of the law enforcement mission is reflected in the Coast Guard's budget: over one-third of all operating expenses go towards the enforcement of laws and treaties. Although many people are aware of the large drug seizures made by Coast Guard cutters in the waters off the southeastern United States, fewer people realize the tremendous team effort that goes into those and other law enforcement activities. Each operational unit is supported by a network of units providing communications, surveillance, intelligence, maintenance, and personnel services.

The need for a strong Coast Guard law enforcement program is more urgent than ever. Drugs have invaded large areas of the United

Figure 23-1. Coast Guard personnel receive extensive training in law-enforcement procedures.

States and have created an unprecedented social crisis in many American cities. In addition, the effect of illegal narcotics has threatened stability throughout the world. The drugs that cause broken families, crime, and serious accidents in the United States are paid for by funds that help to support the drug cartels in their terror and murder campaigns in Central and South America. Aliens from poorer countries are seeking to enter this country illegally in ever-increasing numbers. Fishery stocks are presently in great danger of being overfished and depleted. Lastly, more and more Americans are purchasing and using recreational boats, resulting in greater danger of boating accidents. The Coast Guard's law enforcement mission will remain an important one for years to come.

LAW ENFORCEMENT DUTIES

The Coast Guard is the federal government's principal agency for law enforcement on waters subject to United States jurisdiction. As such, the Coast Guard is charged with enforcing a wide range of federal laws and regulations.

Figure 23-2. Law enforcement personnel need thorough training.

Narcotics

Perhaps the most well-known law enforcement mission for the Coast Guard is drug interdiction. Coast Guard boats, cutters, and aircraft patrol along the entire United States coastline and into Central and South American waters to stop drug-smuggling vessels and aircraft from reaching the United States. Coast Guard boarding teams go aboard vessels at sea and conduct thorough inspections. If it appears that a vessel may be smuggling narcotics, the boarding team may conduct a more thorough search to detect hidden drugs or secret compartments. In addition to stopping smugglers, the Coast Guard also enforces the "Zero Tolerance" program by issuing summonses when personal-use quantities of drugs are found, or, if appropriate, by seizing the vessel and/or arresting the drug user.

Aliens

The Coast Guard is heavily involved in stopping illegal immigration into the United States. Many would-be immigrants, who are unable or unwilling to seek legal immigration, attempt to enter the country though illegal means, often by boat. Many of those ventures are extremely perilous. Boats are often unseaworthy, overcrowded, and dangerously unsanitary. The people who arrange the trips are often unscrupulous criminals who have caused a number of deaths. Coast Guard units intercept many such immigration ventures, provide short-term health care to the passengers, and return them to their native countries.

Fisheries

The fish off the coasts of the United States are a vital natural resource for both this country and the world. They contribute to the food supply, economy, and health of several nations, including the United States, and provide recreational opportunities. Yet those resources are jeopardized by increased fishing and by environmental problems. The Coast Guard enforces a number of federal laws and international treaties to ensure that fishery stocks are not overfished. Those laws affect both domestic fishing close inshore as well as foreign vessels fishing out to 200 miles offshore. Coast Guard boarding teams go aboard fishing vessels at sea and inspect fishing gear, catch logs, and the fish actually caught. In the process, the boarding teams are on the lookout for overfishing, illegal equipment, catches of prohib-

Figure 23-3. Coast Guard personnel check the size of nets aboard U.S. and foreign vessels.

ited species or undersized fish, and for violations of marine mammal protection and endangered species acts.

Recreational Boating Safety

The Coast Guard is the federal agency charged with overseeing and enforcing boating safety throughout the United States. While the primary responsibility for recreational boating safety law enforcement has recently been shifted to the individual states, the Coast Guard remains responsible for coordinating those local efforts. Coast Guard boarding officers have broad authority to enforce federal boating safety regulations. That law enforcement work has contributed to a tremendous increase in the safety of recreational boating in the United States. Over the past twenty years, although the number of recreational boats has tripled, the number of fatalities has actually decreased. The Coast Guard has also recently begun to enforce new federal laws against boating while intoxicated (BWI). (See figure 23-4.) During the course of a routine Coast Guard boarding, the boarding team will conduct a thorough inspection of the vessel and its safety equipment. Where the equipment is not up to the federal safety standards, the boarding officer will advise the operator of the boat how to bring the equipment up to the standards, and explain why it is so important. In addition, the boarding officer may issue the operator a citation noting any safety violations. A citation is like a traffic "ticket" ashore, and may subject the vessel operator to a civil fine.

Other Laws

As federal law enforcement officers, Coast Guard boarding officers are also charged with enforcing a wide variety of other federal laws, including criminal laws, pollution laws, and marine traffic regulations. Even today, Coast Guard personnel are called upon to break up mutinies at sea, prevent demonstrators from hazarding naval vessels, and recover stolen vessels, among many other law enforcement missions.

BOARDINGS

Although maritime law enforcement involves a wide range of activities, one of the most important and common evolutions is the boarding of vessels at sea. Because law enforcement is carried out under a wide range of circumstances and conditions, actual equipment, boarding situations, and procedures may vary throughout the Coast

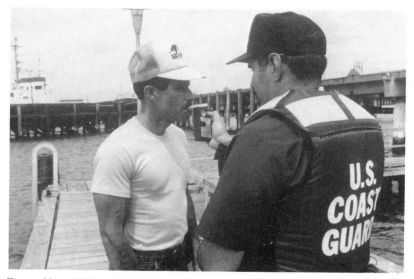

Figure 23-4. BWI can bring fines and jail sentences.

Guard. Nonetheless, there are a number of fairly standard elements for every boarding. The following section describes a "standard" Coast Guard boarding.

Boarding Units

Boardings may be conducted by any Coast Guard unit, but they are generally conducted by floating units such as cutters and small boats. Larger cutters, such as medium- and high-endurance cutters (WMECs and WHECs) often conduct extensive boardings well offshore, using their small boats. Patrol boats (WPBs) conduct a number of boardings from inshore waters to areas hundreds of miles off the coast, also using attached small boats. Small boats from stations and groups usually conduct their boardings in inshore waters. All Coast Guard units board a wide range of vessel types, in all sorts of circumstances.

Types of Vessels Boarded

The Coast Guard boards virtually every type of vessel afloat, from small rowboats to large supertankers. Most vessels boarded in the course of general maritime law enforcement, though, are either pleasure craft such as sailing vessels or sportsfishing boats, fishing vessels, or small freighters.

Boarding Teams

A boarding team consists of at least two Coast Guard people and may be as large as eight or more persons, depending upon the size of the vessel to be boarded, the size of the unit doing the boarding, and the situation involved. For example, while a two-person boarding team may be fine for a small powerboat in inland waters, an eight-person boarding team may be necessary to board a coastal freighter off the Bahamas. The person in charge of the boarding team is called the "boarding officer." Although all Coast Guard officers and petty officers have law enforcement authority, the boarding officer will be the person whose authority will be used for the actual boarding. All others on the boarding team assist the boarding officer.

Equipment

Every person in the boarding team must wear the proper Coast Guard uniform. In addition, boarding team members wear spe-

Figure 23-5. Boarding team conducts inspection.

cialized equipment for their law enforcement activities, including:

Soft body armor. A vest designed to minimize injuries from shots fired at the body of the wearer.

Equipment belt. Also known as "ballistic nylon," the belt holds the person's weapons and equipment.

Chemical irritants (may be optional). A chemical agent that is contained in a spray can. Similar to mace or tear gas, it creates a burning sensation on the skin of the target and leads to severe eye, nose, and throat irritation.

Service pistol. All Coast Guard boarding team members are armed during law enforcement boardings, generally with the M-9, nine-millimeter semiautomatic pistol.

Impact weapon. An expandable steel baton.

Handcuffs and key.

Flashlight.

Head gear. Boarding personnel may wear either a blue ball cap with the words "U.S. Coast Guard" and appropriate Coast Guard cap insignia according to their rank or a white plastic safety helmet with a Coast Guard emblem.

Personal flotation device (PFD). Because of the amount of equipment carried by boarding team members, all boarding team members must wear an approved PFD to ensure their safety if they should go into the water.

Communication equipment. The boarding team will carry a radio to communicate with the unit. Those radios are usually "scrambled" so that others cannot listen in to the law enforcement conversations. In addition, many boarding teams have small personal radios so that team members may communicate with each other during the course of the boarding.

Anti-exposure coveralls. In cold weather, boarding team members wear specialized coveralls that combine protection against the cold with flotation.

Riot shotgun. In some instances, where the boarding officer has specific reasons for suspecting a greater than normal degree of risk in the boarding, one of the boarding team members may carry a riot shotgun.

Boarding bag. In addition to the personal equipment, the boarding officer will carry a bag with miscellaneous forms and equipment required for the boarding. The bag will include boarding forms, check-off lists, hand tools, tape measures, mirrors, Narcotics Identification Kits (NIK kits), a camera, and other specialized gear.

Access kit. In cases in which the boarding officer suspects that the boarding vessel has hidden compartments concealing drugs or other contraband, the boarding team may bring a kit containing equipment to locate, open, and inspect compartments. The kit may include such things as a power drill, a "borescope" for looking through a drill hole into a dark compartment, saws, crowbars, and sledges.

Boarding Procedure

The boarding process begins with the Coast Guard unit establishing the identification and nationality of the vessel to be boarded. The unit will send the name and description of the vessel to a communications center ashore, where they are checked in a federal computer system to see if there is any information available on the vessel or the crew. Once the person in charge on the Coast Guard unit decides to conduct a boarding, the vessel is told to stand by for a boarding, and the boarding procedure is explained. The boarding team forms up on board the cutter or small boat, checks on the available intelligence, double-checks their equipment, then proceeds to the vessel, often by inflatable small boat.

When the boarding team arrives on board the other vessel, the team members take prearranged stations about the vessel to establish and maintain control for the boarding. The boarding officer will meet with the vessel's master, explain the purpose and the process of the boarding, and answer any questions. If the boarding officer has any specific, justifiable concerns about the safety of the boarding, due either to dangerous conditions on the boat or suspicions about the crew, the boarding team may conduct an initial safety inspection (ISI). In the ISI, team members conduct a brief survey of the vessel to ensure that the vessel is safe enough to continue with the boarding.

The boarding officer then conducts the boarding, checking for compliance with a wide range of federal laws and regulations. If, during the course of the boarding, the boarding officer develops probable cause to believe that the vessel is engaged in illegal activity, the scope of the boarding may be expanded to include a complete search of the vessel for evidence. If evidence of criminal activity is found, such as illegal drugs or other contraband, the crew is arrested and the vessel is seized, brought into port and turned over to other agencies. If only minor safety violations are found, the master is given a "citation" listing the violations, much like a traffic ticket. If there are no violations detected during the boarding, the master is thanked for cooperating, and the boarding team departs.

USE OF FORCE

As federal officers, Coast Guard personnel are armed when carrying out their law enforcement duties. They are authorized to use appropriate force to defend themselves and others, and to carry out their duties. The use of force by Coast Guard personnel is closely regulated by federal law and by Coast Guard policy.

Policy

Coast Guard personnel may only use such force as is *reasonably necessary under the circumstances*. Force may not be used where assigned duties can be carried out without it. Where force is necessary, the force used must be limited to the minimum needed, and must be designed to achieve the intended result with minimum injury to persons and property. Although personnel are encouraged to consult with higher authority before using force, in most instances, they will have to make on-the-spot use of force decisions based on their training and experience. In general, Coast Guard personnel may use force in the following circumstances:

Self-defense
Prevention of a crime
Effecting an arrest
Protection of property

Weapons Qualifications

Coast Guard personnel must be highly trained in the use of the weapons they will carry as law enforcement officers. All personnel receive weapons training in the use of the M9 sidearm and the M16 during their initial training. In addition, personnel at operational units must requalify every six months to be considered qualified to carry a weapon. Coast Guard personnel also receive training in the use of riot shotguns, chemical agents, and impact weapons. In addition, everyone who may carry a weapon in the course of duty must qualify every six months on a judgmental "shoot—no shoot" course, in which the person must make split-second use of force decisions. The commanding officer/officer-in-charge of the unit will make the final determination as to who may actually carry a weapon.

Warning Shots/Disabling Fire

Occasionally, cutters encounter vessels that refuse to stop despite a lawful order to do so. In those cases, the cutter involved may fire warning shots across the bow of the vessel, if the shots can be fired safely. Warning shots are generally fired from the largest deck gun available on the cutter, although they may also be fired from mounted machine guns, which may be either .50 calibers or M60s. If the vessel fails to stop despite warning shots, signals, and radio warnings, the cutter may be authorized by higher authority to fire disabling fire into the vessel. Disabling fire is used *only against vessels*. It is intended to disable the vessel, not to cause unnecessary damage or injury to persons. Disabling fire is therefore directed against the engines and steering equipment, not against personnel or living spaces. Disabling fire is generally fired from machine guns or smaller deck guns.

COOPERATION WITH OTHER AGENCIES

Because of the wide-ranging nature of the Coast Guard's law enforcement duties, the Coast Guard works with a wide variety of other law enforcement agencies from states, local governments, and the federal government, as well as from other countries.

State and Local Agencies

The Coast Guard works with local police departments and state maritime patrols to enforce boating safety regulations, boating while intoxicated laws, and drug crimes involving small quantities of narcotics. In addition, the Coast Guard and local agencies share information about criminal activity.

Federal Agencies

The Coast Guard also works with a large number of federal law enforcement agencies to enforce laws ranging from narcotics interdiction to fisheries protection. Some of the principal agencies that the Coast Guard works with are:

United States Customs Service (USCS). Customs is charged with enforcing laws against all smuggling. Although its primary duties involve airports, border crossings, and marine terminals, the Customs Service does have some agents who operate small boats. In addition, Customs operates small aircraft that assist the Coast Guard in detecting and interdicting air smuggling. The Coast Guard has a number of joint projects and operations with Customs, including operations control centers.

Drug Enforcement Agency (DEA). The DEA is the agency charged with investigating and arresting drug-smuggling groups.

The Department of Defense (DoD). Military units currently assist the Coast Guard in detecting possible drug smugglers approaching our borders. As the country has become more aware of the threat posed by the drug crisis, Congress has called for the other armed forces to use their large number of personnel and their powerful equipment even more in the fight against drugs. Coast Guard personnel also deploy on board U.S. naval vessels as part of law enforcement detachments (LEDETS).

National Marine Fisheries Service (NMFS). NMFS has the primary responsibility for managing and conserving our nation's fisheries stocks. Therefore, the Coast Guard works closely with NMFS in enforcing fisheries laws. In many cases, NMFS agents actually go out with cutters on fisheries patrols.

International Cooperation

Many crimes, particularly drug smuggling, are international in scope and have wide-ranging effects. For example, the Medellin Cartel, which smuggles drugs into the United States, is currently involved in a "war" of terrorism against the Colombian government. That war is funded principally by the money the cartel makes from its drug smuggling. The Coast Guard is heavily involved in a wide range of international law enforcement activities, including joint operations with other countries' law enforcement agencies and training foreign Coast Guards so that no area is safe for international criminals.

LAW ENFORCEMENT TRAINING

The Coast Guard's law enforcement mission is highly demanding and can be dangerous. To meet these demands, Coast Guard law enforcement personnel must be highly trained and remain proficient. The Coast Guard accomplishes its law enforcement training needs through a number of ways.

Maritime Law Enforcement School (MLE School)

Primary training for boarding officers is conducted at the MLE School (East), Reserve Training Center, Yorktown, Virginia. Training for boarding team members is conducted at the MLE School (West), Training Center, Petaluma, California.

Area and District-Level Training Teams

Most districts and both Atlantic and Pacific Areas have training teams that visit operational units to conduct law enforcement training. The training often parallels the MLE School curriculum, but is tailored to the specific local circumstances of the individual unit.

Unit Training and Personal Qualification Standards

Most units with law enforcement duties also have their own law enforcement training and qualification requirements. In that training, Coast Guard-wide procedures are custom-tailored to fit the specific unit and personnel available, and the commanding officer can evaluate the abilities of the unit's personnel. Personal Qualification Standards (PQS) ensure that each individual is fully trained and able to perform law enforcement duties before being sent "over the gunwale" to conduct maritime law enforcement at sea.

CHAPTER 24

Ship Construction

Joining the Coast Guard is somewhat like entering any other business or profession—you will have to learn the language that is used there. Most of the words will be familiar, but they will have new meanings. And along with learning a new language, you will have to learn a good deal about ships. A modern cutter is an extremely complicated craft (figure 24-1).

Ship is a general term for any large floating vessel that moves through the water under its own power. A *boat* is essentially the same as a ship, only smaller, and can be hoisted and carried aboard a ship.

In the Coast Guard, a *cutter* is defined as any Coast Guard vessel 65 feet in length or more, having adequate accommodations for the crew to live on board. Coast Guard *boats* are classified as any craft under 65 feet in length.

PARTS OF A SHIP

No matter how specialized your professional training may be, you must be thoroughly familiar with basic nautical terminology and ship construction. This is necessary to carry out routine orders and commands and to act quickly during combat or in emergency conditions.

Figure 24-1. The *Northland* is one of the 270-foot Famous cutter class equipped with modern electronics for surveillance, navigation, and communications.

In some respects a ship is like a building. It has outer walls (called the *hull*), floors (called *decks*), inner walls (called *partitions* and *bulkheads*), corridors (called *passageways*), ceilings (called *overheads*), and stairs (called *ladders*). But a ship moves and is never in the same place twice, so you have to learn new terms for directions and getting about. When you go up the stairs from the pier to a ship, you use the *accommodation ladder* to go on board, and what might be an entrance hall or foyer in a building is the *quarterdeck* in a ship.

The forward part of a ship is the *bow*; to go in that direction is to *go forward*. The after part is the *stern*; to go in that direction is to *go aft*. The topmost, open deck of a ship that runs from bow to stern is the *main deck*; anything below that is *below decks* and anything above it is *superstructure*. The forward part of the main deck is usually the *forecastle* (pronounced foc'sul); the after part is the *fantail*. The forecastle and fantail will be on the same (main) deck on a *flush-deck* ship; the fantail will be one deck lower on a *broken-deck* ship. To proceed from the main deck to a lower deck you *go below*; going back up again you *go topside*. As you face forward on a ship the right side is the *starboard* side and the left side is the *port* side. An imaginary line running full length down the middle of the ship is the *centerline*; the direction from the centerline toward either side is *outboard*, and from either side toward the centerline is *inboard*. A line from one side of the ship to the other runs *athwartships*.

If the interior hull of a ship were all one space, a single large hole made below the waterline would quickly cause the ship to flood and sink. To prevent this, the interior of the ship is divided by bulkheads and decks into *watertight compartments*.

In theory, any large ship could be made virtually unsinkable if it were divided into enough small watertight compartments. There is a limit to this, however, since compartmentation interferes with the arrangement of mechanical equipment and with the operation of the ship. Engineering spaces must be large enough to accommodate bulky machinery and cannot be subdivided.

Hull

The *hull* (figure 24-2) is the main body of the ship below the main outside deck. It consists of an outside covering, or *skin*, and an inside

Figure 24-2. This cut away drawing shows the construction of a typical hull.

structural framework to which the skin is fastened. In almost all types of modern ships, both the framework and the skin are made of steel. The steel skin is called the *shell plating*. The parts of the hull are usually fastened together by welding, although riveting is still used in some places.

Keel

The *keel* is the principal structural part of the hull. It runs from the *stem* at the bow to the *sternpost* at the stern. *Frames* are fastened to the keel; they run athwartships and support the shell plating. *Bulkheads, deck beams,* and *stanchions* are joined together and fastened to the frames; they support the decks and resist the pressure of the water on the sides of the hull. The system of interlocking steel bulk-heads and decks of a warship furnishes a large part of the hull strength.

Large ships have an outer and inner bottom, often called *double bottoms*. These are divided into many compartments. Many of the compartments aboard ship are used as tanks for fuel-oil storage, or fresh water, or for trimming ship. Tanks at the extreme bow and stern, used for trimming ship fore and aft, are called *peak tanks*. A heavy watertight bulkhead just abaft the forward peak tank is called the *collision bulkhead*. All compartments and tanks have pump and drain connections for pumping out sea water and for transferring fuel or water from one part of the ship to another.

Hull Reference Terms

Waterline, freeboard, and draft. The line to which a hull sinks in the water is the *waterline*. The vertical distance from the waterline to the edge of the lowest outside deck is the *freeboard*. The vertical distance from the waterline to the lowest part of the ship's bottom is the *draft*. The draft may also be thought of as the least depth of water in which the ship will float. The waterline, freeboard, and draft will, of course, vary with the weight of the load carried by the ship; as freeboard increases, draft decreases. (See figure 24-3.)

Draft is measured in feet, and numbered scales are painted on the sides of the hull at bow and stern. The relation between the drafts at the bow and the stern is the *trim*. When the ship is properly balanced fore and aft, she is "in trim." When the ship is "out of trim," because of damage or unequal loading, she is said to be "down by the head" or "down by the stern." When the ship is out of balance laterally or athwartships, she has a *list*; she is said to be "listing to starboard" or "listing to port." Both trim and list are adjusted by emptying or filling tanks and compartments in various parts of the hull.

The bow and the stern. The part of the bow structure above the waterline is the *prow*, although this word is not used as generally as the terms *bow* and *stem*. The part of the weather deck nearest the stem is called the *eyes* of the ship. The general area of the weather deck in the forward part of the ship is the *forecastle*, even though the ship may not have a forecastle deck. The edges of the weather deck from bow to stern are usually guarded by removable light wire ropes and stanchions called *life lines*, or by extensions of the shell plating

Figure 24-3. Hull of a typical ship, showing principal parts.

above the deck edge, called *bulwarks*. The main deck area at the stern of the ship is the *fantail*. The part of the stern that literally fhangs over the water is the *overhang*. The lower part of the bottom of a ship is called the *bilge*. The curved section where the bottom meets the side is called the *turn of the bilge*.

Propellers. The *propellers*, or *screws*, that drive the ship through the water are attached to *propeller shafts* and are turned by them. Ships with only one propeller are called *single screw*; ships with two propellers are *twin screw*. Ships with more than two propellers, usually four, are called *multiple screw*. In twin- or multiple-screw ships, the exposed length of propeller shafts is so great that they must be supported by braces extending from the hull, called *propeller struts*. Because of the shape of the hull at the stern, the screws may be damaged when the ship is close by a pier. To prevent this, metal frames called *propeller guards* are built out from the hull above the water.

Decks

The *decks* of a ship correspond to the floors of a building. The *main deck* is the highest deck that extends over the entire ship from stem to stern. The *second deck, third deck, fourth deck*, etc., are other complete decks below the main deck, numbered in sequence from topside down (figure 24-4).

A partial deck above the main deck is named according to its position on the ship; at the bow it is called a *forecastle deck*; amidships it is called an *upper deck*; at the stern it is called a *poop deck*.

A partial deck between two complete decks is called a *half deck*.

A partial deck below the lowest complete deck is called a *platform deck*.

The term *weather deck* includes all parts of the main, forecastle, upper, and poop decks that are exposed to the weather. The *quarterdeck* is not a structural part of the ship, but is a location on or below the main deck, designated by the commanding officer as the place for masts and ceremonies.

Any deck above the main deck, upper forecastle deck, or poop deck is called a *superstructure deck*.

Compartmentation Numbering

Almost every space on a ship is assigned a compartment number. This number is marked on a label that is secured to the door or hatch, and painted on the bulkhead of the compartment. The Coast Guard uses two systems to number compartments: one is for cutters built before March 1949, and the other is for cutters built later. Both of the systems are the same in the following respects:

All compartments on the port side end in an even number.

All compartments on the starboard side end in an odd number.

A zero precedes the deck number for all levels above the main deck; for example, 01, 02, etc.

Figure 24-4. Deck arrangement of a typical ship.

Ships Built Before 1949

When reading the following explanation, use C - 202 - A as your example:

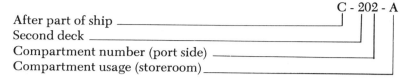

On ships built before 1949 the first letter in a compartment number is always A, B, or C. This letter indicates the section of the ship in which the compartment is located as follows:

A-section—compartments extending from the bow of the ship to the forward transverse bulkhead of the propulsion machinery spaces.

B-section—all compartments amidships between the forward bulkhead of the propulsion machinery spaces to the after transverse bulkhead of the propulsion machinery spaces.

C-section—compartments located abaft the transverse bulkhead of the propulsion machinery spaces to the stern.

After the division letter comes the three- or four-digit deck and compartment numbers. The first number represents the deck number, the next two the compartment number. Main deck compartments are indicated by 100 series numbers (i.e., 102, 109, etc.). Second deck compartments are indicated by 200 series numbers (i.e., 204, 213, etc.). The remaining decks are listed as 300 series, 400 series, etc. Double-bottom compartments are always listed in the 900 series regardless of the number of decks above.

The last letter in a compartment number is the compartment usage number. The letters and their meanings are as follows:

A	Supply and storage
C	Control
E	Machinery
F	Fuel
L	Living Quarters
M	Ammunition
T	Trunk
V	Voids
W	Water

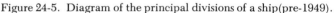

Figure 24-5. Diagram of the principal divisions of a ship(pre-1949).

Ships Built After March 1949

When reading the following explanation, use 4 - 75 - 3 - M as your example:

4 - 75 - 3 - M

Fourth deck
Forward frame number
Second compartment to starboard
    outboard of the centerline
Compartment usage (ammunition)

Ships built after March 1949 have compartment numbers that consist of: a deck number, frame number, relation to centerline of the ship number, and a letter showing the use of the compartment.

Deck Numbers

The deck numbers of a ship (with corresponding names) are shown in figure 24-6. Where a compartment extends down to the bottom of the ship, the number assigned to the bottom compartment is used. The deck number becomes the first part of the compartment number.

Frame Number

The frame number at the foremost bulkhead of the enclosing boundary of a compartment is its frame location number. Where these forward boundaries are between frames, the frame number forward is used. Fractional numbers are not used. The frame number becomes the second part of the compartment number.

Relation to the Centerline

Compartments on the centerline carry the number 0. Compartments completely to starboard are given odd numbers, and compartments completely to port are given even numbers. Where two or more compartments have the same deck and frame number and are entirely starboard or entirely port of the centerline, they have consecutively higher odd or even numbers (as the case may be) numbering from the centerline outboard. In this case, the first compartment outboard of the centerline to starboard is 1; the second, 3; etc. Similarly, the first compartment outboard of the centerline to port is 2; the second, 4; etc. When the centerline of the ship passes through more than one compartment, the compartment having that portion of the forward bulkhead through which the centerline of the ship passes carries the number 0, and the others carry the numbers 01, 02, 03, etc. These numbers indicate the relation to the centerline, and are the third part of the compartment number.

Compartment Usage

The remaining element of the compartment number is the letter that identifies the primary usage of the space. On dry- and liquid-cargo

Figure 24-6. The system of naming and numbering decks of a ship.

ships a double-letter identification is used to designate compartments used for carrying cargo, as follows:

"A"   Storage area, such as:
         Store rooms
         Issue rooms
         Refrigerated stores
         Ordnance related stowage (Non-hazardous)
         Clothing and cleaning gear lockers

"AA"   Cargo holds

"C"   Cutter and fire-control operating areas, such as:
         CIC, Electronic operating spaces (manned)
         IC Rooms, Radio rooms
         Communication office
         Pilothouse, Plotting rooms

"E"   Machinery compartments, including:
         Main machinery spaces
         Auxiliary machinery spaces
         Evaporator rooms
         Pump rooms
         Refrigerating machinery rooms
         Steering-gear rooms
         Windlass rooms

"F"   Fuel compartment, including:
         Fuel oil
         Lubricating oil

"G"   Gasoline compartments (including gasoline
            cofferdams)

"J"   JP-5 compartments

"L"   Living compartments, medical and dental spaces, and
            horizontal passageways, including:
         Officers' quarters
         Crew's quarters
         Water closets and washrooms
         Medical and dental spaces
         Passages

"M"   Ammunition spaces, including:
Magazines
Small arms magazine

"Q"   All spaces not otherwise covered, such as:
Engineering, electrical, and electronics spaces that are
not covered in "E"
Galley
Pantries
Scullery
Laundry
Offices
Shops
Wiring trunks
Fan rooms

"T"   Vertical access trunks

"V"   Voids and cofferdams, other than gasoline tank cofferdams

"W"   Water tanks, including:
Freshwater tanks, Reserve feed-water tank
Peak tanks, Ballast tanks
Bilge tanks, Sump tanks
Built-in sewage-holding tanks

Superstructure

The superstructure of a ship is everything above the weather deck (figure 24-7). There is a great deal of variation in the superstructure layout on different types of Coast Guard cutters, but the same elements will be found in all of them in one form or another. A large part of the superstructure in passenger ships consists of living quarters and recreation facilities. The superstructure of a fighting ship is made up of the actual armament and controls necessary for operating the ship.

Bridge

The bridge is the primary control position for the ship when under way, where all orders and commands affecting the ship, its move-

Figure 24-7. Topside arrangement of a typical cutter.

ments, and routine originate. The OOD is always on the bridge when the ship is under way; the captain will be on the bridge during GQ and during most operations.

Some ships can also be handled from a secondary control station, called *secondary conn*, the GQ station for the executive officer; thus, if the bridge is knocked out or the captain disabled in battle, the executive officer can take over.

Pilothouse

The pilothouse, sometimes called the wheelhouse, contains equipment and instruments used to control the movements of the ship. Usually the bridge extends out on both sides of the pilothouse. Some pilothouse equipment is duplicated on the bridge.

Bridge and pilothouse equipment. Some ship control consoles consist of the engine order section and propeller order section that control speed and direction (ahead or astern) of the ship. The engine order section has a dial for each engine, divided into sectors marked flank, full, standard, $2/3$ and $1/3$ speed ahead, stop, and $1/3$, $2/3$ and full speed astern. When a hand lever is moved to the speed sector ordered by the OOD, the engineroom watch sets the engine throttle for the same speed and notifies the bridge by moving an answering pointer to the same sector. The ship control console is manned by the lee helmsman, who is sometimes the 1JV phone talker. The propeller order section enables the OOD to make minor changes in speed by

Figure 24-8. An HH-65 helicopter returns to WMEC.

ordering the enginerooms to increase or decrease the RPM of the propellers.

The steering control console contains the controls and indicators required to control the course of the ship. The steering wheel (helm) is operated by the helmsman. On the panel in front of the helmsman are various indicators and switches. The ship's course indicator is a gyrocompass repeater, which indicates the ship's true course. Another indicator shows the course to be steered. Two more important indicators show the rudder angle (number of degrees left or right or amidships) and the helm angle (number of degrees left or right of amidships).

Tachometer. This is the same type of instrument that is used on a sports car; it shows shaft RPMs. There is a tach for each propeller.

Lighting panels. The two primary lighting panels in the pilot-house are the *signal and anchor light supply-and-control panel* and the *running lights supply-and-control panel.*

Lights installed on cutters usually include *aircraft warning lights; blinker lights; breakdown, man overboard,* and *underway replenishment lights* and *steering lights.* Switches are located on the signal and anchor light supply-and-control panel.

The location of bridge equipment varies among ship types and may even be different on ships of the same type. A bridge watchstander has to learn where everything is in order to find it in the dark.

Charthouse

The charthouse is normally just abaft the pilothouse and on the same deck, but it may be on another deck some distance away. It contains charts, a chart desk, and the chronometers. On some ships, the dead-reckoning tracer (DRT) may be in the charthouse. The charthouse will also contain navigational instruments such as sextants, stadimeters, bearing circles and stopwatches, parallel rulers, protractors, position plotters, and navigational books and tables.

Secondary Conn

This area contains *steering equipment, engine order telegraph, phone circuits,* etc., necessary for ship control in the event the primary control station is unable to perform because of battle damage. A magnetic compass may be located here.

The Signal Bridge

The signal bridge is an open platform near the navigational bridge and equipped with yardarm blinker controls, signal searchlights, and flag bags, where trained personnel can maintain visual communication with other ships.

Radio

Radio is the station of the *communication watch officer*, where outgoing traffic is prepared for transmission, and incoming messages are readied for local delivery. All messages, except tactical signals received and sent direct from shipboard control stations, go through the message center.

Combat Information Center (CIC)

The CIC is the nerve center of the ship. It has a fivefold function: to collect, process, display, evaluate, and disseminate information from sources both inside and outside the ship. A wide range of electronic equipment is installed in CIC: radar, sonar, electronic warfare intercept receivers, IFF (Identification Friend or Foe), radio and visual communications, PPI (Plan Position Indicator) repeaters, display screens, and computers. Radar installations include both air and surface search and fire control.

Damage-Control Central

Damage-control central maintains damage-control charts, machinery charts, and liquid-loading diagrams, and is responsible for seeing that the proper conditions of readiness are set and maintained. The conditions of stability and damage throughout the ship are known in damage-control central at all times and reported by direct communication to the bridge. All repair parties report to damage-control central.

Masts and Stacks

In some modern ships the masts are included as part of the main superstructure assembly. On older ships and on the smaller types of escort and patrol craft, masts still are a distinct feature of the superstructure. If a ship has two masts, the forward one is the *foremast* and the other is the *mainmast*. On single-masted ships, the mast is amidships or forward, is usually part of the main superstructure assembly, and is called the foremast or simply the mast.

Masts vary greatly in size and shape, some being built of several structural steel members and others being a single steel, aluminum, or wooden pole. On all ships, at least one mast, together with a spar running athwartship called a *yard*, is used for flags and other signal devices. These must be rigged in such a way as to be visible from other ships. The lighter types of masts are supported by *standing rigging*, consisting of wire rope *stays* running fore and aft and *shrouds* running athwartships down to the deck or bulwarks.

The small cap at the top of a pole mast or flagstaff is called a *truck*. The top of any mast may be called the *truck*. Above the truck there is frequently a slender vertical extension of the mast, called a *pigstick*. Almost every naval vessel has a pigstick on the mainmast, from which the *commission pennant* or an admiral's *personal flag* is flown. Extending abaft the mainmast is a small spar that is known as the *gaff*, from which the national ensign is flown when the ship is under way.

The small vertical spars at the bow and stern of a ship are the *jackstaff* and *flagstaff*, respectively. When a ship is at anchor or moored, it flies the union jack on the jackstaff and the national ensign on the flagstaff from 0800 to sunset.

Pipes for the expulsion of smoke and gases from the boilers are called *stacks*. There are many different varieties—short, high, vertical, raked, single, double, split trunk, etc. On most vessels, stacks are located on the centerline approximately amidships. Many new ships, especially those with diesel or gas turbine propulsion, have twin stacks side by side. Stacks, their number and arrangement, are important aids in correctly identifying ships at a distance.

Macks

In some new ships, the mast and stack are combined to form a large tower called a *mack*.

Accommodation Ladder

This is a "stairway" suspended over the side of the ship, with a platform at the bottom that serves as a landing for boats and is so designed that, as it is adjusted up and down, the steps remain level. A *boat rope* or *sea painter* is provided to secure boats alongside while they load and unload.

Brow

The "brow" is basically a gangplank used when the ship is moored alongside a pier or "nested" alongside other ships. Its size and construction will depend on the size of the ships and the distance from the ship to the pier.

Living Quarters

A considerable portion of the interior of a ship must be devoted to living spaces and facilities for the ship's complement of officers and crew. Officers' quarters and mess facilities are generally near the bridge. Quarters for the crew may be distributed throughout a large ship. Other facilities include the galleys, washrooms and heads, various storerooms, and sick bay. The location, size, and arrangement of living quarters are secondary considerations in the design of a ship. Its primary missions are considered first.

Ship's Equipment and Other Spaces

Much of the hull space of most ships is taken up by the engines, engineering equipment, and related piping and electrical systems. Storage and living space may be limited.

Engineering Plant

The enginerooms contain the main engines that drive the ship; these may be diesel, diesel-electric, or gas turbines. Auxiliary enginerooms contain generators that produce electricity, and evaporators and condensers that convert salt water to fresh water. The steering room contains the machinery that powers the rudder. Fuel oil tanks carry fuel for the engines.

Electrical System

A large ship has hundreds of electric motors driving everything from fans and tape decks to gun mounts. Every other system in the ship depends on electric motors. The main power supply is produced in the engineering spaces by diesel-driven generators.

Emergency diesel-electric generators in other parts of the ship automatically cut in to supply power if the main generators are disabled for any reason.

Drainage System

The drainage system includes the piping, valves, and pumps that discharge water from the ship. This includes water in flushing systems, water used in fire fighting, or seawater that enters the hull as the result of damage, collision, or heavy weather. The main eductor is a large pipe in the bottom of the ship to which other drain pipes are connected; the secondary eductor is a smaller pipe running lengthwise in the ship. This system includes connections to all watertight compartments.

Ventilation System

The ventilation system includes air supply, exhaust, and air-conditioning equipment. There are many separate systems so that ducts do not have to run through watertight bulkheads.

Freshwater System

The freshwater system provides water for the crew—for drinking, showers, and cooking—and for the boilers. Freshwater tanks may be filled in port from shore supplies; at sea, fresh water is made from salt water by condensers and evaporators.

Saltwater System

The saltwater system provides water for fire protection, including turret sprinkling, magazine flooding, CBR washdown, and flushing. Flushing water may come directly from the fire main or from separate lines. The fire main is a large pipe running the length of the ship, with risers and branch mains connected to it.

Fuel-Oil System

The fuel-oil system includes fuel storage tanks, filling lines, feed lines to the boilers or diesel engines, and lines and connections for pumping oil from one tank to another to control trim or list when the ship is damaged.

Compressed-Air System

The compressed-air system includes compressors, storage tanks, and high-pressure lines used for testing and blowing out compartments, and for operating pneumatic tools and other equipment.

Magazines

Ammunition for all guns is stored in magazines, which are placed well below the waterline when possible. Projectiles and powder may be stored in separate compartments. All magazines can be flooded by remote control in case of fire. Ammunition is passed to handling rooms, where hoists take it up to the gun mounts or turrets.

Storerooms

Storerooms are spaces in which a ship carries her own supplies; these may be clothing, dry or refrigerated provisions, and various types of spare parts and supplies.

Crew Accommodations

There are many compartments throughout the ship, designated as wardroom, officers' cabins, berthing compartments, pantries, messes, heads, washrooms, and sick bay. Other spaces provided for the health and comfort of the crew may include a barber shop, laundry, galley, library, and ship's store, depending on the size of the ship.

CHAPTER 25

Damage Control and Fire Fighting

Damage control includes all efforts to prevent damage to a ship, as well as all action taken to reduce the harmful effects of damage after it happens. The primary purpose of damage control is to keep a ship in condition to perform its assigned mission; a secondary purpose is to return the ship to port after damage so it can be repaired. The need for damage control is not limited to combat operations; any routine operation can result in an accident calling for prompt damage control.

DAMAGE CONTROL

The three main objectives of the damage control organization of a ship are as follows:

- Taking all necessary action before damage occurs. This means making the ship watertight and airtight in those parts that were so designed, removing all fire hazards, and maintaining and distributing necessary emergency equipment.
- Reducing damage by controlling flooding, fighting fires, and providing first-aid treatment to injured personnel.
- Providing emergency repairs or restoring services after damage occurs. This means manning essential equipment, supplying emergency power, and repairing important parts of the ship that were damaged.

Figure 25-1. Many Coast Guard cutters and craft are equipped to fight fires.

The ship's ability to perform any assigned task depends upon the actions of its damage-control organization. It is important that you realize your responsibility in damage-control procedures. Damage control must be considered an offensive as well as a defensive weapon. Damage control is concerned not only with battle damage but also with damage from fire, collision, grounding, or explosion. Damage control may be necessary in port as well as at sea.

Learn all you can about your ship—the whole ship, not just the part to which you are assigned. In an emergency, you may have to work anywhere on the ship, depending upon the location and the extent of the damage.

The important damage-control systems are drainage, ballasting, fire main, sprinkling and washdown, communications, and casualty power. The most effective people in any repair party are those who can find their way to any compartment in the dark and close any valves, doors, or hatches by touch alone. Much of this you will learn from drills and practical experience.

Damage-Control Repair Lockers

When a ship is placed in commission, damage-control repair lockers are set up in the ship's organization. The number of such lockers depends upon the size and type of ship and the number of personnel available. A Coast Guard cutter will usually have two repair lockers.

Each damage-control locker contains a number of different ratings in order to provide skilled personnel for any type of work. For example, an engineering repair locker may include machinery technicians, electrician's mates, and damage controlmen.

The engineer officer, as the *damage-control officer*, is responsible for damage control. The *damage-control assistant* (DCA), who is under the engineer officer, is responsible for establishing and maintaining an effective damage-control organization. Specifically, the DCA is responsible for the following:

The prevention and control of damage, including control of stability, list, and trim. The DCA supervises placing the ship in the material condition of readiness (to be explained later) ordered by the commanding officer.
The training of the ship's personnel in damage control, including

firefighting, emergency repairs, and nonmedical defensive measures against chemical, biological, and radiological weapons. The operation, care, and maintenance of auxiliary machinery, piping, and drainage systems not assigned to other departments.

Duties of Repair Parties

All repair parties must be able to:

Control and extinguish all types of fires.

Repair hull damage and remove flooding and firefighting water.

Correctly and promptly evaluate the extent of damage in their areas and make accurate "on scene" reports.

Repair electrical and sound-powered telephone circuits.

Detect, identify, and measure dosage and intensity of radiation, and decontaminate after CBR attack.

Give first aid and transport injured to battle dressing stations without seriously disrupting other functions.

All available personnel are assigned to repair lockers. A main propulsion repair party will consist largely of engineering rates and firemen. Repair parties assigned to areas in which magazines are located will have gunner's mates as part of their personnel. Storekeepers are assigned to repair parties that have storerooms located in their areas.

The number and ratings of personnel assigned to a repair party or station, as specified in the Battle Bill, are determined by the location of the station, the portion of the ship assigned to that party, and the total number of personnel available for all stations.

Each repair locker has a locker leader, either an officer or chief petty officer. The second person in charge of a repair party is, in most cases, a senior petty officer who is in charge of the repair party at the scene, and is designated "scene leader."

Investigating and Reporting Damage

In order to make a complete, thorough investigation of any damage, you must know your ship and be familiar with the basic principles of investigating and reporting damage—be cautious, be thorough and persistent, and report all the damage you see.

Damage Repair

Repairs made to a vessel damaged in action, or otherwise in operation, are termed *damage repairs*. These are emergency, usually temporary, repairs necessary to allow the vessel to continue its mission and permit its return to port for permanent repairs. Such repairs are made with whatever material is at hand. The important thing is to keep the ship afloat and maintain as much of its operational capability as possible.

Damage-Control Kits

At each repair locker a number of repair kits are made up and stowed in canvas bags. These kits are kept ready to be taken to the scene of damage. The kits should be constructed and packaged so that they will fit through the smallest watertight scuttle on your ship. These kits are commonly called plugging kits, pipe-patching kits, shoring kits, investigator kits, electrical repair kits, and CBR monitoring kits.

Plugging and Patching Holes

There are two general methods of making temporary repairs to a hole in the piping or hull: put something in it or put something over it. In either case, the patches will reduce the area through which water can enter the ship or through which water can pass from one compartment to another.

Temporary repairs do not call for elaborate tools or equipment. They involve principles that can be applied when using wooden plugs, prefabricated patches, or other readily available materials.

Shoring

Shoring is often used aboard ship to support ruptured decks, to strengthen weakened bulkheads and decks, to build up temporary decks and bulkheads against the sea, to support hatches and doors, and to provide support for equipment that has broken loose. Shores are made of either softwood or metal.

Battle Dressing Stations

Most ships have at least two battle dressing stations equipped to handle personnel casualties. These stations are manned by personnel

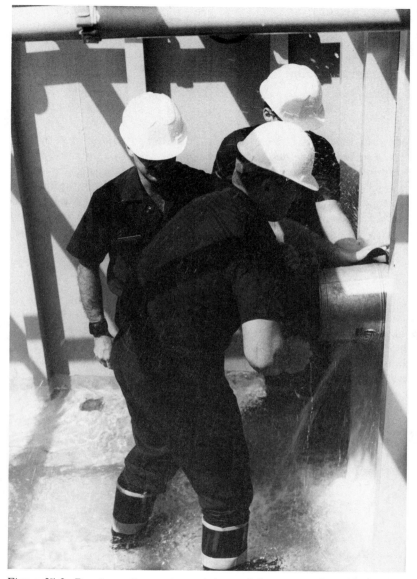

Figure 25-2. Repair parties receive training to help prepare them for the real thing.

of the medical department and are so located that stretcher cases may be brought directly to the station by the repair party stretcher bearers. Besides the battle dressing station, emergency supplies of medical equipment are placed in first aid boxes at various stations throughout the ship.

Decontamination Stations

Most ships have two decontamination stations, primary and secondary, which are provided in widely separated parts of the ship, preferably in the vicinity of battle dressing. These stations provide a place where, after CBR attack, personnel go through decontamination. Stations are manned by medical department and repair party personnel who make certain that proper decontamination procedures have been followed.

Damage-Control Communications

Effective communications are of vital importance to the damage-control organization. Without adequate means or proper procedures of communications among the units of the damage-control organization, the whole organization would break down and fail in its primary mission.

The normal means of damage-control communication aboard large ships are:

- Battle-telephone circuits (sound-powered)
- Interstation two-way systems (4MC intercoms)
- Ship's-service telephones
- Ship's loud-speaker system (1MC general announcing)
- Voice tubes (where installed)
- Messengers

Watertight (WT) Integrity

One of the most important aspects of any operation at sea is to keep the ship watertight. It may sustain any degree of damage, but if the proper degree of watertight integrity is maintained, the ship will stay afloat.

Entering Closed Compartments After Damage

Watertight doors, hatches, manholes, and scuttles should be opened only after making sure that the compartment is dry or so little flooded that no further flooding will be produced by opening the closure. Compartments should never be opened until permission is obtained from the damage-control officer. Extreme caution is always necessary in opening compartments below the waterline in the vicinity of any damage.

Closing and Opening Watertight Doors

Doors, hatches, and scuttles giving access to all compartments must be securely dogged. Double-bottom scuttle covers should be bolted at all times except when they must be open for inspection, cleaning, or painting. They must never be left open overnight or when crew members are not actually engaged in work.

You must obtain permission from the OOD or Damage-Control Central before opening any secured watertight fitting, and you must report back after you have secured the space.

Watertight doors and hatches will retain their efficiency longer and require less maintenance if they are properly closed and opened. To close a door, first set up a dog opposite the hinges, with just enough pressure to keep the door shut. Then set up the other dogs evenly to obtain uniform bearing all around. To open a door, start with the dogs nearest the hinges. This procedure will keep the door from springing and make it easier to operate the remaining dogs.

General-drill orders call for closing all watertight doors, hatches, and ventilator openings designed to be closed during maneuvers, in fog, or as a matter of routine at night.

The strongest doors are those classified as *watertight doors (WT)*. Many of these are used in watertight bulkheads of the compartments in the second deck. They are designed to resist as much pressure as the bulkheads through which they give access and usually have eight dogs. Some doors have dogs that must be individually closed and opened (figure 25–3); others, known as *quick-acting watertight doors*, have handles that operate all the dogs at once.

Nonwatertight doors (NWT) are used in nonwatertight bulkheads. Usually they have fewer dogs than WT doors and are made with dogs that require individual operation.

Airtight doors are also fume-tight and gas-tight. When such doors

DOGS

HINGES

Figure 25-3. Watertight door with individually operated dogs. Dogs are shown in closed position, but would have to be opened before door could be closed.

are used in air locks, they usually have lever-type quick-acting closures, but most others have individually operated dogs.

Panel doors are ordinary shore-type doors that are made of metal and used to provide privacy closures for staterooms, wardrooms, etc.

Hatchways are access openings in decks; hatches are the coverings for the hatchways. Raised lips (coamings encircling the hatchways) keep water and dirt from entering the compartment when the hatch is not secured. Hatches operate with quick-acting devices or may be secured with individually operated drop bolts or individual dogs.

Quick-acting escape scuttles are often provided for rapid access through a hatch.

Manholes are small openings to the water and fuel tanks and voids. They are usually secured by bolting steel plates (provided with gaskets) over them. Occasionally, however, manholes are provided with hinged covers and dogs or drop bolts. Manholes may also be placed in bulkheads.

Gaskets are rubber strips mounted in the covering part of doors or hatches to close against a fixed-position *knife-edge.* Gaskets of this type are either pressed into a groove or secured with retaining strips held in place by screws or bolts.

Watertight closures must have clean, bright (unpainted), and smooth knife-edges for gaskets to press against. A well-fitted WT door with new gaskets will still leak if knife-edges are not properly maintained.

MATERIAL CONDITIONS OF READINESS

In order to use compartmentation to its maximum advantage, and to provide for maximum preparedness, all tight doors, hatches, scuttles,

Figure 25-4. On a quick-acting WT door, a control wheel operates all dogs at once.

access, valves, and fittings having damage-control value are classified and marked. Ships maintain different material conditions of
readiness according to whether contact with an enemy is improb-
able, probable, or imminent. Each condition represents a different
degree of tightness and guarantees the maximum protection against
possible damage, with proper regard for the health and comfort of
personnel and the essential operation of the ship.

Three-Condition Ships

All ships are classified as three-condition ships. These conditions are
the number of progressive steps required to achieve maximum protection for the ship and its personnel against the spread of fire, flooding, smoke, dangerous fumes, and gases, and the effects of nuclear,
biological, and chemical agents. These material conditions of readiness through which all ships progress are *X-ray*, *Yoke*, and *Zebra*.
They are described and defined in the following paragraphs.

X (X-ray). This condition provides the least protection and is set
when the ship is in no danger of attack. A *black X* is placed on all
fittings that shall be closed at all times when not in actual operations.

Y (Yoke). This condition is set and maintained at sea and in port
during wartime. For peacetime cruising, Yoke may be modified during regular working hours. A *black Y* is placed on all fittings that
shall be closed for wartime cruising conditions.

Z (Zebra). This condition provides the maximum protection for
ship and personnel for battle and emergency situations, such as fire,
collision, or General Quarters, and is set when entering or leaving
port during wartime. A *red Z* is placed on all fittings that shall be
closed for battle or emergency conditions.

Yoke and Zebra fittings in condition X-ray, or Zebra fittings in
condition Yoke, which are secured by lock or other obstruction that
makes them inoperable, will be logged closed in damage-control
central. Yoke and Zebra fittings in condition X-ray, or Zebra fittings
in condition Yoke, which are secured but not locked or obstructed,
need not be logged.

The setting of material conditions X-ray and Yoke is normally a
ship division responsibility, and is accomplished by referring to the
compartment check-off lists provided. At General Quarters, the setting of and maintaining of condition Zebra is the responsibility of
personnel stationed within a compartment or area, and of the damage-control organization.

Designation W (William). Certain fittings that serve vital systems such as cooling water and firemain systems shall be open and operating at all times. They are closed only to prevent the spread of damage. These fittings receive the letter classification W (William) which, in itself, is not a material condition of readiness. When contact with significant amounts of radioactive material in the water is expected, sea-suction fittings (classified *W*), except those essential to main engine operation, shall be closed. Particular attention is to be given to the timely securing of evaporators.

Special Classifications

Special classifications are placed on various fittings to meet special requirements. These are described and defined in the following paragraphs.

Circle X and Circle Y. These classifications are indicated by a *black letter within a black circle.* These classifications indicate that the fittings may be opened without special permission by personnel proceeding to battle stations or as required in routine inspection checks. The fittings shall be secured immediately after use.

Circle Z. This classification is indicated by a *red letter within a red circle.* This classification indicates that the fittings may be opened by permission of the commanding officer for health and comfort of the crew during prolonged periods of General Quarters. However, they will be guarded for immediate closure if necessary.

Circle W. This classification is indicated by a *black letter within a black circle* and shows fittings that are normally open and operating. The fittings are closed only to prevent the spread of CBR contamination or for defense.

Dog Zebra. This classification is indicated by a *red Z enclosed by a large black D.* It is placed on fittings that must be secured to prevent light escaping outside the ship.

Figure 25–4 demonstrates the use of these classifications to mark material conditions of closure.

FIRE FIGHTING

The danger of fire is always present. Fire can start in the aviation-fuel stowage area of a cutter, or it can start in an office wastebasket.

If not handled promptly and properly, one can be as dangerous as the other. There are three basic elements in fire fighting:

- *Prevention.* Eliminate the possibility of fire before it starts.
- *Equipment.* Ships and stations are supplied with the items needed to fight fire. Know where they are.
- *Technique.* The best equipment is useless if not handled properly. Know how to use it.

No one wins against a fire. It may be fought efficiently and well, the damage may be minimized, and the fighters may receive commendations for their work. The fact remains that in any fire some property is lost, personnel may be injured, lives may be lost, and valuable time is lost for all concerned.

Fire Prevention

The best way to combat fires is to prevent them. Fire prevention must become a daily habit. Keep equipment squared away; keep working areas shipshape. When things are properly stowed and handled, they don't start fires. Remember:

- Keep containers of volatile liquids tightly closed.
- Prevent the accumulation of oil and grease in the bilges or in the exhaust from galley hoods.
- Keep quarters and workshops free of waste material.
- Properly stow bedding, unseasonable clothing, flammable liquids, paints, acids, gases, and chemicals.
- Be careful how you use open lights and electrical equipment where an explosive vapor might exist.

Fire Triangle

Requirements for Combustion

Three things are required for combustion: *fuel* (to vaporize and burn), *oxygen* (to combine with fuel vapor), and *heat* (to raise the temperature of the fuel vapor to its ignition temperature). The fire triangle illustrates these requirements. It also illustrates two facts of importance in preventing and extinguishing fires:

- If any side of the fire triangle is missing, a fire cannot start.
- If any side of the fire triangle is removed, the fire will go out.

Solid fuels. The most obvious solid fuels are wood, paper, and cloth. These are found aboard ship as insulation, canvas, packing, electrical cabling, wiping rags, and mattresses.

Types of liquid fuels. The flammable liquids most commonly found aboard ship are JP-5, Diesel Fuel Marine, lubricating oil, hydraulic oil, and oilbase paints and their solvents.

Gaseous fuels. Flammable gases found on board a ship include acetylene, propane, and hydrogen.

Oxygen. The oxygen side of the fire triangle refers to the oxygen content of the surrounding air. Ordinarily, a minimum concentration of 16 percent oxygen in the air is needed to support flaming combustion. However, smoldering combustion can take place in an atmosphere with as little as three percent oxygen.

Heat. Heat is the third side of the fire triangle. When sufficient heat, fuel, and oxygen are available, the triangle is complete and fire can exist. Heat of ignition initiates the chemical reaction that is called combustion. It can come from the flame of a match, sparks, heat generated by friction, an oxyacetylene torch cutting or welding metal, an electrical short circuit, or an electrical arc between conductor and motor casing.

The fire triangle is a simple means of illustrating the three requirements for surface glowing or smoldering to exist. However, an additional requirement must be met for flames to exist. This requirement is an uninhibited combustion chain reaction.

Uninhibited combustion chain reaction. The fire tetrahedron includes the uninhibited chain reaction in the combustion process. (A tetrahedron is a solid figure with four triangular faces. It is useful for illustrating the combustion process because it has room for the chain reaction and because each face touches the other three faces.) The basic difference between the fire triangle and the fire tetrahedron is that the tetrahedron illustrates flaming combustion.

Halon and dry-chemical fire extinguishing agents directly attack and break down the chain reaction process. These are discussed later.

Theory of Extinguishment

A fire can be extinguished by cooling, oxygen dilution, or fuel removal. Another method of extinguishment is by chemical flame inhibition.

Removing the fuel. One way to remove the fuel from the fire is to physically drag it away. It is often possible to move nearby fuels away from the immediate vicinity of a fire, so that the fire does not extend to these fuels.

Sometimes the supply of liquid or gaseous fuel can be cut off from a fire. When a fire is being fed by a fuel line, the fire can be extinguished by closing the proper valve.

Removing the oxygen. A fire can be extinguished by removing its oxygen or by reducing the oxygen level in the air to below 16 percent. Many extinguishing agents (for example, CO_2) extinguish fire with a smothering action that deprives the fire of oxygen.

Removing heat. Water, when applied in fog or straight stream, is the most effective means of removing heat from ordinary combustible materials such as wood, paper, and cardboard. Cooling with water can ultimately stop the release of combustible vapors and gases associated with the burning of solid fuels.

Breaking the combustion chain reaction. Flaming combustion occurs in a complex series of chemical chain reactions. Once the chain reaction sequence is broken, a fire can be extinguished rapidly. The extinguishing agents commonly used to attack the chain reaction and inhibit combustion are dry chemicals and Halons. These chemical agents directly attack the molecular structure of compounds formed during the chain reaction sequence. The breakdown of these compounds adversely affects the flame-producing capability of the fire. The attack is extremely rapid.

Classification of Fires

There are four classifications of fire: Class A, Class B, Class C, and Class D. The different classifications are briefly described in the following paragraphs.

Class A fires. Class A fires involve wood and wood products, cloth, textiles, fibrous materials, and paper and paper products, and are extinguished with water in straight or fog pattern.

Class B fires. Class B fires involve gasoline, jet fuels, oil, and other flammable liquids. These fires are extinguished with AFFF (aqueous film-forming foam), Halon 1211, Halon 1301, Purple-K-Powder (PKP) and CO_2.

Class C fires. Class C fires are energized electrical fires that are attacked using nonconductive agents such as CO_2, Halon 1211, PKP, or water spray at prescribed distances. The most effective tactic is to first de-energize and then handle the fire as a Class A fire.

Class D fires. Class D fires involve combustible metals such as magnesium. Water in quantity, using fog patterns, is the recommended agent. When water is applied to burning Class D materials, there may be small explosions. The fire fighter should apply water from a safe distance or from behind shelter.

Fire-fighting Agents

Many materials may be used as fire-fighting agents. The primary agents discussed in the following paragraphs are the most extensively used aboard Coast Guard ships. The primary fire-fighting agents are water, AFFF, CO_2, Halon, PKP, and Aqueous Potassium Carbonate.

Water

Water is a cooling agent, and on board ship the sea provides an inexhaustible supply.

For many years, the principle method of extinguishing a fire was the direct application of a solid water stream at the base of the fire. Although this method is still used, a more efficient method is to apply water in spray form.

Water will absorb heat until it changes to steam. The steam carries away the heat, which cools the surface temperature.

A secondary method of water extinguishment is steam smothering. When water changes into steam by absorbing heat, it expands 1,700 times in volume. The large quantity of steam displaces the air from the fuel, which smothers the fire.

Aqueous Film-Forming Foam

AFFF is composed of synthetically produced materials similar to liquid detergents. These film-forming agents are capable of forming water-solution films on the surface of flammable liquids. The Coast Guard proportions AFFF by volume, six parts of AFFF concentrate mixed with 94 parts water.

AFFF concentrate is a clear to slightly amber-colored liquid concentrate.

Fire-fighting advantages. When proportioned with water, AFFF provides three fire-extinguishing advantages. First, an aqueous film is formed on the surface of the fuel, which prevents the escape of the fuel vapors. Second, the layer of foam effectively excludes oxygen from the fuel surface. Third, the water content of the foam provides a cooling effect. The principal use of foam is to extinguish burning flammable or combustible-liquid spill fires (Class B).

Carbon Dioxide

A method of extinguishing fires by smothering is the use of the inert gas, CO_2. CO_2 is 1.5 times heavier than air. This makes CO_2 a suitable extinguishing agent because it tends to settle and blanket the fire.

General characteristics. CO_2 is a dry, noncorrosive gas that is inert when in contact with most substances and will not leave a residue and damage machinery or electrical equipment. In both the gaseous state and the finely divided solid (snow) state, it is a nonconductor of electricity regardless of voltage, and can be safely used in fighting fires that would present the hazards of electrical shock.

Method of extinguishing. CO_2 extinguishes the fire by diluting and displacing its oxygen supply. If gaseous CO_2 is directed into a fire so that sufficient oxygen to support combustion is no longer available, the fire will die.

Halon

Halon is a halogenated hydrocarbon. The two types of Halon used aboard Coast Guard ships are Halon 1301 and 1211.

Halon 1301. For shipboard installation, Halon 1301 is super-pressurized with nitrogen and stored in compressed-gas cylinders as a liquid. When released, it vaporizes to a colorless, odorless gas with a density of five times that of air. Halon 1301 is installed and used in fixed flooding systems for extinguishing flammable liquid fires.

Halon 1211. This is used in portable fire extinguishers. The halons act by removing the active chemical species involved in the flame chain reaction.

Dry Chemical Extinguishing Agent, Potassium Bicarbonate

Potassium bicarbonate (Purple-K-Powder [PKP]) is a dry chemical used principally as a fire-extinguishing agent for flammable liquid fires. It is used in portable extinguishers.

Use of Purple-K-Powder. PKP is used primarily to extinguish flammable liquid fires but can be used on electrical fires (Class C).

PKP is highly effective in extinguishing both flammable liquid pool fires and oil spray fires. Although PKP can be used on electrical fires, it will leave a residue that may be hard to clean. PKP can also be used extensively in the galley for such items as the hood, ducts, and cooking ranges.

PKP is not effective on fires involving ordinary combustibles (Class A).

Method of extinguishing. When PKP is applied to the fire, the dry chemical extinguishes the flame by breaking the combustion chain. PKP does not have a cooling capability.

Aqueous Potassium Carbonate

Aqueous potassium carbonate (APC) is used on board Coast Guard ships for extinguishing burning cooking oil and grease in deep-fat fryers and galley ventilation exhaust ducts. Aqueous potassium carbonate solution consists of potassium carbonate and water. A technique often used in combating liquid-grease fires involving animal and vegetable oils and fats is the application of solutions such as APC which, upon contact with the burning surface, generate a soaplike froth that excludes air from the surface of the grease or oil. Because the liquid grease cannot burn, the fire is extinguished.

FIRE-FIGHTING EQUIPMENT

There are many kinds of fire-fighting systems and equipment. Some of them are permanently installed and some are portable. These systems and devices must be maintained at maximum efficiency. All fire-fighting equipment is distributed in readily accessible locations. It is inspected frequently to ensure reliability and readiness for instant operation.

Fire-main System

The fire-main system is made up of piping, pumps, fireplugs, valves, and controls. The system is designed to supply plenty of water for fire fighting, sprinkling the magazines, washing the decks, or other purposes for which salt water is normally used.

The *piping* in a fire-main system is either a single line or a loop system. *Risers* are pipes leading from the fire main, which is usually located below the main deck, to *fireplugs* on the upper deck levels and to others located throughout the ship. The fire-main system is so designed that any damaged section of piping can be isolated. That is why there are so many cross connections and shut-off valves at various locations throughout the piping system.

Standard fireplugs usually have outlets either 2½ inches or 1½ inches in diameter. Some 2½-inch plugs are equipped with wye-gates, which provide two hose outlets, each 1½ inches in size. In other cases a reducing fitting is used so that a single 1½-inch hose line can be attached to a 2½-inch outlet.

Forcible-Entry Tools

To do an effective job when fire fighting, you must gain access to the fire. If the normal means of access are blocked, or locked, you will need to use forcible-entry tools to gain access to the area so that you can fight the fire.

The tools most frequently used for forcible entry are the sledgehammer, ax, crowbar, wrecking bar, claw tool, hacksaw, bolt cutter, and exothermic cutting torch.

The portable pack-type exothermic cutting torch may be used to cut holes in decks or bulkheads so that nozzles may be inserted to fight a fire. The outfit may also be used to cut away debris that would hinder fire fighters or rescue workers. These cutting outfits are to be used for emergencies only, never for routine cutting jobs.

Smoke Curtains

Description. Flame-resistant portable smoke curtains and blankets are stowed in repair stations. These curtains are made of fiberglass or other material. There are two kinds of smoke curtains. One is a two-panel curtain for use at doorways and in passageways to control the lateral spread of smoke; it is provided with five spring clamps. The other is a large blanket, 14 feet square, for use at open hatchways to control the vertical spread of smoke.

Dewatering Pump-Model CG-P1A

Designed for the purpose of dewatering boats in danger of sinking, this pump has a rated output of 140 gallons of water per minute.

Submersible Pumps

The portable submersible pump used aboard naval ships is a centrifugal pump driven by a water-jacketed constant-speed ac or dc electric motor. The latest design is rated to deliver 140 gallons per minute against a maximum head of 70 feet. When the head is reduced to 50 feet, the output rises to 180 gallons per minute. Basket strainers are always used with submersible pumps when flood water is being pumped.

To dewater a compartment with a submersible pump, lower the pump into the water using the attached nylon handling line and lead the 2½-inch discharge hose to the nearest point of discharge. The amount of flooding water taken from a flooded space increases as the discharge head decreases. Therefore, dewatering is accomplished most efficiently if the water is discharged at the lowest practicable point and if the discharge hose is short and free from kinks.

Eductor

Eductors are jet-type pumps that contain no moving parts. An eductor moves liquid from one place to another by entraining the pumped liquid in a rapidly flowing stream of water (venturi effect). The eductor can perform low-head dewatering operations at a greater rate of discharge than can be obtained by straight pumping with available emergency pumps. Eductors are used to pump liquids that cannot be pumped by other portable pumps. Also, liquids that contain fairly small particles of foreign matter can be pumped by using an eductor.

Atmosphere Testing Devices

All closed or poorly ventilated compartments, particularly those in which a fire has just occurred, are potentially dangerous. The atmosphere may lack oxygen, contain poisonous gases, or present fire and explosion hazards.

Oxygen Analyzer

The oxygen analyzer is used to verify the percentage of oxygen within a space.

The Navy's Bureau of Medicine requires a space to have an oxygen content of 20 percent before personnel can enter the space without an OBA or an air-line mask. The normal oxygen percentage level at sea level is 20.8 percent.

The oxygen analyzer provides a continuous reading of the oxygen content concentration from 0 percent to 25 percent oxygen in any environment. An oxygen level below 20 percent or above 22 percent should be considered as a potentially dangerous situation.

Combustible-Gas Indicators

The combustible-gas indicator is an instrument used to detect various flammable gases and vapors.

The combustible-gas inductor does not identify combustible gas or gases; it merely indicates that one or more combustible gases are present in a certain proportion.

Drager Multigas Detector

The Drager multigas detector is used to test the atmosphere within a space for toxic gases such as carbon dioxide, carbon monoxide, nitrogen dioxide, and hydrogen sulfide. A separate detector bulb is used for each type of gas. For safety and accuracy, use only Drager detector tubes with Drager multigas detectors.

FIRE FIGHTING TECHNIQUE

Ships are in constant danger of sudden fire that can spread quickly and place the ship and its crew in the gravest danger. Fire on board ship must be handled promptly and effectively wherever it may occur. Every moment of delay increases the danger that the fire will spread.

Fighting fire on board ship is complicated. It involves the teamwork and efficiency of all shipboard personnel. All hands must learn their fire-fighting duties thoroughly. Then when fire strikes, they will be prepared to fight it promptly and efficiently.

A fire party follows these four steps in fighting a fire:

- Locates and reports the fire.
- Isolates the area and fights the fire.
- Sets a reflash watch.
- Overhauls the area.

Locating the Fire

Many fires break out in unattended spaces such as storage areas and gain considerable headway before they are discovered. The first sign of fire may be smoke pouring from a ventilating system outlet or seeping around a door or hatch cover. Smoke may have traveled a considerable distance from the fire, so locating the fire is usually the first job.

Repair locker investigators examine all bulkheads, decks, and vents for abnormal heat. A compartment may be clear, but a hot bulkhead would indicate a fire in the next compartment. Follow up any odor or trace of smoke. Even though the main fire is located, there may be fires in other compartments, and they must all be fought at the same time. When the fire has been definitely located and its extent determined, a complete report of the situation is made to the repair locker.

Isolating the Fire

While the fire party fights the fire, it also sets up fire boundaries to isolate it. If a single compartment is involved, it is isolated from above and below, as well as from all four sides. If a number of compartments are involved, the fire party treats them as a unit and protects all adjacent spaces, to keep the fire from spreading.

Materials on the deck above are removed or thoroughly cooled to prevent the spread of fire. Usually, an inch of water on the deck is enough to absorb the heat from the burning compartment below. Spaces below the fire must not be neglected or paint on the overhead may blister and ignite. Fog should be used to cool the overhead and prevent ignition of materials in such spaces.

All ventilation systems in the fire area are secured to prevent heat and unburned vapors being carried to other compartments, and to help starve the fire by cutting off its air supply.

If there is any doubt that the fire can be kept within the established boundary, a secondary or emergency boundary is set up. Additional hose lines are made ready for use at the secondary boundary.

Fighting the Fire

While the fire is being isolated, it should also be fought. The first step is to de-energize electric circuits in the compartments to protect personnel against shock. Always check fire-hose water pressure at the nozzle before entering any space. All members of the fire party will be dressed in fire-fighter ensemble. Heat and unburned gases build up pressure that should be vented by undogging the door slowly before it is opened completely for entry.

Reflash Watch

Fires that seem to be out may start again from a smoldering fragment of material or through vapor ignition. The next step after extinguishing a fire aboard ship is to set up a reflash watch for each compartment involved, and to maintain it as long as the possibility of reflash exists.

Overhauling the Area

After all fire is extinguished, the area must be overhauled to prevent a reflash of the fire. To do this, members of the fire party break up all smoldering or charred material and saturate it. Whenever possible, materials are immersed in buckets of water. Compartments are desmoked and dewatered. All compartments involved are checked for explosive vapors or liquids that may remain. At this time, a full report is made to the commanding officer on fire and smoke damage and flooding.

Special Problems

In some spaces of the ship, fire fighting is more hazardous than in others, and special equipment is needed. Magazine fires are extremely dangerous. In these spaces, sprinkling systems are installed, which are either automatically or manually operated to cool the ammunition and bulkheads until the fire can be extinguished by fire fighters.

Dangerous oil fires may occur in machinery spaces. Therefore, a steam smothering system is usually installed in addition to standard fire-fighting equipment. Smothering is used first to smother the fire. If the fire spreads, water-fog and foam must be used to extinguish it.

Bedding and other combustibles in living and berthing spaces are potential sources of fire. Some of these spaces contain fixed fog systems that are manually connected to fire plugs with hose lines. The fog will beat down the surface flames until fire hoses can be turned on the fire.

Caution

Some plastics and curtains used in living areas can burn easily and produce toxic gases. Fire parties must be aware of such dangers. The person in charge must know what is burning and how best to handle it, in order to protect personnel.

CHAPTER 26
Maintenance

Every Coast Guard item, no matter how simple or complicated, must be clean and operable for us to safely carry out our many missions. You may think that cleaning and painting aren't important, but they are. Rusted or dirty equipment is not only harder to operate, but eventually fails. That failure could come at a time when *your* life depends upon it.

This chapter describes the general procedures for compartment cleaning, basic paint ingredients, how to prepare surfaces for painting, the basic use and care of paints and paint applicators, safety precautions, and items you should not paint. If you ever have any doubt about the proper way to do any maintenance, ask your supervisor for help!

CLEANING

Maintaining clean conditions aboard ship and ashore has always been an important part of Coast Guard activity. Cleaning is a job that involves practically every member, from the compartment cleaner to the inspecting officer. The close surroundings of Coast Guard life require each of us to have a personal interest in our living and working areas, not only for the sake of appearance but for our health and safety as well.

Figure 26-1. It takes a lot of hard work to keep Coast Guard equipment and facilities in first-class shape.

The Cleaning Bill

Each area of a ship or station is assigned to one of its various departments for upkeep. The Cleaning, Preservation, and Maintenance Bill describes these areas and outlines which department is responsible for them. This bill is carefully planned to ensure that all interior and exterior areas of a ship or station are assigned, and that no areas overlap or are left out. Each division within a department assigns its personnel to the spaces it is responsible for to carry out the duties of cleaning, preservation, and maintenance.

Compartment Cleaning

The term *compartment cleaner* generally applies to persons assigned to clean the living or berthing compartments or spaces such as passageways and heads.

If you are assigned compartment cleaner duties, you will be responsible for keeping your spaces exceptionally clean, preserved, and in good order. Newly assigned personnel are closely supervised to make sure they understand what to clean and how to clean it. Items that may be unfamiliar to you, such as electrical and mechanical devices, are in almost every space aboard ship. With this in mind, caution must be observed at all times. Ask your supervisor to point out hazardous items in your compartment, and observe all special cleaning instructions.

To reduce waste and provide for bulk storage, cleaning gear is stocked in and issued from the Bosun's Hold. Each division is periodically issued cleaning gear and is responsible for its proper storage and care. Because cleaning compounds and solvents are usually either flammable or toxic or both, they must never be left unattended or stored improperly. Always read warning labels and follow their directions carefully. Gear such as brooms and swabs must be cleaned after each use and placed in their storage racks. Gear adrift, such as rags, clothing, or personal gear, must be "policed up" immediately. Any items, if left adrift, could cause serious damage to the ship.

Sweepers

"Sweepers" is piped shortly after reveille, at the end of the regular working day, and at other times as scheduled. At these times, all persons assigned as sweepers draw their gear and sweep and swab down their assigned areas. All trash and dirt should be picked up in a dustpan and placed in a trash receptacle. If dirt is swept over the side, the wind may blow it back on board or the dirt may stick to the side of the ship. In either case, additional work is necessary to clean the ship. At this time you should empty all butt kits (ensure no butts are still burning) and trash receptacles as instructed. Never dump trash or garbage over the side of the ship without first obtaining permission from the officer of the deck. There are various times when all trash must be kept in a safe area aboard the ship until it can be properly disposed of.

The Cleaning Process

Dirt, soil, and contamination all describe the same thing: a foreign material on a surface where it is not wanted. Soil includes grease, oil, tarnish, rust, food residue, and stains. Most exposed surfaces that have been soiled may be cleaned by the proper use of cleaning agents.

Detergents are materials that have the ability to remove contamination and soil. There are other ways of cleaning besides the use of detergents or cleaning compounds. These include purely mechanical processes, such as removing rust from steel by sandblasting or cleaning decks by sweeping. For many cleaning problems, chipping, sweeping, sanding, or brushing may be needed. When detergent compounds are coupled with the mechanical action, however, a cleaner surface is usually produced with less time and labor.

The steps used in most detergent cleaning operations are as follows:

Wetting. The soil and the surface of the object being cleaned must be wetted. If the surface is not wetted properly, the cleaning results will be poor. Contrary to popular belief, water has very poor wetting properties. Its wetting ability, and therefore its cleaning ability, is improved greatly by the addition of materials such as soap or synthetic detergents, which cause the water to flow into tiny crevices and around small particles of soil.

Scrubbing. Dirt is loosened by the mechanical action of rubbing or scrubbing. Oil droplets, for example, are emulsified; that is, they are coated with a thin film of soap. The coating prevents them from recombining, and they rise to the surface. In a somewhat similar manner, solid particles are suspended in solution.

Rinsing. The rinse is very important. It removes loosened dirt from the surface along with the cleaning material.

Zone Inspection

Frequent inspections ensure that all spaces, machinery, and equipment are in a satisfactory state of operation, preservation, and cleanliness. One type of inspection, the zone, divides the ship or station into zones. Each zone is assigned to an inspection party or team. Usually the commanding officer will head one team, while an officer or chief petty officer will head each of the remaining teams. If you are assigned to present a compartment, you present the space to the inspecting officer by saluting and greeting the inspector in the following manner: "Good morning (afternoon), sir/ma'am; Seaman Apprentice Jones (your rank and name) standing by compartment (name or number), for your inspection, sir/ma'am." You will stay with the inspecting officer during the inspection of your spaces to answer questions and provide assistance. Such things as storage cabinets, lockers, and drawers should be unlocked prior to the inspection for easy access. Usually the inspecting officer will give an overall grade to the space; for example, a grade of "outstanding" would indicate that no new discrepancies were noted and all previous discrepancies have been corrected. This is a grade you can be proud of.

Field Day

Periodically, a field day is held. Field day is cleaning day. All hands "turn to" and thoroughly clean the ship inside and out, usually in preparation for an inspection. Fixtures and areas that sometimes are neglected during regular sweepdowns (overhead cables, piping, corners, spaces behind and under equipment, and so on) are cleaned; bulkheads, decks, ladders, and all other accessible areas are scrubbed; knife edges and door gaskets are checked, and any paint, oil, or other substances are removed; all brightwork is shined; and clean linen is placed on each bunk. Field days improve the appearance and sanitary condition of the ship, aid in the preservation of the ship by extending paint life, and reduce the dirt taken into operating equipment. Dirt intake must be held to a minimum to prevent the overheating of electrical equipment and abrasive action in rotating machinery.

Because of weather conditions, there will be many days at sea when the ship's topside areas cannot be cleaned. At the first opportunity, all topside surfaces should be cleaned with fresh water and an inspection made for signs of rust and corrosion. If such signs are discovered, you should tend to the area immediately. A little work at that time will save you a lot of work later.

Deck coverings aboard ship receive more wear than any other material. Unless proper care is given to them, costly replacement is required. There are several materials used for covering decks, but we will discuss only two: the resilient and the nonslip (nonskid paint) types.

Resilient deck coverings include vinyl tile, vinyl asbestos tile, and linoleum. These deck coverings do not need painting; however, daily sweeping and wiping away of spills as soon as possible is necessary. This type of deck covering is cleaned with a damp swab frequently, allowed to dry, then buffed with an electric buffing machine. For more thorough cleaning, when the deck is unusually dirty, apply a solution of warm water and detergent with a stiff bristle brush or circular scrubbing machine and rinse with clean water to remove residual detergent. Stubborn dirt and black marks left by shoes can be removed by rubbing lightly with a scouring pad, fine steel wool, or a rag moistened with mineral spirits.

After the deck covering is washed and dried, it can be polished (with or without waxing) with a buffing machine, or it may be given a coat of self-polishing wax and allowed to dry without buffing. Deck coverings can be buffed several times before rewaxing.

Nonslip (nonskid paint) deck coverings contain pumice, which helps to provide a better footing. To clean a nonskid painted deck, use a cleaning solution consisting of one pint of detergent and five tablespoons of dishwashing compound. This is mixed with fresh water to make 20 gallons of cleaning solution. Apply the solution with a hand scrubber, let it soak for five minutes, then rinse with fresh water. Nonskid deck coverings should not be waxed or painted because to do so will reduce their nonskid properties. If it becomes necessary to spruce up the appearance of a nonskid deck cover, it may be brushed with deck paint diluted with mineral spirits. The diluted paint should be as thin as possible so that the nonskid properties are not affected.

The Coast Guard uses paints primarily for the preservation of surfaces. It seals the pores of steel and other materials, prevents decay, and arrests rust and corrosion. Paint also serves several other purposes. It is valuable as an aid to cleanliness and sanitation because of its antiseptic properties and because it provides a smooth, washable surface. Paint also is used to reflect, absorb, or redistribute light. For example, light-colored paint on a ship's interior distributes natural and artificial light to its best advantage.

Learning to paint properly requires the selection of suitable paints for the surfaces to be covered, the proper preparation of the surfaces before painting, and the correct methods of applying paint. Though the selection of suitable paints will not concern you at this time, you should know how to prepare the surface and how to apply paint with a brush and roller. Improper surface preparation and paint application, in that order, are the greatest reasons for paint failure.

Gaskets, Dogs, Air Ports

Rubber gaskets used for watertight, weather-tight, and airtight purposes should *not* be painted. The metal-bearing edges that come in contact with the gasket should be kept free from rust, grease, and paint. Emery should not be used. The dogs, dog bolts, nuts, hinges, and hinge pins or other parts of watertight doors, and the hatches, manholes, and air ports upon which the watertight security of vessels depends must not be removed except for repair or adjustment. The removal of these parts for other purposes, such as cleaning or polishing, is prohibited, as this practice often results in the loss of the parts or their being replaced without correct adjustment.

PAINTING

Keeping cutters and boats in first-class condition means a constant battle against corrosion, and the only effective protection against corrosion is good paint properly applied to metal surfaces that have been carefully prepared for painting.

This section covers the basic procedures and safety precautions you should observe while painting. More detailed information can be found in the *Coatings and Colors Manual*.

Types of Paint

Anticorrosive paint is used on underwater hull areas to prevent salt water from acting on metal, and for boot topping. It is always used with antifouling paint and *must* go on first. It contains heavy pigments and must be stirred frequently. It dries very rapidly so that it must be applied in short, quick strokes.

Antifouling is applied to a ship's bottom to prevent marine growth—barnacles, worms, and plants. It contains copper oxide, which will pit steel plating wherever it touches, so it must always be used *over* anticorrosive paint.

Boot topping is a special paint applied to the hull at the waterline, covering the area between light load and full load drafts.

Pretreatment coating is applied to all bare metal surfaces, if possible, before the primer coat is applied. It dries fast—within 30 minutes—and if not used within eight hours, must be discarded. It is highly flammable; observe all safety precautions. Modern paint systems, such as Formula 150, incorporate both pretreatment and primer in the same application.

Primers are base coats applied to wood and metal to make a smooth surface for final coats. Always apply two coats of a primer, and a third at all outside edges and corners.

Exterior topside paints consist of white or spar for vertical surfaces and deck gray for horizontal surfaces; spar is used on certain other areas.

Deck paints are green for officers' quarters and wardrooms, gray for other living and working spaces, and red for machinery spaces and shops.

Interior bulkhead and overhead paint is usually fire retardant. White is commonly used on both bulkheads and overheads; other colors are green for offices, radio rooms, pilothouses, and medical spaces; gray for electronic and flag offices; acid-resisting black for compartments in which acids are used; and various pastel shades in crew's living and messing compartments.

Machinery paint is usually gray enamel.

Surface Preparation

For paint to stick to a surface, all salt, dirt, oil, grease, rust, and loose paint must be removed completely, and the surface must be thoroughly dry.

Salt and most dirt can be removed with soap or detergent and fresh water. Firmly imbedded dirt may require scrubbing with scouring powder. When oil and grease fail to yield to scrubbing, they may be removed with paint thinner or other approved solvents. After scrubbing or scouring, always rinse the surface with fresh water.

Equipment and Procedures

The removal of rust, scale, and loose paint requires the use of hand tools or power tools, and paint and varnish removers. Hand tools usually are used for cleaning small areas; power tools are for larger areas and for completely cleaning decks, bulkheads, and overheads covered with too many coats of paint. Paint and varnish removers are used to remove paint from wood.

Hand Tools

The most commonly used hand tools are sandpaper, wire brushes, and hand scrapers. Sandpaper is used to clean corners and to feather paint—that is, to taper the edges of chipped areas down to the cleaned surface so that no rough edges remain. Paint will bond best to a clean surface that has been lightly sanded.

Sandpaper is graded according to the size of the abrasive grit on its surface. For example, it is graded from 12 to 600, the coarsest being 12 and the finest, 600 grit. Very fine emery (a natural abrasive) paper is sometimes used to polish unpainted surfaces.

A wire brush is a handy tool for light work on rust or on light coats of paint. Such a brush also is used for brushing weld spots and cleaning pitted surfaces.

Hand scrapers are made of tool steel. The most common type is L-shaped, with each end tapered to a cutting edge like a wood chisel. They are most useful for removing rust and paint from small areas and from plating less than one-fourth of an inch thick when it is impractical or impossible to use power tools.

Occasionally it is necessary to use a chipping or scaling hammer, but care must be taken to exert only enough force to remove the paint. Too much force dents the metal, resulting in high and low areas. The paint is naturally thinner on the high areas. Consequently, thin paint wears off quickly, leaving spots where rust will form and, in time, spread under the good paint.

Power Tool Safety Precautions

You must be properly trained and qualified before you operate portable power tools. The following safety precautions must be observed when working with electrical and pneumatic (air) tools.

- Wear eye and ear protection while chipping, grinding, sanding, or wire brushing. If dust is excessive, wear a respirator. Do not wear jewelry or loose-fitting clothing.
- Do not use defective tools. If you have any doubt about the condition of any tool, show it to your petty officer, who will have its condition determined.

- Make certain that electrical power tools are grounded properly. Every portable electrical power tool must be provided with a ground lead that connects the tool casing to the ship's structure.
- Give your full attention to your job.
- Do not operate power tools in areas where flammable vapors, gases, liquids, or exposed explosives are present.
- Do not allow power cords and air hoses to kink or come into contact with oil, grease, hot surfaces, or sharp objects.
- Power cords and air hoses must not be laid over ladders, steps, scaffolds, or walkways in such a manner as to cause a tripping hazard.

Aluminum Surfaces

Aluminum surfaces aboard ship present a special problem because if they are not treated properly, considerable corrosion will result. Corrosion is greater when dissimilar metals (such as aluminum and steel) are in contact with each other and are exposed to an electrolyte (seawater, for example), which causes an electric current to flow between them, resulting in galvanic corrosion of the aluminum. The first sign of aluminum corrosion is a white, powdery residue in the area where the two dissimilar metals make contact, later by pitting and scarring of the aluminum surface, and finally by the complete deterioration of the aluminum in the area. Holes in aluminum plating enlarge, and the screws, bolts, or rivets pull out or may even disintegrate.

When painted aluminum surfaces are prepared for repainting, power sanders, if used, must be used with great care. It is best to use hand scrapers, hand and power wire brushes, or sandpaper of a very fine grit. *Never use scaling hammers.*

Steel Surfaces

The most important task in painting a steel surface is the preparation of the surface to be painted. Steel surfaces must be completely free of rust, loose paint, dirt, scale, oil, grease, salt deposits, and moisture. Old paint in good condition is an excellent base for repainting. When a surface is to be repainted and the old paint is not to be removed, the surface must be smoothed and thoroughly cleaned and dried before new paint is applied.

In touch-up painting, when only small areas or spots need repainting, it is essential that the removal of old paint be carried back around the edges of the spot or area until an area of completely intact paint, with no rust or blisters underneath, is reached. The edges of the remaining paint should be feathered.

When an old painted surface is to be completely redone, the old paint should be taken down to bare metal and a primer put on before painting. Never leave a bare metal surface exposed overnight. *Always* put on a primer coat before you quit for the day to prevent oxidation from starting.

Paint and Varnish Removers

Paint and varnish removers are used mostly on wood surfaces but may be used on metal surfaces that are too thin to be chipped or wire-brushed. The three types of removers in general use are flammable, nonflammable, and waterbase alkali. They all are hazardous, and their safety precautions must be strictly observed. The removers should be used only in well-ventilated spaces. The alkali type should not be used on aluminum or zinc because of its corrosive properties.

Safety precautions. Paint and varnish remover must never be used around an open flame, because some types are highly flammable. Removers must not be used in confined spaces because of their dangerous anesthetic or toxic properties that can kill or cause injury if you are exposed to them for long periods. Moreover, paint and varnish removers should not be used by persons having open cuts or sores on their hands unless rubber gloves are worn. Avoid letting the remover touch your skin; watch out particularly for your face, eyes, and mouth. If paint or varnish remover should come in contact with the skin, wash it off immediately with cold water; if it gets into your eyes or mouth, seek medical attention as soon as possible. Read the product label for full details.

What Not to Paint

The following items must not be painted:

- Knife edges, rubber gaskets, dogs, drop bolts, wedges, and the operating gear of watertight doors, hatches, and scuttles.
- Start-stop mechanisms of electrical safety devices and control switchboards on machinery elevators.
- Bell pulls, sheaves, annunciator chains, and other mechanical communication devices.

- Condenser heads and outside surfaces of condensers made of composition metal.
- Sprinkler piping within magazines.
- Glands, stems, yokes, toggle gear, and all machined external parts of the valves.
- Heat-exchange surfaces of heating or cooling equipment.
- Identification plates.
- Joint faces of gaskets and packing surfaces.
- Lubricating gear, such as oil holes, oil or grease cups, grease fittings, lubricators, and surfaces in contact with lubricating oil.
- Lubricating oil reservoirs.
- Machined-metal surfaces (working surfaces) of reciprocating engines or pumps.
- Metal lagging.
- Rods, gears, universal joints, and couplings of valve-operating gear.
- Rubber elements of isolation mounts.
- Ground plates.
- Springs.
- Strainers.
- Threaded parts.
- Zincs.
- Working surfaces.
- Hose and applicator nozzles.
- Electrical contact points and insulators.
- The original enamel, lacquer, or crackle finish on all radio, electrical, and sound equipment, unless damage makes refinishing essential.
- Decorative plastic, such as tabletops.

Painting Safety Precautions

Painting can be dangerous if one is careless. Many paints are highly flammable, others are poisonous, and some are both flammable and poisonous. To increase your chances of remaining alive and healthy, observe the following precautions:

- When burning off paints, do not leave the burned-off paint on the deck where it may become powdered when stepped on. Do not play the torch on the paint long enough to produce smoke. The fumes and powders from paints are poisonous. Do not burn off paint in a closed compartment.

- Keep paint off your skin as much as possible. Wash your hands, arms, and face with soap and warm water before eating. Do not put your fingers, cigarettes, or food in your mouth if they are contaminated with paint.
- Be sure you have adequate ventilation, and wear an approved paint/spray respirator whenever there is reason to believe the ventilation is inadequate in the place you are painting.
- Do not smoke, use an open flame, or use spark-producing tools in the vicinity of painting operations.
- Use only explosion-proof lights near painting operations.
- Do not wear nylon, orlon, or plastic clothing or covering. These materials generate static electricity, which may spark and ignite paint vapors.
- Do not carry matches or cigarette lighters, or wear steel buckles or metal shoe plates. Too often one forgets and strikes a match or lights a cigarette lighter in areas filled with explosive fumes. Steel buttons, buckles, and tabs can strike sparks that are invisible to your eyes, perhaps, but wholly capable of igniting paint vapors.
- When pouring solvents, make sure the containers are touching each other to prevent sparks.
- Never paint during electrical storms.
- Keep food and drink away from areas being painted.
- Do not use gasoline, turpentine, mineral spirits, or other solvents to remove paint from the skin, as the skin will absorb them.
- Follow carefully the instructions of your supervisor.

Paint Issue

Before paint, primers, or paint applicators are issued, your division petty officer will inspect the area to be painted to ensure that all preparations have been properly made. For example, are all items not to be painted properly identified or masked? Are all safety precautions understood and properly observed? Is the surface ready to be painted?

Remember, if you spill paint (oil, grease, whatever) you are responsible for cleaning it up. At the end of working hours, all paint and brushes must be returned to the paint locker. Paint must be stored in its proper container, and all brushes and rollers cleaned as described later in this chapter.

MAINTENANCE   489

PAINTING METHODS

Three means of applying paint are used in the Coast Guard—brush, roller, and spray. The majority of personnel have no occasion to use paint sprayers; hence, their use will not be described here. Instead, this section will concentrate on brushes and rollers, with which everyone in the Coast Guard should be familiar.

Paint Application by Brush

Smooth and even painting depends as much on good brushwork as on good paint. There is a brush for almost every purpose, so use the proper brush and keep it in the best condition.

The two most useful brushes are the flat brush and the sash brush. With a flat brush, a skillful painter can paint almost anything aboard ship. Flat brushes are wide and thick, carry a large quantity of paint, and provide a maximum of brushing action. Sash brushes are handy for painting small items, for cutting in at corners, and for hard-to-get-at spaces. The fitch brush also is useful for small surfaces. The painter's dusting brush is used for cleaning surfaces.

The following are some general hints to help you use a paintbrush properly:

Grip the brush firmly, but lightly, as shown in figure 26-2. Do not put your fingers on the bristles below the metal band (ferrule). The grip shown permits easy wrist and arm motion. To hold it otherwise restricts your movements and causes undue fatigue.

When using a flat brush, do not paint with the narrow edge. This practice wears down the corners and spoils the shape and efficiency of the brush. When using an oval brush, if you revolve it too much, it soon wears to a pointed shape and becomes useless. Do not poke oversized brushes into corners and around moldings. Such a practice bends the bristles, eventually ruining a good brush. Use a smaller brush that fits into such odd spots.

Dip the brush into the paint, but not over halfway up the bristles. Remove the excess paint by patting the brush on the inside of the pot. Avoid overfilling the brush, otherwise paint will drip on the deck or other surfaces and run down the handle.

Hold the brush at right angles to the surface being painted, with the ends of the bristles just touching the surface. Lift the brush clear of the surface when starting the return stroke. If the brush is not held correctly and is not lifted, the painted surface will be uneven, showing

Figure 26-2. Proper technique with a brush saves paint, time, and the brush.

laps and spots and a daubed appearance. Also, a brush that is held at any angle other than a right angle will soon wear away at the ends.

For complete and even coverage, first lay on, then lay off. Laying on means applying the paint first in long strokes in one direction. Laying off means crossing your first strokes. Using the recommended method and crossing your strokes distributes the paint evenly over the surface, covering it completely and using a minimum amount of paint.

Always paint the overhead first, working from the corner that is farthest from the entrance to the compartment. By painting the overhead first, you can wipe drippings off the bulkhead without smearing the bulkhead paint.

When overhead surfaces are being painted, sections should normally be painted in a fore-and-aft direction; beams, in an athwartship direction. But where sections of the overhead contain many pipes running parallel with the beams, it is often difficult to lay off the paint in a fore-and-aft direction. In such situations, better results are obtained by laying off the paint parallel with the beams.

To avoid brush marks when finishing up an area you have painted, use strokes directed toward the last section finished, gradually lifting the brush near the end of the stroke while the brush still is in motion. Every time the brush touches the painted surface at the start of a stroke it leaves a mark. For this reason, never finish a section by brushing toward the unpainted area. Instead, always end up by brushing back toward the area already painted.

When painting pipes, stanchions, narrow straps, beams, and angles, lay the paint on diagonally. Lay off along the long dimension.

Always carry a rag for wiping up dripped or smeared paint. Carefully remove loose bristles sticking to the painted surface.

Cutting In

After you master the art of using a paint brush properly, you should learn to cut in. Cutting in is a simple procedure, and anyone with a fairly steady hand can learn it in a short time.

Suppose you have to cut in the angle between an overhead and a bulkhead. Start at one corner. Hold your brush at an angle of 75 degrees to 80 degrees from the bulkhead and ten degrees from the overhead. Draw your brush along in fairly long, smooth strokes. This is one job where working slowly does not produce better results. The slower you stroke, the wavier your line will be.

Use of Rollers

Large areas, such as ships' decks and sides (free of rivets, bolts, cable, pipes, and so on), can be painted quickly by the roller method. The paint should be laid on and laid off in the same fashion as when brushes are used. A moderate amount of pressure must be applied to the roller to make sure that the paint is worked into the surface. If pressure is not applied, the paint does not stick and soon peels off. When the paint roller is properly used, it will apply a more even coat and use less paint than is possible with a brush.

Care of Brushes and Rollers

Unfortunately, far too many good paint brushes and rollers are ruined simply because painters have little or no idea how to care for them, or they are too lazy to clean them. Consequently, you should pay particular attention to the following hints, and heed them at all times. Treat applicators as though you paid for them yourself, and replace them when they are no longer usable.

Do not let a brush stand on its bristles in a pot of paint for more than a few minutes. The weight of the brush bends the bristles, making it almost impossible to do a good job. Never allow paint to dry on a brush. If you intend to leave a paint-filled brush for long periods, as over the noon hour, fold wax paper or other heavy paper around the bristles and ferrule in such a way that air is kept away from the bristles. Twist the paper around the handle and secure it with rope yarn or sail twine. Cover your pot of paint, and place both it and the brush in a safe place. Before starting to paint again, stir the paint thoroughly with a paddle—not the brush. At the end of the day, before turning in your paint and brush to the paint locker, clean as much paint from the brush as possible by wiping it across the edge of the paint pot or mixing paddle.

Ordinarily, the person or persons working in the paint locker will clean and stow the brushes turned in. Occasionally, though, they require help, and you may be detailed to the job. If so, follow instructions carefully, and do a thorough job of cleaning the brushes. Only brushes that can be cleaned with soap and water are to be cleaned. Others, unless they are to be used again right away, should be allowed to dry and then thrown away. The cost of disposing of thinners as hazardous waste precludes the reuse of these brushes.

Paint lockers usually have containers with divided compartments for stowing different types of brushes (that is, paint, varnish, shellac, and so on) for short periods of time. These containers normally have tight covers and are equipped for hanging brushes so that the entire length of the bristles and the lower part of the ferrule are covered by the solvent or cleaning oil kept in the container. Brushes are suspended so that the bristles do not touch the bottom, thus preventing them from becoming permanently misshapen.

Brushes to be used the following day should be cleaned in the proper cleaner and placed in the proper compartment of the container. Those not to be used again soon should be cleaned, washed in soap or detergent and water, and hung to dry. After drying, they should be wrapped in heavy paper and stowed flat. Do not leave a brush soaking in water. Water causes the bristles to separate into bunches, flare, and become bushy.

The proper cleaners for paint applicators are as follows:

Paint/Finish	*Solvent/Cleaner*
Natural and synthetic oil-base paints and varnishes; chlorinated alkyd resin paints	Turpentine or mineral spirits
Latex emulsion paints	Water
Chlorinated rubber paints	Synthetic enamel thinner xylene
Shellac	Alcohol (denatured)
Lacquer	Lacquer thinner

Paint rollers are cleaned in a different fashion. After use, the fabric cylinder should be stripped from the frame, washed in the cleaner recommended for the paint used, washed in soap and water, rinsed thoroughly in fresh water, and replaced on the frame to dry. Combing the pile of the fabric while it is damp prevents matting.

CHAPTER 27

Safety and Environmental Health

We perform many tasks every day that are dangerous. If you do not follow three basic rules, you or someone else may become sick, injured, or killed. You are responsible for reporting hazardous conditions, using protective equipment, and observing safety precautions. The *Safety and Environmental Health Manual*, COMDTINST M5100.47, contains information about the programs the Coast Guard has developed to protect you.

This chapter gives you an overview of the Coast Guard Safety and Environmental Health Program. The program includes your rights and responsibilities, procedures for reporting hazardous conditions, and methods of protection against the hazards.

THE COAST GUARD SAFETY AND ENVIRONMENTAL HEALTH PROGRAM

Current law provides rights and responsibilities for Coast Guard employees.

Your Rights and Responsibilities

As an employee of the Coast Guard, you have the right to a safe and healthful workplace. Your participation in the program is essential in providing such an environment. You have the right to:

- *Have access* to copies of Coast Guard standards, procedures, and injury and illness statistics.

Figure 27-1. Safety is crucial to many dangerous shipboard evolutions.

- *Comment* on proposed Coast Guard occupational safety and health standards.
- *Assist safety and health officials* in conducting inspections of Coast Guard facilities.
- *Request an inspection* of a work area alleged to possess unsafe or unhealthful conditions. You may make these requests either orally or in writing, and they must be recorded and maintained on file. You may remain anonymous if you wish.
- *Appeal* if you disagree with the action taken on unsafe or unhealthful conditions. If you have exhausted all means available to achieve a satisfactory resolution of the conditions and you remain dissatisfied, you may write the Office of Federal Agency Safety and Health Programs, Occupational Safety and Health Administration, Department of Labor, 3rd & Constitution Avenue, N.W., Washington, D.C. 20207.

You may exercise these rights without fear of reprisal, coercion, discrimination, restraint, or interference. If you think you are being treated unfairly because you exercised your rights, report it to the most immediate safety and health official. If you are not satisfied with the action taken by this official, you may contact Commandant (G-CCS), Chief of Staff, for additional review.

The "Occupational Safety and Health Rights and Responsibilities" poster is required to be displayed in all workplaces. This poster spells out your rights and responsibilities and lists the safety representatives' names and phone numbers.

The Hazard Communication Standard expands on the previous rights to include a *right to know what hazards exist* in your workplace. All known hazards should be pointed out to you during a unit indoctrination.

"Learn your job and the safety issues related to that job." You must comply with all occupational safety and health standards of the Department of Labor, the Department of Transportation, and the Coast Guard that apply to your own actions and conduct.

Identifying Hazards

Your ability to recognize hazards is directly related to your experience and familiarity with the task you are performing. Unfortunately, experience and job familiarity are often the cause of safety mishaps because people tend to be less careful in familiar situations.

Awareness of the ways people can be injured is a key element in recognizing hazards.

Reporting Hazards

You must report safety and health hazards when you find them. Never leave a hazardous condition for the next person to find the "hard way." There are two ways to report a hazardous condition.

The first is a simple oral report to the person responsible for the area in which the hazard exists. Most hazards reported in this way can be corrected on the spot.

The second is a written report submitted on a *Hazardous Condition Notification, Form CG-5082. Fill out Blocks 1 through 5 at a minimum.* Instructions for completing the entire form are contained in COMDTINST M5100.47. Submitting this form creates a record in a computerized information system so that other people can use it to correct similar hazards or document a widespread problem. Even if you make an oral report, a CG-5082 should be submitted for record purposes. Figure 27–2 shows a blank form.

Hazard Abatement

Abatement is the action taken to reduce, control, or eliminate risk. All reported hazards must be abated. Requiring the use of protective equipment, clothing, and devices, and following safety procedures are examples of abatement methods.

Personal Protective Equipment (PPE)

Personal Protective Equipment, or PPE, is a form of guarding against hazards. PPE *does not* eliminate hazards, it only reduces the risks associated with the hazards. Examples of PPE are steel-toe boots, ear plugs, safety eyeglasses, hard hats, and rubber aprons. Let's look at some of the equipment you will use to do your jobs. (Figure 27–3)

Eye Protection

Loss of eyesight is probably one of the most traumatic experiences a person can endure. The eyes are very delicate organs and must be protected. Eyes can be damaged from flying objects or debris, chemical splashes including acids and alkalis, and bright light, like that found in arc-welding or in the glare from sunlight.

DEPARTMENT OF TRANSPORTATION **U. S. COAST GUARD** CG-5082 (8-76)	**HAZARDOUS CONDITION NOTIFICATION**	Identification Number **047069**	
1. NAME AND ADDRESS OF UNIT		**2. OPFAC NUMBER (7-13)**	**3. DATE (14-19)** MO DA YR

4. TYPE OF NOTIFICATION (20) (Check one only)

☐ SAFETY SPECIALIST NOTIFICATION
A

☐ EMPLOYEE NOTIFICATION
B

☐ SAFETY SPECIALIST INVESTIGATION OF EMPLOYEE NOTIFICATION
C

5. NARRATIVE (Describe condition, suggest solution, cite standard violated, give exact location, identify equipment, etc.) (Use additional paper as required)

6. ADP DATA — NARRATIVE BASE

(21-45)

(46-70)

(71-95)

(96-120)

7. ADP DATA — STANDARD VIOLATED

(1-25)

8. ADP DATA — LOCATION

(26-50)

9. ADP DATA — COST, TIME CRITICALITY

EST. COST DOLLARS (51-57)   EST. COMP. TIME (58-60)   CRITICALITY (61)

10. SAFETY SPECIALIST CODE AND SIGNATURE

CODE (62-63)   SIGNATURE _____

11. ADP DATA — COST AND COMP. DATE (Completed by Unit C.O.)

ACT. COST DOLLARS (64-70)   COMP. DATE MO DA YR (71-76)   SIGNATURE _____

Figure 27-2. CG-5082 form—Hazardous Condition Notification.

Figure 27-3. Personal protective equipment.

The most common forms of eye protection are safety eyeglasses. They look like regular eyeglasses with shields along the sides to prevent objects from bouncing off the inside of the glasses into your eye. The lenses are made of special high-impact shatter-proof plastic. They are available with prescription lenses, however, the Coast Guard does not usually provide prescription safety eyeglasses unless your job requires it.

If you wear prescription glasses, you can use safety goggles designed to fit over the outside of them. They offer the same level of protection as safety eyeglasses.

Face shields are worn on your head like a hat. They are usually built with the capability of being flipped up and down on a hinge, and they protect your face from flying debris or chemical splashes while offering additional protection over the eyeglasses or goggles. If a job calls for the use of other forms of eye protection, you should also wear a face shield.

Gas-welding goggles are used for gas welding or standing a fire watch. The lighter shade of the lenses in the goggles will protect your eyes from reflected ultraviolet, but not direct, rays. Never look at the arc of an arc-welding operation when wearing these goggles. Before using them, hold them up to a light source and check for cracks. Even small cracks will let harmful rays into your eyes and cause flash burn. Flash burn feels as if you have sand in your eyes.

You can best protect your eyes from the glare of reflected sunlight by wearing polarized sunglasses.

Hearing Protection

You should strive to protect your hearing with the same priority given to eyesight. Many jobs we do every day present high-noise-level hazards. There are two basic types of hearing protectors, ear plugs and aural protectors.

Ear plugs may be reusable or disposable. Disposable plugs are rolled between the thumb and forefinger and inserted into the ears. Once in the ear, they expand to form a sound-reducing barrier. They are maintenance free, inexpensive, and convenient, and offer the same level of protection as the reusable type.

Reusable plugs offer adequate protection, but must be fitted to the person wearing them. They are available in various types and sizes as shown in Table 1.

Table 1. Personal Hearing Protection, Ear Plugs

STYLE	SIZE	COLOR	NSN (6515-00-...)
Sterilizable plastic, single flange	Extra small	White	442–4765
	Small	Green	467–0085
	Medium	Orange	467–0089
	Large	Blue	442–4807
	Extra large	Red	442–4813
Sterilizable silicone rubber, triple flange	Small	Green	442–4821
	Medium	Orange	442–4818
	Large	Blue	467–0092
Silicone rubber, cylindrical, disposable	Universal		135–2612
Vinyl foam, cylindrical, reusable	Universal		137–6345

When you first begin wearing ear plugs, there may be some discomfort. This is normal and usually goes away after a few minutes. Continued discomfort may be corrected by trying a different size or style. It is very important that you protect your hearing, so, get a proper fit and *wear them*.

Respiratory Protection

Respiratory protection is required to prevent death or illness caused by harmful dusts, fumes, smoke, aerosols, mists, gases, vapors, and atmosphere without enough breathable oxygen. The Coast Guard strives to prevent contamination by confining the hazard, providing adequate ventilation, or substituting a less toxic material. Additional information on respirators can be found in the *Technical Guide: Practices for Respiratory Protection*, COMDTINST M6260.2.

If the above protection is not practical or not in place, you *must* wear a respirator appropriate to the task. When respirators are required, you are responsible for using them properly and reporting any malfunctions such as leaks, problems with fit, and air flow.

Maintenance and Logistics Commands (MLC) safety officials will assist your unit in selecting the right respirator for any given situation.

There are three basic types of respiratory protection: air purifying, atmosphere providing, and atmosphere supplying/air purifying.

Air-purifying respirators. Air-purifying respirators (APR) in use in the Coast Guard fall into four basic categories:

- Single use (disposable)
- Chemical cartridge, both full- and half-face
- Paint spray
- Gas mask

Their use is dependent upon several requirements.

- There *must* be adequate oxygen in the atmosphere.
- The contaminant(s) *must* be identified.
- There *must* be a distinct odor from the contaminant.
- The respirator *must* have the correct cartridge or filter.
- The contaminant *cannot* be absorbed through the skin.

Atmosphere-providing respirators. Atmosphere-providing respirators, sometimes called supplied-air respirators, provide breathable air. They *must* provide a positive pressure to the user. The Coast Guard uses the following three types of atmosphere-providing respirators:

- Self-Contained Breathing Apparatus (SCBA)
- Hose mask
- Air line

Atmosphere-providing/air-purifying. This type of respiratory protection offers the benefits of an SCBA as a backup to the hose mask or air-line respirators. Certain operations require this level of protection.

Approved Respirators

The respirator being used *must* be an approved type. The National Institute of Occupational Safety and Health, NIOSH, and the Mining Enforcement and Safety Administration, MESA, offer standards and specifications for approving respirators for various uses. *Approved respiratory protection will have an approval number beginning with the letters "TC."*

Protective Clothing and Equipment

So far, we have talked about eye protection, hearing conservation, and respiratory protection. This section will introduce you to protective clothing and equipment for the rest of your body.

Certain operations can result in injuries whether they are wounds, burns, or broken bones. Sickness, and even death, can be the result of absorbing a chemical through the skin. The choice of protective clothing and equipment depends on the hazards you expect to find when doing a job.

Some of the various forms of protective clothing and equipment you may use in the Coast Guard are listed below.

- Hard hats
- Combat helmets
- Hard hat/face shield combination
- Foul-weather clothing
- Personal flotation devices (PFD)
- Body armor
- Aprons (leather, rubber, canvas)
- Gloves (leather, rubber, cotton)
- Boots (steel-toe, rubber)
- Full-body chemical-exposure suits
- Industrial safety harnesses

The job will dictate which clothing or equipment you need. Be sure you get the training you need to wear or use *any* protective equipment or clothing.

Potentially Hazardous Operations

Our jobs are inherently dangerous. Table 2 lists some of the jobs presenting hazards you can expect to be exposed to and the equipment you need to protect yourself.

Table 2. Common Hazards and Protective Measures

Potentially Hazardous Operation	Protective Clothing and Equipment
All industrial jobs	Foot protection (safety shoes)
Anchor detail	Hard hat, eye protection (goggles), PFD, and safety shoes
Engineering watch	Single hearing protection below 104 dBA, double protection above, and safety shoes
Fire watch (welding)	High efficiency particulate filter type respirator or airline mask, welding goggles, cover exposed skin to avoid burns from UV radiation, and safety shoes
Firing range or gunnery exercise	Single hearing protection, eye protection (goggles or glasses)

Fuel handling inside (poor ventilation)	Chemical goggle eye protection, organic vapor respirator and cartridge, chemical resistant neoprene rubber gloves. Safety shoes, review material safety data sheet
Fuel handling outside (good ventilation)	Chemical goggle eye protection, chemical resistant neoprene rubber gloves. Safety shoes, review material safety data sheet
Handling corrosive chemicals	Face shield eye protection, chemical resistant neoprene apron, boots, and gloves, review material safety data sheet
Lawn care (mowing and brush clearing)	Single hearing protection and eye protection (goggles), and safety shoes
Line handling (mooring, getting underway, lowering and recovering boats)	Hard hat (boat lowering and recovery only), PFD, no gloves, and safety shoes
Parts cleaning and degreasing	Eye protection (goggles and face shield), ventilation, organic vapor respirator and cartridge, chemical resistant neoprene gloves, review material safety data sheet
Painting (brush) and paint mixing	Eye protection (goggles and face shield), ventilation, organic vapor respirator and cartridge, chemical resistant neoprene gloves, review material safety data sheet
Painting (spray)	Eye protection (goggles and face shield), ventilation, organic vapor respirator and cartridge with paint prefilter, chemical resistant neoprene gloves, review material safety data sheet
Preparing surfaces (chipping and grinding)	Eye protection (goggles), hearing protection, dust mask, gloves, and long sleeve shirt
Towing detail	Hard hat, PFD, and safety shoes
Working aloft	Industrial safety harness with safety line and observer and other equipment for task being performed aloft
Working over the side	Industrial safety harness with safety line and observer, PFD, and other safety equipment for task being performed over the side
Working in or entering a confined space	Air supplied respirator (positive pressure demand type), industrial safety harness with safety line and observer and other safety equipment for task being performed in the confined space

General Safety Hazards and Precautions

This section presents some general hazards and precautions you may find useful. Keep in mind, however, that there may be other hazards and appropriate precautions. They may be specific to your unit or the result of a new system or technology since this was written. Check with your supervisor or safety representative.

Confined Spaces

Closed compartments and unvented spaces may contain unexpected dangers. They may contain liquids or gases that are poisonous, explosive, or deficient in oxygen. The liquids or gases may be under high pressure. All confined spaces should be considered dangerous until proven otherwise. You should *never* enter any of these spaces on your own. The spaces presenting this danger should be clearly marked, but don't be too sure. Enter *only* when directed and when you have taken these precautions:

- Break the seal on the entrance cover *before* removing hold-down bolts or other fastenings.
- Have the space certified as safe by a gas-free engineer.
- Wear appropriate respiratory protection as directed by the gas-free engineer.
- Wear a tending line when working in the space.
- Make sure you have a reliable safety tender standing by and a reliable method of communicating with each other. If you are the safety tender, and the person working in the space is overcome, *do not* enter the space without a self-contained breathing apparatus (SCBA). See the section on respiratory protection.

Boat Safety

Most people in the Coast Guard will be aboard small boats at one time or another either as a passenger or a crew member. When you are boarding a boat or on the boat, follow these general guidelines:

- Obey all orders of the coxswain.
- *Do not* distract the boat crew.
- *Do not* engage in horseplay or move about, causing instability.
- *Do not* smoke in the boat.
- *Do not* sit on life jackets . . . *wear them!*
- Keep all parts of your body in the boat and *do not* sit on gunwales.
- If the boat capsizes or gets swamped, *do not* panic.
- Stay with the boat. Help others.

Deck Safety

A ship's deck presents numerous tripping hazards. These include cleats, bitts, padeyes, and the larger objects like boat davits and winches. Learn where these hazards are before you need to go topside at night. When you are on deck, *do not* sit or lean on lifelines. Stand inboard of them and hang on at all times.

Larger ships have flight decks for helicopter operations. This deck has additional hazards. Rotating propellers are nearly invisible and will kill or maim you if you come into contact with them. Only personnel necessary to flight operations should be on the flight deck.

Lifting

The correct method of lifting certain loads is often neglected. If you do not lift loads properly, you may wind up with a hernia or injured back. Or you may lose control of your load and drop it onto one of your crew mates.

When moving loads that are too heavy or bulky, get help or use a hand truck or dolly. There is no shame in doing a job safely and efficiently.

If you are going to carry a load, follow these guidelines:

- Face the spot where you are going to put the object.
- Crouch down close to the object with feet spread to a comfortable width.
- Pull the object toward you.
- Get a good grip on the object.
- Make sure you can see over the top of the object.
- While keeping your back straight and nearly vertical, tuck in your chin and lift with your legs. *Do not* use a jerking motion.
- Pull the object in closer to center the weight.
- *Do not* twist your body when lifting or carrying. Twisting your body causes most back injuries.
- *Do not* change your grip while carrying the load. Set it down and change your grip.
- If placing a load on a bench or table, set it on the edge and push it away from you.

Handling Cargo

In addition to the lifting precautions, you should exercise the following precautions when handling cargo.

- Remove rings, watches, and bracelets.
- *Do not* throw or drop items from elevated places. Lower them on a line or carry them.
- Wear appropriate protective clothing and equipment such as steel-toe shoes, PFDs, and hard hats.
- Secure hatch covers or doors to avoid interference with traffic flow.
- Use the nonworking side of the ship or an alternate path ashore to avoid traffic.
- *Never* stand in the bight of a line or near lines under strain.
- When using a hand truck, pull the load up, and lower (or push) the load down, ramps.
- When steadying a load, *do not* stand between the load and a fixed object or under a suspended load.
- *Do not* ride a load in any direction, up, down, or horizontally.
- *Do not* engage in horseplay.

Lifelines

Lifelines are lines constructed around the edges of a ship's deck. They are protective barriers to keep people from being thrown or washed over the side. To ensure your safety, and the safety of your crew mates, you should observe these precautions:

- *Never* sit, stand, or lean on lifelines.
- *Never* hang or secure any weight on a lifeline.
- *Never* remove a lifeline without permission. If you do remove one, rig a temporary line in its place.

Ladders

Ladders are a common source of injury if precautions are not followed. In addition to shipboard ladders, the Coast Guard uses straight ladders, extension ladders, multiple-angle ladders, and stepladders. Some ladders are permanently installed, like fire escapes and on towers.

Aboard ship, most ladders are removable. If you have to remove one, be sure to secure hatches and gangways leading to the ladder. The steps of ladders seem to gather paint cans, tools, spilled liquids, and other hazards. Watch your step!

Stepladders are available in several heights. They are portable and are made of wood or aluminum. When using a stepladder, make sure that the legs are open as far as possible for maximum stability. If you are painting or using tools, set the paint can, pan, or unused tools on the shelf provided.

Straight and extension ladders are used for heights greater than those reached by most stepladders. They must be leaned against something to hold them up. If possible, secure the upper end of the ladder to the structure to prevent it from tipping over.

Some general rules for using ladders are summarized below:

- *Do not* leave anything on the steps of ladders.
- *Never* stand on the top two steps of a stepladder.
- *Never* use an aluminum ladder of any type when using electrical tools or working near electrical circuits.
- *Have* someone hold the ladder steady while you are climbing.

Working Aloft

Working aloft can be quite hazardous. If safety precautions are not followed, you can be injured by falling or you can injure someone else by dropping something. Other hazards aloft include being poisoned by stack gases, electrocuted, or burned by radio transmissions. To avoid these hazards, follow these precautions:

- *Never* go aloft without permission from the OOD.
- *Ensure* that electrical and electronic equipment is turned off and tagged to stay off.
- *Always* use an industrial safety harness with safety line and working line.
- *Always* attach tools to the harness with preventer lines to keep them from being dropped.
- If working in the path of stack gases, *always* use self-contained breathing apparatus (SCBA).
- *Always* have a ready-to-climb safety observer watching you.
- *Never* throw or drop anything from aloft. Lower the items with a hand line or suitable tackle.
- *Always* keep a safety line or snap-hook on a closed-loop hold. Radio and radar equipment on other ships create a charge you may feel when climbing. The shock won't hurt, but it may startle you and cause you to fall.
- *Do not* touch antennas, aloft or otherwise. You could be burned by the energy from your own ship or from nearby equipment ashore or from another ship.

- Watch for rotating radar antennas. They could knock you to the deck.
- When finished with the work, report it to the OOD.
- Report any unsafe rigging aloft to the OOD.

Working Over the Side

Working over the side can include painting or welding. You may work over the side when under way *only* with the permission of the commanding officer. While over the side, you must wear an industrial safety harness, an inherently buoyant life preserver, and a tending line. The line must be attached to the ship and tended by someone on the deck at all times.

Electrical and Electronic Equipment

All electrical and electronic equipment is hazardous. This does not mean you should be afraid it, but you should respect the potential danger and observe these safety precautions:

- *Always* inspect the equipment before using it. Look for damaged, cracked, or frayed power cords or defective parts. Return them to the electrician or electronics technician.
- *Always* remove equipment from service that causes a shock, regardless of how slight the shock may be.
- *Never* remove the third pin of a three-wire cord. This connection provides a ground that protects you in case the tool shorts inside. The ground is required on tools with metal cases.
- Use the plug when disconnecting a power cord.
- When using an extension cord, plug the equipment into the extension cord first, then plug the extension cord into the receptacle. Reverse the process when finished.
- *Never* remove or replace fuses. Only qualified personnel are allowed to make these repairs.
- *Never* attempt to make temporary repairs to electrical equipment. Take it to the electrical shop.
- *Do not* touch anyone who has been electrocuted—you will be electrocuted, too. Secure the power, then remove the victim. Administer artificial respiration or cardio-pulmonary resuscitation (CPR) as needed. (You may pull a fire alarm, but *do not* leave the victim.)
- If you cannot secure the power when rescuing an electrical

shock victim, use a wooden pole or cane, or a dry piece of line or a belt to pull the victim free from the circuit.

Rotating Machinery

Knowing the correct operating procedures for machinery is vital to your safety. Many safety precautions for machinery are specific to the equipment, but the following general precautions apply to most equipment. *Do not* operate machinery you have not been trained to operate.

- *Never* place any part of your body into moving machinery.
- *Do not* ride machinery unless it is designed to carry you.
- *Do not* wear jewelry, neckties, or loose clothing when operating machinery.
- *Always* wear PPE appropriate to the operation, i.e., eye protection, hearing protection.
- *Always* remove from service any machinery requiring maintenance or adjustment. Tag it out if necessary.
- *Do not* use compressed air to clean parts of your body or clothing or to do cleanups. Use a vacuum cleaner or a broom. Compressed air can be used for cleaning machine parts as long as the air supply pressure is less than 29 psi.
- Ensure that all safeguards are in place when operating any equipment.
- Check safety devices, alarms, and sensors for proper operation, and report any problems.
- Clean up oil leaks and report them for repair.
- *Do not* allow tripping and fire hazards to accumulate. Keep all machinery spaces clean.

Power Tools

You will be using a variety of portable power tools. They may be electrical, hydraulic, or pneumatic. Regardless of the type, you must protect yourself against the hazards associated with the tool.

- *Always* wear protective equipment.
- *Always* use the installed guards supplied with the equipment.
- *Always* use tools that are in good repair. Return tools with defects for repair.
- *Do not* use tools that produce sparks near explosive or flammable vapors, gases, liquids, or materials.

• Make sure electrical tools are off before plugging them into a receptacle.

Tag-out Procedures

Use DANGER and CAUTION tags for identifying equipment that is hazardous. However, your supervisor may prefer to tag-out the equipment after you report the hazard. You must not remove these tags. They can be removed only by the person who placed them. If your job requires you to operate a tagged-out switch, valve, or control, *do not* operate it; report it to your supervisor. These tags are shown in figure 27–4.

Hazardous Materials

You may have to use, store, handle, or dispose of hazardous materials in your job. A standard labelling technique is used for identifying hazardous materials in three principal categories: health, fire, and reactivity (instability). Each category is rated on a scale from zero to four to indicate the severity of the hazard. Four is most severe.

The sample label in figure 27–5 shows how the information is presented. The four diamonds are color-coded as follows: Blue—Health Hazard; Red—Fire Hazard; Yellow—Reactivity; and White—Specific Hazard. The specific hazard diamond is used to identify the type of material. Fire fighters and health officials use this information to deal with spills or releases of the material. You must pay particular attention to the principal categories.

All workplaces are required to maintain an inventory of all hazardous chemicals and a *Material Safety Data Sheet*, or *MSDS*, for each chemical on board. The MSDSs *must* be available to you before using, handling, storing, or disposing of chemicals. An MSDS gives specific information on the type of hazard presented by the chemical, handling instructions, required and recommended safety precautions and protective equipment, and information on how to contact the manufacturer.

Motor Vehicles

You will probably operate some form of motor vehicle for the Coast Guard. Most people are able to drive an automobile. There are other forms of vehicles, however, including buses, trucks, forklifts, and tractors. Before operating these other types, you must be trained in

BLACK LETTERING ON YELLOW TAG

BLACK LETTERING ON RED TAG

Figure 27-4. Danger and caution tags.

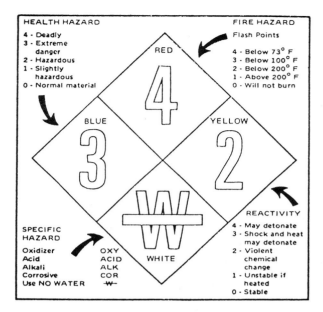

Figure 27-5. Hazardous material label.

their operation, the safety precautions necessary, and emergency procedures. Do not operate equipment for which you have had no training.

Regardless of the type of transportation you are using, Coast Guard regulations require you to wear seat belts, if available. Seat belts save lives. You've heard it all before, but the evidence is very clear.

In addition to seat belts, PPE is sometimes required when operating certain types of vehicles. For example, wear a hard hat when operating a forklift or hearing protection when driving a tractor.

Recreation and Sports

Many people enjoy participating in some kind of sports and recreation. Unfortunately, off-duty injuries do occur when engaging in these activities. To reduce the risk of injury, follow these rules:

- Get a physical examination. Talk with a physician about the activity in which you are going to engage.
- Condition yourself before engaging in it. The physical ensures

that you are healthy. Conditioning ensures that you are fit. Health and fitness are not the same.

- Before exercising or playing a game, be sure you warm up and stretch your muscles out.
- Use protective equipment appropriate to the activity, i.e., goggles for racquetball, knee and elbow pads.
- After strenuous exercise like aerobics, take the time to cool down. This will help reduce muscle soreness.

Aircraft Operations

No matter what career field you choose in the Coast Guard, you may at some time fly on Coast Guard aircraft. Many personnel not normally involved in aviation take flights occasionally, when they need to look at something from the air or when flying is the fastest way to get needed people somewhere. Oil spills requiring monitoring teams to scan large areas quickly or situations where law enforcement teams must be put in place rapidly are two such cases.

Non-aviation personnel need to be aware of the hazards around operating aircraft. Helicopter rotor blades and tail rotors and transport aircraft propellers are deadly when turning. Jet engines can create enough suction at high power to pull people into them if they get too close, and the exhaust is extremely hot and dangerous. Antennas on the outside of the aircraft carry hazardous electrical charges and must not be touched.

If you have the opportunity to fly on a Coast Guard aircraft, one of the crew members should brief you on all the hazards and the procedures for avoiding them. If you have any questions, ask a crew member.

There are some general safety precautions you should always follow when near aircraft:

- Never approach an aircraft unless the crew knows you are there and has signaled you to approach.
- Always approach helicopters from the side, never from the front or back.
- Always wear hearing protection around operating aircraft.
- Never touch anything painted red or yellow without the crew's permission. These colors indicate hazards or emergency equipment.

- Aircraft emergency exits are indicated by yellow markings on the inside of the aircraft. Make sure you know where they are and how to operate them. Ask the crew during your briefing.
- In case of emergency, obey the crew members' orders.
- *Do not* touch helicopters or hoisted loads before discharging the static charge.

CHAPTER 28

Other Vessels and Mariners

To fulfill the many missions of the Coast Guard, our personnel have always had to deal directly with other mariners and the marine industry. The Coast Guard has always done well in dealing with these people. Although this relationship has not always been one of affection and admiration, it has usually been marked with a mutual respect. A general understanding of the types of vessels, and the personnel who operate them, will help acquaint new Coast Guard personnel with the marine industry.

Vessels are characterized as fitting into one of three general categories: commercial vessels and personnel; private vessels; and public vessels.

COMMERCIAL VESSELS AND PERSONNEL

Before beginning a discussion of different vessel types, it is important to understand that the basic underlying purpose of commercial vessels is to make money. Unlike other vessels with which you may be familiar (pleasure craft, Coast Guard cutters, etc.), commercial vessels are conceived, designed, and built with this one ultimate goal in mind.

Cargo Vessels

Cargo vessels are designed to carry a variety of dry cargoes in various

Figure 28-1. A familiar sight at every harbor entrance is the pilot boat. Pilots are expert licensed civilian mariners who control and direct merchant ships on coastal waterways. (Courtesy Charleston Branch Pilots' Association)

forms of packaging. They are generally classified as either bulk, break-bulk, or container vessels.

Bulk Carriers

Certain types of dry cargo do not lend themselves to packaging. Materials such as metal ores, grain, and minerals are more efficiently carried in bulk. Bulk carriers are commonly employed on the Great Lakes to carry iron ore from the mines to ports in the area of the steel mills. Other bulk carriers carry grain from the United States to foreign countries. The cargo holds in such vessels are designed to facilitate off-loading through the use of slightly sloping sides so that cargo settles to the middle of the hold. The cargo is usually off-loaded using cranes with large scoops aided by bulldozers lowered into the holds. Bulk carriers carrying either dry-bulk cargo or liquid-bulk cargo usually transport cargo on only one leg of a voyage.

OBOs (Ore/Bulk/Oil)

OBO carriers can carry either ore, dry-bulk cargo such as grain, or oil. With this cargo-carrying capability, the vessel becomes more "fully employed."

Break-Bulk Vessels

This type of cargo vessel corresponds with the general concept of a traditional "freighter." These vessels are sometimes called "general-cargo" vessels. Cargo for this type of vessel is usually in bales, bags, or small crates that are sometimes palletized to speed loading and unloading operations in port. Additionally, these vessels can carry cars, trucks, or heavy machinery. Because of their ability to carry a wide range of cargoes, and their self-contained cargo-handling capability, these vessels usually service ports with limited shoreside pier facilities.

Roll On/Roll Off (RO/RO) Vessels

RO/ROs are designed to carry cargo on multiple decks, usually in trailers, or as individual vehicles that are themselves cargo. Access from one deck to another is by way of ramps or elevators. The "cargo" is driven on board through a stern ramp or side ramp through watertight closures in the side of the vessel. The advantage of this type of vessel is that cargo can be quickly loaded or unloaded at a port without relying on elaborate shore equipment. More and more RO/RO vessels are being used by the military for such applications as support vessels for the Afloat Prepositioning and Ready Reserve Forces, carrying jeeps, tanks, armored personnel carriers, and other rolling military hardware.

Refrigerator Ships

Refrigerator ships are outfitted with refrigerating equipment to preserve a cargo. The number of "reefer" spaces varies on a given vessel depending upon its trade. Usually reefer ships will carry other general cargo as well.

Offshore Supply Vessels (OSVs)

OSVs are special-purpose freight vessels designed to carry drilling supplies from the shore to drilling units operating offshore. They usually have a large deck area for carrying drill pipe and miscellaneous supplies and have internal tanks for carrying dry or liquid drilling mud. Some OSVs are fitted with large winches on the afterdeck for the purpose of anchor handling.

Container Vessels

Containerization of cargo was started in the late 1950s and early 1960s to assist in the intermodal transportation of cargoes. Cargo is placed in a container at the point of manufacture, the container is placed on a truck, transferred to a rail car, transferred to another truck, and finally placed aboard a container vessel. Thus, the cargo itself is touched only two times—once during initial container loading and once at the destination where the container is unloaded. The containers themselves are constructed of fiberglass, aluminum, or steel and are in standard lengths of either 20 or 40 feet.

Certain types of specialized container vessels, known as LASH or Seabee vessels, are specifically designed to carry, load, and unload barges filled with cargo instead of containers. Once unloaded, these barges are towed to discharge ports.

Lighter Aboard Ship (LASH). The typical LASH vessel has a crane that lifts the barges out of a cargo hold, carries them to the stern of the vessel, and lowers them to the water for launching and towing by a tugboat. The reverse process takes place during the loading of the vessel. The barges are relatively small, and when loaded to capacity draw only eight feet of water. Thus, LASH vessels can transport cargo to and from ports that have no deep water or crane facilities. In addition to the savings accrued through the containerization concept, an additional savings is realized from reduced or eliminated port fees, pilot fees, and tug charges.

Seabee. The Seabee is very similar to the LASH type, except that instead of using a crane on the ship, a stern elevator is used. The barges are moved along tracks to the stern of the vessel and placed on the elevator. The elevator is lowered to the water to launch the barge. The procedure is reversed during loading.

Bulk Liquid Vessels

Many types of liquids are transported by ships. Although some liquids are packaged in drums or other small containers and carried on various types of cargo vessels, many liquids are more efficiently transported in bulk form. Vessels designed for this purpose are called tankers. Virtually the entire vessel has tank spaces for either cargo, fuel oil, or ballast.

Tankers. Tankers are essentially floating cargo tanks. Over the years tank ships have increased in size in the interest of fuel economy and the growing consumer need for oil and chemical products. Tankers are usually subdivided into the following categories:

- Ultra Large Crude Carriers (ULCC), 500,000–or-more barrel cargo capacity, over 1,000 feet in length, carry crude oil.
- Very Large Crude Carriers (VLCC), 300,000– to 500,000– barrel cargo capacity, 900 to 1,000 feet in length, carry crude oil.
- Product carriers, various capacities and lengths, carry refined cargoes such as gasoline, aviation gas, and diesel.
- Chemical carriers (commonly called "drugstore" tankers) are specially designed tankers built with coated tanks and piping systems, and carry a variety of corrosive or hazardous chemical cargoes.

Liquified gas carriers (LPG/LNG). For years the oil fields of the world produced natural gas along with various types of crude oil. If a ready market for the gas existed in the vicinity of the wells, pipelines were constructed and the gas was sold. The energy crisis of the early 1970s made Liquified Natural Gas/Liquified Petroleum Gas (LNG/ LPG) transport by ship economically feasible, so a number of ships were built. By cooling these gases to −265 degrees Fahrenheit, or by pressurization, they become liquefied and occupy only 1/600 of their original volume. Many ship designs are in use today, but they all rely on very special materials and construction techniques to withstand unusual vessel-loading conditions and the extremely low temperatures. Most of these vessels utilize a portion of the liquefied gas that "boils off" during voyages for fuel in the vessel's engines.

Tank Barges

Tank barges are distinguished from tankers in that they are not self-propelled. Barges comprise a very large group of vessels that carry many types of cargoes and serve a variety of functions, including lightering of cargo and the fueling (bunkering) of larger vessels. In fact, there are just about as many types of barges as there are cargoes. Most barges are unstaffed, but some carry a small crew. The following is a list of the more common barge types:

- Tank barges
- Hopper barges
- LNG/LPG barges
- Chemical carriers

Passenger Vessels

Passenger vessels, as the name implies, are those vessels that are designed solely to carry passengers. They are diverse in their designs, and it is virtually impossible to address all the possible configurations. If they could be categorized, the categories might look like this:

- Ferries: vessels of various sizes designed for carrying both passengers and vehicles.
- Head boats: small passenger vessels used for taking people on fishing trips, for which they pay "by the head."
- Passenger liners: large ships designed to carry passengers for pleasure purposes.
- Excursion boats: small passenger vessels designed to take people on sightseeing tours or dinner/dance cruises.
- Crew boats: small passenger vessels designed to transport workers involved in the offshore oil industry.

Towing Vessels

There are a number of types of commercial towing vessels common

Figure 28-2. Coast Guard small boat patrols safety zone around the excursion boat *Delta Queen*.

to most United States waters. They are similar in that they are designed to move or maneuver other floating objects, so their design is oriented toward power and maneuverability. Typical towing vessels include harbor tugs, large seagoing tugs, and tow boats or "pushers" that push barges on the Western Rivers and Intracoastal Waterway.

Fishing Vessels

Commercial fishing vessels make up the most numerous single category of commercial vessels. Fishing vessels likely to be encountered by Coast Guard personnel include lobster boats, gillnetters, shrimpers, oyster boats, crabbers, stern trawlers, and clammers. There is no such thing as a typical fishing vessel. Fishing vessels are at the top of the list for the number of lives lost on all commercial vessels.

Mobile Offshore Drilling Units (MODUs)

MODUs are very special types of vessels. They are really movable platforms from which oil wells can be drilled. Actually, they are vessels only when they are moving from one site to another; at other times they are considered offshore facilities. There are three basic types of MODUs:

- *Semisubmersibles* are used in deep-water drilling. Upon arrival on site they are held in place using various multiple anchor systems.
- *Jack-up rigs* are self-elevating units used in shallow-water drilling. They are towed into place, at which time the legs are lowered to the ocean floor and the rig is "jacked-up" above the water level.
- *Drill ships*, built in the shape of regular ships but with the addition of a derrick, move to sites under their own power and are anchored in place; they are typically used for exploratory drilling.

MERCHANT VESSEL ORGANIZATION

Although the primary function of most merchant vessels is to make money by transporting cargo, a vessel is more than just a complex of structural members, fittings, and machinery. A vessel is also the people that crew it. Time has proven that a ship is no better than its crew. The crew directs the vessel from point to point, and by its skill and experience, enables a vessel to survive in the often fierce environment.

For operational and administrative purposes, all merchant vessels are divided into several departments. The two most important of these are the deck department and the engine department.

The single-most important deck department responsibility is that of supervising the handling and storage of cargo. The administrative head of the deck department is the vessel's master. Since the master is also in command of the entire vessel, many of the deck functions are taken over by the chief mate.

Unlike the military sea services where officers are usually given only one responsibility at a time in a ship, the merchant vessel deck officer must constantly assume responsibility for such diverse operations as navigation and piloting, the operation of navigation equipment, ship's maintenance, the use of lifesaving and fire-fighting equipment, vessel handling, and calculations for cargo loading that may affect the vessel's trim and stability.

Within the engine department, the chief engineer is the highest ranking officer. Additional personnel required within the engineering department include "qualified members of the engine department" (QMEDs) and wipers who perform watchstanding duties and maintenance under the supervision of licensed officers.

The third major department on merchant vessels is the stewards department. The chief steward and the chief steward's cooks are responsible for the feeding of the passengers, if applicable, and the officers and crew.

Passenger vessels have a fourth department called the staff department. This department is made up of officers who hold a USCG certificate of registry as chief purser, purser, pharmacist's mate, surgeon, professional nurse, or medical doctor. These officers have nothing to do with the navigation of the vessel, but provide services and medical care for passengers. As mentioned, all of the above staff officers are typically found only on board passenger vessels, with the exception of the purser, who may also serve in certain cargo and container vessels.

The Coast Guard is responsible for specifying the minimum staffing of United States merchant vessels, on the basis of the numerous statutes and the regulations that clarify the application of these statutes. In developing these minimum staffing standards for a particular vessel, the Coast Guard is concerned primarily with the safety of life at sea. In other words, the Coast Guard ensures that the vessel has a sufficient number of qualified personnel to be capable of coping with the normal hazards of the sea. The following licensed and unlicensed mariners are likely to be part of a commercial vessel's crew.

Merchant Vessel Personnel

Master

The master has the overall responsibility for the vessel. The master is not considered a member of the crew, but rather the on-board owner's representative. The master normally does not stand a watch, but must maintain a valid Coast Guard license that certifies competence to navigate and administer the operation of the vessel.

Chief Mate

The chief mate (the "mate") is responsible for cargo loading, regardless of the type of vessel, for maintaining the vessel's stability, and for the general operations of the ship other than in the engineering department. The chief mate is also the deck department administrator for all paperwork and documents.

Second Mate

The second mate works for the chief mate and is normally designated the vessel's navigation officer. In port, the second mate may be responsible for cargo transfer operations.

Third Mate

The third mate assists the chief mate and is responsible for the maintenance of the lifesaving equipment.

Chief Engineer

The chief engineer (the "chief") has the overall responsibility for the engineering department, as well as for the maintenance and repair of the vessel's deck machinery and the hydraulic and electrical systems. By holding the highest level of license within the engineering department, the chief engineer is considered to be on an equal status with the master. However, the chief engineer is a member of the crew and answers to the master, but does not stand watches.

First Assistant Engineer

The first assistant engineer is responsible for the overall supervision of the engineroom and for the major maintenance and repair of machinery and various system components.

Second Assistant Engineer

The second assistant engineer is responsible for the main propulsion machinery, which includes the boilers (if applicable to the plant).

Third Assistant Engineer

The third assistant engineer is responsible for the auxiliary machinery and the general upkeep of the engineering department.

Radio Officer

The radio officer operates and maintains the vessel's radio equipment. Because of the equipment installed on board modern vessels, the radio officer does not normally stand a watch.

Other Crew Members

Able-Bodied Seaman (AB)

An AB acts as the helmsman, and also can serve as the vessel's lookout. The AB is qualified to operate the vessel's lifeboats. At least 65 percent of the deck crew on board a major vessel, exclusive of the licensed officers, are required to be rated "able seamen."

Boatswain

The boatswain is the AB who heads the deck gang. The boatswain is responsible for maintaining the cargo gear and maintaining the general upkeep of the vessel within the deck department. The boatswain reports directly to the chief mate.

Ordinary Seaman

The ordinary seaman is an entry rating in the deck department. For the most part, ordinary seamen carry out the vessel's cleaning and upkeep functions and attend to minor repairs. The ordinary seaman rating equates to a nonrated individual in the Coast Guard.

Qualified Member of the Engine Department (QMED)

Individuals with the following special qualifications make up these ratings: refrigeration engineer, deck engineer, fireman/watertender, junior engineer, electrician, machinist, pumpman, deck engine mechanic, engineman.

Oiler

The oiler is responsible for engineroom upkeep and minor maintenance of machinery. The oiler is a watchstander.

Wiper

The wiper is an entry rating for the engine department. The wiper performs a similar function in the engineering spaces as the ordinary seaman does on deck.

Tankerman

A tankerman is any person holding a certificate issued by the Coast Guard attesting to competency in the handling of certain bulk liquid cargoes.

Lifeboatmen

Lifeboatmen must possess the knowledge and ability to launch and recover the vessel's lifeboats or life rafts, to handle the various types of lifeboats/life rafts in a seaway, and to operate and be familiar with all of the lifesaving equipment and provisions on board the lifeboats/life rafts. The number of certified lifeboatmen varies, depending upon the lifeboat and the life-raft requirements for each vessel.

PRIVATE VESSELS

Private vessels are pleasure boats, yachts, research craft, nonfederal training vessels, exploration vessels, and certain supply and support vessels. Because a vessel is private does not exempt it from federal safety and environmental protection requirements. Service in "passengers for hire" can bring a private vessel into an "inspected vessel" category. Passengers for hire are people on board who contribute some consideration toward their passage, which can include buying a ticket or reimbursing expenses.

For the most part, when we speak of private vessels we are thinking of the millions of state-numbered pleasure craft in the United States. Pleasure craft and other private vessels operating on the United States navigable waters are subject to Coast Guard and state jurisdiction. The fact that a vessel is state-numbered does not exempt that vessel from federal requirements. The applicability of federal law is a matter of the craft's service and economic circumstances.

PUBLIC VESSELS

The term public vessel generally means any vessel owned and operated by a department or agency of the federal government, or of a state or a subdivision thereof, and which is engaged exclusively in official, noncommercial operations. This term also applies to foreign vessels owned and operated by a foreign government recognized by the United States. Public vessels include military vessels of the Coast Guard, Navy, Army, Air Force, and Military Sealift Command, Army Corps of Engineers dredges, and support vessels crewed by civil-service personnel.

Since Coast Guard vessels are public vessels, Coast Guard personnel should be aware that their vessels are in a different category from those in the commercial and private sector.

CHAPTER 29

Duty Ashore

Because the Coast Guard is an agency assigned many and varied missions, our responsibilities are performed by units in a variety of worldwide locations, ashore as well as afloat.

Shore units support our fleets of cutters and aircraft or operate in specific program areas of their own. An assignment ashore may present opportunities to serve in small-boat search and rescue, respond to an environmental hazard, or keep the flow of supplies and personnel "moving to the mission." Signals from Coast Guard Loran stations around the globe provide mariners with a source of reliable and accurate navigation. The radio watchstander at a station or group communication center is often the only link a distressed mariner has with the means for assistance. An icebreaker stranded in the Arctic because of major mechanical failure may have to rely on the assistance and expertise of a mobile ship maintenance detachment's personnel for repairs; a Coast Guard aircraft deployed from one of our air stations will get the team and spare parts on scene.

The *Staffing Standards Manual* (COMDTINST M5312.11) provides a detailed description of each type of Coast Guard field unit, including manning and specific watchstanding responsibilities.

Unit Orientations

After reporting to a unit ashore, you may expect your initial period to be taken up with administrative inprocessing, also known as the

Figure 29-1. The Coast Guard Training Center at Cape May, New Jersey.

check-in process. Often this procedure simply consists of touring the unit with your *sponsor*, completing the paperwork, interviews, required reading, and area familiarization necessary to settle you in at the unit. As discussed later in this chapter, you will begin the required qualification process(es) necessary for the responsibilities you will be assigned in the unit watch organization.

Shore Unit Organization

You learned about basic shipboard organization in this manual. Shore units, too, are organized for order and efficiency to the greatest degree possible, and are headed by a commanding officer or *officer-in-charge*; as with ships, an executive officer or *executive petty officer* serves as the second-in-command and administrator. Similarly, the shoreside "exec" is assisted by unit personnel assigned to collateral duties, boards, and committees. But whereas departments prevail as the major subdivision for most units ashore, further resemblance to a ship's organizational structure is often small.

As explained in chapter 2, field units ashore, such as group offices and small-boat stations, may differ significantly from one another in their organizational arrangement because of the variance in personnel allowances, tenant/landlord command relationships, and assigned functions. Conversely, larger, more complex activities, such as district or area staffs, are identically structured in accordance with the *Coast Guard Organization Manual* (COMDTINST M5400.7 series).

The key to understanding the shore unit to which you are assigned is your familiarity with the specific unit's organizational rules and regulations. These documents, sometimes published as *Standard Operating Procedures (SOP)*, a unit *Organization and Regulations Manual*, or a series of individual directives, parallel the system of shipboard bills discussed in chapter 18, inasmuch as they govern by force of order the operation and administration of the unit and its personnel.

Dual Command Authority

In some instances, the commanding officer of one Coast Guard unit may be concurrently designated as the commanding officer of another unit. This arrangement is made in situations where colocated units share operating facilities, personnel, and mission focus to a degree that best lends itself to a common chain of command. For

Figure 29-2. Coast Guard duty ashore can be just as rewarding and exciting as duty at sea.

example, Commander, Coast Guard Group Cape May is designated also as Commanding Officer, Coast Guard Air Station Cape May. In the Coast Guard, this "two-hat" concept is employed almost exclusively for shore commands.

Standard Routine

The routine of the day for Coast Guard personnel assigned ashore may, as you might expect, differ considerably for each type of activity. Personnel assigned to units within metropolitan office spaces, such as recruiters and staff, often work under conditions and scheduling that closely resemble those of their civilian counterparts. This is certainly not the case for the company of a small boat or air station during the peak of search-and-rescue "season," or for the Coast Guard's thousands of watchstanding personnel serving at a variety of units.

Shore units having berthing and messing facilities will publish and enforce as regulations specific policies for these accommodations, including such specifics as meal hours, reveille and taps, smoking regulations, and material inspection schedules and standards. Additional timely information about the unit's routine may be found in the *Plan of the Week*.

Plan of the Week

The executive or senior administrative officer will prepare and issue a Plan of the Week, which serves as a unit calendar of official events to all hands for the following seven days. The Plan of the Week includes:

The schedule of the normal routine, and any variations or additions.

The orders of the day, detailing the training schedule, duty section, liberty sections, personnel and material inspections, etc.

Notices of matters that should be brought to the attention of all concerned.

Reprints of regulations and orders that are to be brought to the attention of the station's company.

Copies of the plan of the week are widely distributed throughout the unit, and publicly displayed. Everyone is responsible for knowing what is in the plan of the week, as any instruction or direction it provides constitutes an official order.

Watch Organization and Qualifications

As aboard ship, nearly all Coast Guard field units ashore must employ a watch organization to meet round-the-clock mission responsibilities. Such organizations will vary in personnel numbers and complexity in relation to the size and functions of the unit.

Ashore, periods of military responsibility that may encompass one or more watches in addition to boat or flight crew, maintenance, emergency response, or other tasks, are known as *duty*; personnel in the *section* of the command's watch organization remaining on board the unit to perform this rotating responsibility are said to "*have the duty*." The frequency, or *rotation*, of your particular duty will also vary, according to its nature, and may be affected by the seniority of your rate or rank.

Periods of duty are normally of 24 hours' duration, although periods of up to 48 hours are sometimes authorized at small units, such as small-boat stations, to increase the consecutive length of the follow-on liberty period.

Soon after reporting aboard, you will likely begin the training process, sometimes called a *break-in*, which will lead to your qualification for the type of duty you will *stand*.

Duty Days and Watchstanding

Depending upon the unit mission, organization, and your rate and rating, or rank, watchstanding might be either a duty-day responsibility, or your primary responsibility at the unit. The latter case is true, for example, for radiomen assigned to communication stations and centers, and radarmen and quartermasters serving at vessel traffic services.

If you are nonrated, your duty day and accompanying watchstanding responsibilities will vary with the type of unit to which you are assigned. At a small-boat station, you may take a turn at the communication or lookout tower watch, and work at boat maintenance or groundskeeping when off-watch. At a training center, you might serve a period of telephone watch, or perhaps in a standby capacity as the duty vehicle driver. A roving security watch might be a responsibility of your duty day at a base, in addition to housekeeping responsibilities.

V.
Personal Fitness
and Survival Skills

CHAPTER 30

Wellness

Wellness is an important part of Coast Guard life. It is more than simply the absence of illness. Wellness refers to your lifestyle habits, how you live your life. More than half of the diseases affecting us are caused by poor habits: tobacco, diet, lack of exercise, unmanaged stress, etc. To reach and maintain an optimal state of good health, you must actively pursue a healthy lifestyle. If you do, you are guaranteed to look better, feel better, play better, think better, work better, and live longer!

What does it mean to lead a healthy lifestyle? Most important is good nutrition—eating right. Then there is achieving and maintaining a high level of physical fitness. Avoiding tobacco products is an essential part of a healthy lifestyle, as is moderation in drinking alcoholic beverages (or not drinking at all). Next is managing stressful situations successfully—keeping your cool. Lowering your risks for heart disease, cancer, and other long-term problems is also part of a healthy lifestyle. This means keeping your cholesterol and blood pressure under control and periodically visiting your medical and dental department for screening examinations. And finally, a healthy lifestyle means paying attention to simple but critical safety precautions—always wearing your seatbelt in cars and always wearing a helmet when riding a bicycle or motorcycle.

In thinking about wellness, it's sometimes helpful to consider your body as a machine. It's an incredibly complicated and highly efficient machine, and only you are responsible for caring for it. Just as a

Figure 30-1. Regular exercise will keep you healthy and fit for duty.

finely tuned, expensive sports car requires the correct fuel, oil, tires, and maintenance procedures to run properly, your body needs the correct food, exercise, rest, and care to stay healthy. Just as you would avoid putting sand in your gas tank, you should avoid poisoning your body with tobacco, excess alcohol, drugs, or other toxic substances. And just as you would carefully follow the maintenance procedures in your car's owner's manual, you should have periodic physical and dental exams to ensure your overall health.

NUTRITION

Nutrition is the foundation of wellness. Since you literally are what you eat, a healthy lifestyle starts with your diet. There are seven steps to eating right: (1) eat a variety of foods; (2) maintain a healthy weight; (3) limit your intake of total fat, animal fats, and cholesterol; (4) eat plenty of vegetables, fruits, and grain products; (5) use sugars in moderation; (6) use salt and sodium only in moderation; and (7) if you drink alcoholic beverages, do so in moderation (it's okay not to drink!).

PHYSICAL FITNESS

There are five essential parts to being physically fit: aerobic capacity, muscle strength, muscle endurance, flexibility, and maintaining a healthy level of body fat. Each of these is important, and you cannot neglect any of them if you want to be fit. Physical fitness helps make you a more productive and capable member of the Coast Guard and a healthier and happier person in your private life.

Aerobic capacity is a measure of your body's endurance or stamina. Good endurance enables you to maintain activities (either work or play) for extended periods of time. Aerobic capacity depends on the efficiency of your heart, lungs, and muscles to get and use oxygen. To increase your aerobic capacity, you must exercise with your large muscles (your legs and arms) for at least 20 minutes at a time, at least three times per week. Aerobic exercises include running, jogging, cycling, stair-climbing, rowing, swimming, jumproping, cross-country skiing, and fast walking. Aerobic exercise is also an effective way to burn calories, which is important if you want to lower your level of body fat.

Muscle strength is a measure of the force you can produce, allowing you to lift, push, pull, and carry. These are all important in your Coast Guard duties, but they are also important in your recreation and home activities. The only way to build muscle strength is to exercise against resistance, either by lifting weights or by lifting your body-weight against gravity (push-ups, pull-ups, calisthenics, etc.). Strength-training exercises not only help you build muscle, but also help you lose fat. The more muscle mass you have, the higher is your rate of metabolism and the faster you burn calories, even when you are asleep!

Muscle endurance is your ability to perform hard work over a prolonged period of time. Muscle endurance is important in your Coast Guard duties for both emergency situations (e.g., firefighting, damage control, CPR, etc.) and for operational requirements (e.g., boatcrew or cutter duties in rough seas). The best muscle endurance exercises are pull-ups, curl-ups, push-ups, parallel bar dips, and calisthenics. You can also build muscle endurance by lifting weights. But instead of using heavy weights and a small number of repetitions (5–10), as you would do to build muscle strength, you should use light weights and a high number of repetitions (15–20) to build endurance.

Figure 30-2. Coast Guard facilities are equipped to assist you in maintaining a healthy lifestyle.

Flexibility describes your ability to move your joints through a full range of motion. You need good flexibility to develop muscle strength, to prevent injuries to your muscles, tendons, ligaments, and joints, and to protect against back injuries. Proper stretching, both before and after exercise, is the most effective way to develop good flexibility.

Body composition refers to the relative amounts of fat and lean tissue in your body. The more fat you have, the harder it is on your joints and the harder your heart has to work. Trying to carry around an extra 10–20 pounds of body fat is like walking with a 10–20-pound pack on your back. Your goals should be to maximize your muscle mass and minimize your body fat. An ideal body composition for men is a body fat of 15–17 percent, while for women it is 18–22 percent. Try not to think of losing "weight" if you are too heavy; what you really want to lose is fat. The best way to lose fat and preserve muscle is to maintain a low-fat, healthy diet, perform aerobic exercise for at least 20 minutes three times per week, and to perform strength-training and muscle endurance exercises.

TOBACCO

Tobacco is one of the most harmful and addictive substances available in our society. It is responsible for more deaths and more disease than any other single agent. It is as addictive as heroin, so once you start, it's hard to get free of its hold. Cigarette smoking not only leads to heart disease and cancer, but it also causes you to have wrinkled skin, so you look prematurely old. Smokeless tobacco (dip, chew, etc.) can give you mouth and throat cancer while you're still young. Young men (and women too) have died in their teens and twenties from using dip! Don't let this happen to you. Tobacco is definitely not a part of a healthy lifestyle.

ALCOHOL

It's okay not to drink. Alcohol has been a part of our society for a very long time, and people have had problems with it for just as long. If you drink, do so responsibly. "It's okay not to drink" means not only abstinence, but also knowing your limits. It means it's okay to stop after one or two drinks and not to feel pressure from your friends to drink more. It also means that you, in turn, should not pressure your friends to drink more if they want to stop. The Coast Guard can provide you with professional help if you develop a problem with alcohol, but the best medicine is preventive medicine. Drink responsibly or not at all, and remember, it really is okay not to drink.

CHAPTER 31

Swimming and Lifesaving

Anyone who goes to sea, whether in a high-endurance Coast Guard cutter or merely across a harbor in a 14-foot skiff, should know how to swim. Many emergencies—shipwreck, flood relief, and other types of rescue work—require the use of expert swimmers. Just being able to swim is often not enough; you have to be a good swimmer. The following information will help, but the only way to improve is to practice.

Control of Position and Buoyancy

Jellyfish or Tuck Float

Double up, hugging legs, with face submerged. Float like a ball with only part of your back above the water. This is a good exercise for beginners; it acquaints them with body buoyancy, and develops their ability to hold their breath. From this position, beginners learn to open their eyes under water and familiarize themselves with floating. From this position, too, you can slowly but firmly massage cramps in legs or toes. At times, it may serve as a rest for muscles tired from the stretchout of swimming.

Back Float

Lie on your back with your head thrown back, chin and nose above water, arms and legs relaxed. Some people can float well this way,

Figure 31-1. A Coast Guard small-boat crew member demonstrates lifesaving technique.

others keep sinking as they exhale. Try to keep your lungs full of air. Do not become panicky if your face does sink. Gently work your hands so as to raise your chin enough for a quick breath, and then let yourself sink. Your face will soon rise above the surface. Gulp a breath while drifting, rest and relax while sinking. This is the preparatory position for learning the backstroke, and an excellent way of resting and floating during long periods in the water.

Dead Man's Float and Glide

Lean forward, face down in the water, and relax completely. Play "dead man" all over. This float leads to the crawl, or speed stroke, and to the breast, or froglike stroke. It teaches relaxation in the water, how to swim under water with eyes open, and how to get the most out of a glide.

Breathing

In general, breathing for swimming is the same as for any other sport. Try to keep it regular, don't hold your breath too long, don't pant. Breathe through your mouth when your face is out of water; exhale by blowing out through your mouth and nose to keep them clear of water. Try to take air in fast, blow it out slowly.

Treading Water

Being able to tread water is a vital skill and should be practiced until you can do it for minutes at a time, not just a few seconds. It is required for every situation in which you need to raise your head to look around, or call for help, or use your hands.

There are several methods of treading. Practice all of them, and by changing from one to the other, you will be able to stay afloat longer. The most commonly used methods are mentioned here.

Modified frog kick for treading. Stand upright in the water. Draw legs up together with the knees spread out to the sides. Separate and extend legs. Finally press the legs together until the feet are ten to 20 inches apart. The movement of drawing, spreading, and pressing them is then repeated. Pushing the legs out and pressing them together gives an upward thrust to the body. This kick can be practiced while hanging on to the edge of a pool; its advantage is that the slow movement is not so tiring as some of the other treading kicks and it is adjustable; you can tread low in the water or thrust up high by this same kick.

Scissors kick for treading. This is similar to walking and is easy to learn. It is best practiced at first on land. Lie on your side with feet together and legs extended, then draw them slowly up in a semi-tucked-up position. Separate the legs, one moving forward, the other backward, then squeeze them together. The movement should be slow, steady, and continuous. Practice for a while, holding on to the edge of the pool or a firm object. The scissors kick is easy to learn and is a natural movement, effective but not tiring. It also leads to the side-stroke, which is important in distance swimming and lifesaving.

Sculling

Sculling with the hands enables people to control their body in the water in a number of positions, with or without the help of their feet. Sculling and treading combined will save more energy than using the feet or hands alone. Sculling has the advantage of teaching a sense of balance in the water. It develops the muscles of the hands and arms needed for pushing against the water, and it teaches people how to get a "grip" on the water.

Vertical sculling. One method of sculling while holding oneself upright in the water is to weave the hands vigorously back and forth in front of and to the sides of the body in a figure-eight movement. This forces the water downward and keeps the body up.

Another method is to drop the hands down near the hips in the water; then turn them to about a 45-degree angle away from the body, thumbs downward. With the palms of the hands, push the water away from the body until the hands are about two feet out from the sides of the body. Immediately rotate the hands so that the thumbs are up, then turn to the starting position, pulling water toward the sides of the body. When the hands reach the sides, they are again rotated until the thumbs are down, and the movements are repeated. The emphasis is on the push-away part of the stroke.

A third method is to place the hands palms down on the water, press down on the water several feet in depth, and recover again.

All these methods, or combinations of them, will be useful at different times.

Flutter-back sculling. This is one of the best sustaining strokes for staying afloat for a long time or for moving slowly and easily in some direction. Lie on your back and kick slowly up and down, with legs and feet in a knock-kneed and pigeon-toed position, and make a slow sculling movement at the hips with your hands.

Swimming Strokes

In general, there is no need for speed swimming. There may, however, be occasions where speed is needed, such as in swimming away from a sinking ship, catching up with a boat or raft, or swimming against a rapid current.

In the crawl, or speed stroke, it is necessary to lift your arms out of the water, and water-soaked clothing can make this very difficult and tiring. At the same time, a life jacket and other gear can hamper the freedom required for the crawl strokes. The best strokes to use in emergencies are those with underwater arm recoveries, as discussed in the sections that follow.

Dog Paddle or Human Stroke

The dog paddle is a valuable sustaining stroke for people fully clothed or wearing life jackets. It is particularly useful in crowded or narrow places because most of the movements are under the body, and the position of the head enables you to look about.

In the dog paddle the legs execute a slow up-and-down kick; the knees are bent and the feet are extended in a pigeon-toed manner. The arms are moved alternately. Each arm is pushed ahead in the water until extended, then brought downward and backward, held straight the whole time, and a strong grip is taken on the water. At the end of the pull the arm is bent, drawn up, and shoved forward again. Avoid the tendency to hold your breath and to stroke too fast.

Sidestroke

The sidestroke is a well-rounded stroke for long-distance swimming and lifesaving rescues.

Leg Action. Lie on your side, whichever side is the most natural. Start with your feet together, bend your knees and move your heels toward your hips. When your legs are up as far as is comfortable, separate your feet, making your top leg move forward and the bottom one backward. After they are separated as far as possible, straighten your legs and snap them together from this spread position like closing a pair of scissors. Make sure to stop your feet as they come together. This is the "scissor kick." It's the same as used in treading water.

Arm action. Lying on your side with one ear in the water, reach the lower arm ahead of you along the surface of the water and the top arm back alongside the top leg. When beginning the stroke, cup the lower hand a little, as if holding a handful of water, and sweep the hand downward toward the front of the chest. Here it meets the other hand, which (at the same time) has been slowly brought up in front of the chest, with the hand knifing edgewise in the water to lessen resistance. At the meeting position, the hand that has just come up in front of the chest is cupped and pushed down along the body to the top of the upper leg. While this motion is being carried out, the lower arm is returning to its extended position, knifing edgewise through the water. This ending and starting position is then held during the glide portion of the stroke.

Combined stroke. Push or glide into a sideways position, the lower ear in the water, feet together, with the lower arm reaching ahead and the upper arm resting on the top leg. Start moving the arms and legs at the same time, bringing up the heel while pulling with the lower arm. When the hands meet in front of the chest, the feet should begin separating. In a continuous motion, keep moving the arms and snap the feet out and together using the scissor kick motion. Glide for a short distance and repeat the stroke.

Breaststroke

The breaststroke is invaluable for long-distance swimming, swimming through heavy surf, or swimming through debris-filled water. It is frequently used as an approach stroke for water rescues.

The kick. Lie face down, with legs together and fully extended. Bring your heels up toward your hips and spread your knees about the width of your hips, with heels slightly wider than the knees. When the knees are brought up to just beneath the hips, turn your feet outward and move them to the sides until they are past the width of the hips. To finish the kick, push feet back down, making a circle until they return to their starting position.

Arm action. Start face down, and with arms extended, hands together, and palms down. Push palms out and back pushing downward slightly until the hands are in line with shoulders. Bring the elbows up to the sides and the forearms and hands just under the chest and neck. Not stopping, extend hands forward under the water's surface back to starting position. Hold this position for the glide.

Combined Stroke. Start with arms extended forward and legs straight. The hands start pulling to begin the stroke. Just after the hands have pulled a few inches, the legs start their recovery and the head begins to lift for a breath. As the legs move through the propulsive part of the kick, the arms are moved forward to the extended glide position. Take a breath when the mouth lifts out of the water, with hands pressing down and back. The head should be moved back into the water with the neck straight as the power is exerted by the kick. If you want to chat with your shipmate or keep an eye on something ahead, you can keep your head up as you swim, but this reduces your glide and makes the stroke harder.

Backstroke

This stroke will enable you to swim on your back for great distances without becoming tired, and is outstanding for survival swimming. You will also find it to be the easiest stroke to learn and accomplish.

Leg action. Lie on your back, extend your legs, and keep your legs together. Keeping your thighs straight, bend your knees so that your heels drop down and move toward your hips. When your heels are directly underneath your knees, turn your feet outward and spread your feet and legs. Without stopping, push your feet down and back making a circle with your heels until they come together. This is the "breaststroke kick" adapted for the back stroke. You may also hear it called the "whip kick."

Arm action. Perform a back glide to get into position, with arms down along the sides of your body. Slowly bring the hands up underwater, over the front of the body to about mid-chest, with fingertips brushing your ribs. Then stretch your arms straight outward at shoulder height. Continuing, sweep your slightly cupped hands even with the surface of the water in a wide arc until they are back at the starting point, along your sides. Remember to keep your hands underwater at all times and to put your chin to your chest during the arm stroke to prevent getting water in your face.

Combined stroke. The combined movements of the stroke are very easy to learn. Start with feet together and hands at your sides. Move your hands up at the same time as you drop your heels. As you extend your arms, turn your toes out. Now sweep your hands to your sides as you bring your feet together in a circular motion. Make your movements smooth and continuous, and rest only at the end of the stroke to allow a long glide. Keep your head fairly well back, with your ears in the water. Take your time and relax.

Special Instructions

Cramps

Cramps are rarely as dangerous as people believe. Take a deep breath and float quietly for a while. If the cramp is in an arm or leg muscle, massage it slowly and firmly.

Removal of Clothes

If it is necessary to remove your clothes in the water, the heaviest articles should be removed first. To remove trousers, assume a backfloat position, unzip them, slide them down, and flutter-kick out of them.

Remember that shoes are a real protection against sharks and sunburn, and that clothing in general is a protection against exposure. Remove only clothing that interferes with your keeping afloat.

Using Clothing To Keep Afloat

Shirts may be inflated by tying the cuffs and collar, blowing air into the opening, and then holding the garment under water. Trousers make better floats than shirts. After the trousers are removed, they should be floated on the surface with the fly turned up. A single knot should be tied in each leg, then one side of the waist of the trousers should be grasped with each hand, and the garment should be worked around on the surface until the legs are at the back of the head and neck. When this position is reached, the trousers should be flipped over the head, and the waist brought down smartly on the surface, trapping a good pocket of air in each leg. The waist should then be gathered under the water and held in one hand.

Figure 31-2. A muscle cramp in the foot can be worked out by massage.

Mattress covers, sea bags, laundry bags, pillow cases, and sacks may be used for support by capping the openings on the surface.

Swimming in Dangerous Waters

There are several emergency techniques that should be studied and practiced.

Underwater Swimming

The ability to swim underwater is very important in avoiding surface hazards such as floating debris, oil, or flaming oil or gasoline. It has lifesaving value, for it enables a swimmer to rescue a shipmate who has gone under. There are occasions, too, when it is necessary to recover articles lost overboard in shallow water.

Almost any swimming stroke can be used underwater. The breaststroke and the sidestroke lend themselves particularly well to underwater swimming. The main thing is to learn breath control. Practice holding your breath and keeping your eyes open as much as possible.

Swimming in Shark Infested Waters

A lot of research has been done on shark attacks in recent years. During World War II, people in the water were told to splash wildly to drive away sharks, but more recently it has been discovered that sharks seem attracted to frantic movements. Sharks are extremely dangerous and unpredictable predators and have extraordinary sensory receptors. Species of sharks vary in their feeding habits, with the result that some are considered more dangerous than others. Sharks seem to sense fright exhibited by creatures in the water. They also seem to be attracted to bright colors, but most of all, sharks are attracted by blood. Some recent experiments indicate that sharks exhibit a characteristic "S" twist before striking, and immediately before biting they roll their eyes upward losing sight of their prey. These experiments indicate that during the last phase of the attack, the sharks are guided by sensors located in their snouts. For some reason, in these experiments, the presence of metal objects caused the shark to divert that last phase of his attack toward the metal object and away from the original object of the attack.

Although there is no good advice on how a swimmer might avoid shark attacks, except by avoidance, the information that is

Figure 31-3. Swimming in dangerous water; (top) procedure for making surface dive; (center) alternate procedure for submerging; (bottom) in shallow rapids, swim feet first on your back, "fin" the hands at hip level to protect against rocks.

Figure 31-4. Use side stroke or breast stroke in surf to preserve strength. Ride small waves; surface-dive to end the ride before the wave breaks.

Figure 31-5. In shark-infested waters, swim as quietly as possible. Always wear shoes. Try to hold onto some floating object, especially in cold water. Keep moving to maintain circulation. In a current, either swim parallel to the shore or diagonally to it in order to get out of it. In seaweed or underwater plants, move calmly; don't thrash about.

currently available indicates that the following actions may reduce the risk of shark attack.

- Avoid bleeding into the water.

- Wear shoes and other protective clothing, particularly clothing of dark, drab shades; save the bright colors to show above the surface to attract rescuers.
- Remain calm, remembering that all species of sharks are not the same, nor do all sharks have the same level of aggressiveness.
- Swim slowly and quietly to minimize attracting the attention of sharks.
- In the presence of nonattacking sharks, do not strike at them, because that may provoke an attack that might not otherwise occur.
- If the water is clear enough to see sharks swimming beneath the surface, watch for a tell-tale "S"-like twisting by a shark, which may indicate that an attack is imminent.
- If a shark is about to attack, its jaws may possibly be diverted at the last moment by thrusting an object such as a piece of driftwood toward the shark's mouth.
- Do not confuse sharks with dolphins and porpoises, both of which are mammals, known in fact and legend to be friendly and helpful to sailors in the sea.

Swimming in Surf

Along coastlines and on reefs, waves steepen and break, turning into what are called "breakers." Surf consists of more than one of these breakers. Coast Guard boats often cross bars in leaving and entering inlets and harbors, and often encounter broken waves at sea, on bars, and in inlet channels; seldom, however, do Coast Guard boats go deliberately inshore into the surf, except during special emergency operations.

You are most likely to encounter surf after the foundering of a Coast Guard boat or if you are swept overboard from a boat near the beach. Surf conditions in these cases are probably going to be very rough.

You *should* be wearing a PFD. The PFD-equipped swimmer's best chance of avoiding injury is to make sure that the PFD is properly secured, and then to assume a rolled-forward position to protect the neck, back, and limbs. Take deep breaths whenever possible, and keep the eyes open underwater to help you reorient to the surface.

A non-PFD-equipped swimmer must avoid being caught on the surface by a large, plunging breaker. Such a swimmer must dive under approaching crested waves, then surface soon enough after the wave has passed to get another breath before diving under the next wave. Dives should be as deep as possible to avoid getting caught in the surface water as it curls over from the back face of the wave. Waves can be flattened by onshore winds, yet retain all the force of much higher seas. The swimmer in such a surf must watch for approaching seas and rise with them or dive as necessary to conserve air and strength. A swimmer must move quickly onto the beach to avoid the back rush of water after each wave.

Strong inshore feeder currents will set parallel to the shoreline, usually in the direction of the wind and surf. These currents are formed by waves that have been pushed onto the beach and that must find an outlet to return to the level of the sea. These outlets are marked by lower wave heights, slower wave speeds, confused current swirls, and foam. When these feeder currents turn to sea, they are called "rip currents." They flow seaward at angles from 45 to 80 degrees from the inshore feeder currents.

Swimmers must avoid these rip currents. If the swimmer seaward of the breaker line can determine the direction of the wind, or the angle the surf is approaching the beach, it is possible to pick the area where a rip current is least likely. That area will be just downwind of the place in the surf line where the waves seem lower and break farther to sea.

Should a swimmer get caught in a rip current, the best strategy is to swim gently at right angles to the direction of the current, *never* against it. Since most rip currents angle away from the beach, swimming at right angles to the current, down the beach and in the general direction that the wind and surf is moving, will enable the swimmer to make slow progress toward the shore without becoming exhausted. Once clear of the current, the swimmer should head directly toward the beach.

Further information on breakers and surf can be found in *Knights Modern Seamanship* and *The American Practical Navigator, Bowditch*. Because of their unique profession, Coast Guard personnel should learn to swim comfortably in surf, studying its movements and rhythms. Under emergency conditions, experience and knowledge of the surf may make survival possible.

Lifesaving

Effective lifesaving in the water depends upon the rescuer's presence of mind, knowledge of the methods that may have to be used, and strength and skill in carrying them out. Drowning people usually panic. Their one idea is to keep their heads above water. The whole technique of lifesaving is centered upon that fact. If a drowning person grabs or tries to grab some part of the rescuer's body or clothing, the rescuer should sink, taking the victim under water. Under water, the victim usually will let go. Under no circumstances should a rescuer strike a drowning person. A drowning victim's system has already had sufficient shock to cause severe physical reactions, and a severe blow may cause heart failure.

Lifesaving Approaches

There are several ways to approach a drowning person. Practice all of them.

Frontal approach. The rescuer should swim slowly toward the victim and attempt to calm and reassure the victim by talking. The victim should be told exactly what the rescuer is going to do and must be instructed to follow orders. Then the rescuer should grasp with the right hand the victim's left wrist, turn the victim's body slowly, and use one of the carries described below.

Rear approach. If the victim is too excited to pay attention to directions, the rescuer should swim behind the victim, grasp the chin with the right hand, apply pressure to the back with the left hand, and use one of the carries.

Underwater approach. The underwater approach is by far the safest because the drowning person does not have a chance to get a grip on the rescuer. The rescuer should swim within ten feet of the victim and surface-dive to a depth at which the victim's legs can be easily reached. If the victim is facing the rescuer, the rescuer should turn the victim in the opposite direction by pressure on their upper legs. The rescuer should slide the right hand up the drowning person's back and grasp the victim by the chin, applying pressure to the back with the left hand. The victim should be brought to the surface as quickly as possible and one of the carries used.

Lifesaving Carries

All of these methods should be practiced (see figure 31–6).

Hair carry. This is the easiest of the carries because it allows the most freedom of movement on the part of the rescuer. The rescuer turns on the left side, slides the right hand up the back of the victim's head to the top and grasps the hair tightly, using the left arm and legs for swimming sidestroke. The rescuer may swim on either side, changing hands when necessary in order to rest.

Head carry. The rescuer swims on the back, holding the victim's head above the water with both hands meeting under the victim's chin.

Cross-chest carry. The rescuer turns on the left side, places an arm over the victim's right shoulder, across the chest and under the left arm. The victim's body should be supported on the rescuer's right hip, and the rescuer should swim sidestroke, using the free left arm and both legs. This carry may be done from either side, but should not be used unless the victim is in bad condition, nor should it be used for long distances, because it is the most tiring.

Tired swimmer's carry. If the victim has enough control to obey orders, the victim should be ordered to turn on the back, face the rescuer, spread the legs, and place both hands on the rescuer's shoulders with the arms stiff. The rescuer assumes the position for the breaststroke and swims, pushing the victim ahead. The breaststroke is useful because it leaves the arms and legs unhampered for swimming and is only slightly more tiring than ordinary swimming.

Carries from the water. The most common carry is the fireman's carry. On reaching shallow water, the rescuer stands the victim up temporarily, places the right arm between the victim's legs, and throws the helpless person's body over the right shoulder. In this position, the victim's right wrist is grasped in the right hand of the rescuer, whose left arm is free.

A convenient carry for short distances is the *saddle back*. After bringing the victim into waist-deep water, the rescuer moves the victim's body around behind, with the head to the right. The rescuer grasps the victim with both arms around the body, hoists the victim across the back, leans forward, and carries the victim ashore.

Snorkel and SCUBA Diving

Both of these techniques are being used more and more, in military operations and as a form of recreation. Each offers many dangers to an untrained swimmer, and no one should attempt to snorkel or dive with SCUBA gear without training. Certification courses are available and will greatly benefit any swimmer. Any diving done under orders for the Coast Guard must be performed only by trained divers.

Figure 31-6. Approved methods of carrying a person in the water are: (A) head carry; (B) chest carry; (C) tired swimmer's carry.

Figure 31-7. A rescue swimmer is often the difference between life and death.

CHAPTER 32

Survival

Normally, the Coast Guard helps those who get into trouble, and you will be trained to handle such emergencies. But there may come a time when your own ship, boat, or aircraft is in trouble, and the problem of doing something about it may be pretty much up to you. This chapter gives basic information on survival if you should be shipwrecked. Special instructions will be given to members of rescue boats or aircraft crews. No matter where you are, you must familiarize yourself with such other instructions as are available. Perform drills diligently, learn the use of survival equipment, keep your life jacket and other lifesaving gear in good condition, and regularly review instructions so that you can manage in an emergency. Refer to the Coast Guard *Rescue and Survival Systems Manual*, COMDTINST M10470.10 series for detailed information.

PERSONAL FLOTATION DEVICE (PFD)

Personal flotation devices (PFDs) come in a number of forms. Shipboard military personnel are usually provided with specially designed PFDs that are inherently buoyant, meaning they are filled with a substance such as fibrous glass or kapok that provides flotation. Other military PFDs include less cumbersome, inflatable, and formed plastic types. Commercial-type PFDs are used by Coast Guardsmen in certain situations. These are referred to as type I, II, III, or IV PFDs and are assigned a Coast Guard Approval Number.

Figure 32-1. Survival at sea requires being prepared at all times.

Type I commercial PFDs provide similar flotation to military PFDs that are inherently buoyant. PFDs are often termed "life preservers," "life jackets," or "life vests." The official definitions for these terms are somewhat tricky, so if you become involved with this terminology in a legal sense or in a written report, be sure to use the correct term. Generally speaking, the term "life preserver" is correct for PFDs provided on board Coast Guard vessels. The typical Coast Guard life preserver is the Navy vest type with collar. It is an inherently buoyant PFD. This PFD is designed to provide superior flotation characteristics and reliability. It will support the head of an unconscious person.

Navy Vest-Type PFD with Collar

The vest-type PFD uses fibrous glass or kapok pads to provide buoyancy, and has straps to pull tight for a close fit. (See figure 32–2.) Leg straps prevent it from riding up in the water. A webbing body strap helps toward a snugger fit and provides a hold for lifting you out of the water. You can use the strap to attach yourself to a life raft or to other individuals.

Put the vest preserver on over your other clothes. Tie the upper tape at the waist fairly tight; it helps keep the preserver from sliding

Figure 32-2. U.S. Navy vest-type PFD, with collar.

up in the water. Then adjust the chest strap and fasten the snap hook into the ring. Tie the collar tapes to keep the collar under your chin, threading the tapes through the D-rings to hold the collar in the proper position.

The leg straps may be adjusted in the water, but if a person is injured or unconscious, they should be adjusted before the injured person is put overboard. Pull the straps between the legs from behind. Pull the leg straps as tight as possible without producing discomfort. While aboard ship and not in danger of going overboard, you need not use the leg straps.

Care Aboard Ship

When the outer covering or envelope of the vest preserver becomes soiled, the pads should be removed, the envelope—*not the pads*—cleaned, and the pads reinserted. Don't scrub kapok-filled life preservers lest you impair the fire-resistant qualities of the cloth. You may wipe them off, but that is all. Don't tamper with any jacket, or handle it roughly. Keep all jackets away from heat, moisture, oil, and dirt; or you may have a jacket that won't support you when you want it to.

Navy Vest-Type PFD Without Collar, Work Type (Inherently Buoyant)

This is a lightweight PFD that is formed-plastic-filled and provides 17 1/2 pounds of buoyancy. (See figure 32–3.) The unit is composed of three cotton-drill-covered sections that are assembled through a series of straps to form the completed PFD. Each section has a

Figure 32-3. U.S. Navy vest-type PFD, without collar; work type (inherently buoyant).

formed or molded pad two inches thick, notched for flexibility, allowing the PFD to conform more closely to the shape of the body. Because this vest type PFD is light in weight, the wearer is able to work in comparative comfort.

The work-type PFD is buoyant enough to keep the wearer afloat, but it has no self-righting capability and will not keep an unconscious wearer's head out of the water while awaiting rescue.

Coast Guard-Approved Type III PFD, (Inherently Buoyant)

The main advantages of type III PFDs are wearability, ease of donning, simple construction, and neat appearance. The disadvantages are poor flotation characteristics (no righting movement), and minimum buoyancy (15 pounds). Therefore, type IIIs should be worn only where greater freedom of movement is required, and the mission and environment are less hostile.

Navy Inflatable Yoke-Type PFD

This is a lightweight preserver that can be blown up either by a CO_2 cylinder or by mouth. (See figure 32–5.) It is fastened around your

Figure 32-4. Coast Guard–approved Type III PFD.

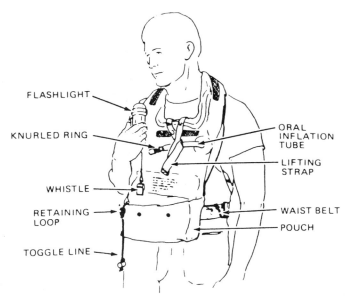

FLASHLIGHT

KNURLED RING

WHISTLE

RETAINING
LOOP

TOGGLE LINE

ORAL
INFLATION
TUBE

LIFTING
STRAP

WAIST BELT

POUCH

Figure 32-5. Navy standard inflatable yoke-type PFD.

waist by a web belt. When blown up, it holds itself closely around your neck. An extra piece of webbing provides a handhold for assisting you out of the water. A length of line with a wood T-toggle enables you to attach yourself to a boat, to float lines, or to other survivors. When not needed, the inflatable preserver is carried in a pouch, normally worn at your back.

When you need the preserver, pull the pouch around to the front, remove the preserver, slip it over your head and inflate it. To inflate the preserver, grasp the lanyard attached to the inflater and jerk downward as far as possible. This will release the carbon dioxide gas into the air chamber. If the preserver has two inflaters, pull both lanyards. For more buoyancy, push in the mouthpiece or the oral inflation valve and blow up the preserver yourself. To deflate the preserver, open the oral valve.

LPU-25/P Survival Vest Assembly/Underwater Escape Rebreather

The LPU-25/P is designed as a constant-wear survival vest for use by helicopter aircrew members. It is a nylon mesh vest, consisting of pockets for personal survival equipment stowage, a casing assembly, and an attached bladder assembly. The bladder assembly has an oxygen section for rebreathing and a carbon dioxide section for flotation.

The LPU-25/P is to be used as a life preserver for flotation and/or a rebreathing device that will supply two to three minutes of rebreathing time to escape from a submerged helicopter. Once inflated, the LPU-25/P provides a minimum of 22 pounds of buoyancy.

In an emergency, inflate the oxygen side by pulling downward and outward on the left-side pull toggle. Place the rebreather mouthpiece in your mouth and pull upon the mouthpiece to start the flow of oxygen. Once clear of the aircraft and at the surface, inflate the CO_2 side by pulling downward and outward on the right-side pull toggle.

ABANDONING SHIP

Preparations

There are two important things to do if time permits; find out the distance and direction to the nearest land, and see that your equipment is in good condition. What clothing and gear to take with you will depend on whether you are in a hot or cold climate and whether you will take to a boat or raft, or depend upon your life jacket to keep you afloat.

Clothing

Clothing is especially important in cold weather, but even in hot weather you need protection from the sun. In cold weather, you need:

- Long woolen underwear, woolen socks, to keep your body warm.
- A windproof jacket to protect your shoulders and arms.
- A helmet or cap to keep your head warm and water out of your ears.
- Gloves to warm hands and to prevent burning them on lines.
- An anti-exposure suit, if available.

Equipment

The more equipment you have, the better. Take these as a minimum:

- Flashlight, knife, whistle.

- Line, at least six feet long, tied under your arms with snap-on free end to make fast to a line on a raft, boat, or rescue ship.
- Sunglasses.
- Wallet, money belt.

Actions Before Leaving Ship

This depends on the amount of time you have. Remember to:

- Keep calm.
- Test life-jacket valves and inflating tubes; don't leave the ship with a leaking jacket.
- If it's available, drink hot tea or coffee to reduce the effects of cold.

Abandon Ship Procedure

The following procedure is a guide to be followed whenever practical.

Leaving the Ship

For survival, it is best that you abandon ship fully clothed. If possible, get away from the ship in a lifeboat or life raft. If it is impossible to leave the ship on a life raft, lower yourself into the water using a firmly anchored hose or line. When you have a choice, leave the ship from the windward side and from whichever end of the ship is lower in the water. If it is necessary to jump into the water, hold the legs together and the body erect. Injured personnel should always have their leg straps adjusted before they are lowered into the water. Inherently buoyant type PFDs must be securely fastened and kept close to the body by folding the arms across the chest and gripping the jacket with the fingers. This procedure will prevent buoyant PFDs from riding up and striking your chin or neck when you hit the water. If you are wearing an inflatable PFD, it must not be inflated until you are in the water. The same procedure is followed for jumping with an uninflated PFD as with the inherently buoyant PFD. The PFD should be inflated as soon as you are in the water and clear of flames.

In the water. When in the water, swim away from the ship as rapidly as possible and climb into a lifeboat if one is available.

Ship surrounded by flames. When the ship is surrounded by burning oil and abandonment is essential, jump feet first through the flames and swim to windward under the surface of the water for as long as possible. When the air in your lungs is exhausted, spring above the water in a vertical position, push the flames away with a circular motion of your hands, quickly take a deep breath, and turn around to swim to windward, submerge feet first in a vertical position and swim under the surface again. This procedure should be repeated until you are well clear of flames. Any buoyant articles of clothing and shoes should be discarded. Only the inflatable PFD should be worn, insofar as possible during this abandon-ship procedure, and the preserver should be inflated only after you are clear of the flames. Inherently buoyant PFDs will not permit the wearer to swim beneath the surface.

Survival in Cold Water

When forced to abandon ship in cold waters, put on as much clothing as possible (including hat and gloves), or an anti-exposure suit, if available, and be sure your life jacket is properly adjusted. Once in the lifeboat or raft, huddle up close to your shipmates to conserve body heat. If there is water in the lifeboat, immersion-foot can be prevented by untying shoe laces, elevating legs, and exercising ankles and toes at regular intervals. However, if you develop frostbite or immersion-foot, do *not* rub the affected parts.

If you must enter the water, make sure you are heavily dressed and wearing a life jacket. Enter the water as slowly as possible in order to reduce the shock of initial entry. Once in the water, remember that any movement will increase the rate of body-heat loss and reduce your chance for survival. Swim only to a nearby boat, raft, or piece of debris that you may be able to use to escape from the water. If you must remain in the water, cross your legs, bring your knees up toward your chest and hold your arms around your chest (heat-escape-lessening posture). This posture will help reduce body-heat loss.

If you should find yourself in the water, especially cold water in a survival situation, follow these tips:

- Keep as much of your body out of the water as possible. If you can, climb onto an overturned hull or piece of debris. Do so immediately.
- Wear a personal flotation device. This will eliminate the need for physical activity to stay afloat, thereby saving body heat.

- If you have time, put on extra clothing and be sure to cover your head.
- Protect yourself against the wind by staying to leeward.

If forced to remain in the water, keep your head above water and as dry as possible. Swimming will produce a faster cooling rate; therefore, once flotation is assured and essential survival actions have been taken, stop swimming and assume the heat-escape-lessening posture. If there are other people in the water, assume a huddle position with them. All survivors face inward, with sides and chests close together and arms around each other. Either of these two actions will increase survival time by up to 50 percent.

Hypothermia is a killer. Its danger is not restricted to freezing the body to death. Prolonged exposure to cold renders the body incapable of coordinated movement and the mind incapable of rational thought. Long before victims are unconscious, they may be unable to take the steps necessary to save their own lives.

Survival in Hot Climate

Wear shirt, trousers, hat, and shoes. They may be a hindrance in the water, but if you are adrift for any time, they are necessary to protect against the effects of sun, wind, and salt water. Take the same equipment as for cold weather, and take the same actions before leaving the ship.

Avoid panic; keep calm. If you panic, others may, and all of you may be in more trouble. Nonswimmers are most likely to lose their

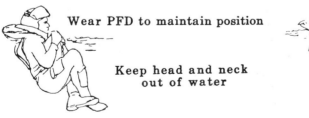

Wear PFD to maintain position

Keep head and neck out of water

Conserve heat by huddling

Figure 32-6.   Heat-preserving postures.

heads after abandoning ship, so encourage them, help them, and keep talking to them. Keep your wits about you, keep control of the situation, and you will come through.

ADRIFT IN A BOAT OR RAFT

Ingenuity and foresight are required to make the most of all available equipment. In a powerboat, use the fuel for making the most distance, not speed. The best mileage will be made at the slowest speed that can be held with the clutch fully engaged. If the boat has sails, use them and save the fuel for an emergency. If there are no sails, try to jury-rig a mast and sail with oars, boat hooks, pieces of wreckage, clothing, and tarpaulins.

The most serious situation is to be adrift in a life raft with no way to rig a sail. In that case, make your rations and water last as long as possible. The longer you hold out, the better your chances for rescue or a safe landing. People have endured for more than a month in a raft, with practically no rations.

Rescue units will start looking for you at your last-known position. Don't leave that area unless you can make it to shore or to a well-traveled shipping lane.

Organizing for Survival

The first thing to do is to secure all gear to the raft or boat. Anything not lashed down is liable to go overboard and be lost.

- Rig a tarp or sail for protection from the sun, and get under it. The water will reflect enough sun to burn your skin, so stay out of the sun as much as possible. Remember that the same tarp or sail will catch drinking water when there is rain.
- Inventory the provisions on board, and store them where they will be safe, even against high seas. Plan for rationing food and water. No one should eat or drink during the first 24 hours. However, in cold climates, eating every two hours will help you to stay warm.
- Don't get excited and don't rush. Do things deliberately to conserve energy and to avoid perspiring.
- Save your clothes. Although it is warm during the day, you may need something to wear at night.
- Arrange watches and cooperate in standing them. Stow your signaling gear—mirror, marking dye, flares, and smoke signal—where they can be reached in a hurry.

First Aid

In general, the first-aid procedures afloat are the same as those ashore. There are some special considerations, however, that apply to survivors at sea.

Fuel oil from a sinking ship will float on the water and accumulate on the skin of survivors. If swallowed, it may cause vomiting. In the eyes, it will cause redness and smarting. Ordinarily these symptoms will disappear in a day or two. Wipe oil from the eyelids with a clean cloth or bandage.

Petrolatum (vaseline) may be used to ease chapped skin and cracked lips. But it is better to prevent sunburn by wearing or rigging whatever protection is available against the sun. Even a dark tan is not a sure protection against sunburn. Reflected light from the ocean may burn the eyeballs as well as the skin. Guard against the sun when it is directly or almost directly overhead.

Boils often appear on the skin of people who have been in lifeboats or rafts for several days. Unless skilled medical assistance is at hand, no treatment should be attempted. Simply cover them with protective bandages and do not try to open them. Resist exhaustion and conserve strength by sleeping and resting as much as possible.

Coast Guard-Approved Rafts

The standard features of Coast Guard-approved rafts are listed below.

- Constructed of neoprene-coated nylon.
- CO_2 overpressurized inflation system with relief valves that provide for cold inflation.
- Two independent buoyancy tubes.
- Self-erecting canopy.
- Boarding ladder/towing bridle.
- Survival equipment (drinking water, signal flares, etc.).
- Inflatable floor.
- Exterior/interior lights.
- Stabilizing pockets (water).
- Rainwater catchment assembly.
- Rescue line (throwable).
- External/internal life line.
- Sea anchor.

Crew survival rafts can be released and inflated either manually or automatically by use of the hydrostatic release.

The life rafts can be deployed manually by releasing the raft from the stowage rack and pulling the operating painter from the raft container. The container should preferably be placed in the water prior to inflation to allow ample room for expansion of the raft. If practical, personnel should board the raft directly from their vessel to avoid unnecessary boarding problems and exposure to the water, especially in cold oceans. Immediately upon boarding the raft, complete these steps:

- Get clear of sinking vessel in case of explosion or surface fire.
- Search for survivors.
- Salvage floating equipment that may be useful; stow and secure all items.
- Ensure sea anchor is properly deployed.
- Check raft for proper inflation, leaks, and points of possible chafing. Bail out water that may have entered the raft. Be careful not to snag the raft with shoes or sharp objects.
- In cold oceans, inflate floor immediately, put on exposure suit, if available. Rig entrance cover. If with others, huddle together for warmth.
- Check the physical condition of all aboard. Give first aid as necessary. Take seasickness pills if available. Wash oil or gasoline from clothing and body.
- If there is more than one raft, keep close together to expedite rescue operations. If possible, rafts should be tied together about 50 feet apart bow to stern from towing bridle to towing bridle.
- Make a calm estimate of the situation and plan a course of action carefully.
- Ration water and food; assign duties.
- Keep a log. Record time of entry into water, names, and physical condition of survivors, ration schedule, winds, weather, direction of swells, times of sunrise and sunset, and other navigation data. Inventory all equipment.

Rescue and Assistance

Although shipboard rafts are intended for crew survival, these rafts may be used, at the discretion of the commanding officer, for other purposes such as rescue and assistance. If the raft is used as a rescue platform for recovering survivors, the canopy fabric may be cut away.

Four-Man Rescue and Survival Raft

The four-man rescue and survival raft (RR-4) was modified to provide SAR boats with a multipurpose raft. This raft is a basic Coast Guard-approved raft modified to incorporate a stowable canopy and a heavy, water-ballast system for stability. The four-man rescue and survival raft incorporates most of the features required for Coast Guard-approved rafts except:

> The canopy is stowable. This raft is packed with the canopy stowed.
>
> The exterior and interior lights and the rainwater catchment assembly have been removed from the canopy.
>
> A heavy, water-ballast system has been added for increased stability in heavy weather. Because of this system, the raft will not be as affected by wind as conventional rafts would be.

1. SEA ANCHOR
2. RETRORELECTIVE MATERIAL
3. CANOPY COVER
4. BALLAST BAG
5. FLOOR
6. BUOYANCE TUBE (UPPER)
7. BUOYANCE TUBE (LOWER)
8. BALLASTING PORT
9. DEBALLASTING HANDLE
10. BOARDING LADDER
11. TOWING BRIDLE

Figure 32-7. Life raft, four-man (RR-4), SAR boat, rescue and survival (typical).

Survival Items

Signal Whistle

This whistle is used to attract the attention of rescue ships or personnel in foggy weather or at night. It is made of plastic with a lanyard attached for easy access and to prevent loss. The whistle's range is 1,000 yards.

Survival Knife

The survival knife is a multipurpose survival tool stowed in its sheath when not in use. It is a hunting knife with a five-inch steel blade. One side of the blade is honed and the other side is serrated.

The survival knife is the most valuable general-purpose survival tool. It can be used for cutting wood and material and opening cans, and it is a hunting knife as well as a weapon. At all times, the survival knife should be kept clean and sharpened, and returned to the sheath when not in use.

Signal Kit MK-79 MOD-0

The MK-79 MOD-0 signal illumination kit is a distress signaling device. It is small and light in weight so that it can be carried in flight suits or life rafts.

The MK-79 signal kit consists of one MK-31 projector and seven MK-80 screw-cartridge flares. Included with the launcher and flares is a bandolier, which stores the flares until use, protective caps for the flares, and an instruction sheet.

The projector aims and fires the flares. Each flare consists of a red pyrotechnic star. Upon activation, this star is propelled to heights of from 250 to 650 feet. The star burns for a minimum of 4 1/2 seconds and has 12,000 candlepower.

The kit is operated by pulling the thumb trigger into the safety catch, screwing the cartridge into the projector, pointing the cartridge in a safe, upward direction, and releasing the thumb trigger.

Full safety and operation instructions are in the *Coast Guard Ordnance Manual*, M8000.2 and NAVORD OP 2213.

Smoke and Illumination Signal Marine MK-13 MOD-0

The MK-13 MOD-0 is used for day or night signaling with smoke or flare. (See figure 32–8.) This marine smoke and illumination signal consists of a metal cylinder five inches long and 1.5 inches in diameter, each end of which is fitted with a protective plastic cap. The cap on the flame (night) end is molded so that there are three prominent protrusions or beads across its face. These beads positively identify this end, by the sense of touch, for nighttime use. The face of the cap at the smoke end is smooth. A label adhered to the outer surface around the whole body of the signal further identifies the smoke (day) and flame (night) end and provides precise instructions for use. Beneath each plastic end cap is a pull ring to which is tied a nylon cord or lanyard. A large washer on the cord at the flame end provides additional identification in darkness. The pull ring at each end is attached to a pull strip seal, which is attached to a friction wire that extends inward through a pull wire igniter cup containing ignition composition.

The MK-13 MOD-0 illumination signal is intended for either day or night signaling on land or sea. Because of its weight (6.5 ounces) and size, the MK-13 MOD-0 may be carried in life vest, flight suit, or life raft. It emits orange smoke for day use and a red flare for night use. Burning time is 20 seconds.

A sharp, quick pull on the pull ring of the MK-13 MOD-0 causes a friction wire that is attached to the pull strip seal to move through the ignition cup and ignite the flare mixture (night) or the smoke mixture (day), depending upon which type of display is desired.

The MK-13 Mod-0 signal must be operated, stored, and handled in accordance with procedures found in the *Coast Guard Ordnance Manual*, M8000.2 and NAVORD OP 2213.

Emergency Signaling Mirror

The emergency signaling mirror is used to attract rescue ships or aircraft. It measures two inches by three inches and replaces the three-inch by five-inch mirror. There is a hole in the corner through

Figure 32-8. Mk-13 MOD-0 marine smoke and illumination signal.

which a lanyard passes so that the mirror may be looped around the neck.

The emergency signaling mirror is intended to reflect sunlight at ships, aircraft, or rescue parties. Instructions for using the mirror are printed on its back.

Distress Signal Lights

SDU-5/E

The SDU-5/E is a battery-operated strobe light used to signal rescue parties. The light is a lightweight, compact, battery-operated portable unit with all circuitry encapsulated within the case. The battery entry and the case are completely watertight when the battery is installed. The case is provided with a push-ON, push-OFF type switch to permit one-handed operation. A flexible switch boot further ensures watertight integrity. A three-foot nylon cord attaches the light to the equipment case by either of two attachment loops on the light case.

The SDU-5/E is intended for equipping aircrew members and shipboard personnel with a high-intensity, visual distress signal in the event of abandonment of aircraft or a man overboard.

Personnel Marker Lights

The personnel marker light (PML) is a chemical light developed for use on personal flotation devices. It is used to attract the attention of SAR aircraft, ships, or ground parties. Once activated it provides light for eight hours. The PML is equipped with a pin-type clip and should be attached in the same location on the PFD as the one-cell flashlight.

To activate the PML, slide the protective sleeve from the PML breaking the sealing band. Firmly squeeze the lever against the light tube until the ampule inside the light breaks.

Equipment in Rafts and Boats

The following items should be in all rafts or lifeboats:

Air pump	Paddles
Canned water	Sea anchor
Dye marker	Signal gear

First aid kit   Signaling mirror
Flashlight (waterproof)   Sponge
Food packet   Water desalting kit
Knife   Whistle

Other Survival Kit Items

Concentrated food. The Navy emergency rations for life rafts meet minimum nutrition requirements for personnel shipwrecked with limited supplies of water. Each can contains a total of 15 sugar-type tablets, eight malted milk tablets, two multivitamin tablets, and two packs of chewing gum. The daily ration would normally be one of these cans per person.

Dye marker. The dye marker consists of a can of *fluorescein* (a material that glows in very little light) packed in a waterproof container. On the water, it forms a yellow-green patch that usually is visible for two hours for a relatively long distance. At night, it can be seen only in bright moonlight, and rough water quickly disperses it.

First-aid kit. The camouflaged kit for life rafts contains an assortment of bandages and some tubes of petrolatum (for burns). The bandages consist of compresses to cover open wounds, long strips of gauze to hold the compresses in place, and triangular all-purpose gauze bandages, which may be used to hold other bandages in place, or as slings, head bandages, and so on.

Fishing kit. The fishing kit contains gloves, a knife that will float, sinkers, pork rind for bait, an assortment of hooks and fishing rigs, a dip net, a bib with pockets to hold the equipment, and directions printed on waterproof paper. The kit is enclosed in a can with a key opener.

Flashlight. One of the most commonly used night signals as well as a most useful piece of equipment is the flashlight. A waterproof model is standard; but any flashlight should be kept out of the water to ensure the best service and longest life. The equipment containers are provided with spare batteries; nevertheless, flashlights should be used only when necessary.

Food and Water in the Environment

Fish caught in the open sea are healthful and nourishing, cooked or raw, and will supplement and even replace canned rations as long as sufficient drinking water is available.

When fish are caught near shore, avoid the poisonous kinds. Poisonous fish can be used as bait but must not be eaten.

Drying Fish

Well-dried fish will stay unspoiled for several days. To dry large fish, clean them, cut them in thin narrow strips, and hang them in the sun. Small fish, a foot long or less, should also be cleaned before drying, the backbone removed, and slits cut across the inside about a quarter of an inch apart. They should then be hung in the sun. Fish not cleaned will spoil in a half day. Do not eat dried fish unless you have plenty of drinking water.

Fishing Tips

Never tie a fishing line to finger, hands, feet or boat. A big fish can cut or break your line or carry off your tackle. Don't pay out all your line, but leave slack in the boat. Have someone hold the end of the slack line.

Don't lean over the side of the boat when a fish is hooked. A boat can be capsized in this fashion.

* Try to catch small fish rather than big ones.
* Keep the bait moving to make it look alive.
* Keep parts of any bird or fish you catch and use them for bait.
* Clean hooks and lines of fish and fish slime, and dry them in the sun.
* Don't get your lines tangled or let hooked fish tangle them. Two people can fish at the same time, but they must be careful.
* In a rubber boat, be careful that your knife and fishing hook never get a chance to prick, stick, or make a hole in your boat.
* Make a fair division of your catch.
* Keep fishing. You never know when fish may bite.
* Fish will be attracted by a light at night. Often a bright moon or flashlight shining on a cloth will draw fish.

Solar (Sun) Stills

Solar stills are sometimes provided. They can distill two pints of water each day. Usually, a still is provided for each person the boat is designed to accommodate. The stills operate most efficiently in direct sunlight. They will function to a certain degree during cloudy or overcast days, but they cannot distill water at night, on dark days, in

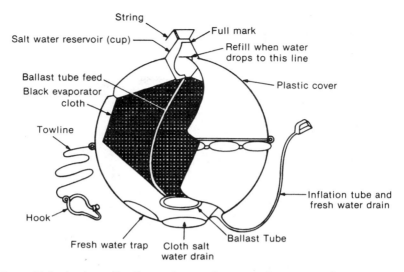

Figure 32-9. A solar still will provide enough water to keep a man alive.

polar waters, or during inclement weather. The solar still is one of the most reliable sources of potable water at sea. The water is pure, but may appear somewhat milky because of talc sprinkled on the inside of the plastic cover to keep it from sticking to itself.

Eating on Land

Most tropical fruits are good to eat. It is safe for humans to eat the same things that monkeys eat. Unknown roots, fine shoots, and other herbs must be experimented with cautiously. Eat any unfamiliar plants in very small quantities until their effect is ascertained.

Turtles and their eggs may be eaten cooked or raw. All animals are safe to eat. Snakes, even poisonous ones, are edible, but their heads should be removed. Grubs and grasshoppers can be eaten if the wings and legs are picked off before cooking. Caterpillars should not be eaten.

All birds are good to eat, cooked or raw. Their blood and liver are edible. The feathers, meat, guts, and even the toes make good lures or bait for fish. Birds can sometimes be caught in nets; the larger ones will often take a bit of fish on a hook dragged on top of the water. Some birds will go after a baited hook tossed into the air.

Water Discipline

If possible, take a drink of water before abandoning ship. After abandoning ship, conserve body water; try to keep cool and avoid sweating.

Unless you become very thirsty, drink no water for the first 24 hours on the raft. Thereafter, drink a pint (16 ounces) of water a day if your supply is limited. Drink a pint and a half (24 ounces) a day, or more if necessary, if you have an abundant supply of rain water and the one-pint allowance does not satisfy you. It is better to keep up the rate of 16 ounces a day (four ounces—half a glass—four times a day) until only ten ounces are left, rather than to use smaller amounts for a longer time. When only ten ounces are left, use it only to moisten the mouth. (Sea water and urine should never be drunk. Sea water will cause vomiting, diarrhea, and delirium.)

When the supply of water is limited, bird and fish flesh should be consumed sparingly. The moisture in fish flesh is more than offset by the increase in urine resulting from the body's assimilation of the fish protein. Use fish for food, not water.

On land, water can be obtained from a hole dug at low tide just below the high-water mark. The water in the hole may be salty and discolored, but it can be drunk in small quantities. Large amounts will cause sickness.

Mental Attitude

The most important factor in survival after shipwreck in any except the coldest waters is the element of mental and emotional stability. How well people adjust to the psychological stress of being cast adrift may mean the difference between their rescue and loss. Superior equipment is useless when people are emotionally and mentally disorganized.

Cold-Weather Protection

Many cutters and aircraft operate in cold climates where exposure to cold weather and frigid water can cause hypothermia and death. To protect crews from these dangers, cutters and aircraft have hypothermia protective devices.

The anti-exposure coverall, or "work suit," is designed for routine work on deck when operating in cold environments. In addition, the anti-exposure coverall provides protection against hypothermia in

Figure 32-10. Survival suits protect the body against hypothermia.

the water. Similar to insulated coveralls, the anti-exposure coverall is water resistant and buoyant, but still provides the mobility necessary for working and climbing.

The survival suit is provided as an abandon-ship garment aboard cutters operating in cold climates. The suit is a one-piece garment with high flotation characteristics that completely covers the body except for the face. The survival suit is designed so that one size will fit all. The thermal qualities of the 3/16–inch nylon-lined neoprene foam will keep a person warm, wet or dry.

CHAPTER 33

First Aid

First aid is emergency treatment for injured or wounded people. It consists only of immediate, temporary assistance to save life, prevent further injury, and preserve the victim's vitality and resistance to infection. The way to remember your first aid priorities is to simply go by the *ABCs*. First, ensure the victim has an adequate *airway*. Then check for *breathing*. Next check *circulation* by checking for a pulse and obvious bleeding. When these are under control, treat for or prevent *shock*. *The ABCs are the serious life threats*, and should be corrected first before things such as splinting fractures.

Take Immediate Action

Know what to do and do it. When coming upon a victim, take care to protect *yourself* by surveying the scene to be sure there are no hazards such as live electrical wires or loose gear that may have caused the injury and may be dangerous to you. Secure any hazards before starting treatment. Next, check to see if he or she is awake—a victim who is conscious and speaking obviously has an adequate airway, can breath, and has a pulse, so the next priority is to check for hemorrhage, control it, then treat for shock. Don't move victims unless absolutely necessary to save them from fire, gas, drowning, or gunfire. A fractured bone may cut an artery or nerve; a broken neck or back may result in spinal cord injury and paralysis, or death.

Figure 33-1. Coast Guardsmen and Red Cross workers on a rescue mission after hurricane Camille hit Mississippi.

Make an injured person comfortable and cover to keep warm. If a victim must be moved, know how to do it.

Control the Situation

Ask for medical assistance if possible. Use a telephone, radio, messenger, or send someone in a car. Have someone keep bystanders clear. Loosen clothing about the victim's neck, chest, and abdomen. Examine the victim to determine the extent of injuries. Look for bleeding, wounds, fractures, or burns. Notice the color of the skin. Determine the state of consciousness by asking the victim questions. Bleeding from the nose and ears is often a symptom of a fractured skull. Bloody froth coming from the mouth often indicates damaged lungs. Check the pulse rate and strength. Check dogtags if present for blood type; see if the victim carries anything (bracelet, tag, or card) about drugs or medicines required or forbidden.

Frequently, loss of blood is not as serious as it may look, but lack of breathing is very dangerous. Breathing must be restored first. For that reason, artificial respiration is covered first in this chapter. After that, all other first-aid treatments follow in alphabetical order.

RESCUE BREATHING AND CARDIOPULMONARY RESUSCITATION

Symptoms

Absence of or insufficient breathing, and/or cyanosis (blueness of the skin, lips, fingernails, tongue, or mucous membranes of the mouth) are symptoms that indicate the need for rescue breathing. If these symptoms are present and the victim has no pulse, the victim is in cardiac arrest and cardiopulmonary resuscitation is needed.

Securing the Scene

Before you can recognize or treat a victim's condition, you must first secure the scene. This is done by removing the cause, or removing the victim from the cause. For example, if your victim was electrocuted, secure the power.

Recognition and Treatment

After you have secured the scene, perform your ABCs:

- Airway: open then look, listen, and feel for;

- Breathing: if victim is not breathing, call for help, then give two full breaths. Next, check for;
- Circulation (pulse): if there is a pulse, continue artificial respirations (rescue breathing). If there is no pulse, start external cardiac massage along with artificial respiration (cardiopulmonary resuscitation).

Rescue breathing and/or CPR must be continued until:

- normal breathing and pulse have resumed;
- until the victim is pronounced dead by a doctor or until;
- you are no longer able to continue.

Frequently, after recovery of respiration, the victim will again stop breathing. Closely monitor your victim. If natural breathing stops, artificial respiration should be resumed at once.

Rescue Breathing

This is always your first step of treatment, followed by a pulse check which will determine the necessity for external cardiac massage. (See figure 33-2.) The steps to follow are:

- Place the victim on their back and kneel beside the head. (a)
- Shake and shout, to establish the victim's level of consciousness. (b)
- Place one hand under the chin and the other hand on the forehead, so that your thumb and forefinger can pinch the nose closed. (c)
- Tilt the head back gently by lifting the chin and pushing the head down. This will open the airway in the majority of cases. (c) Note: If neck or back injuries are suspected, use an alternate method for opening the victim's airway called the modified jaw thrust. (k)
- Look, listen, and feel. Bend over the victim so that your ear is a few inches from the mouth and you're looking at the chest. Look for the chest to rise while listening and feeling with your ear for the movement of air. (d)
- Take a deep breath (about twice the normal), open your mouth widely, and place your mouth over the victim's mouth and blow, giving two full breaths. (e)
- Watch for the victim's chest to rise. As soon as this happens, remove your mouth from victim and allow the air to escape naturally after each breath. Give two breaths initially then repeat—

a. Kneel beside victim

b. Shake and shout

c. Open the airway

d. Look, listen and feel

e. Give two full breaths

f. Check the pulse

g. Locate correct hand position

h. Compress breastbone

i. Breastbone

j. Correct hand position

k. Modified jaw thrust

l. Clearing the mouth

12–14 times per minute for adults
18–20 times per minute for children and infants

If the chest does not rise, one or more of the following conditions exist and must be corrected:

Air leak. Make sure you have an airtight seal between your mouth and the victim's.

Airway obstruction (more likely). Reposition the head to attempt to open the airway and try again. If the chest still fails to rise, look into the victim's mouth and remove any foreign bodies (false teeth, etc.), vomit, or blood clots, then try another breath. If the chest still will not rise, the choking sequence should be followed.

Children and infants require less air to sufficiently ventilate. Infants only require the amount of air you can hold in your cheeks. However, as long as you watch the chest as you puff (rather than blow) and remove your mouth when the chest begins to rise, no damage will occur.

Mouth-to-nose breathing may be carried out using the same techniques as mouth-to-mouth, except, of course, the victim's mouth is held closed while your mouth is placed over the victim's nose.

Airways and tubes should be used only by personnel trained in their use or by medical officers. Not only are they dangerous when used by untrained personnel, but they usually are not available when an emergency arises.

After mouth-to-mouth breathing has been started and only after it has been determined that the heart has stopped should external cardiac massage be started and combined with rescue breathing to give cardiopulmonary resuscitation (CPR). It is most important to realize that external cardiac massage is unnecessary and actually dangerous unless the heart has stopped beating. Many cases will be encountered in which the person has stopped breathing but whose heart is still beating, and these cases require only rescue breathing.

Cardiopulmonary resuscitation must be started without delay. You have only four to six minutes in which to initiate this rescue technique. After that time, irreparable damage begins to occur in the victim's brain. Therefore, do not leave the victim to summon aid. Send another person for help, and start resuscitation immediately.

Don't waste time moving the victim except when absolutely necessary.

External Cardiac Massage

After mouth-to-mouth breathing has been instituted with two full breaths, check to see if external cardiac massage should be started. It is needed only if the heart has stopped beating. Perform external cardiac massage as follows:

- Check for a pulse. The best place to check is the carotid artery in the neck (f), close to the surface on either side of the adam's apple. Practice feeling your own.
- Find proper hand placement. Locate the notches at the upper and lower ends of the breastbone. (g) Place the heel of one hand over the lower third of the breastbone, (point "X" in i), and the other hand on top of the first. (j)
- Compress breastbone toward the backbone by exerting downward pressure on hands (1½ to 2 inches for adults) with the weight of your upper body. Keep elbows straight. Pressure is then released smoothly. (h) This cycle is repeated at a rate of 80–100 times per minute in adults and children. Children and infants' breastbones are not as strong; therefore, external cardiac massage should be done with one hand for children, and two fingers for infants. Compress the breastbone 1 to 1½ inches for children and ½ to 1 inch for infants at a rate of 100–120 per minute.

Timing

Timing is one of the most critical aspects of CPR. Without correct timing, CPR is useless. Remember the following while performing CPR as a rescuer performing chest compression or rescue breathing; it could be the difference between life or death for your victim.

- The rescuer performing chest compressions (compressor) must maintain a steady tempo and rate. A helpful way to maintain this tempo is count aloud as you compress the chest (one and two, and three and four, etc.). During two-rescuer CPR the compressor must pause after the fifth compression to allow the rescuer performing the rescue breathing (ventilator) to administer a breath.
- During one-rescuer CPR, the rescuer must administer both the breaths and chest compressions. This is performed as a cycle of 15 compressions, then two breaths. If your timing is right, you should be completing four cycles per minute.

While performing CPR, check the following: Hand placement: fingers should be kept away from the ribs to avoid fractures. Pulse: should be checked frequently to see if the heart has restarted. Note: Good CPR should generate a pulse, which can be checked at the carotid artery by the rescuer doing the rescue breathing.

While performing CPR, the stomach may become distended with air. This is especially true if the airway is not clear. It is not dangerous and should be left alone. Often during CPR the victim vomits, so you must be ready to turn the head to one side and clean out the mouth with fingers or a cloth. (l)

Summary

Cardiopulmonary resuscitation should be started at once in any case where breathing and the heart have stopped. If only breathing has stopped, use rescue breathing. Don't waste time seeking help or equipment. Begin treatment at once, by following these simple instructions:

- Put victim on a firm surface, face up.
- Start rescue breathing.
- Check for pulse.
- If pulse is absent, start CPR.
- Continue CPR until someone of higher authority takes over, until victim recovers, or until you are physically unable to continue.

GENERAL FIRST AID TREATMENT

Animal Bites

The dangers in an animal bite are rabies and infection; if the bite is by a pet, the pet must be kept under observation to determine if rabies treatment is required. Bites by wild animals or unknown domestic animals should be checked by a doctor to determine if rabies treatment is necessary.

Rinse the wound under running water, then wash with soap and water. Apply antiseptic. Treat for bleeding and shock as necessary.

Bandages

Bandages are used to hold dressings (compresses) to the wound. Dressings should be sterile. But bandages can be of any material that will sufficiently keep the dressing in place. The bandage may be applied in turns: circular, spiral, or figure eight. Triangular bandages may be tied on the head or face, shoulder or hip, chest or back, foot or hand. Cravat bandages are employed for wounds of the head, neck, eye, temple, cheek, ear, elbow, knee, arm, or leg. Roller bandages are wrapped on the hand and wrist, forearm or leg. *The First Aid Textbook* prepared by the American Red Cross is invaluable for learning the application of bandages and any first aid problem.

Bleeding

An average human body contains twelve pints of blood. One pint can be lost without harmful effect. A loss of two pints will usually produce shock. If half the blood is lost, death almost always results. Bleeding must be stopped quickly.

In arterial bleeding, bright red blood spurts out; this bleeding is very serious. In venous bleeding, dark red blood flows steadily; this also can be very serious. Capillary bleeding—usually not serious—comes from a cut or small abrasion. Practically all bleeding can be stopped if pressure is applied to the wound. If direct pressure does not stop the bleeding, pressure should be applied at the right pressure point (see below). Where severe bleeding cannot be controlled by either of these methods, pressure by means of a tourniquet should be applied.

Direct Pressure

Use a sterile dressing or the cleanest cloth available—a freshly laundered handkerchief, a towel, or an article of clothing. Fold it to form a pad, place it directly over the wound, and fasten it in position with a bandage. If the bleeding does not stop, try applying direct pressure by hand steadily, for five or six minutes, over the pad (figure 33–3).

Figure 33-3. Control of bleeding by direct pressure on the wound.

In cases of severe bleeding, don't worry about infection—stop the flow of blood. If nothing else is available, jam a shirt or other large material into the wound. Remember, direct pressure is the first method to use to control bleeding.

Pressure Points

Bleeding from a cut artery or vein may often be controlled by applying pressure to the right pressure point and elevating the part if it is a limb. A pressure point is a place where a main artery lies near the skin surface and over a bone. Pressure there compresses the artery against the bone and shuts off the flow of blood to the wound. Remember to apply pressure at the point nearest the wound and *between* the wound and the heart.

It is very tiring to apply finger pressure, and it can seldom be maintained for more than 15 minutes. As soon as possible, use a compress held securely over the wound by a bandage.

Tourniquet

If the bleeding is still severe, you may have to apply a tourniquet. Remember, this may result in gangrene when left on too long.

A tourniquet consists of a pad, a band, and a device for tightening the band so that the blood vessels will be compressed. The type found in many first aid kits consists of a web band two inches wide by five feet long, with a buckle for fastening. Wrap it once about the limb, then run the free end through the slit in the felt pad and through the buckle. Draw the band tight enough to stop the flow of blood.

An improvised tourniquet should be a band approximately two inches wide. Do not use rope, wire, string, or very narrow pieces of cloth; they will cut into the flesh. A short stick may be used to twist the band and tighten the tourniquet. The band should be placed two inches above the wound. A tourniquet is never used unless bleeding cannot be controlled in any other way. Once a tourniquet has been applied, it should be released only by medical personnel. By the time the tourniquet is put on, the victim has already lost a considerable amount of blood. The additional loss resulting from loosening the tourniquet may easily cause death. If a tourniquet is used, mark the patient's forehead with a "T" and the time. Improper use may produce gangrene. Do not use a tourniquet except as a last resort.

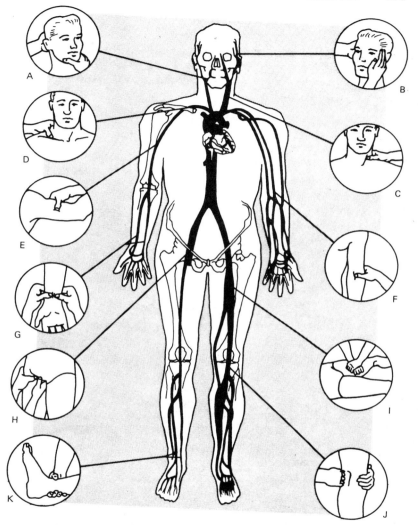

Figure 33-4. Control of bleeding by application of pressure at points where artery lies near the skin and over a bone.

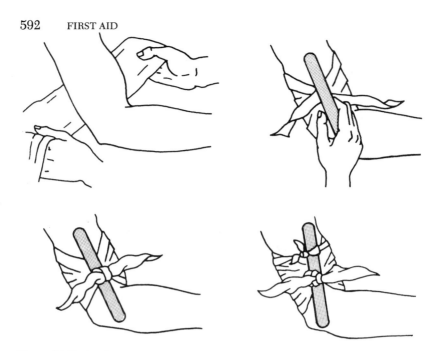

Figure 33-5. Applying a tourniquet: tie bandage with overhand knot, tie square knot over stick, twist to tighten the tourniquet.

Internal Bleeding

If a patient is bleeding internally, they may be thirsty, restless, fearful, and in shock. Nothing should be given by mouth, even if the victim is thirsty, for if anesthesia has to be given, the patient might vomit and aspirate material into the lungs.

Bleeding in the stomach may be indicated by a wound in that area and bloody vomiting (often resembling coffee grounds), or bloody stools. The treatment to be administered for internal bleeding is the same as for shock. Immediate medical care should be sought, since internal bleeding may be rapidly fatal, or may cause death by slower bleeding over a longer period of time.

Blisters

The skin covering a blister is better protection than any bandage and should therefore be left alone. If the blister is where it might be broken, open it with a sharp knife or needle that has been heated in flame. Press out fluid with a bit of sterile gauze and apply a sterile bandage.

Treatment of Burns and Scalds

Burns and scalds are caused by exposure to intense heat (fire, bomb flash, sunlight, hot metal solids, hot gases, or hot liquids). Contact with electric current may cause severe burns.

Burns are classified according to the depth of injury to the tissues. A burn that reddens the skin is called a first-degree burn. A burn that raises a blister is a second-degree burn. A burn that destroys the skin and actually chars or cooks the tissues is a third-degree burn. In some third-degree burns the destruction extends down to muscles and bones.

The size of the burned area may be far more important than the depth of the burn. Third-degree burns frequently appear as blanched areas surrounded by reddened or blistered skin. A first-degree burn that covers a very large area of the body may be more serious than a small third-degree burn.

The main dangers from burns are shock and infection. First aid treatment must be directed toward relieving pain, combatting shock, and preventing infection.

Minor Burns

Cool the burns immediately. Cool-water treatment has proved both comforting and effective. Submerge the burned part in cool water, but don't freeze. Continue until no pain is felt when the burned part is withdrawn from the water. Be careful not to over-cool. If the victim begins to shiver, stop cooling and dress the burns. Do not apply ointments or other medicines to the burned area. Cover the burn with a sterile bandage to prevent infection. The pain will be greatly lessened if the bandage is airtight and fairly firm. Commercially available clear plastic food wrap makes an excellent airtight burn dressing; just apply the wrap and cover with a bandage.

Serious Burns

Immediate care is to cool the burns. Tissues continue to burn after removed from the heat source. Keep the victim's head slightly lower than the feet, and see that the victim is warm enough. Do not remove clothing immediately. Cover the victim with a blanket. Do not overheat. Remember that exposure to cold will increase shock. Seriously burned victims should be given nothing by mouth except on direct order of a physician or medical officer.

Chemical Burns

Chemicals in contact with the skin or other body membranes may cause chemical burns by direct chemical destruction of the body tissue. This kind of injury can be caused by acids (nitric acid, sulfuric acid, hydrochloric acid, etc.), and caustic alkalies.

Here are some guidelines for treating chemical burns. Wash off the chemical immediately with large amounts of clean, fresh, cool water. If it is not possible to put the victim under running water, immerse the affected areas in water, or pour great quantities of water over the burns. If the chemical is a dry powder, do not apply water but remove the agent by "dusting" and removing the clothes.

Dry gently with sterile gauze. Do not break the skin or open any blisters.

Treat for shock. See also "Eye Injuries."

Information on chemicals can be obtained through the *Chemical Hazards Response Information System* (CHRIS) (COMDTINST M16465.12 series).

Choking

Choking occurs when an object obstructs the airway. The obstruction even may be the tongue in an unconscious victim. This is relieved by the airway-opening methods explained in the CPR section. Most commonly it is caused by a piece of food in adults or small toys or food in children. The universal choking sign is one or both hands clutching the throat. If the obstruction is not removed, the eventual outcome is death; therefore, *first aid action must be immediate.*

Ask the victim, "Are you choking?" If the victim can speak and is getting enough air, encourage them to relax and try to cough the object up. Do not attempt to remove the object yourself. Get help if the obstruction is not cleared in a short time.

In complete obstruction or in partial obstruction where the victim is not getting enough air, abdominal thrusts should be performed. The choking sequence follows:

Call for assistance.
Stand behind the victim. Wrap your arms around his or her waist.

First Aid For Choking

1
- **ASK: Are you choking?**
- If victim cannot breathe, cough, or speak...

2
- **Give the Heimlich Maneuver.**
- Stand behind the victim.
- Wrap your arms around the victim's waist.
- Make a fist with one hand. PLACE your FIST (thumbside) against the victim's stomach in the midline just ABOVE THE NAVEL AND WELL BELOW THE RIB MARGIN.
- Grasp your fist with your other hand.
- PRESS INTO STOMACH WITH A QUICK UPWARD THRUST.

3
- **Repeat thrust if necessary.**

- **If a victim has become unconscious:**
  - Sweep the mouth.

American Red Cross

4

5
- Attempt rescue breathing.

6
- Give 6-10 abdominal thrusts.
- Repeat Steps 4, 5, and 6 as necessary.

Figure 33-6. First aid for choking. (Courtesy American Red Cross)

Make a fist and place the thumb side of your fist just above the navel but below the lower margin of the ribs.

Grasp your fist with your other hand and press into the victim's abdomen with six to ten quick upward thrusts.

Repeat until the object is coughed up or until the victim goes unconscious.

For unconscious victims perform the airway, breathing sequence as in CPR. If you are unable to get air into the lungs, reposition the head and try again. If there is still no air exchange, abdominal thrusts are needed.

Straddle the victim at the knees.

Place the heel of one hand just above the navel. Place the other hand on top of the first.

Give six to ten upward abdominal thrusts.

Open the mouth and with the index finger attempt to remove the object.

Reposition the head and attempt artificial respiration.

If no air exchange, repeat above steps until obstruction is cleared or until you are relieved by another rescuer.

Electrocution

A person knocked unconscious by electrical current may need artificial respiration or CPR at once. If the victim is still in contact with any object that might carry current, cut the contact. Pull the switch if you know where it is, but don't waste time looking for it. Pull or push the victim away from contact with a dry rope, piece of clothing, pole, oar, or board. Rubber gloves are good if you have them, but they will not protect against very high voltage. Most work gloves will be damp and sweaty; don't use them. Don't touch the victim until he or she is clear of contact. Commence artificial respiration or CPR. Send for medical assistance.

Exposure to Extreme Cold

This can result in loss of body heat, frostbite, and immersion foot.

In the treatment of all injuries from exposure to extreme cold, it is essential to get the victim into a warm place as soon as possible. It is almost impossible to give effective first aid treatment while the victim is still exposed to the cold.

Remember, however, that there may be other life threats that must be treated before the victim can be moved into a warmer place.

General Loss of Body Heat (Hypothermia)

This abnormally low body temperature usually results from total immersion in cold water or exposure to cold temperatures without adequate clothing, and can result in loss of consciousness. The victim will appear pale and unconscious and may be taken for dead. Breathing is slow and shallow and the pulse faint or unobtainable. Body tissues feel semirigid, and the arms and legs may be stiff.

First aid treatment consists mainly of bringing the body temperature to normal. The victim should be wrapped in warm blankets in a warm room. Take care to warm the body and not the arms and legs as cold blood from the extremities can cause cardiac arrest if circulated to the body too fast. If the victim has been immersed in cold water, remove the wet clothes. Be alert for further complications such as respiratory or cardiac arrest. It is very important to handle the victim very gently and move the victim only if necessary. Get the victim to a medical officer as soon as possible.

Frostbite

Exposure to dry cold causes frostbite, especially in the cheeks, nose, chin, ears, forehead, wrist, hands, and feet. The skin turns white or gray, then bright pink.

Frostbite may also be caused by contact with certain chemicals that have rapid freezing action, such as industrial gases. Injuries caused by these substances are often referred to as chemical burns, but the body tissue is actually frozen rather than burned.

When the frostbitten area is warmed up, it immediately becomes red and swollen and large blisters develop. Severe frostbite causes gangrene, in which body tissues, and sometimes even bone, are permanently destroyed. If deep tissue has been destroyed, the injured part may have to be amputated.

The first aid treatment for frostbite is rewarming the frozen tissue, but only if there is no danger of the part refreezing. Get the victim into the warmest available place as soon as possible and undressed. If feet or legs are frostbitten, do not allow the victim to walk. Do not handle the frostbitten area unnecessarily, and do not exert any pressure against it.

Place the victim in bed and covered. Don't let anything touch the frostbitten parts. Keep sterile gauze or cloth pads between the toes and fingers, and keep frostbitten parts slightly elevated. Obtain medical assistance as soon as possible. *Caution: Never rub or massage frostbite with ice or snow. Do not apply cold water. Do not expose a frostbitten area to cold air.*

Immersion Foot (Trench Foot)

This results from prolonged exposure to a combination of moisture and cold. People on life rafts or in unprotected lifeboats are most likely to get immersion foot from exposure to near freezing seawater, but cases have occurred as a result of longer immersion in warmer water. This condition sometimes affects other parts of the body, such as knees, hands, buttocks.

A person who remains for a long time in a cold, wet place, standing or crouching in one position, is also very likely to develop this condition.

Immersion foot causes a feeling of heaviness or numbness. All sensitivity may be lost. The affected areas become swollen. The skin is first red, then waxy white, then yellowish, and finally a mottled blue or black. The injured parts remain cold, swollen, discolored, and numb; or they thaw, and the swelling increases and the skin becomes hot, dry, red, and blistered. In severe cases, there may be gangrene.

The first aid treatment should be given while medical aid is being summoned.

Get the victim off the feet as soon as possible; keep the victim as warm as possible.

Expose the injured part to warm, dry air.

If the skin is not broken or loose, the injured part may be left exposed; however, if it is necessary to move the victim, cover the injured part with loosely wrapped fluff bandages of sterile gauze.

Do not apply salves or ointments. Be careful not to rupture blisters.

Eye Injuries

For wounds of the eye, apply thick, dry sterile bandages. If the eyeball is injured, do not allow any pressure of the bandage against the eyeball. If soft tissue around the eye is injured, apply a pressure bandage. Keep the victim lying down while being transported and until medical aid is available.

To remove an object in the eye, such as a floating speck of dirt, have the victim look upward, and remove the object with the corner of a clean handkerchief or with a cotton swab moistened with clean water. Either gently pull the lower lid down with your finger, or turn the upper lid back over a match stick or cotton swab applicator by grasping the lashes of the upper lid between the fingers and everting it. If these methods fail, cover the eye by bandaging and obtain medical help. *Never* attempt to remove an object that is *imbedded* in the eye.

Chemical Burns

Flush the eye immediately with large quantities of fresh, clean water. Hold the victim's head over a drinking fountain so that the water flows from the inside corner of the eye toward the outside corner, or have the victim lie down with the head turned slightly to one side; then pour water into the inside corner of the eye and let it flow gently across the eyeball to the outside corner. If the victim is unable to open his or her eyes, hold the eyelids apart so that the water can flow across the eyeball. Do not use anything except water.

Another way to wash chemical substances from the eye is to have the victim open and close the eyes several times while the face is immersed in a pan of fresh water.

Cover the eye with a small, thick compress; fasten the compress in place with a bandage or an eyeshield, and get medical care as soon as possible. Refer to CHRIS, if the manual is available.

Fainting

This is a reaction of the nervous system that slows down the flow of blood to the brain. To prevent fainting, a person should lie flat for ten minutes with the head lower than the rest of the body. If a person who appears to have fainted does not recover consciousness almost immediately, that is not simple fainting. Unconsciousness may be caused by asphyxia, deep shock, poisoning, head injury, heat stroke, heart attack, stroke, or epilepsy. Get medical help at once.

Fish Hooks

If the barb is buried in the flesh, bandage the hook so that the flesh is protected from further injury and seek medical help.

Fish Stings

Many sea creatures (Portuguese men-of-war, jellyfish, stingrays, scorpion fish, toadfish) are poisonous. The symptoms range from burning, stinging, reddening of the skin, hives, pus sores, abdominal cramps, numbness, dizziness, pain in the groin and armpits, nausea, muscular pain, breathing difficulty, and constriction of the chest, to prostration and shock.

For Portuguese men-of-war and jellyfish stings, remove the tentacles immediately and wash the skin with rubbing alcohol. Apply ammonia, vinegar, or a soothing lotion. If available, an excellent remedy is meat tenderizer. Make a paste with it and apply to the sting area. Treat for shock. Care must be taken that you do not come in contact with the tentacles. Use a stick or some other means to remove them. Do *not* rinse with *fresh* water. A stingray wound should be washed immediately with cold salt water. Much of the toxin will wash out, and the cold water causes blood vessels to constrict, slowing circulation, and acts as a mild pain-killing agent. The wound should then be immersed in hot water for 30 minutes to an hour, with the temperature as high as the victim can stand without injury. (Hot compresses can be applied for wounds in areas that cannot be immersed.) A sterile dressing should then be applied.

Fractures

A closed fracture is one in which a bone is broken, but there is no break in the skin. An open fracture is one in which the skin is broken. All fractures require careful handling; send for medical aid as soon as possible. Don't move a fracture victim until the fracture has been splinted, unless necessary to save life or prevent further injury. Do not attempt to "set" a broken bone.

Treat for shock. Stop the bleeding in an open fracture. Use direct pressure or the pressure point system.

Apply splints over clothing if the victim is to be moved a short distance or if a doctor will see them soon. Otherwise, apply well-padded splints after the clothing has been cut away. Be careful when you handle any fracture to avoid additional shock or injury. Splints vary according to the area and nature of the fracture. Follow these rules:

> For a bone fracture, place the splint(s) so that the joint above and the joint below the fracture cannot move.
> For a joint fracture, place the splint so that the bone above and the bone below the fracture are immobilized.

Collarbone

On the injured side, place the forearm across the chest, palm turned in, thumb up, with the hand four inches above the elbow, and support the arm in this position with a sling. Fasten the arm to the body with several turns of bandage around the body and down over the hand to keep the arm close against the body.

Skull

It is not necessary to determine whether or not the skull is fractured when a person has had a head injury. The primary aim is to prevent brain damage. Do not let the victim move. Try not to move the victim more than necessary. Do not let the victim get cold, do not give anything to drink. Stop the bleeding and get immediate medical assistance. Do not plug the ears and nose to stop bleeding or leaking of fluid from these areas.

Spine

Pain, shock, and partial paralysis result from damage to the spine. Severe pain in the back or neck after injury should be treated as a fractured spine. Treat for shock. Keep the victim flat, and do not move his head.

If the victim cannot move his legs, feet, or toes, the fracture is probably in the back; if the victim cannot move his fingers, it is probably in the neck. If transportation is necessary, carry the victim face up on a backboard, rigid stretcher, door, or wide frame. Never try to lift such a victim with fewer than four people; pick up the victim by the clothing and slide the stretcher underneath.

Pelvis

Treat a victim with a pelvis injury for shock, but do not move unless absolutely necessary. If a victim must be moved, handle the same as for a victim of a fractured spine. Bandage legs together at ankles and knees; place a pillow at each hip and fasten them in place. Fasten the victim securely to the stretcher.

Heart Attack

Heart disease is the number one killer in the United States today. Heart attacks are caused by a lack of blood supply to the heart muscle. Fortunately, new ways of treatment are reducing the number of deaths due to heart attack. These new treatments must be started early, making recognition and prompt transport of victims of prime importance.

Symptoms of a heart attack include chest pain that may radiate to the arm, jaw, or neck, and cause shortness of breath, nausea, sweating, dizziness, anxiety, and/or weakness.

Treatment includes making the victim comfortable by loosening clothing. Keep the victim calm and quiet, do not allow a heart attack victim to walk around. Give the victim oxygen if you're trained in its use. Get the victim to a medical officer as soon as possible. Monitor the pulse and breathing—be ready to do CPR if necessary.

Heatstroke

Heatstroke and heat exhaustion are caused by excessive exposure to heat, direct rays of the sun, or heat of machinery spaces, foundries, bakeries, etc. Under similar circumstances, one person may develop heatstroke and another heat exhaustion. There are important differences between the two afflictions. Each represents a different bodily reaction to excessive heat, and for this reason, the symptoms and treatment are different.

Heatstroke results from a failure of the heat-regulating mechanism of the body. The body becomes overheated, the temperature rises to between 105 and 110 degrees Fahrenheit, but there is no sweating or cooling of the body. The victim's skin is hot, dry, and red. The victim may have preliminary symptoms such as headache, nausea, dizziness, or weakness, but very often the first signs are sudden collapse and loss of consciousness. Breathing is likely to be deep and rapid. The pulse is strong and fast. Convulsions may occur. Heatstroke may cause death or permanent disability; at best, recovery is likely to be slow, and complicated by relapses.

The longer the victim remains overheated, the greater the danger of death. Follow these first aid measures to lower body temperature:

- Move victim to a cool place, remove the clothing, place victim on back with head and shoulders slightly raised.
- Sponge or spray the body with cold water, and fan victim so the water will evaporate rapidly.
- Get victim to a medical facility as soon as possible. Keep victim cold while being transported.
- Do not give the victim anything to drink unless directed to do so by a doctor.

Heat Exhaustion and Heat Cramps

In heat exhaustion, there is no failure of the heat-regulating mechanism, but there is a serious disturbance of the blood flow, similar to the circulatory disturbance of shock. Through prolonged sweating, the body loses large quantities of salt and water.

Heat exhaustion may begin with a headache, dizziness, nausea, weakness, and profuse sweating. The victim may collapse and lose consciousness, but can usually be aroused rather easily. The temperature is usually normal or even below normal; sometimes it may go down as low as 97 degrees Fahrenheit. The pupils of the eyes are usually dilated, the pulse is weak and rapid, and the skin is pale, cool, and sweaty. Sometimes there may be severe cramps in the abdomen, legs, and arms.

Follow these first aid measures:

- Move the victim to a cool place, but not to where victim will be exposed to strong drafts or become chilled.
- Loosen clothing and make the victim as comfortable as possible.
- Keep the victim quiet and lying down, with the feet and legs somewhat elevated. Be sure that the victim is kept comfortably warm. You may have to cover victim with blankets, even if the air is quite warm. The pain of severe cramps may be relieved by the application of heat to the affected muscles or by stretching the affected muscle group. If the victim is conscious and able to swallow, give water to drink. If available, a commercially prepared electrolyte beverage is helpful. Replacement of the salt and water that has been lost by sweating is probably the most important part of the treatment and often brings rapid recovery. If recovery is not prompt, get medical attention as soon as possible.

Insect Bites

Wash insect bites with soap and water. Itching can be relieved by using cold-water compresses. Ice, applied to bee stings, will prevent pain and swelling. Some people experience severe allergic reactions to bee and other insect stings. The person stung should be carefully observed and given immediate medical attention if allergic reactions are either observed or are part of that person's medical history.

Ticks can be dislodged by applying mineral oil to the tick; be careful not to crush the insect or leave its jaws embedded in the flesh. Certain types of ticks carry Rocky Mountain Spotted Fever or Lyme Disease, which can be fatal. Inflamed bites require medical assistance.

Poisoning

First aid treatment for poisoning depends partly upon whether the poison enters the body by ingestion (taking the poison into the stomach by way of the mouth), by inhalation (breathing poisonous gases), by skin contact, or by injection. (Poisoning by injection is covered under "Snakebite" and "Spiders and Scorpions.")

Symptoms

Intense pain frequently follows poisoning; nausea and vomiting may occur. The victim can become delirious, or may collapse and become unconscious, and almost always is likely to have trouble breathing. Some poisons characteristically cause paralysis; others cause convulsions. Shock is always present in acute poisoning.

Emergency treatment is usually required, because poisons act very rapidly. Treatment by a physician should be obtained as soon as possible.

The first treatment for ingested poisoning is to dilute with several glasses of water. Contact should be made with a Poison Control Center, if available. The Poison Control Center may direct you to induce vomiting in the victim. Vomiting should not be induced if the victim has ingested a strong acid or alkali, or if the victim is unconscious. Vomiting may be brought on by tickling the throat, or by administering a nauseating fluid such as salt dissolved in water or syrup of ipecac.

Activated charcoal can absorb poisons in the body. It is given as a mixture of two to four tablespoons dissolved in a glass of water after the victim stops vomiting. Always save empty containers of the offending agent and send to the hospital with the victim.

Inhaled poisons can come from refrigeration machinery, firefighting equipment, paints and solvents, photographic materials, and many other types of shipboard equipment that contain volatile and sometimes poisonous chemicals. Fuel oil and gasoline vapors constitute special hazards.

Carbon monoxide is present in all exhaust gases of internal combustion engines.

First aid treatment for carbon monoxide, and for all gases, follows:

- Get the victim out of the toxic atmosphere into a well-ventilated space. Remove contaminated clothing.
- Watch the breathing. Give artificial respiration if necessary. Give oxygen if it is available and you know how to use it.

• Keep the victim lying down and quiet. Treat for shock. Call a medical officer as soon as possible.

Poisoning by skin contact is not usually a first aid problem. Such poisoning can be fatal; some types build up over a long period of time. There is no real cure. Know the substances that can poison by contact and be careful in handling them. They include gasoline, benzene, naphtha, lead compounds, mercury, arsenic, carbon tetrachloride, and TNT.

Shock

Shock is a term used to describe events that take place when one of the components of the circulatory system fails. It can be pump failure (the heart), pipe failure (blood vessels), or fluid failure (the blood). The result is a lack of blood supply to the brain and vital organs, which can lead to death. Shock can be caused either by injury to the nervous system causing the dilated blood vessels, injury to the heart causing loss of pump function, or most commonly because of severe bleeding (not enough blood to go around). In an attempt to compensate for the lack of blood supply to the vital organs, the heart rate increases. The pulse, however, is weak, and the blood flow to the brain is reduced. Unconsciousness or confusion may result.

Most injuries will cause shock, which may be slight, lasting only a few seconds, or serious enough to be fatal. Shock may begin immediately, or it may be delayed as much as several hours.

Shock is recognized by the following symptoms: The pulse is weak and rapid; breathing may be shallow, rapid, and irregular; the skin feels cold to the touch and may be covered with sweat; the pupils of the eyes are usually dilated. A shock victim may complain of thirst, may feel weak, faint or dizzy, and nauseated. The victim may be very restless and feel frightened and anxious. As shock deepens, these signs gradually disappear and the victim becomes less and less responsive, even to pain. Shock victims may insist they feel fine, and then pass out.

Keep the victim flat on the back, with feet higher than the body. Keep the victim warm by using blankets. Do not use artificial heat. Do not give anything by mouth. A shock victim is often thirsty. Moisten lips with cool water, but don't give anything to drink.

Snakebite

Poisonous snakes in the United States include "pit vipers" (rattlesnakes, copperheads, water moccasins) and coral snakes. Identifying the snake, in some cases, is not easy. Check these points:

Fangs mean the snake is poisonous.
Rattles identify rattlesnakes, but not always; sometimes a rattler loses the rattle.
Snakes with a sensory organ, a "pit," between nostrils and eyes, are pit vipers and are poisonous.
Snakes striped fore-and-aft are not poisonous, except for one very rare native of the Far East.

Pit viper bites may produce the following symptoms:

Tissue swelling at the bite gradually spreading to surrounding areas. Swelling occurs between three to five minutes following the bite, but may continue for as long as an hour and be so severe as to burst the skin.
Severe pain.
Escape of blood from the capillaries. Accumulation of blood in the tissues may cause severe pain.
Severe headache, thirst.
Bleeding from internal organs into the intestines, blood in urine or stools.

Bites of coral snakes, cobras, or kraits may produce some of the following symptoms:

Irregular heartbeat, generalized weakness and exhaustion, shock.
Severe headache, dizziness, mental disturbances such as incoherent speech, stupor, mental confusion, and possible unconsciousness. Extreme pain is not characteristic.
Muscular incoordination, such as inability to reach for and pick up an object or to move from place to place; sometimes muscle spasms and twitching.
Difficult or labored breathing and even respiratory paralysis.
Numbness and tingling of the skin, particularly of the lips and soles of the feet, excessive sweating.
Chills, fever.
Nausea, vomiting, diarrhea.

A snakebite victim should lie down and keep calm. Remind the victim that very few people are even disabled by snakebite. Keep the victim at rest (dry, warm, and quiet), and immobilize the affected part below the level of the heart.

For a bite on the arm or leg, place a restricting band two to four inches above the bite. The restricting band should be tight enough to stop the flow of blood in the veins but not the arteries.

Treat for shock. It may be necessary to give artificial respiration. Victims have been kept alive for two hours after becoming unconscious and have been saved by delayed injection of antivenin.

If you are alone and have been bitten by a snake, keep your emotions under control. If you can kill the snake and look for fangs, do so. Apply a restricting band two to four inches above the site of the bite, remain as quiet as possible and keep the wound lower than your heart.

If pain is great, if there is swelling, numbness, tingling, or continued oozing of blood at the bite site, you can be fairly sure that the snake is poisonous. If it is evident that no help is coming, walk slowly with a minimum of exertion.

Spiders and Scorpions

Brown Recluse and Black Widows are probably the most common of the poisonous spiders. The Black Widow spider bite causes pain almost at once, and the pain spreads quickly from the region of the bite to the muscles of the back, shoulders, chest, abdomen, and limbs. The pain is usually accompanied by severe spasms of the abdominal muscles.

A bite from any other poisonous spider may be felt as a sharp sting, but it is not usually accompanied by severe pain. About half an hour after the bite, the victim begins to feel painful muscle cramps near the bite, which soon spread to other muscles of the body. Shock usually develops at about the same time, though it may be delayed for as much as an hour or two. The victim becomes restless and anxious and may be very thirsty. Nausea and vomiting may occur.

Scorpions have a stinger and venom sac in the tail. Their sting causes immediate, intense pain. The area near the sting will become numb and paralyzed.

First aid measures for spider bites and scorpion stings are limited. Clean the wound and surrounding area. Treat the victim for shock: lying down, quiet and warm. Severe muscle cramps and pain may sometimes be relieved by warm-water baths. Do not apply suction and do not incise (cut the wound in an attempt to remove the poison). It does no good. Always seek medical care.

Splinters

If a splinter is under the skin where it can be seen, it can be removed by pulling it out the same way it went in. Clean the broken skin, and cover with a sterile dressing.

Transportation of the Injured

Take these precautions before transporting an injured person: Give necessary first aid. Locate all injuries to the best of your ability. Treat airway, breathing, and circulation problems, shock, fractures, sprains, and dislocations. Make the victim as comfortable as possible.

Use a regular stretcher. If you must use an improvised stretcher, be sure that it is strong enough to hold the victim. Have enough people to carry the stretcher; don't drop the victim.

Fasten the victim in the stretcher so the victim cannot slip, slide, or fall off. Tie the feet together unless injuries make this impractical.

Use blankets, garments, or other material to pad the stretcher and to protect the victim from exposure.

An injured person should usually lie on his back while being moved, but one having difficulty in breathing because of a chest wound may be more comfortable if his head and shoulders are slightly raised. Fracture cases should be moved very carefully, so that the injury will not be made worse. A victim with a severe injury to the back of the head should be kept on one side. A patient should always be carried feet first, unless there is some special reason for carrying him head first.

The four-person lift and the fireman's carry are recommended ways to lift an injured person, and the fireman's drag is used to transport a patient under special circumstances.

Fireman's Carry

This method is used if transporting the patient is required immediately. For instance, if there is immediate danger to the victim or rescuer such as a fire or explosion.

Turn the victim face up (figure 33-8.a.). Bend the victim's knees, place your feet against the victim's, then grab the arms and lift the victim's back off the ground (figure 33-8.b.). Quickly bend at the knees, pull the victim up over your shoulder, and lift from the legs, keeping your back as straight as possible (figure 33-8.c.).

To lower the victim, kneel on your left knee. Grasp the left knee

Figure 33-7. Transporting an injured person: fireman's drag.

with your right hand. Slide the victim around in front of you and down your right thigh into a sitting position. Shift your hands to the head and place the victim gently on his back. This is an emergency move designed to get a person out of immediate danger; do not use it if there is time, equipment, and personnel resources available to use one of the more preferred patient handling maneuvers (using a Miller body splint, Stokes litter, or four-person lift).

Four-Person Lift

The four-person lift should be used when you need to move a patient but you do not have a stretcher or litter. In the four-person lift the number one person stabilizes the head and neck; number two takes the shoulders and back; number three takes lower back and buttocks; and number four takes the legs and feet (figure 33-8.d.). The number one person is in charge of directing the lift. Number one will say, "Ready, lift," and all will lift together to the kneeling position (figure 33-8.e.). Number one will check with the rest of the team and if all is stable, will say, "ready, lift" again. The victim is lifted and carried as needed (figure 33-8.f.). The number one person directs the lift-and-carry process, and all rescuers try to keep victim's body straight with minimal bounding, etc.

a. Victim face-up

b. Pull victim up toward you

c. Victim ready for transport

d. Preparing to lift

e. Lift to one knee

f. Victim ready for transport

Figure 33-8.   Transporting an injured person: four-person lift.

Fireman's Drag

Use this method when you must remain close to the deck. Lay the victim on his/her back. Tie the wrists together with a handkerchief, belt, or other available material. Place the victim's arms over around your neck, then crawl forward (figure 33-7).

Stokes Litter

This is a wire basket supported by iron or aluminum rods. It is adaptable to a variety of uses and will hold a person securely in place even if it is tipped or turned. The Stokes litter is generally used aboard ship, and especially for transferring injured persons to and from boats. It can be used to rescue people from the water and for direct ship-to-ship transfer of injured persons (figure 33–9).

The litter should be padded with two blankets placed lengthwise, so that one will be under each of the victim's legs, and a third folded in half and placed in the upper part of the litter to protect the victim's head and shoulders. Victims should be lowered gently into the litter and made as comfortable as possible. The feet must be fastened to the end of the litter to prevent sliding up and down, and the victim must be fastened into the litter by straps over the chest, hips, and knees. The straps should go over the blanket or other covering.

Figure 33-9. Stokes stretcher being lifted into a rescue helicopter.

APPENDIX A

Code of Conduct

As a member of the armed forces of the United States, you are protecting your nation. It is your duty to oppose all enemies of the United States in combat or, if a captive, in a prisoner of war compound. Your behavior is guided by the Code of Conduct, which has evolved from the heroic lives, experiences, and deeds of Americans from the Revolutionary War to the Southeast Asian Conflict.

Your obligations as a United States citizen and a member of the armed forces result from the traditional values that underlie the American experience as a nation. These values are best expressed in the United States Constitution and Bill of Rights, which you have sworn to uphold and defend. You would have these obligations—to your country, your service and unit, and your fellow Americans—even if the Code of Conduct had never been formulated as a high standard of general behavior.

Just as you have a responsibility to your country under the Code of Conduct, the United States government has an equal responsibility—always to keep faith with you and stand by you as you fight for your country. If you are unfortunate enough to become a prisoner of war, you may rest assured that your government will care for your dependents and will never forget you. Furthermore, the government will use every practical means to contact, support, and gain release for you and for all other prisoners of war.

To live up to the code, you must know not only its words but the ideas and principles behind those words.

The Code of Conduct is an ethical guide. Its six articles deal with your chief concerns as an American in combat; these concerns become critical when you must evade capture, resist while a prisoner, or escape from the enemy.

Experiences of captured Americans reveal that to survive captivity honorably demands great courage, deep dedication, and high motivation. To sustain these personal values throughout captivity requires that you understand and believe strongly in our free and democratic institutions, love your country, trust in the justice of our cause, keep faithful and loyal to your fellow prisoners, and hold firmly to your religious and moral beliefs in time of trial.

Your courage, dedication, and motivation supported by understanding, trust, and fidelity will help you endure the terrors of captivity, prevail over your captors, and return to your family, home, and nation with honor and pride.

ARTICLE I

I am an American, fighting in the forces which guard my country and our way of life. I am prepared to give my life in their defense.

All men and women in the armed forces have the duty at all times and under all circumstances to oppose the enemies of the United States and support its national interests. In training or in combat, alone or with others, while evading capture or enduring captivity, this duty belongs to each American defending our nation regardless of circumstances.

ARTICLE II

I will never surrender of my own free will. If in command, I will never surrender the members of my command while they still have the means to resist.

As an individual, a member of the armed forces may never voluntarily surrender. When isolated and no longer able to inflict casualties on the enemy, members of the armed forces have an obligation to evade capture and rejoin friendly forces.

Only when evasion by an individual is impossible and further fighting would lead only to death with no significant loss to the enemy should one consider surrender. With all reasonable means of resistance exhausted and with certain death the only alternative, capture does not imply dishonor.

The responsibility and authority of a commander never extends to the surrender of a command to the enemy while the command has the power to fight and evade. When isolated, cut off or surrounded, a unit must continue to fight until relieved or able to rejoin friendly forces through continued efforts to break out or evade the enemy.

ARTICLE III

If I am captured I will continue to resist by all means available. I will make every effort to escape and aid others to escape. I will accept neither parole nor special favors from the enemy.

The duty of a member of the armed forces to use all means available to resist the enemy is not lessened by the misfortune of captivity. A POW is still legally bound by the Uniform Code of Military Justice and ethically guided by the Code of Conduct. Under provisions of the Geneva Convention, a prisoner of war is also subject to certain rules imposed by the captor nation. When repatriated, a prisoner of war will not be condemned for having obeyed reasonable captor rules, such as sanitation regulations. The duty of a member of the armed forces to continue to resist does not mean a prisoner should engage in unreasonable harassment as a form of resistance. Retaliation by captors to the detriment of that prisoner and other prisoners is frequently the primary result of such harassment.

The Geneva Convention recognizes that a POW may have a duty to attempt escape. In fact, the Geneva Convention prohibits a captor nation from executing a POW simply for attempting escape. Under the authority of the senior official (often called the senior ranking officer, or SRO), a POW must be prepared to escape whenever the opportunity presents itself. In a POW compound, the senior POW must consider the welfare of those remaining behind after an escape. However, as a matter of conscious determination, a POW must plan to escape, try to escape, and assist others to escape.

Contrary to the spirit of the Geneva Convention, enemies engaged by U.S. forces since 1950 have regarded the POW compound as an extension of the battlefield. In so doing, they have used a variety of tactics and pressures, including physical and mental mistreatment, torture and medical neglect, to exploit POWs for propaganda purposes, to obtain military information, or to undermine POW organization, communication, and resistance.

Such enemies have attempted to lure American POWs into accepting special favors or privileges in exchange for statements, acts, or information. Unless it is essential to the life or welfare of that person or another prisoner of war or to the success of efforts to resist or escape, a POW must neither seek nor accept special favors or privileges.

One such privilege is called parole. Parole is a promise by a prisoner of war to a captor to fulfill certain conditions—such as agreeing not to escape nor to fight again once released—in return for such favors as relief from physical bondage, improved food and living conditions, or repatriation ahead of the sick, injured, or longer-held prisoners. An American POW will never sign nor otherwise accept parole.

ARTICLE IV

If I become a prisoner of war, I will keep faith with my fellow prisoners. I will give no information or take part in any action which might be harmful to my comrades. If I am senior, I will take command. If not, I will obey the lawful orders of those appointed over me and will back them up in every way.

Informing or any other action to the detriment of a fellow prisoner is despicable and is expressly forbidden. Prisoners of war must avoid helping the enemy identify fellow prisoners who may have knowledge of particular value to the enemy and who may, therefore, be made to suffer coercive interrogation.

Strong leadership and communication are essential to discipline. Discipline is the key to camp organization, resistance, and even survival. Personal hygiene, camp sanitation, and care of sick and wounded are imperative. Officers and noncommissioned officers of the United States must continue to carry out their responsibilities and exercise their authority in captivity. The senior, regardless of service, must accept command. This responsibility and accountability may not be evaded.

If the senior is incapacitated or is otherwise unable to act, the next senior person will assume command. Camp leaders should make every effort to inform all POWs of the chain of command and try to represent them in dealing with enemy authorities. The responsibility of subordinates to obey the lawful orders of ranking American military personnel remains unchanged in captivity.

The Geneva Convention Relative to Treatment of Prisoners of War provides for election of a "prisoners' representative" in POW camps containing enlisted personnel but no commissioned officers. American POWs should understand that such a representative is only a spokesman for the actual senior-ranking person. Should the enemy appoint a POW chain of command for its own purposes, American POWs should make all possible efforts to adhere to the principles of Article IV. As with other provisions of this code, common sense and the conditions of captivity will affect the way in which the senior person and the other POWs organize to carry out their responsibilities. What is important is that everyone support and work within the POW organization.

ARTICLE V

When questioned, should I become a prisoner of war, I am required to give name, rank, service number, and date of birth. I will evade answering further questions to the utmost of my ability. I will make no oral or written statements disloyal to my country and its allies or harmful to their cause.

When questioned, a prisoner of war is required by the Geneva Convention and this code to give name, rank, service number (Social Security number), and date of birth. The prisoner should make every effort to avoid giving the captor any additional information. The prisoner may communicate with captors on matters of health and welfare and additionally may write letters home and fill out a Geneva Convention "capture card."

It is a violation of the Geneva Convention to place a prisoner under physical or mental duress, torture, or any other form of coercion in an effort to secure information. If under such intense coercion, a POW discloses unauthorized information, makes an unauthorized statement, or performs an unauthorized act, that prisoner's peace of mind and survival require a quick recovery of courage, dedication, and motivation to resist anew each subsequent coercion.

Actions every POW should resist include making oral or written confessions and apologies, answering questionnaires, providing personal histories, creating propaganda recordings, broadcasting appeals to other prisoners of war, providing any other material readily usable for propaganda purposes, appealing for surrender or parole, furnishing self-criticisms, and communicating on behalf of the enemy to the detriment of the United States, its allies, its armed forces, or other POWs.

Every POW should also recognize that any confession signed or any statement made may be used by the enemy as false evidence that the person is a "war criminal" rather than a POW. Several countries have made reservations to the Geneva Convention in which they assert that a "war criminal" conviction deprives the convicted individual of prisoner-of-war status, removes that person from protection under the Geneva Convention, and revokes all rights to repatriation until a prison sentence is served.

Recent experiences of American prisoners of war have proved that, although enemy interrogation sessions may be harsh and cruel, one can resist brutal mistreatment when the will to resist remains intact.

The best way for a prisoner to keep faith with country, fellow prisoners, and self is to provide the enemy with as little information as possible.

ARTICLE VI

I will never forget that I am American, fighting for freedom, responsible for my actions, and dedicated to the principles which made my country free. I will trust in my God and in the United States of America.

A member of the armed forces remains responsible for personal actions at all times.

A member of the armed forces who is captured has a continuing obligation to resist and to remain loyal to country, service, unit, and fellow prisoners.

Upon repatriation, POWs can expect their actions to be reviewed, both as to the circumstances of capture and conduct during detention. The purpose of such reviews is to recognize meritorious performance as well as to investigate possible misconduct. Each review will be conducted with due regard for the rights of the individual and consideration for the conditions of captivity; captivity of itself is not a condition of culpability.

Members of the armed forces should remember that they and their dependents will be taken care of by the appropriate service and that pay and allowances, eligibility, and procedures for promotions and benefits for dependents will continue while the service member is detained. Service members should make sure that their personal affairs and family matters (such as pay, powers of attorney, current will, and provisions for family maintenance and education) are properly and currently arranged. Failure to do so can create a serious sense of guilt for a POW and place unnecessary hardship on family members.

The life of a prisoner of war is hard. Each person in this stressful situation must always sustain hope and resist enemy indoctrination. Prisoners of war standing firm and united against the enemy will support and inspire one another in surviving their ordeal and in prevailing over misfortune with honor.

Nautical Terminology

Sailors aboard ships of the Coast Guard and Navy speak in a "language" of terms and expressions that is as unique and traditional as the life they lead. The nautical glossary that follows contains most of the terminology you will need for effective and professional communication aboard your unit. Many words and phrases not appearing here, or appearing only briefly, are developed and explained in the text of this manual. It is suggested that the reader refer to the chapter(s) covering the related subjects after looking up a word here.

Abaft: behind or farther aft; astern or toward the stern.
Abeam: at right angles to the centerline of and outside a ship.
Aboard: on or in a vessel. **Close aboard** means near a ship.
Absentee pennant: special pennant flown to indicate absence of commanding officer, admiral, chief of staff, or officer whose flag is flying (division, squadron, or flotilla commander). Also called **absence indicator.**
Accommodation ladder: a portable flight of steps down a ship's side.
Adrift: loose from moorings, or out of place.
Aft: in, near, or toward the stern of a vessel.
Aground: resting on or touching the ground or bottom.
Ahead: forward of the bow.
Ahoy: term used to hail a boat or a ship, as "Boat ahoy!"
All hands: entire ship's company, both officers and enlisted personnel.
All night in: having no night watches.

Allowance: numbers, ranks, and ratings of officers and crew assigned to a ship when it is impracticable to assign a full complement. See **complement**.

Aloft: above the ship's uppermost solid structure; overhead or high above.

Alongside: by the side of the pier or ship.

Amidships (or midships): in middle portion of ship, along the line of the keel.

Anchorage: suitable place for a ship to anchor. Area of a port or harbor.

Anchor's aweigh: said of an anchor when just clear of the bottom.

Anchor ball: black shape hoisted in forepart of a ship to show that ship is anchored in a fairway.

Anchor cable: chain, wire, or line running between anchor and ship.

Anchor detail: group of ship's personnel who handle ground tackle when the ship is anchoring or getting under way.

Anchor light: white light displayed by ship at anchor. Two such lights are displayed by a ship over 150 feet in length.

Anchor watch: detail of ship's personnel standing by at night as a readiness precaution while ship is at anchor.

Anemometer: instrument to measure wind velocity.

Astern: toward the stern; an object or vessel that is abaft another vessel or object.

Athwart, athwartships: at right angles to the fore and aft or centerline of a ship.

Auxiliary: an assisting machine or vessel, such as an air-conditioning machine or fuel ship.

Avast: a command to cease or desist from whatever is being done.

Awash: so low in the water that the water is constantly washing across the surface.

Aweigh: position of an anchor just clear of the bottom.

Aye, aye: reply to an order or command to indicate that it is understood and will be carried out. ("Aye, aye, sir/ma'am," to officers.)

Backstay: a stay supporting a mast from aft.

Backwash: water thrown aft by turning a ship's propeller.

Bail: to dip water out of a boat with a bucket. A hoop or ring; a half hoop or yoke.

Ballast: heavy weight in the hold of a vessel to maintain proper stability, trim, or draft. A ship is **in ballast** when it carries no cargo, only ballast.

Barge: craft used to haul material, as a coal barge; a power boat used by flag officers, as admiral's barge.

Barnacle: small marine animal that attaches itself to sides and bottoms of hulls and piers.

Barometer: instrument that registers atmospheric pressure; used in forecasting weather.

Batten: long strip of steel or wood that wedges the edge of a tarpaulin against the hatch.

Batten down: to cover and fasten down; to close off a hatch or watertight door.

Battle lantern: a battery-powered lantern used for emergency lighting.

Battle lights: dim red lights that furnish sufficient light for personnel during darken-ship period.

Beam: width; breadth; greatest athwartships width of a vessel.

Bear: to lie in a certain direction from the observer.

Bear a hand: speed up the action; lend a helping hand.

Bearing: direction of an object, expressed in degrees either as relative or true bearing.

Beaufort Scale: a table of scales indicating various velocities of winds.

Becket: circular metal fitting on a block; a rope eye or grommet.

Belay: to cancel an order; to stop; to firmly secure a line.

Below: short for **below decks**; below the main deck.

Bend: a general class of knots used to join two lines together.

Bend on: to secure one thing to another, as bend a flag onto a halyard.

Berth, berthing: space assigned a vessel for an anchoring or mooring.

Bight: middle part of a line as distinguished from the end and the standing part; a single complete turn of line; bend in a river or coastline.

Bilge: lower part of vessel where waste water and seepage collect.

Billet: a crew member's assigned duties within the ship's organization.

Binnacle: large stand used to house a magnetic compass and its fittings.

Bitt: strong iron post on ship's deck for working or fastening lines; almost invariably in pairs.

Bitter end: the utmost end of line.

Black gang: slang for engineroom force.

Blackout: darken ship.

Blinker: lamp or set of lamps, triggered to a telegraph key, used for sending flashing light message.

Block: an item of deck gear made of one or more grooved sheaves, a frame (casing or shell), supporting hooks, eyes, or straps; may be metal or wood.

Boat chock: a strong deck fitting that supports one end of a boat that is resting on deck.

Boat fall: rigging used to hoist or lower ship's boats.

Boat gripe: lashing used at sea to secure a boat hanging from the davits against the strongback and away from the ship's side.

Boat hook: wooden staff with metal hook and prod at one end; used to fend off or hold on.

Boat painter: rope attached to the stern ringbolt of a boat; used for securing it. Also a short piece of rope secured to the bow of a boat; used for towing or making fast. Not to be confused with the sea painter, which is a much longer rope.

Boat plug: metal or wood plug used to stop up boat's drain hole.

Boats: small open or decked-over craft propelled by oars, sails, or some type of engine. This term also applies to larger vessels built to navigate rivers and inland waters.

Boat skid: heavy wood and metal frame on ship's boat deck used to support a boat's keel.

Boat sling: rope or chain sling used for hoisting or lowering large-size boats with a single davit or crane.

Boat station: allotted place for each person when boat is being lowered.

Boatswain: warrant officer in charge of deck work. Pronounced "bosun."

Boatswain's call: see **boatswain's pipe**.

Boatswain's chair: line-secured board on which a worker sits while aloft or over the side.

Boatswain's locker: compartment where deck gear is stowed.

Boatswain's Mate of the Watch (BMOW): Petty officer responsible for ensuring that all deck watch stations are properly manned and in order.

Boatswain's pipe: small, shrill silver whistle used by boatswain's mate to pass a call or pipe the side.

Bollard: wooden or iron post on a pier or wharf to which mooring lines are secured.

Boom: projecting spar or pole that provides an outreach for extending the foot of sails, or for mooring boats, handling cargo, and so on. Rigged horizontally or nearly so.

Boot camp: slang for recruit training center.

Boots: slang for recruits or new hands on board.

Boot topping: surface of the outside plating of ship or boat's side between light and load lines.

Bow: forward section of a vessel.

Bower anchor: either of the two anchors usually carried at the ship's bow. Most ships anchor by using one of the bowers.

Bowline: one of the most used knots; used to make a temporary eye in the end of a line. Pronounced "bo'lin."

Bow painter: see **boat painter.**

Boxing the compass: naming all compass points and quarter points in their proper order, from north, east, south, through west.

Break: to unfurl a flag with a quick motion. In ship construction, an abrupt change in the fore-and-aft contour of a ship's main deck.

Breaker: a small container for stowing drinking water carried by boats or rafts; a wave that breaks into foam against a shore.

Break out: to unstow or prepare for use.

Breakwater: a structure used to break the force of waves.

Breast line: a mooring line running at right angles from the ship's fore-and-aft line.

Bridge: raised platform from which ship is steered, navigated, and conned; usually located in forward part of the ship.

Bridle: span of rope or chain with both ends secured.

Brig: prison on a ship or shore station.

Brightwork: metal work that is kept polished rather than painted.

Broach to: turning suddenly into the wind; to be thrown broadside in a surf.

Broad command pennant: personal command pennant of an officer, not a flag officer, commanding a division of battleships, aircraft carriers, or cruisers, a force, flotilla, or squadron of ships or craft of any type, or air wing.

Broad on the starboard or port beam: bearing 090° or 315° relative to the bow of the ship.

Broad on the starboard or port quarter: bearing 135° or 225° relative to the bow of the ship.

Broadside to: at right angles to the fore-and-aft line of a ship.

Broken water: an area of small waves and eddies in otherwise calm water.

Brow: large gangplank leading from a ship to a pier, wharf, or float; usually equipped with rollers on the bottom and hand rails on the side.

Buckler: plating fitted over the hawsehole to prevent entry of water.

Bulkhead: one of the vertical wall-like structures enclosing a compartment.

Bull nose: a closed chock at the head of the bow on the forecastle deck.

Bulwark: raised plating or woodwork running along the side of a vessel above the weather deck. Helps keep decks dry and prevents crew and gear from being swept overboard.

Bunker: storage space for fuel.

Buoy: floating marker anchored by a line to the bottom, which by shape and color conveys navigational information; may be lighted or unlighted, and may be equipped with whistles, bells, or gongs.

Burdened vessel: see **give-way vessel**.

Burgee: swallow-tailed flag.

Burgee command pennant: personal command pennant of an officer not a flag officer, commanding any of the following units: a division of ships or craft other than battleships, aircraft carriers, or cruisers; a major subdivisions of an aircraft wing.

By the head: ship's appearance with a greater draft forward than aft. For example, "down by the head."

By the stern: opposite of **by the head**.

Cabin: Aboard ship, the captain's living quarters; covered compartment of a boat.

Cable: see **anchor cable**.

Cable jack: crowbar-like tool used on forecastle for working the anchor cable.

Cable-laid rope: three or four plain-laid, three-stranded ropes twisted in the opposite direction to the twists of each rope; used for ropes much exposed to water.

Cable markings: a series of turns of wire or stripes of paint on certain links of each anchor chain, indicating the **scope** or amount of chain that has run out.

Cadet: a student officer of the United States Coast Guard Academy.

Camber: the arch in a ship's deck that makes the centerline section higher than the extremities.

Camel: large fender float used for keeping vessel off wharf, pier, or quay; usually of one or more logs.

Can buoy: cylindrical metal buoy used to mark the left side of a channel, entering from seaward, and painted green.

Capstan or capstan head: that part of a vertical-shaft windlass around which a working line is passed.

Cardinal point: one of the four principal points of the compass—north, east, south, and west.

Cargo whip: rope or chain used with a boom for handling cargo. One end has a heavy hook; the other end is rove through a block and taken to the winch. Also called **cargo hoist, cargo rope.**

Carrick bend: most usually seen as a double carrick bend, a much-used knot for bending two lines or hawsers together.

Carry away: to break loose, tear loose, or wash overboard.

Carry on: an order to resume work or duties.

Cast: act of heaving the lead into the sea to determine depth of water; to throw the ship's bow in one direction or another when getting under way.

Cast loose: to let go a line or lines.

Cast off: to throw off; to let go; to unfurl.

Cat's paw: a quickly formed twist in the bight of a line by which two eyes are formed.

Centerline: imaginary line running from ship's bow to stern.

Chafe: wearing away the surface of line, spar, or chock by rubbing.

Chafing gear: guard of canvas or rope around spars, hawsers, chocks, or rigging to prevent chafing.

Chain cable: see **anchor cable.**

Chain grab: see **wildcat.**

Chain locker: compartment in which chain cable is stowed.

Chain of command: succession of commanding officers through which command is exercised from superior to subordinate.

Chain pipe: heavy steel pipe that leads the chain cable through the deck to the chain locker.

Chains: platform or a general area on either side of forward part of a ship where leadsman stands as he or she takes soundings.

Chain stopper: short length of chain fitted with a pelican hook and secured to an eyebolt on the forecastle; used for quickly letting go the anchor or for securing the anchor in stowed position.

Chart: nautical map used as an aid to navigation.

Charthouse or chartroom: compartment on or near the bridge for handling and stowage of navigation equipment.

Check: to slack off slowly; to stop a vessel's way gradually by a line fastened to some fixed object or to an anchor on the bottom; to ease off a rope a little, especially with a view to reducing the tension; to stop or regulate the motion, as of a cable when it is running out too fast.

Chipping hammer: small hammer with a sharp peen and face set at right angles to each other; used for chipping and scaling metal surfaces. Also called **scaling hammer** or **boiler pick**.

Chock: steel deck member, either oval or U-shaped, through which mooring lines are passed. Usually paired off with bitts.

Chronometer: an especially accurate timepiece used for navigation.

Clamp down: going over a deck with damp swabs; a lesser form of swabbing down.

Clap on: to clap on a rope means to catch hold in order to haul on it; to clap on a stopper or tackle means to put on a stopper or tackle; to clap on canvas means to put on more sail.

Clear: to straighten out a tangled line or chain; make ready for running.

Cleat: a small, metal deck fitting with horns; used for securing lines; also called **belaying cleat**. Short piece of wood nailed to brow or gangplank to give surer footing.

Clinometer: bridge and engineroom instrument that indicates amount of a ship's roll or degree of list.

Close aboard: nearby.

Clove hitch: a knot much used for fastening a line to a spar or stanchion.

Coaming: raised framework around deck or bulkhead openings and cockpits of open boats to prevent entry of water.

Cofferdam: empty space between two bulkheads separating two adjacent compartments. Its purpose is to isolate one compartment from another, preventing liquid contents of one from entering the other in the event one bulkhead loses its integrity.

Coil: laying down line in circular turns, usually one turn atop the other.

Collision bulkhead: watertight athwartships bulkhead a few feet abaft the stem; used to isolate the damage due to a head-on collision.

Colors: national ensign; distinguishing flag flown by a vessel to indicate her nationality. Also, the ceremonies performed at a naval activity when colors are hoisted at eight o'clock and hauled down at sunset.

Command: a term applied to a naval unit or group of units under one officer; a definite and direct form of order.

Commission: to activate a ship or aircraft; a written order giving an officer rank and authority; the rank and authority itself.

Commission pennant: long, thin, seven-star pennant flown by a ship to indicate that the ship is commissioned for service in the Coast Guard or Navy.

Companionway: set of steps or ladders leading from one deck level to another.

Compartment: space enclosed by bulkheads, deck, and overhead, corresponds to a room in a building.

Compass: instrument to indicate geographic direction.

Compass rose: diagram of a compass card on a chart, assists navigator in laying out courses and directions on chart.

Complement: numbers, ranks, and ratings of officers and enlisted personnel as are determined to be necessary to fight the ship most effectively, or to perform such other duties as may be required.

Conn: to direct helmsman as to movement of helm, especially when navigating in narrow channels or heavy traffic. (For example, to conn the vessel.)

Counter: part of a ship's side at the stern.

Country: living quarters, such as officer's country, wardroom country, CPO country.

Coupling: metal fitting at the ends of a length of fire hose.

Course: direction steered by a ship.

Court-martial: military court for the trial of more serious offenses.

Cowl: bell- or hood-shaped opening of a ventilator; it increases the amount of air forced into or drawn out of the ventilator.

Cow's tail: frayed end of a rope.

Coxswain: enlisted man in charge of a boat; acts as helmsman. Pronounced "koksun."

Cradle: a stowage rest for ship's boat.

Crossing the line: crossing the earth's equator.

Crosstree: superstructure member at top of a low mast or between two such masts; runs athwartships.

Crow's nest: lookout's stand high on a mast or crosstree.

Cumshaw: a gift, or something procured by trade or without payment.

Cut of the jib: general appearance of a vessel or of a person.

Cutter: a Coast Guard vessel 65-feet in length or longer; a type of sailing vessel.

Cutwater: forward edge of the stem at and below the waterline.

Damage control: measures necessary to keep ship afloat, fighting, and in operating condition.

Davit: shipboard crane that can be swung out over the side; used for hoisting and lowering boats and weights. Often found in pairs.

Davy Jones's locker: the bottom of the sea.

Day's duty: tour of duty on shipboard lasting 24 hours.

Dead ahead: directly ahead of the ship's bow; bearing 000° relative.

Dead in the water: said of an underway ship that is making neither headway or sternway.

Dead reckoning: navigator's estimate of ship's position from the course steered and the distance run.

Deck: on a ship corresponds to the floor of a building on land.

Deck seamanship: branch of seamanship embracing the practical side, from the simplest rudiments of marlinspike seamanship up to navigation; includes small-boat handling, ground tackle, steering, heaving the lead, signaling, etc.

Deep: the distance in fathoms between two successive marks on a lead line, as "By the deep, four."

Deeps: in a lead line, the fathoms that are not marked on the line.

Deep six: slang meaning to dispose of by throwing over the side. Also, when referring to lead line use, a depth of six fathoms of water.

Degaussing gear: electrical gear that sets up neutralizing magnetic fields to protect the ship from magnetic-action mines. Pronounced "degow'sing."

Department: an organizational subdivision of ship's crew into specialized functions, e.g., Engineering Department, Operations Department, Supply Department, etc.

Deployment: dispersal or disposition of ships for mission execution.

Depth charge: explosive charge used against submarines.

Derelict: abandoned vessel at sea, still afloat.

Diesel: a type of oil-burning, internal-combustion engine used on some ships and boats of the Coast Guard.

Dip: lowering a flag part way in salute or in answer, and hoisting it again. A flag is "at the dip" when it is flown at about two-thirds the height of the halyards.

Director: electromechanical device for directing and controlling gunfire.

Displacement: weight of water displaced by a ship.

Distance line: a light line spanning ships engaged in underway refueling or replenishment. Marked off in 20–foot lengths, it helps station keeping.

Ditty bag: small bag used by sailors for stowage of personal articles, toilet articles, or laundry.

Division: in shipboard organization, a subdivision of a ship's department for further specialization.

Dock: artificial basin for ships, fitted with gates to keep in or shut out water; water area between piers.

Dock trials: four- to six-hour trial of main engines while ship is moored alongside a pier.

Dog: metal fitting used to secure watertight doors, hatch covers, scuttles, etc.

Dogwatch: one of the two-hour watches betweem 1600 to 2000.

Doldrums: areas on both sides of the equator where light and variable breezes blow.

Dolphin: cluster of piles for mooring.

Double-bottoms: watertight subdivisions of ship, next to the keel and between outer and inner bottoms.

Double up: to increase the number of ship-to-pier turns of a mooring line.

Doubling: rounding a point of land; for example, doubling Cape Horn.

Draft: depth of water from the surface to the ship's keel; a detail of crew members.

Draft marks: numeral figures on either side of the stem and sternpost, used to indicate the amount of ship's draft.

Dressing ship: to display the national ensign at all mastheads and the flagstaff; **full dressing** further requires a rainbow of flags bow to stern over the mastheads.

Drift lead: sounding lead and line dropped over side of a ship to detect dragging of the vessel.

Drogue: floating anchor usually made of spars and canvas; used to keep the head of a vessel to the wind, to lessen leeway, or to check headway. Also called **drag sheet, sea anchor.**

Duct: large sheet-metal pipe that leads air from blowers to enclosed spaces.

Duty: the responsibility to adequately perform military obligations; a period of specific military responsibility, such as a watch. See **duty day.**

Duty day: a period of duty wherein one section of the ship's in-port watch organization remains onboard for a 24–hour period in order to ensure safety aboard, to operate the ship as may be required, and to maintain it in readiness. The section "**having the duty**" is called the **duty section.** One or more watches of varying types may be stood by members of the duty section during the duty day; ship's work may also be assigned to duty section members when off-watch. Most Coast Guard ships operate a four-section duty organization, wherein each section has the duty every four days. A duty organization is also employed aboard most shore units of the Coast Guard.

Ease her: a command to reduce the amount of rudder or helm.
Ease off: to ease a line; slacken it when taut.
Easy: carefully, gently.
Ebb tide: tide falling or flowing out.
Echo counter: fathometer; device for measuring depth of water by sending out vibrations that bounce back from the bottom. It measures time taken from the echo to return, and from that the distance is calculated.
Eddy: a small whirlpool.
Embark: to go on board a ship preparatory to sailing.
End for end: reversing positions of an object or line.
End on: head-to-head or stem-to-stem.
Engineer Officer (EO): an officer who is responsible for the ship's machinery, fuel, and water.
Engineer of the Watch (EOW, EOOW): an officer in charge of the engineering department while on watch.
Engine order telegraph: signaling gear for transmitting speed and direction orders from bridge to engineroom.
Ensign: colors, national flag. Also, junior commissioned officer in the Coast Guard or Navy. Pronounced "en'sin."
Escape hatch: in general, any hatch, usually small, that permits escape from a compartment when ordinary means of egress are blocked.
Even keel: floating level, no list.
Executive Officer (XO): an officer directly subordinate to the commanding officer, and who is second in command of the ship. The XO is in charge of the ship's administration, personnel, and routine.
Executive Petty Officer (XPO): an enlisted person directly subordinate to the officer-in-charge of a unit. The XPO is in charge of the ship's administration, personnel, and routine.
Eyebolt: a metal bolt ending in an eye.

Eyebrow: curved metal arc mounted above a porthole, used to shed water.

Eyes: foremost part of weatherdeck in the bow of the ship.

Fag: Frayed or untwisted end of rope.

Fairlead: an eye, block, or fitting furnishing a clear lead for a line. Pronounced "leed."

Fair tide: tidal current running in same direction as the ship.

Fairway: in inland waters, an open channel or midchannel.

Fair wind: a favoring wind.

Fake: a single turn of line when line is coiled down.

Fake down: coiling down a line so that each fake of rope overlaps the one underneath and makes the line clear for running.

Fall: entire length of rope in a tackle; the end secured to the block is called the **standing part**; the opposite part, the **hauling part**. Also, the line used to lower and hoist a boat.

Falling glass: lowering atmospheric pressure as registered by the barometer; normally a sign of approaching bad weather.

False keel: thin covering secured to lower side of main keel of ships; affords more protection.

Fancy work: intricate, symmetrical rope work used for decorative purposes.

Fantail: main deck section in the after part of a flush-deck ship.

Fast: snugly secured; said of a line when it is fastened securely.

Fathom: a six-foot unit of length.

Feather: a preparation technique whereby irregularities are leveled by sanding to produce a smooth surface for painting.

Feel the way: to proceed cautiously, taking soundings while doing so.

Fender: canvas, wood, rope gear, or old rubber tire used over the side to protect a ship from chafing when alongside a pier or another ship.

Fend off: to push away; pushing away from a pier or another ship when coming alongside, to prevent damage or chafing.

Fiber rope: general term for cordage made of vegetable fibers such as hemp, manila, flax, cotton, or sisal.

Fid: a wooden marlinspike.

Field day: general cleaning day aboard ship; usually before inspection.

Field strip: to disassemble without further breakdown the major groups of a piece of ordinance for routine cleaning and oiling; as opposed to **detailed stripping**, which may be done only by authorized technicians.

Fife rail: a wood or metal rail near the base of the mast bored with holes to take belaying pins, usually at the head of the flag bag.

Figure-eight fake: method of coiling rope in which the turns form a series of overlapping figure-eight's advancing about one or two diameters of the rope for each turn; usually done over the lifelines.

Figure-eight knot: knot forming a large knob; easily tied.

Fire control: shipboard system of directing and controlling gun, missile, or torpedo fire; the compartment wherein fire-control functions are carried out.

Fire main: system of pipes that furnish water to fireplugs.

First lieutenant: officer in charge of cleanliness and general upkeep of a ship or shore station; the officer in charge of the deck department. This is a duty, not a rank.

Fix: determination of a ship's position by using one or more navigational methods.

Flag bag: container for stowage of signal flags and pennants; rigged with different slots to take the flag's snaps and rings.

Flag officer: an officer of the rank of rear admiral or above; so called because of that officer's entitlement to fly a **personal flag**, which by the numbers of stars upon it, indicates the officer's rank.

Flagstaff: small vertical spar at the stern on which the ensign is hoisted.

Flank speed: a certain prescribed speed increase over standard speed; faster than full speed, but less than emergency full speed.

Flap: hinged surface of airplane wing; used to increase the lift on take-off and landing.

Flare: outward and upward curving sweep of a ship's bow; outward curve of the side form waterline to deck level. Also, a pyrotechnic device used to illuminate or attract attention.

Flash burn: burn received from the heat of explosion of a projectile or bomb or inflammable liquid.

Flash plate: protective metal plate over which the anchor cable rides. It is part of the forecastle.

Flat-top: slang for an aircraft carrier.

Fleet: a naval organization of ships and aircraft under one commander; normally includes all types of ships and aircraft necessary for major operations. Also, to draw the blocks of a tackle apart.

Flemish: to coil line flat on deck in a clockwise direction, each fake outside the other, all laid snugly side by side; begins in the middle and works outward.

Floating drydock: movable dock floating in water; ships of all sizes are floated into it and repaired.

Flood tide: tide rising or flowing toward land.

Flotsam: floating wreckage or goods thrown overboard. See **jetsam.**

Fluke: flat end of an anchor that bites into the bottom.

Flush deck: continuous upper deck extending from side to side and from bow to stern.

Flying boat: type of seaplane that can float on its own hull in the water.

Flying bridge: an area aloft of the pilothouse often employed for lookout stations.

Fore and aft: running in the direction of the keel.

Forecastle: upper deck in the forward part of the ship. Pronounced "foke'-sul"; abbreviated fo'csle.

Forecastle deck: partial deck of the main deck at the bow.

Forestay: a stay supporting a mast from forward.

Forward: toward the bow; opposite of aft.

Foul: jammed; not clear for running.

Foul anchor: anchor with its cable twisted around it.

Founder: to sink.

Frame: ribs of a vessel.

Frap: to bind lightly by passing lines around; to draw together the parts of tackle or other combinations of ropes to increase tension.

Frapping lines: lines passed around the boat falls to steady them.

Freeboard: height of a ship's sides from waterline to main deck.

Full speed: a prescribed speed that is greater than standard speed but less than flank speed.

Funnel: ship's smokestack; stack.

Furl: gathering up and securing a sail or awning; opposite of **spread.**

Fuselage: the body to which the wings and tail of an airplane are attached.

Gaff: small spar abaft the mainmast from which the national ensign is flown when the ship is under way.

Gale: a wind between a strong breeze and a storm; characterized as moderate (28–33 knots), fresh (34–40), strong (41–47), or whole gale (48–55 knots).

Galley: the ship's kitchen.

Gangplank: see **brow**.

Gangway: opening in the bulwarks or the rail of the ship to give entrance at the head of the gangplank or brow; an order to stand aside and get out of the way.

Gantline: a rope and a block on top of a mast, stack, etc., used to hoist rigging, staging, boatswain's chairs, etc.

Gather way: to gain headway.

Gear: general term for lines, ropes, blocks, fenders, etc.; personal effects.

General quarters: battle stations for all hands.

Gig: a ship's boat designated for the commanding officer's use.

Gimbals: a pair of rings, one within the other, with axes at right angles to each other. Supports the compass and keeps it horizontal despite the ship's motion.

Gipsey, gypsy: cathead; drum on a horizontal shaft windlass or winch for working lines.

Give-way vessel: the vessel which by the Rules of the Road must keep out of the way of another vessel. Formerly called the burdened vessel. See **stand-on vessel**.

Glass: barometer or quartermaster's spyglass.

Glasses: binoculars.

Go adrift: to break loose.

Grab-rope: a rope secured above a boat boom or gangplank; used to steady oneself.

Granny knot: a knot somewhat similar to a square knot; does not hold under strain.

Grapnel: small anchor with several arms; used for dragging for lost objects or for anchoring skiffs or dories.

Gratings: wooden or iron openwork covers for hatches, sunken decks, etc.

Gripes: metal fastenings for securing a boat in its cradle; canvas bands fitted with thimbles in their ends and passed from the davit heads over and under the boat for securing for sea.

Grommet: ring of rope formed by a single strand laid three times around a metal ring set in canvas, cloth, or plastic.

Ground: to run ashore; to strike the bottom through ignorance, violence, or accident.

Ground tackle: term referring to all anchor gear.

Gudgeon: support for a rudder; consists of metal braces bolted to the sternpost and having eyes to take the pintles, or pivot pins, on which the rudder swings.

Guesswarp: a line at the outer end of a boat boom, used for securing a boat to the boom. Also a hauling line laid out by a boat.

Gun mount: a gun structure with one to four guns; may be open or enclosed in a steel shield. Enclosed mounts are not as heavily armored as **turrets** and carry no gun larger than five inches.

Gunwale: upper edge or rail of a ship or boat's side. Pronounced "gun'nle."

Guy: a line used to steady and support a spar in a horizontal or inclined position.

Gyrocompass: compass used to determine true direction by means of gyroscopes.

Gyrocompass repeaters: compass cards electrically connected to gyrocompass and repeating the same readings.

Gyropilot: automatic steering device connected to the repeater of a gyrocompass; designed to hold a ship on its course without a helmsman. Also called **automatic steerer, "iron mike," "iron quartermaster."**

Hack chronometer: spare or comparison chronometer, not quite as accurate as standard chronometer.

Hail: to address a nearby boat or ship. Also a ship is said to "**hail from**" a particular home port.

Halfdeck: partial deck below the main and above the lowest complete deck.

Half hitch: usually seen as two half hitches; a knot used for much the same purposes as a clove hitch.

Half-mast: position of the ensign when hoisted halfway; usually done for a day or more at a time in respect to a deceased person.

Halyard: line used for hoisting flags, pennants, or balls.

Hand lead: a lead weighing from seven to 14 pounds, secured to a line and used for measuring the depth of water or for obtaining a sample of the bottom. Pronounced "led."

Handsomely: to ease a line gradually; to execute something deliberately and carefully, but not necessarily slowly.

Handy billy: small, portable, power-driven water pump.

Hangfire: gun charge that does not fire immediately upon pulling the trigger, but some time later.

Hatch: an opening in the ship's deck, for communication or for handling stores and cargo.

Haul: to pull.

Hauling part: that part of the fall of a tackle to which power is applied.

Hawsepipes and hawseholes: the steel castings in the bow through which anchor cables run are hawsepipes; the openings are hawseholes.

Hawser: heavy line, five inches or more in circumference, used for heavy work such as towing or mooring.

Head: compartment of a ship having toilet facilities.

Heading: the direction a ship's bow points at any given moment.

Headroom: clearance between decks.

Headway: forward motion of a ship.

Heave: to throw or toss; to pull on a line.

Heave away: an order to start heaving on a capstan or windlass, or to pull on a line.

Heave in: an order to haul in a line or the anchor cable

Heave 'round: to revolve the drum of a winch or windlass so as to pull in a line or anchor cable.

Heave short: an order to heave in on anchor chain until the ship is riding nearly over her anchor.

Heave the lead: to employ the lead line.

Heave to: to bring the ship's head into the wind or sea and hold her there by the use of engines and rudder.

Heaving line: a small line with a weight on one end; weighted end is thrown to another ship or to a pier so that a larger line attached to it may be passed.

Heel: to list over.

Helm: the helm proper is the **tiller,** but the term is often used to mean the rudder and the gear for turning it, such as the ship's wheel. See **joystick.**

Helmsman: the person at the wheel; the person who steers the ship.

Highline: line running between ships that are replenishing or transferring at sea.

Hitch: general class of knots by which a line is fastened to another object, either directly or around it. Also, a slang expression for a term of enlistment.

Hoist: display of signal flags on halyard. Also, to raise a piece of cargo or gear.

Hoisting pad: metal piece bolted to boat's keel; has an eye to which hoisting rod is bolted.

Hold: space below decks for storage of ballast, cargo, etc.

Holiday: an imperfection or vacant space in an orderly arrangement; spots in painted work left unfinished.

Holiday routine: routine followed aboard ship on authorized holidays and Sundays.

Horns: horizontal arms of a cleat or chock; projecting timbers of a stage to which rigging lines are secured.

Horse latitudes: latitudes on outer margins of trade winds (around 30 north and south) where prevailing winds are light and variable.

House: to stow or secure in a safe place; to run an anchor's shank up into the hawsepipe.

Housing anchor: anchor having one stock; houses itself in hawsepipe when hove in.

Housing chain stopper: chain stopper fitted with a screw turnbuckle, used for securing anchor in hawsepipe.

Hove taut: pulled tight.

Hug: to keep close. A vessel might hug the shore.

Hulk: a worn-out and stripped vessel unable to move under its own power.

Hull: framework of a vessel, together with all her decks, deckhouses, inside plating or planking, but exclusive of masts, rigging, guns, and all superstructure items.

Hull down: said of a distant vessel when only her stack-tops and mast are visible above the horizon.

Idler: member of ship's company who does not stand night watches. Also known as a **dayworker**.

Inboard: toward the ship's centerline.

Inland Rules: rules enacted by Congress to govern the navigation of certain inland waters of the United States. Part of the Rules of the Road.

Inner bottom: top of the double bottom; consists of watertight plating.

Inshore: toward land.

Intercardinal points: the four points midway between the cardinal points of the compass: northeast, southeast, southwest, northwest.

Interior communication (I.C.): communications and announcement systems inside a ship.

International Rules: the rules established by agreement among maritime nations and governing the navigation of the high seas. Part of the Rules of the Road.

Jack: flag similar to the union of the national ensign; flown at the jackstaff when in port; plug for connecting an electrical appliance to a power or phone line.

Jack-o'-the-dust: enlisted person serving as assistant to the ship's cooks.

Jackstaff: spar on the bow of a ship from which the Union Jack is flown when the vessel is in port.

Jacob's ladder: light ladder made of rope or chain with metal or wooden rungs; used over the side and aloft.

Jetsam: goods that sink when thrown overboard. See **flotsam**.

Jettison: to throw goods overboard.

Jetty: a landing; a small pier.

Jew's-harp: anchor shackle; ring to which the anchor cable bending shackle is secured; found at upper end of the anchor shank.

Jigger: light handy tackle for general work about the deck.

Joystick: a type of helm employing a stick instead of a wheel to steer the ship.

Junior Officer of the Deck (JOOD): The officer or petty officer acting as an assistant to the OOD. When the ship is moored or anchored, the term **Junior Officer of the Day** is generally employed.

Jury rig: makeshift rig of mast and sail or of other gear, as jury anchor, jury rudder; any makeshift device.

Kapok: water-resistant fiber stuff packed into life jackets to make them buoyant.

Kedge: anchor used for kedging; that is, moving a ship a short distance at a time by taking one of the anchors out in a boat, letting it go, and then hauling the ship up to it. If this is done merely to change the heading of the ship, it is called **warping**. See **warp**.

Keel: backbone of a ship; running from stem to sternpost at the bottom.

Keelhaul: to reprimand severely.

Keelson: timber or steel fabrications bolted on top of a keel to strengthen it.

Kenter shackle: a patent shackle used in connecting shots of anchor chain; similar to detachable links.

King post: short mast supporting a boom.

Knife edge: smooth, polished edge of the coaming against which the rubber gaskets of watertight doors and scuttles press when closed; furnishes better watertight integrity.

Knock off: to cease what is being done; to stop work.

Knot: one nautical mile per hour. Also, a knob, tie, or fastening formed with rope.

Lacing: line used to secure canvas by passing through eyelets or grommets in the canvas.

Ladder: in a ship, corresponds to stairs in a building.

Landfall: first sighting of land at the end of a sea voyage.

Landlubber: seaman's term for one who has never been to sea.

Landmark: any conspicuous object on shore, used for piloting.

Lash: to tie or secure by turns of line.

Lay: a preliminary order, such as "Lay aloft," "Lay below," etc. The direction of the twist of strands of rope.

Lead line: line secured to the lead used for soundings.

Lead or sounding lead: weight used for soundings; that is, for measuring the depth of the water. Pronounced "led."

Leadsman: crew member detailed to heave the sounding lead.

Leave: authorized absence of an individual from a place of duty, chargeable against the individual in accordance with applicable law.

Lee: direction away from the wind.

Lee helmsman: assistant or relief helmsman.

Leeward: in a lee direction. Pronounced "lu'ard."

Left-hand rope: twisted from right to left. Strands and cables are usually left-handed.

Let go by the run: allowing a line to run free.

Liberty: any authorized absence granted for short periods to provide respite from the work environment or for other specific reasons. Liberty is not chargeable to the member.

Lie to: said of a vessel when under way with no way on.

Life buoy or life ring: a ring or U-shaped buoy of cork or metal to support a person in the water; a type of personal flotation device.

Lifejacket or life preserver: a belt or jacket of buoyant or inflatable material; worn to keep a person afloat; a type of personal flotation device.

Lifeline: line secured along the deck to lay hold of in heavy weather; line thrown on board a wreck by a rescue crew; knotted line secured to the span of lifeboat davits for the use of the crew when hoisting and lowering.

Life raft: inflatable float craft for use in survival at sea.

Lighter: small vessel used for working (loading and unloading cargo) ships anchored in harbor.

Lightship: small ship equipped with a distinctive light and anchored near an obstruction to navigation or in entrances or shallow water to warn shipping. There are no longer any lightships in U.S. waters.

Line: seagoing term for rope or cable; the equator.

Line-throwing gun: small-caliber gun that projects a weighted-at-one-end line a long distance; surpasses a heaving line in gaining distance.

List: inclination or heeling over of a ship to one side.

Lizard: line fitted with a thimble or thimbles and used as a leader for running rigging. A **traveling lizard** is fitted to the middle of a lifeboat's falls for use in taking up the slack when hoisting.

Lock: compartment in a canal for lowering or lifting vessels to different levels.

Locker: small metal or wooden stowage space; either a chest or closet.

Log: instrument for measuring a ship's speed through the water. Also, a short term for **logbook**.

Longitudinal frame, longitudinal: The part of a ship's "skeleton" that runs fore and aft.

Look alive: admonishment to work faster or more diligently.

Lookout: seaman assigned duties involving watching and reporting to the OOD any objects of interest; the lookouts are "the eyes of the ship."

Loran (Long-Range Aid to Navigation): a navigational system that fixes the position of a ship by measuring the difference in the time of reception of two synchronized radio signals.

Lubber's line: line marked on inner surface of compass bowl to indicate direction of ship's bow.

Lucky bag: locker for stowage of personal gear found adrift.

Magazine: compartment; used for stowage of ammunition and explosives.

Main battery: the largest-caliber guns carried by a warship.

Main deck: highest complete deck extending from stem to stern and from side to side.

Mainmast: second mast from the bow of a ship that has two or more masts. If a vessel is considered a ship but has one mast, that mast is considered the mainmast.

Manhole: round or oval hole cut in deck, bulkhead, or tank top to provide access.

Man-of-war: fighting ship; warship.

Manrope: side rope to a ladder used as a handrail; rope used as a safety line anywhere on deck; rope hanging down on the side of a ship to assist in ascending the ship's side.

Maritime: pertaining to the sea.

Mark: call used in comparing watches, compass readings, or bearings; fathoms in a lead line that are marked. Also, a model or type of a piece of equipment, as Mark XIV torpedo.

Marlinspike: pointed iron instrument used in splicing line or wire.

Marry: placing two lines together, as in hoisting a boat; to sew together temporarily the ends of two lines for rendering through the block.

Mast: upright spar supporting signal yard and antennas in a naval ship. Also the term applied to the hearing of cases of offense against discipline, or for requests or commendations.

Meal flag: ECHO flag, which may be hoisted from port yardarm of a Navy or Coast Guard ship at anchor when the crew is at mess.

Meet her: an order to shift the rudder in order to check the swing of a ship during change of course.

Mess: to eat; group of crew members eating together; the compartment or location for the dining of a select group aboard ship, such as the CPO mess.

Messcook: nonrated crew members assigned to clean the galley and messdeck, and to help serve the meals.

Messdeck: the compartment where enlisted personnel mess.

Messenger: light line used for hauling over a heavier rope or cable; for example, the messenger is sent over from the ship to the pier by the heaving line and then used to pull the heavy mooring lines across. Also, an enlisted crew member who runs errands for the OOD.

Midshipman: a student officer of the United States Naval Academy.

Mind your rudder: warning to helmsman to watch the ordered course carefully.

Misfire: powder charge that fails to fire when the trigger has been pulled.

Monkey fist: a knot, with or without a weight enclosed, worked in the end of a heaving line to form a heavy ball to facilitate throwing the line.

Mooring: securing a ship to a pier, buoy, or another ship; or anchoring with two anchors.

Mooring buoy: a large, well-anchored buoy to which one or more ships moor.

Mooring line: one of the lines used for mooring a ship to a pier, wharf, or another ship.

Morse code: code of dots and dashes used in radio and visual signaling.

Motor launch: large, sturdily built powerboat used for liberty parties and heavy workloads.

Mousing: small stuff seized across a hook to prevent unhooking.

Muster: to assemble the crew; roll call.

Nautical mile: 6,080.2 feet, or about a sixth longer than a land mile.

Naval stores: oil, paint, turpentine, pitch, and other such items traditionally used for ships.

Neap tide: tide that twice a lunar month rises and falls the least from the average level; that is, the tide with the least amount of change from high to low, occurring every 28 days.

Nest: two or more vessels moored alongside one another; boat stowage in which one boat nests inside another.

Net: a group of intercommunicating radio or landline communication stations; a barrier of steel mesh used to protect harbors and anchorages from torpedoes, submarines, or floating mines.

Netting or snaking: small stuff crisscrossed and strung around the forecastles and fantails of a ship. Extending up about two feet from the deck, it furnishes a lifesaving device to exposed personnel.

Nothing to the right (left): order to the helmsman not to let the ship go to the right (left) of the ordered course.

Not under command: said of a ship when disabled and uncontrollable.

Nun buoy: cone-shaped buoy used to mark channels; it is anchored on the right side, entering from seaward, and is painted red.

Oakum: a caulking material made of old, tarred, hemp fiber rope.

Occulting light: a navigational aid light that blinks **on** an equal or greater amount of time than it blinks **off**; differs from **flashing light**, which blinks **off** more than it blinks **on**.

Officer-in-charge (OINC): an enlisted person in charge of a unit where no officer is assigned. OINCs are *not* commanding officers, but have many of the responsibilities of a commanding officer.

Officer of the deck: the officer on watch in charge of the ship. When moored or anchored, the term **officer of the day** is generally employed.

Officer of the watch: See **Watch officer.**

Oiler: a tanker—a vessel especially designed to carry and dispense fuel.

Oiling: taking fuel oil on board.

Oil king: petty officer in charge of fuel-oil storage.

Old Man: seaman's term for the captain of a ship or other naval activity.

On the bow: bearing of an object somewhere within 45° to either side of the bow.

On the quarter: bearing of an object somewhere astern of the ship, 45° to either side of the stern.

OOD: officer of the deck (day).

Order: directive telling what to do, but leaving the method to the discretion of the person ordered. See **command.**

Orlop: partial deck below the lower deck; also the lowest deck in a ship having four or more decks.

Oscar: Traditionally, the name given to the dummy employed for ship's "Man overboard" drills; the flag hoisted by a ship to indicate a man/woman overboard.

Outboard: toward the side of the vessel, or outside the vessel entirely.

Out of trim: to carry a list or to be down by the head or stern.

Overhand: projection of ship's bow or stern beyond the stem or sternpost.

Overhaul: to separate the blocks of a tackle; to overtake a vessel; to clear or repair anything for use.

Overhead: on a ship, equivalent to the ceiling of a building ashore; ships have overheads rather than ceilings.

Pad eye: metal eye permanently secured to deck or bulkhead.

Painter: a line in the bow of a boat for towing or making fast.

Palm and needle: sailor's thimble made of leather, and a large needle, used for sewing heavy canvas or leather.

Paravanes: torpedo-shaped devices towed on either side of ship's bow to deflect and cut moored mines adrift.

Parbuckle: device for raising or lowering a heavy object along an inclined or vertical surface. A bight of rope is thrown around a secure fastening at the level to which the object is to be raised or lowered. The two ends of the rope are then passed under the object, brought all the way over it, and led back toward the bight.

The two ends are then hauled or slackened together to raise or lower the object, the object itself acting as a nonmovable pulley.

Parceling: wrapping a rope spirally with long strips of canvas, following the lay of the rope and overlapping like the shingles on a roof as of a rope or line.

Part: to break, as of a rope or line.

Passageway: corridor or hallway on a ship.

Pass a line: to carry or send a line to or around an object, or to reeve through and make fast.

Pass the word: to repeat an order or information to all hands.

Pay: to fill the seams of a wooden vessel with pitch or other substance.

Pay off: to turn the bow away from the wind.

Pay out: to increase the scope of anchor cable; to ease off or slack a line.

Peak: topmost end of the gaff; from this point the ensign is flown while the ship is under way.

Peak tank: tank in the bow or stern of a ship; usually for water ballast.

Pelican hook: hinged hook held in place by a ring; when the ring is knocked off, the hook swings open.

Pelorus: navigational instrument used in taking bearings; consists of two sight vanes mounted on a hoop revolving about a dumb compass or a gyro repeater.

Pendant: length of rope with a block or thimble at the end.

Pennant: three- or four-sided flag that tapers off toward the end.

Periscope: optical instrument used to observe at a level about eye level.

Pier: a harbor structure projecting out into the water with sufficient depth alongside to accommodate vessels.

Pigstick: a small spar that projects above the top of the mainmast; commission pennants are usually flown on this.

Pile: pointed spar driven into the bottom and projecting above the surface of water; when driven at the corners of a pier or wharf, they are termed **fender piles.**

Pilot: an expert who comes aboard ships in harbors or dangerous waters to advise the captain as to how the ship should be conned; also, the person at the controls of an aircraft.

Pintles: pivot pins on which a rudder turns.

Pipe: an announcement over the ship's general announcing system, as in "What was that last pipe?" See also **boatswain's pipe.**

Pipe down: an order to keep silent; also used to dismiss the crew from an evolution.

Pipe the side: ceremony at the gangway in which side boys are drawn up and the boatswain's pipe is blown when a high-ranking officer or distinguished visitor comes aboard.

Pitch: the forward heaving and plunging motion of a vessel at sea.

Pivot point: point in a ship about which the ship turns.

Plan of the day: schedule of day's routine and events ordered by the executive officer; published daily aboard ship.

Platform deck: partial deck below lowest complete deck; called first, second, etc., from the top where there is more than one.

Plimsoll mark: a mark on the side of merchant ships to indicate allowed loading depths.

Pointer: member of gun crew who controls vertical elevation of a gun in aiming at a target; that is, the pointer positions the gun up and down. See **trainer.**

Pollywog: person who has never crossed the line (equator).

Poop deck: partial deck at the stern over the main deck.

Port: left side of the ship facing forward; a harbor; an opening in the ship's side. The usual opening in the ship's side for light and air is also a port. The glass set in a brass frame that fits against it is called a **port light.**

Preventer: line used for additional safety and to prevent loss of gear under heavy strain or in case of accident.

Pricker: small marlinspike.

Privileged vessel: see **stand-on vessel.**

Prolonged blast: blast on the ship's whistle of from four to six seconds' duration.

Protective deck: deck fitted with heaviest protective plating.

Punt: rectangular, flat-bottomed boat usually used for painting and other work around waterline of a ship.

Purchase: general term for any mechanical arrangement of tackle that increases the force applied by a combination of pulleys.

Pyrotechnics: chemicals, ammunition, or fireworks that produce smoke or lights of various colors and types.

Quadrant: metal fitting on rudder head to which steering ropes are attached.

Quadrantal correctors or spheres: two iron balls secured at either side of the binnacle; these help compensate for ship's magnetic effect on compass.

Quarter: that part of ship's side near the stern.

Quarterdeck: that part of the main (or other) deck reserved for honors and ceremonies and as the station of the OOD in port.

Quartermaster of the Watch (QMOW): Assists the OOD navigate when the ship is under way; a ship's quarterdeck watchstander in port.

Quarters: living space; assembly of the crew; all hands assembled at established stations for muster, drills, or inspections.

Quay: a wharf; a landing place for receiving and discharging cargo. Pronounced "key."

Rack: a sailor's bed.

Radar (Radio detection and ranging): the principle and method whereby objects are located by radio waves; a radio wave is transmitted, reflected by an object, received, and illuminated by an oscilloscope or cathode-ray screen.

Radio detection finder: apparatus for taking bearings on the source of radio transmission.

Rail: top pipe of the lifeline pipes that extend along various outboard sections of weather decks; uppermost edge of a bulwark.

Rail loading: loading a davit- or crane-supported boat while it is swung out and even with the deck.

Rake: angle of a vessel's masts and stacks from the vertical.

Rakish: having a rake to the masts; smart; speedy in appearance.

Range: distance in yards from ship to target; two or more objects in line to indicate direction.

Rank: grade of official standing of commissioned and warrant officers.

Rate: grade of official standing of enlisted personnel. A rate identifies an enlisted member by paygrade or level of advancement with a **rating**; a rate reflects levels of aptitude, training, experience, knowledge, skill, and responsibility. See **rating**.

Rat guard: a sheet-metal disk constructed in conical form with a hole in the center and slit from the center to the edge. It is installed over the mooring lines to prevent rats from boarding ship from the shore over the mooring lines.

Rating: name given to an enlisted occupational specialty that requires basically related aptitudes, training, experience, knowledge, and skills.

Ratline: short length of small stuff running horizontally across shrouds, used for a step.

Recognition: process of determining friendly or enemy character of a ship, plane, or other object or person.

Reducer: metal fitting between fire-main outlet and hose coupling of smaller diameter.

Reef: chain or ridge of rocks, coral, or sand in shallow water.

Reeve: to pass the end of a rope through any lead, such as a sheave or fairlead.

Relative bearing: bearing or direction of an object in degrees in relation to the bow of the ship. The bow of the ship is taken as 000° and an imaginary circle is drawn clockwise around the ship; objects are then reported as being along a line of bearing through any degree division of this circle.

Relieving (the watch, the duty, etc): to take over the duty and responsibilities, as when one sentry relieves another. Those who relieve are **reliefs.**

Request mast: mast held by captain or executive officer to hear special requests for leave, liberty, etc.

Rig: general description of a ship's upper works; to set up, fit out, or put together.

Rigging: general term for all ropes, chains, and gear used for supporting and operating masts, yards, booms, gaffs, and sails. Rigging is of two kinds: **standing rigging,** or lines that support but ordinarily do not move; and **running rigging,** or lines that move to operate equipment.

Rig ship for visitors: word passed as a warning to all hands to have the ship and their persons in neat order for expected visitors.

Riser: vertical branch pipe; that is, a pipe going up and down between decks and having branch connections or offshoots.

Roll: the side-to-side motion of a ship at sea.

Rope: general term for cordage over one inch in diameter. If smaller, it is known as cord, twine, line, or string. It is constructed by twisting fibers or metal wire. The size is designated by the diameter (for wire rope) or by the circumference (for fiber rope). The length is given in fathoms or feet.

Ropeyarn Sunday: a time for repairing clothing or other personal gear.

Round line: three-stranded, right-handed small stuff, used for fine seizing.

Rouse in: to haul in, especially by manpower.

Rudder: a flat, vertical, mobile structure at the stern of a vessel; used to control the vessel's heading.

Ruffles: roll of the drum used in rendering honors.

Rules of the Road: regulations enacted to prevent collisions between watercraft.

Runner: line fastened at one end to a fixed object, such as an eyebolt, on deck and rove through a single block. It has an eye on its other end to which a tackle is clapped on. The term is also loosely applied to any line rove through a block.

Running bowline: bowline made over the standing part of its own rope so that it forms a free-sliding noose.

Running lights: lights required by law to be shown by ship or plane when under way between sunset and sunrise.

Salvage: to save a ship or cargo from danger; to recover a ship or cargo from disaster and wreckage.

Samson post: in small craft, a single bitt amidships.

Scope: length of anchor cable out.

Scow: large, open, flat-bottomed boat for transporting sand, gravel, mud, etc.

Screw: the propeller; the rotating, bladed device that propels a vessel through the water.

Scullery: compartment for washing and sterilizing eating utensils.

Scupper: opening in the side of a ship to carry off water.

Scuttle: small opening through hatch, deck, or bulkhead to provide access; similar hole in side or bottom of ship; cover for such an opening; to sink a ship intentionally by boring holes in the bottom or by opening seacocks.

Scuttlebutt: drinking fountain. Also, a rumor, usually of local importance.

Sea anchor: see **drogue.**

Seabag: large canvas bag for stowing a sailor's gear and clothing.

Sea chest: intake between ship's side and sea valve or seacock.

Seacock: valve in pipe connected to the sea; a vessel may be flooded by opening the seacocks.

Sea ladder: rope ladder, usually with wooden steps, for use over the side.

Sea lawyer: enlisted member who likes to argue; usually one who thinks the regulations and standing orders can be twisted to favor his or her personal inclinations.

Sea marker: dye for brightly coloring the water to facilitate search and rescue.

Sea painter: a long line running from well forward on the ship and secured by a toggle over the inboard gunwhale in the bow of a boat.

Seaworthy: capable of putting to sea and meeting usual sea conditions.

Second deck: complete deck below the main deck.

Section: a unit of a shipboard division.

Secure: to make fast; to tie; an order given on completion of a drill, exercise or evolution, meaning to withdraw from the corresponding stations and duties.

Secure for sea: extra prescribed lashings on all movable objects.

Seize: to bind with small rope.

Seizing stuff: small cordage for seizing.

Semaphore: code indicated by the position of the arms; hand flags are used to increase readability.

Sennet, sennit: ornamental, braided, fancy ropework, formed by plaiting (interweaving) a number of strands.

Service stripes: diagonal stripes on the lower left sleeve of an enlisted member's uniform denoting periods of enlistment. Usually referred to as "hash marks."

Serving: additional protection over parcelling, consisting of continuous round turns of small stuff.

Serving mallet: wooden mallet with a groove cut lengthwise in its head; used for serving large rope.

Set: direction of the leeway of a ship or of a tide or current.

Set taut: an order to take in the slack and take a strain on running gear before heaving it in.

Set the course: to give the helmsman the desired course to be steered.

Set the watch: the order to station the first watch.

Shackle: U-shaped piece of iron or steel with eyes in the ends through which a bolt passes to close the U.

Shaft alley: spaces within a ship surrounding the propeller shaft.

Shakedown: cruise of newly commissioned ship to test and adjust all machinery and equipment and to train the crew as a working unit.

Sheave: wheel of a block over which the rope reeves. Pronounced "shiv."

Sheer: longitudinal upward curve of a deck; amount by which the deck at the bow is higher than the deck at the stern. Also, a sudden change of course.

Sheer off: to turn suddenly away.

Shell: casing of a block.

Shellback: person who has crossed the equator and been initiated.

Shell room: compartment for stowage of projectiles.

Shift the rudder: an order to swing the rudder an equal distance in the opposite direction.

Ship: a general term for large oceangoing craft or vessels; to enlist or reenlist, as to **ship over.**

Ship's company: all the enlisted members and officers serving in, and attached to, a ship; **all hands.**

Shipshape: neat, orderly.

Shore patrol: naval personnel detailed to maintain discipline, to aid local police in handling naval personnel on liberty or leave, and to assist naval personnel in difficulties ashore.

Shore up: to prop up.

Short blast: whistle, horn, or siren blast of about one second's duration.

Short stay: when anchor chain has been hauled in until amount of chain out is only slightly greater than depth of water and ship is riding almost directly over the anchor.

Shot: short length of chain, usually 15 fathoms.

Shove off: to leave; an order to a boat to leave a landing or a ship's side.

Shroud: side stay of hemp or wire running from masthead to rail to support the mast.

Sick bay: ship's hospital or dispensary.

Side boys: nonrated personnel manning the side when visiting senior officers or distinguished visitors come aboard.

Side lights: red and green running lights carried on port and starboard sides respectively.

Single up: to reduce the number of mooring lines out to a pier preparatory to sailing; that is, to leave only one easily cast off line in each place where mooring lines were doubled up for greater security.

Sister hooks: twin hooks on the same swivel or ring; closed, they form an eye.

Skeg: continuation of the keel aft to protect the propeller.

Skids: beams fitted over decks for stowage of heavy boats.

Skivvies: slang for underclothing.

Slack: the part of a line hanging loose; to ease off; state of the tide when there is no horizontal motion.

Slings: fittings for hoisting a boat or other heavy lift by crane or boom; they consist of a metal ring with four pendants. Two of these pendants are for athwartships steadying lines, the other two shackle to chain bridles permanently bolted to the keel of the boat.

Slip: to let go by unshackling, as an anchor cable; space between two piers; waste motion of a propeller.

Small craft: generally, all vessels less than small-ship size.

Small stuff: small cordage designated by the number of threads (nine-thread, twelve-thread, etc.) or by special names, such as marline, ratline stuff, etc.

Smart: snappy, seamanlike.

Smoking lamp: a lamp aboard oldtime ships used by personnel to light their pipes; now used in phrase "The smoking lamp is lit (or out)" to indicate when smoking is allowed or forbidden throughout the ship or a specified area therein.

Snub: to check suddenly.

Snipes: slang for members of the engineering department.

Sonar (Sound navigation and ranging): device for locating objects under water by emitting vibrations similar to sound and measuring the time taken for these vibrations to bounce back from anything in their path.

Soogie: to wash or scrub. In the Coast Guard, scouring powder is called **soogie powder.**

SOPA: senior officer present afloat.

Sound: to measure depth of water by means of a lead line. Also, to measure depth of liquids in oil tanks, voids, blisters, and other compartments or tanks.

Sound-powered phone: shipboard telephone powered by voice alone.

Span: line made fast at both ends with a purchase hooked to its bight; wire rope located between davit heads and set up by a turnbuckle. Also, to bridge or reach across.

Spanner: a tool for coupling hoses.

Spar: steel or wood pole serving as a mast, boom, gaff, pile, etc.

Spar buoy: long, thin, wooden spar used to mark channels.

Speed cone: cone-shaped, bright yellow signal used when steaming in formation to indicate engine speeds.

Speed light: white or red light mounted high on a ship to indicate changes in speed at night.

Spitkit: derisive term for small, unseaworthy vessel; slang for a sailor's toilet kit.

Splice: to join two lines by tucking the strands of each into the other.

Splinter screen: protective plating around a gun mount.

Spring: mooring line leading at an angle of about 45° off centerline of vessel; to turn a vessel with a line.

Spur shore: wooden spar used to hold vessel clear of a pier.

Squall: a sudden stormlike gust of wind and rain.

Square away: to get things settled down or in order.

Squilgee: drier for decks and glass made of a flat piece of wood with a rubber blade and a long wooden handle. Pronounced "squeegee."

Stack: ship's smoke pipe. See **funnel.**

Stadimeter: instrument for measuring distance from an object.

Stage: platform rigged over ship's side for painting or repair work.

Stanchion: wood or metal upright used as a support.

Stand: condition of tide when there is no vertical motion. See **slack.**

Stand by: preparatory order meaning "Get ready," or "Prepare to."

Standard speed: speed set as basic speed by officer in command of a unit.

Stand-on vessel: the vessel with the right of way. Formerly called the privileged vessel. See **give-way vessel.**

Starboard: right side of a ship looking forward.

Starboard pennant: a trapezoid-shaped green and white pennant indicating that the commanding officer of the ship from which it flies is the Senior Officer Present Afloat (SOPA). Also called the **SOPA pennant.**

Station keeping: the art of keeping a ship in its proper position in a formation of ships.

Stay: piece of rigging, either wire or fiber, used to support a mast.

Steady: order to helmsman to hold ship on course.

Steerageway: slowest speed at which a ship can be steered.

Stem: upright post or bar at most forward part of the bow of a ship or boat. It may be a casting, forging, welding, or made of wood.

Stern: after part of a ship.

Stern sheets: space in a boat abaft the after thwart.

Sternway: backward movement of a ship.

Stopper: short length of rope or chain firmly secured at one end; used in securing or checking a running line.

Stove: broken in; crushed in.

Stow: to put gear in its proper place.

Strake: continuous line of planks or plates running the length of a vessel.

Strand: part of a line or rope made up of yarns.

Striker: enlisted member in training for a particular rating.

Strip ship: to prepare ship for battle action by getting rid of any unnecessary gear.

Strongback: spar lashed to a pair of boat davits; acts as a spreader for the davits and provides a brace for more secure stowage of a lifeboat at sea.

Superstructure: all equipment and fittings, except armament, extending above the hull.

Superstructure deck: partial deck higher than the main, forecastle, and poop decks, and not extending to the ship's sides.

Survey: examination by authorized competent personnel to determine whether a piece of gear, equipment, stores, or supplies should be discarded or retained.

Swab: a rope or yarn mop.

Swamp: to sink by filling with water.

Swash plates: plates pierced with a number of holes, fixed in tanks to prevent liquids from moving too violently when ship rolls or pitches.

Swing ship: moving the ship through the compass points to check the magnetic compass on different headings and make up a deviation table.

Swivel: metal link with an eye at one end, fitted to revolve freely and thus keep turns out of a chain.

Tachometer: mechanical device indicating shaft revolutions.

Tackle: arrangement of ropes and blocks to give mechanical advantage; a purchase, that is, a rig of lines and pulleys to increase available hauling force. Pronounced "take-el."

Tackline: short length of line used to separate flags in a hoist.

Taffrail: a rail at the stern of a ship.

Taffrail log: device that indicates the speed of the ship through the water. It is trailed on a line from the taffrail and consists of a rotator and a recording instrument.

Take a turn: to pass a turn around a cleat, bitts, or bollard with a line and hold on.

Taps: lights out for the night.

Tarpaulin: heavy canvas used as protective covering.

Task force: temporary grouping of units under one commander; formed for purpose of carrying out a specific operation or mission.

Taut: with no slack. Also, strict as to discipline and orderliness.

Telephone talker: crew member who handles sound-powered phone for drills and evolutions.

Tend: direction the cable leads when ship is anchored. Also, to oversee (for example, to tend to your duties).

Tender: an auxiliary vessel that supplies and repairs ships or aircraft.

That's high: an order to cease hoisting.

Thimble: iron ring grooved on outside for rope grommet.

Thrum mat: mat used to prevent chafing.

Thrums: short strands of rope yarn stuck through a mat to make a rough surface.

Thwart: crosspiece used as a seat for a boat.

Tide: the vertical rise and fall of the sea caused by gravitational effect of sun and moon.

Tier: to stow cable in chain locker.

Tiller: short piece of metal or wood fitted into the head of the rudder and used to turn a boat's rudder.

Toggle: wooden or metal pin slipped into a becket; furnishes a rapid release.

Tompion, tampion: plug placed in muzzle of gun to keep dampness and foreign objects out. Pronounced "tompkin."

Top: platform at top of mast; to **top a boom** is to lift up its end.

Topping lift: line used for topping a boom and taking its weight.

Topside: above decks.

Tow: to pull through the water; vessels so towed. The usual towing vessels in naval talk are **tugs,** not **towboats.**

Towing lights: special white lights displayed by a towing vessel at night.

Track: path of a vessel.

Tracking: keeping a gun directed at a moving target.

Trades: generally steady winds of the tropics that blow toward the equator; northeast in the Northern Hemisphere, and southeast in the Southern Hemisphere.

Train: auxiliary vessels; also, to move a gun horizontally onto a target.

Trainer: gun-crew member who controls horizontal movement of gun in aiming it at a target.

Transom: athwartships piece bolted to sternpost; planking across stern of square-sterned boat.

Trice up: to hitch up or hook up, such as trice up a rack.

Trick: period of time a helmsman is at the wheel, as "to take a trick at the wheel."

Trim: angle to the horizontal at which a ship rides; that is, how level the ship sits in the water; shipshape.

Trimming tanks: tanks used for water ballast. By flooding or emptying these tanks, the ship may be trimmed, that is, balanced in water at various angles.

Truck: flat, circular piece secured at top of mast or at top of flagstaff and jackstaff. Also, uppermost part of a mast.

Trunk: a vertical shaft.

Tumble home: amount vessel's sides come in at the deck from the perpendicular.

Turbine: high-speed rotor turned by steam or other hot gases.

Turnbuckle: metal appliance, consisting of a thread and screw capable of being set taut or slacked and used for setting up standing rigging.

Turn to: an order to begin work.

Turret: heavily armored housing containing a grouping of main battery guns. It extends downward through decks, and includes ammunition handling rooms and hoists. See **gun mount**.

Two-blocked: when two blocks of a tackle have been drawn as closely together as possible.

Veer: to let anchor cable, line, or chain run out by its own weight. Also, when the wind changes direction clockwise or to the right, it is said to veer.

Very well: reply of a senior (or officer) to a junior (or enlisted person) to indicate that information given is understood, or that permission is granted.

Void: empty compartment below decks.

Wake: the track left in the water behind a ship.

Wale shores: stout timbers of various lengths used to prevent a drydocked vessel from toppling over. They are rigged between the vessel's sides and the sides of the drydock.

Walk back: an order to keep the gear in hand but to walk back with it toward the belaying point.

Wall knot: knot made at the end of a rope by back-splicing the ends, thus forming a knot. Used for finishing off seizing and, on the end ope, to prevent the rope from unreeving.

Wardroom: officer's mess and lounge aboard a ship.

Warp: to move a vessel by a line or laid-out anchor, "Warp the ship into the slip." See **kedge.**

Watch: a period of duty, usually of four hours' duration. Watches call for a variety of duties, and are of many types: quarterdeck watch, messenger watch, signal watch, radio watch, etc.

Watch and watch: alternating four hours of watch time with four hours of off-watch time. Most off-watch periods are of eight to 12 hours duration.

Watchcap: knitted wool cap worn in cool or cold weather; canvas cover placed over a stack when not in use.

Watch officer: an officer regularly assigned to duty in charge of a watch or of a portion thereof; for example, the OOD, or the engineering officer of the watch.

Watch, quarter, and station bill: a large chart showing every crew member's location and duties in a Coast Guard or Navy ship's organization of drills and evolutions.

Water breaker: drinking water cask or container carried in boats.

Waterline: point to which the ship sinks in water; line painted on hull showing point to which ship sinks in water when properly trimmed.

Waterlogged: filled or soaked with water but still afloat.

Watertight integrity: system of keeping ship afloat by maintaining watertightness.

Waterway: gutter at side of ship's deck to carry water to scuppers.

Weather: exposed to wind and rain; to the windward, as "to face the weather," or "to weather a storm."

Weather cloth: canvas spread for protection from wind and weather.

Weather deck: portion of main, forecastle, poop, and upper deck exposed to weather.

Weather eye: to "keep a weather eye" is to be on the alert.

Weigh: to lift the anchor off the bottom.

Well deck: a low weather deck.

Whaleboat: sharp-ended lifeboat; when equipped with an engine, called a **motor whaleboat.**

Wharf: harbor structure alongside which vessels moor. A **wharf** generally is built along the water's edge; a **pier** extends well out into the harbor.

Wheelhouse: pilothouse; the topside compartment where on most ships the OOD, helmsman, quartermaster of the watch, etc., stand their watches.

Where away: answering call requesting location of object sighted by lookout.

Whipping: keeping the ends of a rope from unlaying, by wrapping with turns of twine and tucking the ends.

Wildcat: sprocket wheel on windlass for taking the links of the chain cable.

Winch: hoisting engine secured to the deck; used to haul lines by turns around a horizontally driven drum or gypsey.

Windlass: anchor engine used for heaving in the anchor.

Wind scoop: metal scoop fitted into a port to direct air into the ship for ventilation.

Wind ship: to turn a ship end for end, usually with lines at a pier. Pronounced "wined."

Windward: into the wind; toward the direction from which wind is blowing; opposite of **leeward**.

Wire rope: rope made of wire strands, as distinguished from **fiber rope**.

With the sun: in clockwise direction; the proper direction in which to coil a line; right-handed.

Work a ship: to handle ship by means of engines and other gear; for example, to work a ship into a slip using engines, rudder, and lines to dock.

Worming: filling the lays of a wire rope preparatory to parceling and serving.

Yard: spar attached at the middle of a mast and running athwartships; used as a support for signal halyards or signal lights; also a place used for shipbuilding and as a repair depot, as the Coast Guard Yard, Baltimore, Maryland.

Yardarm: either side of a yard.

Yardarm blinker: signal light mounted above the end of a yardarm and flashed on and off to send messages.

Yarn: twisted fibers used for rough seizings, which may be twisted into strands; also, a story, as to "spin a yarn," meaning to tell a story not necessarily true.

Yaw: zigzagging motion of a vessel as it is carried off its heading by strong overtaking seas. This motion swings the ship back and forth across the intended course.

Yoke: the piece fitting across the head of a boat's rudder, to the end of which steering lines are attached.

Ribbons of Decorations and Awards

Medal of Honor

Navy Cross

Coast Guard
Distinguished
Service Medal

Silver Star Medal

Legion of Merit

Distinguished
Flying Cross

Coast Guard Medal

Navy and
Marine Corps
Medal

Bronze Star Medal

Meritorious Service
Medal

Air Medal

Joint Service
Commendation
Medal

Coast Guard
Commendation
Medal

Navy
Commendation
Medal

Coast Guard
Achievement Medal

Navy
Achievement Medal

Purple Heart Medal

Combat Action
Ribbon

Presidential Unit
Citation

Coast Guard Unit
Commendation

Navy Unit
Commendation

Coast Guard
Meritorious
Unit Commendation

Navy Meritorious
Unit Commendation

Gold
Lifesaving Medal

Silver
Lifesaving Medal

DOT Outstanding
Achievement Medal

DOT Meritorious
Achievement Medal

DOT Superior
Achievement Medal

Coast Guard
Good Conduct
Medal

Navy
Good Conduct
Medal

Marine Corps
Good Conduct
Medal

Army
Good Conduct
Medal

| Air Force
Good Conduct
Medal | Coast Guard Reserve
Meritorious Service
Ribbon | Naval Reserve
Medal | Naval Reserve
Meritorious Service
Medal |

Navy Expeditionary
Medal

China Service
Medal

American Defense
Service Medal

American Campaign
Medal

European-African
Middle Eastern
Campaign Medal

Asiatic-Pacific
Campaign Medal

World War II
Victory Medal

Navy Occupation
Service Medal

Medal for
Humane Action

National Defense
Service Medal

Korean
Service Medal

Antarctic
Service Medal

Armed Forces
Expeditionary
Medal

Vietnam
Service Medal

Armed Forces
Reserve Medal

United Nations
Service Medal

United Nations
Medal

Philippine
Presidential Unit
Citation

Republic of Korea
Presidential Unit
Citation

Republic of Vietnam
Gallantry Cross
Unit Citation

Republic of Vietnam
Civil Actions
Unit Citation

Republic of Vietnam
Campaign Ribbon

Coast Guard
Expert Rifleman
Medal

Coast Guard
Expert Pistol
Shot Medal

Coast Guard
Letter of
Commendation

Marine Corps.
Expeditionary
Medal

Note: The ribbons for the DOT Gold Medal, the Bicentennial Unit Commendation, and the Gold and Silver Lifesaving Medals are not shown.

Allied Naval Signal Pennants and Flags and International Alphabet Flags

Pennant	Spoken	Pennant	Spoken	Pennant	Spoken
	PENNANT ONE "WUN"		CODE		SQUAD
	PENNANT TWO "TOO"		BLACK PENNANT		STARBOARD
	PENNANT THREE "THUH-REE"		CORPEN		STATION
	PENNANT FOUR "FO-WER"		DESIG		SUBDIV
	PENNANT FIVE "FI-YIV"		DIV		TURN
	PENNANT SIX "SIX"		EMER-GENCY		FIRST SUB
	PENNANT SEVEN "SEVEN"		FLOT		SECOND SUB
	PENNANT EIGHT "ATE"		FORMA-TION		THIRD SUB
	PENNANT NINE "NINER"		INTER-ROGATIVE		FOURTH SUB
	PENNANT ZERO "ZERO"		NEGAT		PORT
	ANSWER		PREP		SPEED

Flag	Name — Written / Spoken	Flag	Name — Written / Spoken	Flag	Name — Written / Spoken
	A ALFA "AL-FA"		M MIKE "MIKE"		Y YANKEE "YANG-KEY"
	B BRAVO "BRAH-VOH"		N NOVEMBER "NO-VEM-BER"		Z ZULU "ZOO-LOO"
	C CHARLIE "CHAR-LEE"		O OSCAR "OSS-CAH"		ONE - 1 "WUN"
	D DELTA "DEL-TAH"		P PAPA "PAH-PAH"		TWO - 2 "TOO"
	E ECHO "ECK-OH"		Q QUEBEC "KAY-BECK"		THREE - 3 "THUH-REE"
	F FOXTROT "FOKS-TROT"		R ROMEO "ROW-ME-OH"		FOUR - 4 "FO-WER"
	G GOLF "GOLF"		S SIERRA "SEE-AIR-RAH"		FIVE - 5 "FI-YIV"
	H HOTEL "HOH-TEL"		T TANGO "TANG-GO"		SIX - 6 "SIX"
	I INDIA "IN-DEE-AH"		U UNIFORM "YOU-NEE-FORM"		SEVEN - 7 "SEVEN"
	J JULIETT "JEW-LEE-ETT"		V VICTOR "VIK-TAH"		EIGHT - 8 "ATE"
	K KILO "KEY-LOH"		W WHISKEY "WISS-KEY"		NINE - 9 "NINER"
	L LIMA "LEE-MAH"		X XRAY "ECKS-RAY"		ZERO - 0 "ZERO"

APPENDIX E

IALA MARITIME BUOYAGE SYSTEM
LATERAL MARKS REGION B

PORT HAND

Can   Pillar   Spar

Topmark (if any): Single can.

BUOYAGE DIRECTION

STARBOARD HAND

Conical   Pillar   Spar

Topmark (if any): Single cone,
point upward.

Lights, when fitted, may have any phase
characteristic other than that used
for preferred channels.

Examples

Quick Flashing
Flashing
Long Flashing
Group Flashing

PREFERRED CHANNEL
TO STARBOARD

Can   Pillar   Spar

Topmark (if any): Single can.

BUOYAGE DIRECTION

PREFERRED CHANNEL
TO PORT

Conical   Pillar   Spar

Topmark (if any): Single cone,
point upward.

Lights, when fitted, are composite
group flashing Fl (2+1).

APPENDIX F

STORM WARNING SIGNALS
DAYTIME SIGNALS

SMALL CRAFT   GALE   WHOLE GALE   HURRICANE

NIGHT SIGNALS

SMALL CRAFT   GALE   WHOLE GALE   HURRICANE

Beaufort Scale

Estimation of the wind's speed and a constant awareness of the state of the sea are important responsibilities of a mariner. Sea state can have a significant influence upon a ship. Course changes, leeway, dead reckoning, engine speeds, and even rudder angles are affected by wind and sea. The photos represent "steady state" sea conditions.

0   Calm 0–1 kts.
Sea like a mirror.

1   Light air 1–3 kts./1¼-ft waves.
Ripples with appearance of scales; no foam crests.

2   Light breeze 4–6 kts./1½-ft. waves
Small wavelets; crests of glassy appearance, not breaking.

3   Gentle breeze 7–10 kts./2-ft. waves
Large wavelets; crests begin to break; scattered whitecaps.

4   Moderate breeze 11–16 kts./4-ft. waves
Small waves, becoming longer; numerous whitecaps.

5   Fresh breeze 17–21 kts./6-ft. waves
Moderate waves, taking longer form; many whitecaps; some spray.

6   Strong breeze 22–27 kts./10-ft. waves
Larger waves forming; whitecaps everywhere; more spray.

7   Near gale 28–33 kts./14-ft. waves
Sea heaps up; white foam from breaking waves begins to be blown in streaks.

8   Gale 34–40 kts./18-ft. waves
Moderately high waves of greater length; edges of crests begin to break into spindrift; foam is blown into well-marked streaks.

9   Strong gale 41–47 kts./23-ft. waves
High waves; sea beings to roll; dense streaks of foam; spray may reduce visibility.

10   Storm 48–55 kts./29-ft. waves
Very high waves with overhanging crests; sea takes white appearance as foam is blown in very dense streaks; rolling is heavy and visibility reduced.

11   Violent storm 53–63 kts./37-ft. waves
Exceptionally high waves; sea covered with white foam patches; visibility still more reduced.

12   Hurricane 64–71 kts./45-ft. waves
Air filled with foam; sea completely white with driving spray; visibility greatly reduced.

APPENDIX H

Servicewide Exam Study Guide and Notes

Many Coast Guard men and women use the *Coast Guardsman's Manual* as a primary reference document when studying for servicewide exams. This is perfectly acceptable and is certainly encouraged, but you need to be aware that this document is *not* an official document and tends, over time, to become outdated.

The Coast Guard is constantly changing and Headquarters personnel are responsible for ensuring that the latest policies and procedures are documented in official directives and publications. Future editions of the *Coast Guardsman's Manual* will reflect these changes but you need to review current official references to be sure you have the latest information available prior to taking the exam. The extra effort you put in to ensure accuracy may make the difference between being advanced or remaining with the pack.

COMDTINST M9000.6	Naval Engineering Manual (Chap. 555 and 079)
COMDTINST M1650.25	Medals and Awards Manual
COMDTINST M5500.11A	Security Manual (Chap. 1, 2, 3, 4, 5, 8, 10, 11, and 12)
COMDTINST M1000.6A	Personnel Manual (Chap. 2, 5, 6, 7, 8, 10, and 13)
COMDTINST M7220.29	Pay Manual (Chap. 2, 3, and 4)
COMDTINST M5216.4	Correspondence Manual
COMDTINST M2300.7	Radiotelephone Communications Handbook
COMDTINST M4400.13	Comptrollers Manual Vol. III (for E-6th E-9 Servicewide)
NSTM 555	Firefighting-Ships (BASICS)
NSTM 079 Vol. 2	Practical Damage Control (BASICS)
NSTM 070	Radiological Recovery of Ships After Nuclear Weapons Explosion (BASICS)
NSTM 077	Personnel Protective Equipment
NSTM 470	Shipboard Biological/Chemical Defense and Counter Measures (BASICS)

Major Events in Coast Guard History

1790 (4 Aug.) Congress authorizes the construction of ten cutters to enforce tariff laws, creating the Revenue Cutter Service.

1793 (May) Captain William Cooke seizes gold from privateer Francois Henri Hervieux, who tried to land at Brunswick, North Carolina.

1794 (20 Jul.) Cutter *Virginia* seizes the *Unicorn* in Smithville, Virginia, as she is outfitting as a privateer to be used under the French flag.

1799 (Apr.) Cutter *Eagle* captures French privateer *Bon Pere*; this was one of more than a dozen captures made by cutters during the Quasi-War.

1813 (4 Oct.) Cutter *Vigilant* captures British privateer *Dart*, which had seized 30 prizes off the New England coast during the War of 1812.

1819 (31 Aug.) Cutters *Louisiana* and *Alabama* capture pirate *Lefarge* and crew in the Gulf of Mexico.

1833 (Jan.) Revenue cutters enforce the tariff at Charleston, South Carolina, after merchants refuse to pay a sugar tax.

1846 (Nov.) Cutters participate in the attack on Frontera, Mexico; during the Mexican War, cutters are used extensively in riverine and blockade operations.

1848 (14 Aug.) Life-Saving Service begins as a voluntary organization to help those in distress along the coasts.

1851 (31 Oct.) Captain Douglas Ottinger disperses a mob on clipper ship *Challenge*, preserving order during the California Gold Rush.

1861 (5 Apr.) Cutter *Harriet Lane* fires the first maritime shot of the Civil War by firing on *Nashville* at Charleston.

1863 (14 Mar.) Cutter *Agassiz* helps drive away attacking Confederates at New Bern, North Carolina.

1869 (29 Mar.) Idawalley Zorada Lewis, keeper of Lime Rock Lighthouse, makes one of her many rescues.

1876 (31 Jul.) Cadet training program starts, becoming the foundation for the Coast Guard Academy.

1890 Cutter *Bear* introduces reindeer into Alaska to improve the sustenance of the native Americans; the reindeer were purchased from Russian officials in Siberia.

1905 The Revenue Cutter Service Yard is established at Curtis Bay, Baltimore, Maryland.

1909 (23 Jan.) The sinking passenger liner *Republic* makes the first use of the radio in a major distress case that involved Revenue cutters.

1913 Cutters *Seneca* and *Miami* make the first International Ice Patrol after the sinking of the *Titanic*; the Coast Guard has conducted the patrol since that time without a single disaster.

1915 (28 Jan.) The Coast Guard is officially established by combining the Revenue Cutter Service and the Life-Saving Service.

1916 (1 April) Coast Guard aviation starts with the entry of the first Coast Guard officers into Navy flight training at Pensacola, Florida.

1918 (16 Aug.) The Chicamacomico Lifesaving crew rescues the crew of the torpedoed tanker *Mirlo* off the North Carolina coast.

1918 (16 Sep.) While serving on convoy duty, the crew of cutter *Seneca* fails to save the torpedoed British tanker *Wellington*, but picks up the crew who abandoned the ship.

26 Sept.) German U-boat torpedoes cutter *Tampa*, which is

escorting a convoy between England and Gibraltar; the cutter sinks with all hands.

1919 (27 May) Coast Guard Lieutenant Elmer Stone pilots naval NC-4 aircraft across the Atlantic; it is the first transatlantic crossing.

1920 (24 Mar) The first Coast Guard Air Station is established at Morehead City, North Carolina.

1919 (20 Mar.) Cutter *Oliver Wolcott* sinks rumrunner *I'm Alone* in an attempt to enforce Prohibition.

1934 (15 May) Lightship *Nantucket* is rammed and sunk by the ocean liner *Olympic*; lightships were frequently the victims of collisions.

1939 (23 Jun.) The Coast Guard Auxiliary is formed; today, the Auxiliary, a volunteer organization, is almost 40,000 strong.

1939 (1 Jul.) Lighthouse Service joins the Coast Guard, doubling the size of the service.

1940 (10 Feb.) Cutter *Duane* makes the first weather patrol. This became a major Coast Guard duty until 1976 when the ships were replaced by satellites and super buoys.

1941 (30 Jun.) The Coast Guard Reserve is formed; during World War II most of the 240,000 members of the Coast Guard were reservists.

1941 (12 Sep.) Cutter *Northland* seizes Norwegian trawler *Boskoe* and captures a German radio crew on shore. The United States had not yet declared war against Germany.

1942 (21 Feb.) Cutter *Spencer* sinks *U-255*.

1942 (28 Feb.) The Bureau of Marine Inspection joins the Coast Guard.

1942 (27 Sep.) Petty Officer First Class Douglas Munro, U.S. Coast Guard, rescues Marines from Guadalcanal and receives the Medal of Honor.

1942 (Dec.) The SPARS (*Semper Paratus*—Always Ready) are created; during World War II, 10,000 women serve in the Coast Guard.

1943 The first Loran-A chain is established; this long-range electronic aids-to-navigation system has evolved into the maritime communities' primary navigation system.

1944 (3 Jan.) The first helicopter rescue occurs when two cases of blood plasma are delivered to Navy destroyer *Turner* following an explosion on board.

1944 (29 Jun.) *Cobb* conducts the first shipboard helicopter landing. The Navy tasked the Coast Guard to develop the helicopter for wartime service.

1945 (29 Jan.) USS *Serpens*, manned by Coast Guardsmen, blows up at Guadalcanal. (The Coast Guard manned 300 vessels for the Navy and 350 for the Army in World War II, and sank 11 U-boats.)

1957 (Jul.–Sep.) Cutters *Storis*, *Bramble*, and *Spar* transit the Northwest Passage to demonstrate the feasibility of an eastward passage for ships building the DEW line.

1965 (Mar.) Coast Guard participation in the Vietnam War begins. During the conflict, 8,700 Coast Guardsmen serve in Vietnam.

1967 (1 Apr.) The Coast Guard is transferred to the Department of Transportation, ending its 177–year association with the Department of the Treasury.

1967 (Dec.) Oil tanker *Argo Merchant* sinks off New England, which leads to an expansion in the Coast Guard's environmental mission.

1973 Coast Guard Pollution Strike Teams are formed to help fight maritime oil and chemical pollution.

1976 The Fisheries Conservation and Management Act quadruples the offshore fishing area that the Coast Guard is responsible for patrolling.

1980 (May–Jul.) Coast Guard units shepherd 225,000 refugees as they flee Cuba.

1980 (4 Oct.) Coast Guard, Air Force, and Canadian units rescue all of the passengers and crew from the cruise ship *Prinsendam* in the Gulf of Alaska.

1986 (4 Aug.) The Coast Guard formalizes the Maritime Defense Zone arrangement, ensuring the continuity of a wartime role within the Department of the Navy.

1989 (24 Mar.) The Coast Guard responds to our nation's largest oil ⋯⋯⋯ the tanker *Exxon Valdez* grounds in Alaska.

1989 (5 July) *Shearwater* seizes 3,359 pounds of cocaine.

1989 (1 Oct.) *Cushing* seizes 12,000 pounds of cocaine.

1990 (Aug.) Active-duty and Reserve personnel begin deployments with coalition forces of Operation Desert Shield/Desert Storm.

Index

About the Author

Captain George E. Krietemeyer started his military career as a seaman recruit in the USNR at Floyd Bennett Field, Brooklyn, New York. He accepted an appointment to the U.S. Coast Guard Academy and graduated as an ensign in 1959.

His aviation career started at NAS Pensacola, and in 1961 he was awarded his "Wings of Gold." Aviation tours at CGAS Miami, CGAS Elizabeth City, AR&SC, ATTC, and ATC Mobile included search and rescue, law enforcement and engineering test-pilot duties allowing him to amass over 5,000 flight hours in both fixed-wing and rotary-wing aircraft. Command tours included assignment as the first CO of the Aviation Technical Training Center and command of the Aviation Training Center during the transition to Falcon jet aircraft.

Captain "K" now resides in Mobile, Alabama and works as a total quality management consultant to government and private industry.

The **Naval Institute Press** is the book-publishing arm of the U.S. Naval Institute, a private, nonprofit professional society for members of the sea services and civilians who share an interest in naval and maritime affairs. Established in 1873 at the U.S. Naval Academy in Annapolis, Maryland, where its offices remain today, the Naval Institute has more than 100,000 members worldwide.

Members of the Naval Institute receive the influential monthly magazine Proceedings and discounts on fine nautical prints, ship and aircraft photos, and subscriptions to the quarterly Naval History magazine. They also have access to the transcripts of the Institute's Oral History Program and get discounted admission to any of the Institute-sponsored seminars offered around the country.

The Naval Institute's book-publishing program, begun in 1898 with basic guides to naval practices, has broadened its scope in recent years to include books of more general interest. Now the Naval Institute Press publishes more than sixty titles each year, ranging from how-to books on boating and navigation to battle histories, biographies, ship and aircraft guides, and novels. Institute members receive discounts on the Press's nearly 400 books in print.

Full-time students are eligible for special half-price membership rates. Life memberships are also available.

For a free catalog describing the Naval Institute Press books currently available, and for further information about U.S. Naval Institute membership, please write to:

Membership & Communications Department
U.S. Naval Institute
118 Maryland Avenue
Annapolis, Maryland 21402-5035

Or call, toll-free, (800) 233-8764.

THE NAVAL INSTITUTE PRESS
THE COAST GUARDSMAN'S MANUAL
Eighth Edition

Set in Caledonia
by BG Composition
Baltimore, Maryland

Printed on 50-lb. Finch Opaque Smooth White
and 60-lb. Finch Opaque Smooth White
and bound by The John D. Lucas Printing Company
Baltimore, Maryland